PASTORS AS TEACHERS

THE TEACHING MINISTRY OF THE CHURCH AND ITS ROLE IN THE STRENGTHENING OF CHURCH TODAY

By

NELSON NOEL NG'UONO WERE

PASTORS AS TEACHERS

Copyright © 2020 **by Nelson Noel Ng'uono Were**
June, 2020
All Rights Reserved
Printed in the United States of America

ISBN 978-1-7347481-9-2

All Scripture quotes are from the King James Bible except those verses compared and then the source is identified.

No part of this work may be reproduced without the expressed consent of the publisher, except for brief quotes, whether by electronic, photocopying, recording, or information storage and retrieval systems.

Address All Inquiries To:
THE OLD PATHS PUBLICATIONS, Inc.
142 Gold Flume Way
Cleveland, Georgia, U.S.A. 30528
Web: www.theoldpathspublications.com
E-mail: TOP@theoldpathspublications.com

The cover picture is Dr. Were's church in Africa where he is the pastor. It was taken by him.

ABSTRACT

Teaching is an important aspect of the pastoral ministry. Pastoral duties include teaching, and as such, pastoral preparation and equipping must include training of candidates for the ministry. The pastoral office is evolving from the traditional teacher of the Word to the modern corporate executive and motivational speaker. This has been accompanied by discussions on the role of teaching in the church today. Is there a need for theological training today? What is the place of theology in the pulpits and in church ministries? The effect has seen the teaching ministry of the church increasingly subordinated and superseded by other functions.

In the past, the pastoral office was seen as one which revolved around the Word of God and the pastor as one who handled the Word of God. This meant that the pastor had to be thoroughly acquainted with the Word of God in order to fulfil his duties to the flock. Pastoral theology focused on the person and work of the minister, emphasizing the pastor's relation to God, to the word, and to the flock as imperative for his effectiveness in his duties. In recent years, there has risen a group of men who have great influence despite their questionable teachings and practices. The church is increasingly weakened as many follow their pernicious ways, the testimony of Christ is tarnished by them, hence the question is raised "what is the role of teaching in the strengthening of the church today?"

To answer this question, the Bible and Church history will be considered to see what place the Bible accords teaching in the life of God's people and in the work of the ministry. What light does the testimony of history shed on the place, importance and effect of proper teaching in the life of the church? The avenues available for teaching and the current state of the teaching ministry will be considered before prescriptions for strengthening of the teaching ministry are given. All this is aimed at emphasizing the centrality and necessity of teaching in the pastoral ministry and the life of the church. The need for solid biblical teaching in the church and for teachers who would study, know, and rightly divide and handle the Word of God is dire. May God grant that the church would have such men!

DEDICATIONS

The author wishes to acknowledge his indebtedness and express gratitude to the many who have contributed to the completion of this work. This research has benefited from the prayers, concern, and support of many. First and foremost, thanks and praise and glory be to God who has granted grace, strength, wisdom and by His providence availed help when needed in different forms and through different persons.

Secondly, thank God for the Far Eastern Bible College for the opportunity she accorded the author to both study the Word of God and to grow through the studies and for the advice, insight, guidance and corrections her faculty has given in the process of writing this paper. To Dr. Jeffrey Khoo as thesis advisor, the author is grateful for his patience, time, and insights in the course of the research and writing process. The author also thanks Ms Carol Lee for her guidance and input.

Finally, thank God for the Holy Trinity Church in Africa, Faith College of the Bible, and Bomet Bible Institute fraternities for their assistance and above all for their moral support and prayers during the whole period. Rev. Dr. Raymond Carlson played an important role in both challenging and supporting the author in the pursuit of this work. The author also acknowledges his wife and his parents and their role in the completion of the work, especially his late dad, who before passing on to glory was a great inspiration and example in the pastoral work and greatly influenced and guided the author in his pastoral pursuits and studies. Many are they who through encouragement, prayer, insight and support this work has come to its completion, and to them all, the author is indebted.

DEDICATED TO THE MEMORY OF:

My Dad
Rt. Rev. Job Ogutu Were
1946 – 2018
A father, friend, mentor and pastor whose discipline,
discipleship and direction, God used to guide me into
the ministry.

CONTENTS

ABSTRACT	*3*
DEDICATIONS	*4*
CONTENTS	*5*
INTRODUCTION	*8*
Need	18
Presuppositions	20
Purpose	21
CHAPTER I: BIBLICAL BASIS FOR THE TEACHING MINISTRY OF THE CHURCH	*23*
The Place of Teaching in the Bible	24
Teaching is a Calling and a Gift from God	26
Teaching is Part of Pastoral Duty	27
Teaching Is Part of the Church's Life and Commission	27
Biblical Terminology Related to Teaching	28
Teach	30
Deuteronomy 4:1 (*lamadh*)	31
2 Chronicles 15:3 (*yarah*)	36
2 Timothy 2:2 (*didasko*)	39
Doctrine	40
Pastor	43
Biblical Examples on Teaching	46
Deuteronomy 6:1-9 (*Shanan*)	47
Galatians 6:6 (*katecheo*)	48
Injunctions for Teaching in the Assembly (Biblical Basis for Church Indoctrination)	48
Acts 11:26 – Teaching as a Means of Christian Growth	49
1 Corinthians 12:28 – Teaching as a Gift of the Holy Spirit	50
1 Samuel 12:23 – Teaching as a Safeguard against Sinning	51
Ezra 7:10, 25 – Teaching as a Means of Effecting Obedience	52
Injunctions for Teaching and Mentoring Ministers (Biblical Basis for Pastoral Training)	54
CHAPTER II: HISTORICAL EXAMPLES OF SOUND TEACHING MINISTRY	*58*
IN the Home — Richard Baxter at Kidderminster, England	59
Introduction	59
About the Man Richard Baxter	60
The Pastoral Practice of Richard Baxter	63
Biblical Principles for Contemporary Application from Richard Baxter's Ministry	64
From the Pulpit — John Calvin in Geneva, Switzerland	69
Introduction	69
About the Man John Calvin	70
The Pastoral Practice of John Calvin	73
Biblical Principles for Contemporary Application from the Ministry of John Calvin	80
In the Missions Field — William Carey in India	85
Introduction	85
About the Man	86
The Pastoral Practice of William Carey	90
Biblical Principles for Contemporary Application from William Carey's Ministry	95
In PASTORAL Training and Mentoring — John Brown of Haddington, Scotland	98
Introduction	98
About the Man	99
The Pastoral Practice of John Brown	103
Biblical Principles for Contemporary Application from John Brown's Ministry	107

Concluding Observations _____ 109

CHAPTER III: TEACHING AVENUES AVAILABLE FOR THE CHURCH TODAY _____ 112

In the Home _____ 116
Family Worship _____ 121
The Basis for Family Worship _____ 122
Commitment to God is a family issue – Joshua 24:15 _____ 122
Family is the agency for strengthening the faith – 2 Timothy 1:5; 3:15 _____ 122
Family is the agency for spreading the Gospel of the Kingdom – Proverbs 22:6 _____ 122
The Practice of Family Worship _____ 123
The role of the father in family worship – Job 1:1-5 _____ 123
The role of the children in family worship – 1 Timothy 5:4 _____ 124
Practical Steps for a Family Worship Service _____ 125
Why is it Necessary to Introduce and Teach the Catechism in the Church? _____ 135
The Practice of Catechism _____ 138
Practical Steps in Catechism at Home _____ 140
In the Church _____ 142
Christian Education Department and the Teaching Avenues Available to Aid Growth in Grace and Knowledge of Christ _____ 150
Spiritual awareness (2 Pet. 3:17) _____ 150
Spiritual growth (2 Pet. 3:18) _____ 150
The Practice of the Sunday School _____ 154
The Teaching (Content and Curriculum) of the Sunday School _____ 157
The Organisation (Time and Class Grouping) of the Sunday School _____ 158
Mid-week Bible Study and Home Fellowship Programs _____ 159
Vacation Bible Schools and Vacation Bible Training Programs _____ 160
Christian Education Department and the Teaching Avenues Available to Aid in Serving God and Fellow-men _____ 160
Hebrews 5:12-6:3 _____ 160
The Bible College _____ 163
The need for the Bible College as a Teaching Avenue _____ 165
The practice of the Bible College as a Teaching Avenue _____ 170
Training for Christian Ministry (Ephesians 4:11-16) _____ 171
Training for Christian Stewardship and Church Leadership (Ephesians 4:17-28) _____ 173
Concluding Observations _____ 174
Ignorance _____ 175

CHAPTER IV: THE CURRENT STATE OF BIBLE TEACHING IN THE CHURCH IN KENYA _____ 177

The Teaching of Christianity in the Kenyan School Curriculum _____ 180
The Influence of Africa Traditional Culture and Promotion of an "African Theology" _____ 182
The Influence of Popular International Televangelists and their Writings _____ 184
FACTORS CONTRIBUTING TO THE DECLINE OF BIBLE TEACHING _____ 185
The Neglect of Scriptures through Substitution _____ 186
Call to assemble and regulations for gathering (Exod. 19:10-15) _____ 187
The Word of God proclaimed to the assembly (Exod. 20:1-17; 21:1-23:33) _____ 187
Congregational response and covenant (Exod. 20:18-21; 24:3-11) _____ 188
The Neglect of Scriptures through Dilution _____ 188
Neglect through Subordination of Scriptures _____ 190
EVIDENCES OF THE DECLINE OF BIBLE TEACHING _____ 194
Secularism _____ 195
Syncretism _____ 195
Materialism _____ 197
CONCLUDING OBSERVATIONS _____ 198

CONTENTS

CHAPTER V: PRESCRIPTIONS AND SUGGESTIONS FOR STRENGTHENING THE TEACHING MINISTRY OF THE CHURCH — *200*

- The PERSPECTIVE hindering the teaching ministry of the church — 202
- Strengthening, reviving and reforming theological training — 206
- Address The Prevailing Mindset — 207
- Set Clear Standards For Bible Teaching And Theological Training — 208
- Train, Equip and Qualify Men for the Work of the Ministry — 210
- Identify Persons or Groups that Need Discipling, Training and Mentoring for the Work of the Ministry — 211
- Identify Available, Viable, and Credible Training Options — 211
- Promote a Working Ideal — 211
- Affirming the textual basis for the teaching ministry of the church — 215
- What Ought to Be Believed concerning the Text of the Bible? — 217
- The Verbal Plenary Inspiration of the Bible — 217
- The Words of the Bible: — 218
- The Writers of the Bible: — 218
- The Verbal Plenary Preservation of the Bible — 219
- Passages Which Present the Attributes of God — 219
- Passages Which Present the Attributes of God's Word — 220
- Passages Which Warn against the Adulteration of God's Word — 220
- Passages Which Present the Availability and Necessity of God's Word — 221
- Passages Which Confirm and Illustrate the Preservation of God's Word — 221
- Which Text Ought to Be the Basis for Teaching in the Church? — 223
- The Canonicity of the Bible — 224
- Canonicity of the Old Testament Books — 224
- Canonicity of the New Testament Books — 226
- The Transmission and Translation of the Bible — 228
- The Texts to be Translated — 229
- The Translators to do the Work — 235
- The Translation Techniques Employed — 237
- The Theological Considerations of the Translators — 240
- Teaching and pastoral aids for strengthening the church — 243
- Theological Education — 243
- Pastoral Tools and Library — 250
- Concluding Observations — 252

CONCLUSION — *254*

BIBLIOGRAPHY — *255*
- BOOK SOURCES — 255
- ELECTRONIC AND INTERNET SOURCES — 266

ABOUT THE AUTHOR — *272*

CURRICULUM VITAE — *272*
- PERSONAL DETAILS: — 272
- EDUCATION AND TRAINING: — 272
- TEACHING EXPERIENCE: — 272
- WORK EXPERIENCE: — 272
- PUBLICATIONS: — 273

INTRODUCTION

The modern-day understanding of the pastor and the pastoral office has given rise to many varied practices, and with it, varied schools of pastoral and practical theology. What is a pastor? What are his duties and roles in relation to the church? In considering these questions, one cannot disregard the church and its role and purpose. The modern-day pastor has become a corporate executive, a motivational speaker among other roles that were never part of the role of the pastor in the New Testament Church. And these modern-day roles are being performed at the expense of the biblical roles of pastors as taught in the New Testament. Pastoral theology and training have taken the same turn with an increasing emphasis on sociology, humanistic anthropology, psychology and group dynamics, and leadership and marketing principles and a decreasing emphasis on doctrine and theology. This paradigm shift prompts the question: "What is pastoral theology?"

Pastoral theology is a branch of theology that focuses on the pastoral office and what the Bible states about the person, character and office of the pastor and minister of the Gospel of Christ. The question that pastoral theology should address is what the Bible says about the pastor and his office. A survey of pastoral theology textbooks of the past reveals this biblical emphasis, an emphasis that seems to be lacking today. Gregory Bedell defines Pastoral Theology as the "Theory of the practice of theology in Pastoral care."[1] In explaining and clarifying his definition, Bedell goes on to explain that "Pastoral Theology is the science of applying a knowledge of Divine things to the relationships and duties of a Pastor."[2] This means that the pastoral office and duties thus focus on the application of biblical principles and injunctions to everyday situations. This means that the pastor in his pastoral work, deals both with the Scripture and with the people under his care and is to relate what the Scriptures say to what the people experience from day-to-day. Bedell illustrates this by comparing pastoral theology as a study to two other fields, that of law and of medicine. He writes,

> So in Law and Medicine, this department is named the "theory and practice" or more correctly, the theory of the practice. By this knowledge men are prepared, in the one case, to apply principles of law to practice at the Bar; and in the other, to apply their knowledge of the curative powers of medicines, and the modes of administering remedies, to the cure of disease. In like manner Pastoral Theology stands between a knowledge of Divine things, and the application of that knowledge to the cure of souls.[3]

Pastoral theology as a study is thus intended to equip the pastor with principles which he can apply and relate to all of life's situations he encounters in the course of his life's ministry. This branch of study is concerned with the principles and application of the truth of the Word of God to practical everyday situations that the minister faces in his ministry and is thus concerned with the theory and practice of the Gospel ministry. Pastoral theology is by some referred to as Practical Theology[4] because it addresses the is-

---

[1] Gregory Thurston Bedell, *The Pastor: Pastoral Theology* (Philadelphia: J. P. Lippincott & Co., 1880), 45.

[2] Ibid.

[3] Bedell, *The Pastor: Pastoral Theology*, 45-46.

[4] "It is the art of applying usefully, in the ministry, the knowledge acquired in the three other departments of theology, which are purely scientific. It appears, then, that we may very conveniently call Pastoral Theology that collection of rules or directions to which we have given the name of Practical Theology." [A. Vinet, *Pastoral Theology: or the Theory of the Evangelical Ministry*, translated and edited by Thomas H. Skinner (New York: Harper & Brothers Publishers, 1853), 21.]

INTRODUCTION

sues, and aspects of ministry related to the person and work of the pastor and the relationships involved in pastoral ministry. Murphy, in answering the question "What is Pastoral Theology?" writes,

> That department of study whose object is to assist the Christian minister in applying the truths of the gospel to the hearts and lives of men is called Pastoral Theology. It is "theology" because it has chiefly to do with the things of God and his word. It is "pastoral" because it treats of these divine things in that aspect of them which pertains to the pastor. It is practical because it relates to the work of the pastor as he is appointed to influence men by applying to them the teachings of the Holy Scriptures.[5]

Murphy in his explanation highlights three aspects of what pastoral theology chiefly deals with. First, he points out that it deals with the things of God. This was the apostolic understanding found in Acts 6 which led to the choosing of the seven. Priority must be placed on the things of God. Hence training must emphasize the Bible and Theology. Second, it deals with the things of God in relation to the work and office of the pastor. This highlights how the pastor is to handle and relate to, the things of God when discharging his duties and responsibilities. Hence, the training must be pastoral. Third, it gives principles and wisdom on how the Word of God is to be related to daily life and to be applied to particular situations. Hence, the training must be practical.

In explaining the practical aspect, Murphy shows what avenues and means are available to the pastor by which he can use to apply the wisdom attained to the hearers either generally or particularly with respect to their situations, obligations or challenges. He writes that, "pastoral theology deals with sermonizing only in its most general aspects, and at the point of its immediate contact with the hearts of men."[6] Apart from sermonizing as an avenue and means used by the pastor in reaching his hearers, there is also the aspect of character and testimony. The pastor's character is necessary in accomplishing pastoral duties as Murphy observes,

> The pastoral office is one of such overwhelming importance and sacredness that it cannot be successfully exercised unless it enlists the heart of the pastor. His heart, his whole heart, glowing with love to God and men, is one of the chief ingredients of its power. The cultivation of his heart, then, his personal piety, is the first thing that must be studied in this science of the gospel ministry.[7]

The uniqueness, importance and sacredness of the office of the pastor, in comparison to other offices that men may hold, demands of the men who hold this office a clear view and understanding of the duties, responsibilities and obligations required of them by virtue of the office. It is also clear, from Murphy's definition, that the pastoral office cannot be executed without the exercise of the heart or without the faithful interpretation and application of the Holy Scriptures. Functions and duties of the pastor revolve around the Holy Scriptures and its faithful application. Preparation and training of the pastor must thus emphasize and build a mastery of the Holy Scriptures and the wisdom needed in using and applying the Scriptures lawfully.

The pastor as an ambassador of God to men and a teacher of the holy oracles, is not only to present the truths he teaches and preaches but also present himself to those who attend to his words. Thus, the pastoral office does not only have a public aspect but

---

[5] Thomas Murphy, *Pastoral Theology. The pastor in the various duties of his office* (Audubon, New Jersey: Old Paths Publications, 1996), 13.

[6] Ibid.

[7] Murphy, *Pastoral Theology*, 14-15.

also a personal one. Concerning the personal aspect of the pastoral office, W. Walsham How writes that "the work we are to consider is work which depends for its success upon the personal character of the worker more than any other sort of work does."[8] Pastoral work is not about filling churches with people or amassing followers. It is about making disciples of all nations. Disciples who will "love the Church for her own sake, attend her services as a duty and privilege, and lean far less upon the individual than they so often do."[9] But in order to do this successfully, there must be an emphasis on building the inner man, and pointing and leading people to Christ as Scripture states that *"All that the Father giveth me shall come to me ..."* (John 6:37) and that *"... if I be lifted up from the earth, will draw all men unto me"* (John 12:32). From the human agency's perspective, Paul says, *"Be ye followers of me, even as I also am of Christ"* (1 Corinthians 11:1). These point to the fact that pastoral work demands the personal influence of the pastor as Walsham rightly states,

> God has so ordered things that, practically, we must depend much on personal influence to win and attract and retain our people; and he who resolves to go upon the plan of leaving Church principles, Church services, and Church teaching, to win their way by their own intrinsic power, apart from the exercise of personal gifts, will have a limited number of subjects for his experiment. Thus, it is most necessary for one looking forward to the holy office of the ministry to foster those gifts and cultivate those powers by which he may best commend his teaching and his services to his people.[10]

The work of the ministry cannot be divorced from the person of the minister and so Pastoral Theology seeks, with regard to the person of the minister, to address areas such as the call and qualifications, the personal life and pastoral responsibility to self and congregation. Right practice proceeds from right belief and, as evidence of right belief, commends the teachings and instructions of the pulpit to the pew with authority that no words can. This distinguishes the pastoral vocation from any other vocation that man has endeavoured to pursue. The gifting and training of a pastor are therefore intrinsically connected. Anyone seeking to enter into the Gospel ministry does not have the luxury of choosing either one or the other, but of necessity requires both gifting and training for the ministry. Paul, speaking to the Ephesian elders in Acts 20, exhorted them to take heed to themselves and then to the flock of God, showing that the person of the minister is a necessary part of the ministry. Ashton Oxenden observes rightly that the motif of the sheep which is frequently employed in Scripture,

> Describes men not merely as sheep, but as "sheep" that "have gone astray;" and the Son of God is spoken of as the Great "Shepherd of the sheep" "the Good Shepherd," "the Chief Shepherd," "the Shepherd and Bishop of souls," who counted not his life too dear a price to pay for the recovery of his flock.[11]

This motif points out the condition of man as lost, and also identifies the deepest, most urgent need of man as reconciliation, recovery, and restoration to fellowship with his shepherd. This need is fulfilled not through the primacy of social, cultural, political or economic intervention, but rather is fulfilled in Christ the Good Shepherd who laid down

---

[8] W. Walsham How, *Lectures on Pastoral Work: delivered in the Divinity School, Cambridge, 1883* (London: Wells Gardner, Darton & Co., 1884), 5.

[9] Ibid.

[10] How, *Lectures on Pastoral Work*, 5.

[11] Ashton Oxenden, *The Pastoral Office: its Duties, Difficulties, Privileges, and Prospects* (Bible House, New York: Protestant Episcopal Society for the Promotion of Evangelical Knowledge, n.d.), 2.

INTRODUCTION

His life for the sheep. Christ who came to seek and save that which was lost, who laid down His life for the sheep and took it up again as He had received command from the Father, and gave gifts to men (Eph 4:9-11). These gifts were given to men who were once lost and had gone astray, but having been reconciled to the Bishop of their souls, were to take charge, as under-shepherds of the Great Shepherd, over their fellows to feed the flock of Christ which He had purchased with His blood. Oxenden aptly describes this saying,

> The picture, however, yet needs something to make it complete. It represents the sheep of the flock and their condition; and Christ, their loving Shepherd, seeking them out and gathering them together, ordering every thing for their good, watching over them with untiring care, and ready to conduct them at last to that safe and happy fold above which He has purchased for them and prepared for their reception. But this Almighty Shepherd is now in heaven, whilst his sheep are still upon earth; and though He could feed them from thence as easily as if He were still going in and out among them in person, yet He is pleased to employ men poor, feeble, unworthy men to act the Shepherd's part and take charge of His beloved flock. This, then, is the office of the Christian Minister; he is an Under-Shepherd, in subordination to Christ the Chief Shepherd. And happy is it for us in this country, and under our pastoral system, that each minister has his own appointed charge, each shepherd his own allotted portion of the flock to tend.[12]

Representing Christ, the Chief Shepherd, first and above all, demands that none would enter the pastoral ministry uncalled and none would go into any area of the ministry unsent. The rigours and responsibilities of the duties of the ministry, the oversight to be taken over the flock and the example to be set for them, as well as the hope laid and the judgment awaiting those who take up for themselves the office and work of the ministry, require of all that one would make sure he is called to, gifted and prepared for, equipped and trained before venturing into the ministry. Thus, the very notable increase both of churches and preachers in Kenya over the past years is very worrying when it is considered that many have taken upon themselves the work of the ministry of the Gospel with no training or biblical knowledge and in some cases, even no visible evidence of saving grace at work. The decreasing emphasis on theology and Scripture on the one hand, coupled with the increasing emphasis on psychology, sociology, humanism, and consumerism on the other hand, in the courses being offered to students preparing for the pastoral ministry and in the institutions claiming to prepare men for ministry adds to the concern. John Burgon's words in the preface of his treatise on the pastoral office fitly presents the desire of this writer as he addresses the necessity of the teaching ministry in strengthening the church. Burgon says,

> This "strange and well-nigh incredible custom which has prevailed among us, and is only beginning in the rarest instances to be broken through, (of our Clergy being admitted to their holy office without a shadow of training in the duties, but specially in the mind and habit proper to it, and essential to the well-being of the Church)"— must strike the most careless observer. I humbly hope that the day is not far distant when it may be generally deemed as ridiculous as to myself it seems that this most difficult and dangerous of all offices should be entered upon with less preparation than almost any other calling in the world. Professors of every branch of human learning are thought to require a long course of preliminary study. Physicians of the body are carefully trained for their function. By what strange infatuation is it expected that the Physician of souls should have an intuitive acquaintance with every department of his vocation? Or judged reasonable that the teacher of Sacred Learn-

---

[12] Oxenden, *The Pastoral Office*, 3.

ing in a parish should sometimes know no more Divinity than some of the children in his own Sunday-school? Why, there is scarcely a trade or a handicraft but requires a prolonged apprenticeship. Is it expected that men will become Theologians suddenly, and by intuition?[13]

What is it that has reversed the gains that Burgon was beginning to see in his time? What is it that has taken the church back to that sorry state in which men enter the ministry without a shadow of training? Why should men think that "this most difficult and dangerous of all offices should be entered upon with less preparation than almost any other calling in the world"? Why do they think that the ministry is to be left for those who have failed in their attempts at other professions and callings in the world? Why are pastors not acquainted with the Bible today? The lack of biblical, theological and doctrinal understanding in the pulpit definitely results in a similar lack in the pew, and such, in the view of this writer, is a great contributor to the growth of all forms of adulteration of the gospel and the rise of all sorts of personality cults. The church is ailing and weak because the pulpit is weak. Burgon points out the logical and reasonable conclusion that training and preparation is an absolute necessity and prerequisite for service. Those who would enter into service untrained and unprepared, end up doing great disservice. The Word is alive and powerful, a two-edged sword, but those who would wield it faithfully and masterfully are few and thus begins the decay of the church. Commenting on Ephesians 4:14, the Africa Bible Commentary notes,

> Lack of maturity leads to stunted growth, with believers remaining like infants, dependent on others and open to every influence (4:14). A lack of sound doctrine and teaching will result in a fragmented church with a weak faith and inadequate knowledge of Christ. Such a church is vulnerable to the influence of false teachers. Immature Christians accept whatever they are told by teachers who may be motivated by greed or who rely on purely human wisdom. With no stable rock to stand on, weak Christians are tossed around and become unstable.[14]

One of the reasons for the proliferation of false teaching and false teachers is the lack of sound doctrine in the church. Thus, the problem that needs to be addressed is the lack of emphasis on the teaching ministry of both the church and the pastor. The need of the times and age is the propagation of sound doctrine and teaching. This need is highlighted by the increase in apostasy. The need to teach as part of the pastoral ministry is of utmost importance to the church living in the midst of a wicked and perverse generation. The church needs to shine, and it is important the pastor sees this—that he is obligated before God and is duty-bound toward his fellow-men in view of the present danger. As one reads through the pastoral letters in the New Testament, the repetition of *"teaching"* and *"sound doctrine"* is quite clear. 1 Timothy 1:3-4 gives a glimpse of what Timothy was to do in Ephesus as pastor, which is, to take control and oversight of the teachings ensuring that only that which is sound is taught and that no other doctrines are taught, and to face the challenge of men who have strayed and yet desire to teach what they do not know the faith or the truth (1 Tim. 1:7).

Such duties and obligations as those required of Timothy and Titus by the Apostle Paul are outlined in the pastoral epistles, and they require and emphasize the necessity and need to train and prepare pastors for the ministry. To this effect, Enoch Pond observes concerning the training programs of his time that, "The studies pursued in the the-

---

[13] John W. Burgon, *A Treatise on the Pastoral Office: addressed chiefly to candidates for holy orders, or those who have recently undertaken the cure of souls* (London: MacMillan and Co., 1864), x.

[14] *Africa Bible Commentary: a one volume commentary written by 70 African Scholars*. Gen. Ed. Tokunboh Adeyemo (Nairobi, Kenya: Word Alive Publishers, 2006), 1434.

ological seminaries of our country are chiefly calculated to prepare the youthful preacher for the more public duties of the sacred office, — for the devotions and instructions of the sanctuary."[15] The pastoral office comprises not only of public duties alone, but also of private duties, and the oversight exercised by pastors is not limited to church attendance and the numbers that appear to hear the Sunday sermon. As Paul said to the Ephesian elders, the pastor is to teach them publicly and from house to house, setting himself up as an example and pattern for Christian life and conduct, and thus by this way, "exert upon them, in the house, by the way, in their seasons of prosperity and adversity, in sickness and affliction, when rejoicing in hope, or mourning in spiritual darkness and desertion, or anxiously inquiring the way to heaven."[16]

Thus, in reviewing the writings of the 1800s in regard to their perspective and view of pastoral theology as training in preparation for the pastoral office, one sees that their understanding of pastoral theology included the duties and preparations for the pastoral ministry. The preparations go with the whole person: preparation of the heart, the mind and the mouth of the minister. This was so due to their view of both the person and the office of the pastor. This view consistently regards the office as a "sacred office"[17] and "an office beset with the gravest difficulties"[18] and thus an office which has duties and obligations which require the exercise of the heart, the mind, and the strengths, talents and giftings of the person holding the office. The pastor in his duties will be constantly and consistently be required "to visit, to catechize, to prepare candidates for confirmation, or for the Lord's Supper, and must trust throughout to the suggestions of the moment for direction and help."[19] Therefore, as one cannot be involved in something he knows nothing about, the pastor will need to know the duties he is to attend to, first, in the scriptural injunctions governing the duties and controlling principles related to the performance of those duties, and second, in the history, methods, and the objectives used both in the performance of the duties and the attaining of the goals intended. When these are lacking, the pastor will "as a matter of prudence, to deal with generalities: to be rhetorical and vague, instead of precise and instructive"[20] or else even worse still, resort to things unrelated to the call and work of the pastor as is increasingly becoming the norm. The preparations for pastoral ministry, therefore, have to prepare the heart, the mind and the mouth of the minister. His heart needs to be prepared as it is the seat of all his devotions, his mind too as with it he tackles the subjects and with his mouth he is to exhort, rebuke, reprove and instruct the flock. And all this is to be done both privately and publicly.

The practical requirements that the ministry places daily on the minister cannot be presumptuously done. They need preparation of the heart and mind and, as such, the maturing and teaching of the flock becomes intrinsically tied to the preparation of the minister. The "generalities" and "rhetoric" of the untrained and unprepared minister will never work towards the training and maturing of the flock. So the pastor needs preparation and training not only for competency, so that he can handle himself and the duties of the ministry well, but also for the church, so that, when he is able with competence to handle himself and the duty well, he is able to teach and mature the flock committed to

---

[15] Enoch Pond, *Lectures on Pastoral Theology* (Andober: Warner F. Draper, 1866), 3.

[16] Ibid.

[17] Pond, *Lectures on Pastoral Theology*, 3.

[18] Burgon, *A Treatise on the Pastoral Office*, ix.

[19] Ibid.

[20] Ibid.

his charge, and as such he is able both to save himself and them that attend to his ministry. For this, the pastor will require "especially an intellect divinely enlightened and the peculiar ability publicly to expound these great things divinely revealed, as ministering salvation to the soul of man."[21]

This is the consistent testimony and view of Scripture in reference to the person and office of the pastor. The Pastoral epistles, in setting forth the qualifications for those who would attend to the office of the ministry, clearly points out the need for both a moral character above reproach and proper preparation and training. This is seen when one examines both 1 Timothy 3 and Titus 1. In 1 Timothy 3 verses 2 and 6 respectively, Paul points out that he should be apt to teach as well as not a novice. It is to be noted that these are intertwined with moral qualifications that have to do with the character of the man. In Titus 1, verse 9 presents clearly the need for trained men holding the office with verses 10 and 11 presenting what the training will help him accomplish. Generally stated, the work of the ministry is aimed at changing men, influencing their character and way of life, and as such, Balikie rightly notes,

> It is impossible to conceive any change so great or so glorious as that which the Christian ministry is thus designed to effect. It aims at a radical change in the relation of men to God an entire change, too, of character and; life; it aims at bringing men habitually under the influence of the purest motives, and at making their life the best and noblest possible, and the fittest preparation for the life to come. The influence of the Christian minister must not terminate with his public services; it is designed, under God's blessing, to be a silent power with his people during every hour of their lives; in hours of work and in hours of rest, in the market-place and the counting-house, in the family and in the closet prevailing, through the power of the Spirit, above all contrary influences, counteracting some of the strongest natural inclinations, and bringing every thought into captivity to the obedience of Christ.[22]

How is all this to be accomplished? The radical change in relationship to God, in character and life, in motives and world-view and in focus of the life to come is designed to be achieved through the agency and influence of the Christian minister in the pastoral office, and that is why Balikie observes that the minister "must not terminate with his public services." The Pastoral Theology books of the 1800s also consistently agree that the means availed for the effecting of a fruitful and God-honouring pastoral ministry have to be centred and founded on the Word of God. Balikie explains,

> For accomplishing all these changes, the chief instrument furnished to the Christian minister is the Word. He is to come into contact with men chiefly by means of spoken truth. What his Master has committed to him is "the word of reconciliation" (2 Cor. v. 18). As a sower, "he soweth the word" (Mark iv. 14). As a preacher, he preaches the word (2 Tim. iv. 2). That word is "the word of salvation" (Acts xiii. 26). It is the forerunner of faith and all other vital graces faith cometh by hearing, and hearing by the word of "God" (Rom. x. 17). We do not speak at present of the unseen power that makes the instrument efficient; we advert to what is outward and apparent the means furnished to the minister for effecting the change. So far as he is concerned, that change must be effected by the delivery of a message from God a message which, in the first instance, reveals

---

[21] Stephen II Tyng, *The Office and Duty of the Christian Pastor* (New York: Harper & Brothers Publishers, 1874), 12.

[22] William Garden Balikie, *For the Work of the Ministry: A Manual of Homiletical and Pastoral Theology* (London: Strahan and Co., 1873), 1.

the way to his favour, but which has bearings at the same time on the whole sphere of human life and duty.[23]

There is no sphere or area of life that is not affected by the Word of God and there is no duty that is not effected by the Word of God and as such, the Christian's life and duty has to be touched by the work of the pastor. The work of the pastor in order to touch and change the life of the Christian has to centre on the Word of God, thus making the pastor a minister of the Word above all else. Thus, one must ask, "Is it possible to attain the qualifications and duties of the pastor and the office of the minister without seeing the need for the training of men for the work of the ministry as well as in sound doctrine?" One must also ask, "If the need is imperative, then what ought to be the content of the training and preparation for the work of the ministry?" Finally, one must ask, "Can effective preparation for the ministry of the Word discard the Word?"

When those who are set on the pulpit ministry to instruct others on the things of God have not been fully instructed in all aspects of the ministry to which they have entered, they do not only become ineffective, they are harmful to the ministry. The ministry is "the ministry of the Word," and as such the minister must be thoroughly acquainted with the Word.

Whatever training program that is set for those preparing for the ministry has to major upon the Word. Knowing the Word, understanding the Word, practising the Word, rightly dividing the Word and accurately presenting the Word to the flock ought to be the emphasis. The Word is not to be replaced or displaced from its rightful position in the preparation for and subsequently in the work of the ministry. Burgon notes concerning the centrality of the Bible in the pastoral ministry,

> In the front of any treatise on the Christian Ministry, must be placed the study of that much-neglected book, — the Bible. It is the one revelation to man of God's mind and will. Nothing which is not read therein, nor may be proved thereby, is "to be required of any man that it should be believed as an article of the Faith." All other books which relate to the science of Divinity, have grown directly out of this. They are expositions of its teaching, or formularies of its doctrines; commentaries on its meaning, or exhortations based upon its precepts; treatises on its idiom, or discussions of its difficulties; unfolding of its prophecies, or helps to its correct understanding. They all point back to the Bible: appeal to it, refer to it, submit themselves to its decision. From this celestial armoury, the minister of Christ derives all his weapons.[24]

Why then is the emphasis of modern-day pastoral training moving away from the Word? Why is there a neglect of the Bible in the training of ministers of the Bible? In an article in *Christianity Today*, Linda Perkins observes the shift in trends for pastoral training. While quoting Marshall Shelley, she notes that "since the 70s and 80s, pastoral training has emphasized leadership because churches needed pastors who could do more than shepherd."[25] Herein begins the problem. Men have sought to do more than just shepherd the flock, and have pursued the other duties at the expense of pastoring. They have left undone the work that they are supposed to do. And the result is that both the Bible and pastoral office has been used for varied reasons other than that for which they are prescribed.

---

[23] Balikie, *For the Work of the Ministry*, 2.

[24] Burgon, *A Treatise on the Pastoral Office*, 1.

[25] Linda Perkins, "Pastoral Training Is Changing", *CT Pastors*, accessed February 21, 2018, https://www.christianitytoday.com/pastors/2018/February-web-exclusives/pastoral-training-is-changing.html.

The rise in the number of false teachers who draw people after themselves and leading them astray, as well as the rise in the number of those who cannot endure sound doctrine and seek an alternative voice and message to that which was once and for all delivered unto the saints, are a call for the return to sound doctrinal and pastoral teaching. The rise in popularity of "Bible Teachers" and "Bible Messages" that pamper to the flesh, that make the sinner comfortable in his sin, that require no turning away from the world, the flesh, sin and the devil, that does not require sorrow for sin, that presents man as basically good and God as too loving and magnanimous to judge, that puts away the cross as offensive and the blood as unneedful today, that measures spirituality in terms of material and physical wealth and possession, and the message that is all-inclusive, demands a pastoral ministry that teaches and preaches the cross. Sound doctrine is to be clearly and loudly propagated and systematically presented the more when men cannot endure it. The pastoral ministry does the church a great disservice and does the Lord a great dishonour when pastors shy away from the truth and when the whole counsel of God is not declared. The rising apostasy may be a sign of the end times as prophesied and as such must increase and cannot be stopped, but the flock needs to be fed, the church needs to be warned and thus sound doctrinal preaching and teaching need to be the true church's recourse. Silence of the pulpit aids in the propagation of error, hence the need to re-examine the doctrines the church espouses and that which it propagates. Adama Ouedraogo in his article notes,

> Today, numerous Africans are following such illustrious predecessors and proclaiming themselves as prophets or apostles and creating their own religious movements.
>
> The emergence of African prophets and apostles allowed for the proclamation of equality of blacks and whites in faith and ministry (Gal 3:28; Col 3:11). It also established the principle of the separation of the Christian faith from all colonial political connections. These positive effects justify the reputation these men enjoy.
>
> However, there are also some more negative aspects associated with the emergence of African prophets and apostles. Many of them lack biblical and theological training and rely solely on their own gifts. But the growth of the church depends on the exercise of a variety of complementary gifts. An apostle or prophet cannot go it alone without the help of teachers (Eph 4:11-14). Those who want to preach the word of God must therefore study it seriously or surround themselves with those who have done so.
>
> Despite their claim to be promoting mainstream Christianity, many African prophets and apostles do not take the Bible as the basis for their faith and conduct. Instead, their teaching is based on direct revelation that they receive from God for their prophetic and messianic mission. They regard their teachings as additions to the Bible. However, the Bible warns against making the slightest addition to the word (Rev. 22:18-19).[26]

What are these positive effects that justify the reputation of Africa's modern-day apostles and prophets? The first pointed out by Adama is "the proclamation of equality of blacks and whites in ministry" and the second is "the principle of separation of the Christian faith from all colonial political connections." These effects are neither biblical nor theological, but rather social and political, yet men who lay claim to biblical offices justify and use them for aims and effects that are not biblical.

---

[26] Adama Ouedraogo, <u>Prophets and Apostles</u>, *Africa Bible Commentary: A One Volume Commentary Written by 70 African Scholars*, Gen Ed., Tokunboh Adeyemo (Nairobi, Kenya: Word Alive Publishers, 2006), 1434.

INTRODUCTION

The picture that Adama paints stands in stark contrast to the emphasis of the Bible as the fundamental foundation that John Burgon presents when he states: "It is the one revelation to man of God's mind and will. Nothing which is not read therein, nor may be proved thereby, is 'to be required of any man that it should be believed as an article of the Faith.'"[27] The ministry and Scripture have been, here in Africa, by some, used politically to establish "the principle of the separation of the Christian faith from all colonial political connections" and socially to "justify the reputation these men enjoy." Apart from this, Adama also points out that "many African prophets and apostles do not take the Bible as the basis for their faith and conduct." Hence an ailing and weak church.

There is a clear departure from the biblical and theological emphasis to one that emphasizes experience, where the modern-day "apostles and prophets" highly elevate "signs and wonders" as the key to reviving the church, encouraging the saints to holy living, winning of souls to Christ; and where motivational speakers parading as shepherds employ modern-day psychological consumer marketing methods for church growth. There is a vital need to revisit the practice of the pastoral ministry and the theology that governs its practices. With many failing to see that the God-ordained means of growing the church and maintaining spirituality among the saints is through the ministry of the Word to the church, and with the presence of diverse ways and means of doing ministry being presented, there is a dire need to revisit pastoral theology and question whether all that is done in the name of God is truly being done in the right and acceptable way that God would expect of His servants and ministers.

This writer has witnessed some of these churches in Kenya that are attended by many people and watched through the media by millions portraying an image of Christianity that is neither Biblical nor Christian. Maureen Waruinge in her article titled "Five Strange Miracles some Pastors Perform" written for Radio Jambo, a local radio station, noting the gullibility of many, said,

> Wonders will never cease when it comes to our church leaders. Some of them are known to do such crazy things that leave the world in dismay.
>
> Kenyans love miracles and perhaps because of this need by faithfuls, pastors feel the need to pretend they can perform the miracles. It has been said that some Kenyans will spend their life savings to get pastors to perform miracles, and while society has tried to intervene not much has been done to stop fake pastors fleecing their followers.[28]

She then goes on to point out claims that have been made and things that have been done by notable televangelists, prophets and apostles. From "pastors" that claim to look into the book of life to confirm whether one's name is in it for a fee,[29] to those who

---

[27] Burgon, *A Treatise on the Pastoral Office*, 1.

[28] Maureen Waruinge, "Five Strange Miracles Some Pastors Perform Archives – Radio Jambo", *Radio Jambo*, accessed October 28, 2017, https://radiojambo.co.ke/tag/five-strange-miracles-some-pastors-perform/.

[29] In 2014, Bishop Thomas Wahome of the "Helicopter Ministries" shocked many when he claimed he had a direct line to heaven and could check if a person's name was in the Lamb's Book of Life. A leading newspaper, The Daily Nation, carried in their "Sunday Nation" edition of 9 August 2015, a story headlined "Controversy is Wahome's Second Name." The article in part reads, "Controversy does not seem to stop stalking Helicopter Ministries head Bishop Thomas Wahome. Ranging from disputes over church property to his teaching in the church, the Bishop has occasionally attracted debatable opinions on who he is and what he stands for. He has been in and out of court due to disputes between him and persons who felt offended by his actions. **The preacher has also sparked controversy in the past for charging his flock to reveal to them whether they would go to heaven or hell. Each member of the congregation could pay Sh1,100 to book an appointment with the preacher and an additional Sh1,500 to confirm if their name is in the Book of Life** [emphasis added]." ["Controversy Is Wahome's Second Name", *Daily Nation*, ac-

traffic babies in the promise of "Miracle Babies"[30] and others who practised fake healing[31] or make a host of absurd claims which are dutifully believed and followed by adherents.

Indeed, it is disturbing to see the things currently being done and taught in the name of Jesus Christ. Church-goers are made to worship in ways and means that are created by man to suit man. They are entertained, amused and then sent home thinking that they have worshipped God. Does God approve when men gather to entertain themselves in the name of worshipping Him? Does God approve when men make merchandise of the name of Christ? There must be something wrong. Many have found themselves in the pulpit who ought not to be there. And whilst in the pulpit they have driven another agenda, taught another gospel and have led astray many captive and fallen. The question arises, why would men take upon themselves a call they have not received? Why would others ascend to the pulpit but not for the cause of Christ? And further still, why would such men, deceived and deceiving, have a strong following and why is the rest of the church keeping quiet about this? These may be questions to which a blanket answer cannot be given, yet they are issues that the teaching ministry of the church and pulpit can do a great deal to stem. This can proceed in a twofold front. On the one hand, the need to train and teach men in preparation for the ministry; and on the other hand to prepare them for the pastoral function of teaching the flock and maturing them so that they are not tossed to and fro by every wind of doctrine. These two fronts are related in that if the preachers are not trained and do not know the Word of God and cannot handle it skilfully and truthfully, then the members cannot be matured through sound teaching and so will become prey to both false teachers and false brethren who may enter in privily.

Need

What is the role of the teaching ministry in the strengthening of the church today? Or rather, what is the place of teaching in the church today? These are questions this paper will deal with. In doing so, the need of teaching, the place of teaching, the contents to be taught and the methods to be used to effect it will need to be considered. All these will be primarily guided by Scripture. There is much training and education going on today and yet the pastoral ministry is ailing. Many pastors, having gone through years of train-

---

cessed December 20, 2016, http://www.nation.co.ke/news/Controversy-is-Wahomes-second-name/-/1056/2826286/-/iual5yz/-/index.html.]

[30] When the BBC asked Mr Deya during its 2014 investigation how he explained the births of children with DNA different to that of their alleged parents, the 65-year-old Mr Deya said: "The miracle babies which are happening in our ministry are beyond human imagination. It is not something I can say I can explain because they are of God and things of God cannot be explained by a human being." ["UK Extradites 'Miracle Pastor' To Kenya", *BBC News*, accessed October 28, 2017, http://www.bbc.com/news/world-africa-40824267.]

[31] An investigation by Kenya's KTN TV station in November 2014 exposed the tricks Victor Kanyari, a famous televangelist, was allegedly using to fool worshippers at his Salvation Healing Ministry church. He used potassium permanganate, a chemical compound that easily dissolves in water to give a reddish solution, to wash the feet of his members and then claim that blood was oozing from their feet as a sign of healing. One of his former aides demonstrated how the preacher performed the trick. Another video shows him putting his hand under a woman's dress to touch her breast, saying this would cure her from breast cancer. The woman is seen turning away from the camera but the preacher forces her to turn around to face the congregation as he exposes her breast for all to see. He then calls for a church worker to anoint the "diseased" breast with oil. The investigation said Kanyari was the son of "Prophetess" Lucy Nduta, another controversial pastor who was convicted in 2009 for "defrauding vulnerable people" claiming she could cure them from Aids. Shortly afterwards, he appeared on another TV programme, saying his "tribulations" were the work of his enemies. ["The Men Who Claim To Be Africa's 'Miracle Workers'", *BBC News*, accessed October 28, 2017, http://www.bbc.com/news/world-africa-38063882.]

ing, are finding the rigours of the pastoral ministry difficult and exhausting; and they find themselves either ill prepared for the ministry or questioning themselves whether it is what they were called into, and what have they got themselves into. This is the result, mainly, of the shift of emphasis in pastoral training from the preparation focusing on the ministry of the Word and prayer, to the preparation of administrators and marketing gurus who focus on social projects and motivational speaking. The scriptural emphasis of the pastoral ministry has always been the Word of God (1 Tim. 4:13-16; Titus 2:1; 2 Tim. 2:2, 15, 22 and 2 Tim. 4:2).

"... *Preach the word; be instant in season, out of season ...*" (2 Tim. 4:1-4).

This work will highlight the importance of the teaching ministry in the church as the duty of the church especially in these last days. Paul's warning to Timothy does not come without an injunction to preach and teach. The statement that *"they will not endure sound doctrine,"* demands that there has to be a constant proclamation and presentation of sound doctrine for them not to endure. The same is reflected in 1 Timothy 4:1 when Paul again says that in the *"latter times some shall depart from the faith."* This departure from the faith presupposes the presence and knowledge of the faith being departed from. Under such circumstances, what is the role and duty of the true ministers? *"Preach the Word"* is what the pastor is called to in 2 Timothy 4:2, and in 1 Timothy 4:6: *"put the brethren in remembrance of these things."* In both passages, the phrase *"sound doctrine"* appears. The church's response to the rise in false doctrines, false teachers, apostasy, etc. is sound doctrine. The preacher's response to an impatient, wilful flesh-focused man and the preacher's response when the generation he serves turns away from the faith and will not endure sound doctrine is to preach the whole counsel of God.

"Sanctify them through thy truth: thy word is truth" (John 17:17).

Another need for this thesis arises from the place and work of the Word in the life of the believer. The church as the body of Christ is to be subject to her Head, and as the bride of Christ, she is to be pure and holy and separate for her Husband. Thus, the need for the church to submit and obey Christ as well as the need of the church to be pure and holy and separate from the world and unto her Lord require the propagating and teaching of the Word of God and of sound doctrine as this is what is reflected in John 17:17. The Word as a means of sanctification needs to be applied and presented faithfully.

> There are two admitted axioms in every department of human science, which will apply with equal force to the matter before us; — viz., that an effect cannot exist without a cause, and that a cause does not operate without the use of means. Let these admitted propositions form the basis of our reasoning upon this important subject. God has designed the sanctification of his people; he has appointed his truth as the great instrument of effecting their sanctification; and in order to accomplish this, he has declared, that his truth must dwell in the heart in the same richness, fullness, and purity with which it is revealed in his word.[32]

The necessity of the Word of Christ to dwell richly in every believer requires the looking into how the church practices her theology especially with regard to the teaching emphasis of the church. This means that ministers in the kingdom of God ought to look into what doctrines the flock committed to their charge is exposed to and root out any wrong teachings that may hinder growth or lead the flock astray. The ministers in the kingdom of God ought to look into the times and the needs of their flock and to feed their flock with what is necessary for their spiritual growth and what can help them draw nigh to God as well as resist the growing apostasy of the times. Like Paul, they must not

---

[32] Octavius Winslow, *Personal Declension and Revival of Religion in the Soul* (Edinburgh: The Banner of Truth Trust, 1978), 112.

shun to declare the whole counsel of God or to give anything that is profitable for the body, but working according to the gifting of the Holy Ghost and in the power which works mightily in them, they should endeavour night and day even with many tears to feed the flock of God, to warn them and rebuke them and instruct them in righteousness with the aim of presenting every man perfect before Christ at His appearing so that the body of Christ in this age may worship and serve and live for their God in a way that He will take pleasure in and that will be a light in the midst of this wicked and perverse generation, giving glory to God and being a blessing to the nation.

Presuppositions

"All scripture is given by inspiration of God, and is profitable for doctrine, for reproof, for correction, for instruction in righteousness: That the man of God may be perfect, thoroughly furnished unto all good works" (2 Tim. 3:16-17).

All issues that will be discussed by this writer will have for its basis and final authority the Word of God. All scriptural references and quotations will be taken from the King James Bible. This writer believes in the divine, verbal and plenary inspiration and preservation of the Scriptures in their original (Greek, Hebrew and Aramaic) languages, their consequent inerrancy and infallibility, and as the Word of God the supreme and final authority in faith and life.

> The scriptural approach to Scripture is thus to regard it as God's written testimony to himself. When we call the Bible the Word of God, we mean, or should mean, that its message constitutes a single utterance of which God is the author. What Scripture says, he says. When we hear or read Scripture, that which impinges on our mind (whether we realize it or not) is the speech of God Himself.[33]

This "scriptural approach to Scripture" creates a world view in which the chief end of man is to glorify God and therefore makes Scripture (God's written Testimony of Himself) both the rule of faith and of practice. As such this paper also presupposes the authority of the Bible and holds the Bible as the final court of appeal of which its verdict on any matter is to be accepted without question. Where the Bible is silent on any matter, speculations are not to be made and whatever is discussed on such matters remains as opinions of men which are fallible and subject to error. In matters of controversy where opinions differ, Paul's injunction in Romans 3:3-4 is to be observed: *"For what if some did not believe? Shall their unbelief make the faith of God without effect? God forbid: yea, let God be true, but every man a liar; as it is written, That thou mightest be justified in thy sayings, and mightest overcome when thou art judged."* Let God be true and all men liars is the biblical principle to be presupposed when dealing with the Word of God as given in the Scriptures as this is the testimony of the Scriptures on God (Num. 23:19; 2 Sam. 7:28; Jer. 10:10).

From this primary presupposition, others drawn from Scripture are to be affirmed since they form the Testimony of God. This writer affirms that the Bible has only one meaning though the applications may be many, and that it is through the help of the Holy Spirit (1 Cor. 2:14, cf. 1 John 2:20, 27) that the authorial intent is to be sought through God-honouring methods of exegesis letting the Bible speak. The reliance on the Holy Spirit's illumination does not negate the need for diligent study for Scripture does say *"study to shew thyself approved unto God a workman that needeth not be ashamed rightly dividing the word of truth"* (2 Tim. 2:15).

---

[33] J. I. Parker, *"Fundamentalism" and the Word of God* (Grand Rapids Michigan: Wm. B. Eerdmans Publishing Co., 1958), 89.

INTRODUCTION

This writer also affirms the divine, verbal and plenary inspiration and preservation of the Scriptures in the original languages, their subsequent inerrancy and infallibility (2 Tim. 3:16-17, cf. 2 Pet. 1:19-21 and Ps. 12:6-7 cf. Matt. 5:17-18; 24:35; Mark 13:31; Luke. 16:17, 21:33), and as the Word of God the supreme and final authority in faith and life. The Bible is God's inspired Word that is profitable for reproof and doctrine that will guide every believer. All issues that will be discussed here by this writer will be based on the Word of God as the final authority and all scriptural references and quotations will be taken from the King James Bible unless otherwise stated.

This writer further affirms the doctrine of grace as taught in Scripture and that the testimony of Scripture is that God in His dealings with man has done so covenantally, first through the covenant of works which our first parents Adam and Eve failed to keep when they disobeyed God and ate of the fruit of the tree of knowledge of good and evil. Then, since the fall, through the covenant of grace often called Federal Theology in which all men are born in sin and that Scripture has concluded all to be under sin and thus in Adam all die and all who would be saved must be saved through the finished work of Christ as accomplished by and represented in His active and passive obedience (Gen. 2:16-17; 3:15; 2 Kings 13:23; Rom. 5:12-21; 1 Cor. 15:21-22; Eph. 2:8-9). From this also the doctrines of (i) Divine Sovereignty of God and Human Responsibility, (ii) the function of the Law as a school master, and the work of the Holy Spirit in conviction of sin and regeneration respectively, (iii) the sufficiency of Christ as the Saviour and the necessity of the work for sanctification and (iv) the Solas of the 16th century Reformation are affirmed.

Purpose

If an evaluation of the church in Kenya is to be conducted, one would find varied practices from orthodox to liberal, biblical and unbiblical, and the increase of strange practices will most definitely catch the eye.[34] Differing gospels being propagated including the so-called gospel of repentance of the Repentance and Holiness Movement; the gospel of prosperity from the Health and Wealth Movements; the social and liberal gospels and a great many variances to these including the rise of African Liberation Theology will be critiqued.[35]

---

[34] Elizabeth Stoddard in her article speaks of her visual experience of Kenya's religiosity. She writes, "The pervasiveness of religion in the everyday lives of Kenyans struck me forcibly when our team was in Kenya this November. As an American who, by nature, is conditioned to keep religion relegated to the private sphere, the omnipresent manifestations of religion all around the city of Nairobi were almost jarring. The store fronts of local businesses bear the name of Mary, Jesus, or God; for instance, God's Mercy Unisex Hair Salon. If the store name had no mention of religion, you were sure to see crosses or art depicting religious scenes somewhere within the store. It seemed as if churches, mosques, synagogues, and temples dotted every intersection. And Nairobi's numerous schools and health facilities often showed signs of sponsorship or funding from faith-inspired organizations through their insignias or names." [Elizabeth Stoddard, "The Ubiquity Of Religion In Kenya", *Berkleycenter.georgetown.edu*, accessed August 8, 2019, https://berkleycenter.georgetown.edu/posts/the-ubiquity-of-religion-in-kenya.]

[35] The rapidly expanding Charismatic movement is producing a fresh set of as yet unexamined phenomena from interesting theological divergences and the merging of Pentecostalism with indigenous religious practices. In Africa the rise of the NRMs has more to do with the post-colonial political, cultural, and social crisis, and with questions of enculturation and the African desire for healing and help to face life's problems. During the last ten to fifteen years, there has been a bewildering explosion of new religious movements in Africa: open-air rallies, crusades, revival gatherings, miracle centres, healing ministries and so on. Kenya, a country that had already experienced a proliferation of sects and independent churches, has been a propitious ground for these new religious movements. More and more, this is the form that Christianity is taking, outside the confines of the mainline churches. … Kenya like all Africa has her share of NRMs expanding by the day. A most recent one is Repentance and Holiness Movement led by Prophet Dr. David Owuor [Mildred A. J. Ndeda, "The Struggles Of New Religious Movements In The Kenyan Religious Space:

Having stated the need of writing this book, this writer now sets down its aim. First of all this writer endeavours to establish what the Scriptures say concerning the teaching role of the pastor and the place of teaching in the life of both the believer and the church. This will serve as the foundation, so that as the writer progresses, it would be within biblical perimeters.

This writer believes that laying the foremost foundations on Scriptures will guide him to achieve the goal of discussing the topic of true biblical and sound teaching and its place and significance in the life of the church. This work is not intended to be an exhaustive or novel work and there may be issues and cases that may be unique to different settings and areas to which the book may not address. This writer will try to deal with those cases that are conspicuous and pertinent at the present time and within the East African context, particularly in Kenya, as that is the context in which he minsters and is acquainted with. On account of this, it will be needful to highlight some areas in which the Kenyan context may present a unique case in point in the study of practical pastoral ministry.

The Case Of Repentance And Holiness Movement", *Les Cahiers D'Afrique De L'Est / The East African Review*, accessed May 5, 2019, http://journals.openedition.org/eastafrica/404.]

CHAPTER I

BIBLICAL BASIS FOR THE TEACHING MINISTRY OF THE CHURCH

Christianity is not merely a system of abstract truths, but it is a life. Yet it is a new life. It is a life which, even on the practical side, one must learn to live. No man lives the Christian life naturally, automatically. Like swimming, it must be learned. One must receive instruction as to the effects of sin, as to how God loves the sinner and gave His Son to die for his salvation, as to how Christ "gave himself up for our sins that he might deliver us out of this present evil world" (Gal. 1:4), how God freely forgives the repentant sinner and gives him grace through the channel of faith to begin and continue the living of the pure, altruistic, sacrificing, but joyous, triumphant life of the Christian.[36]

In his observation above, Charles B. Williams presents the Christian life on the basis of understanding truths that influences practices. This understanding of truths is one that is achieved, not naturally, but through systematic, continual and graded instruction of Scripture. The Christian must learn Scripture in order to live the Christian life, and so he must be taught to know sin and its effects, God and His attributes, Christ and His work, salvation and its requirements, etc. All this is to be accomplished by the application of Scripture to the life of the believer. As such, Williams gives an apt introduction to the starting point of the place and role of the teaching ministry of the church, which is the Scriptures, which is the biblical basis. The understanding of Christian life and how it is effected, as well as the understanding of Christian growth and how it is achieved, will doubtless lead to the consideration of the teaching ministry of the church in pastoral care.

The Christian life is not natural to man, even to those born from above. The Christian life is to be learned and hence to be taught. This is the testimony of the Scriptures, and can be exemplified in Christ, as seen from His words in Matthew 11:29 where He exhorts: *"Take my yoke upon you, and learn of me"* and from the perception of the people of Jesus' time of Him with scripture testifying that *"the people were astonished at his doctrine: For he taught them as one having authority, and not as the scribes"* (Matt. 7:28-29); and even the Pharisees referred to Him as *"a teacher come from God"* (John 3:2).

Both in the Old and New Testaments the teaching and instruction motif is clearly brought out with various people given the responsibility of teaching others to obey God. Beginning with the parents (who have a duty in the Old Testament to teach and rehearse to their children the words and works of God from generation to generation) to Jesus being a teacher and His sayings presented as teachings in the Gospel accounts, and the apostolic church continuing in the apostles' doctrines or teachings. In addition to this, with the pastor being required to be apt to teach (1 Tim. 3:2; 2 Tim. 2:24), there is necessity to consider what the Bible says concerning teaching and what place it has in the pastoral ministry.

In Exodus 4, God directs Moses to go, promising him His presence and instruction. The LORD tells Moses that He will teach him what to say. The Bible says, *"Now therefore go, and I will be with thy mouth, and teach thee what thou shalt say."* (Exod. 4:12) From this example, one principle that can be drawn in regard to the ministry of God's Word is that the minister must be taught of God. The same principle can be further noted in verse 15 of Exodus chapter 4, where Moses is to put words into Aaron's mouth.

---

[36] Charles B. Williams, *The Function of Teaching in Christianity* (Nashville, Tennessee: Sunday School Board Southern Baptist Convention, 1912), 19.

The Bible says, "*And thou shalt speak unto him, and put words in his mouth: and I will be with thy mouth, and with his mouth, and will teach you what ye shall do*" (Exod. 4:15) in comparing the two verses, the principle of teaching is presented in a two-fold manner: that of the divine instruction as in Exodus 4:12 where the LORD teaches Moses what he was to say, and that of providential instruction as in Exodus 4:15 where the LORD will teach Aaron through Moses. And as Moses teaches Aaron, the LORD teaches both Moses and Aaron as can be seen in the change from the singular personal pronouns to the use of the plural personal pronouns. Thus in searching the Scriptures, one can draw injunctions on teaching and examples which provide a clear view of the place of teaching in the pastoral ministry.

The Place of Teaching in the Bible

The current distinction on what is secular and what is spiritual has affected the church greatly and undermined Christian growth in varying degrees. Since the Christian life is a life that is learned, the Bible has to have pre-eminence in the learning of the Christian, and what is not distinctly Christian undermines the Christian's life when it is brought into the education and teaching of the Christian. The effects of the increasing secularization is made more pronounced by the absence of biblical teaching. In the face of rising secularization, the subordination of the place of teaching in the pastoral ministry of many churches presently has greatly contributed to the rise of church goers considering themselves Christians and yet are unacquainted with the teachings of Christ, and people considering themselves believers and yet do not know what they believe or affirm and cannot discern between truth and falsehood and are taken advantage of and preyed upon by the many false teachers who have invaded the sheepfold. The Daily Nation, a local newspaper carried an article on the Kenyan church in which some of these issues were raised. The article reads in part,

> A senior pastor at one of the evangelical churches in the city who holds a Bachelor of Arts degree in Bible and theology from the East Africa School of Theology asks a simple question; what is good news to you? That, in her view, is what changed. Preaching today is done to meet the needs of the 21st century congregation. "We are a fast-moving society and the message can be adjusted," she adds.
>
> During a recent Sunday service in the city, one evangelical reverend introduced his main message for the day as "12 secrets to an effective prayer life". One of the points under this was "creative miracles". He went on to expound: "Imagine what you want. Call things which are NOT as though they ARE. In your prayer, prophesy to dry bones." ...
>
> After four years at St Paul's University taking Bachelors of Divinity and five years as a Methodist preacher, Reverend David Manyera is convinced that nothing has changed in the message. In his view, it is the mode and medium of delivery that changed. "These days you may use secular issues as an opportunity to pass the message," he says. They call it accommodation, enculturation and, at times, Christianisation of African ideologies.
>
> But there is an elephant in the Christian room. And that elephant is called "Prosperity Gospel". "Give and it will be given to you. A good measure, pressed down, shaken together, and running over will be poured into your lap. For with the measure you

CHAPTER I: BIBLICAL BASIS FOR THE TEACHING MINISTRY OF THE CHURCH

use, it will be measured to you," reads Luke 6:38. Well, let us just call it... the elephant in the room.[37]

This shift has not only affected those who are trained in the work of the ministry; subordination of teaching in the pastoral ministry has also given rise to a Christian Education program that is neither pastoral nor doctrinal with pastors not considering the importance of and necessity for theological training, and delegating and leaving all avenues of education to laymen who are ill-equipped for the work leading to the propagation of the ever increasingly popular social and prosperity gospels.

What does the Bible say about teaching? What is its place in the life of the church? If there is to be teaching in the church, who are responsible for teaching and what qualifications are required of them who would teach? 2 Timothy 3:16-17 gives a biblical description of Scripture which uses two adjectives. The first is being inspired of God: *"All Scripture is given by inspiration of God."* (2 Tim. 3:16a). This first attribute or description of Scripture points to its nature and source. Peter says no prophecy of Scripture is of any private interpretation and this is because all Scripture is given by inspiration of God and the holy men of God spoke as they were moved by the Holy Spirit. The second adjective given by Paul is profitable: *"All Scripture is ... profitable for doctrine, for reproof, for correction, for instruction in righteousness."* (2 Tim. 3:16b-17). This second attribute or description of Scripture points to its functions. Scripture is useful, serviceable, advantageous in the areas of (i) doctrine or teaching, (ii) reproof or convicting by giving evidence; (iii) correction or straightening up again and reforming, and (iv) instruction or disciplining and nurturing through tutoring in righteousness. This clearly presents teaching as one of the primary avenues by which Scripture can be applied profitably.

Christ in speaking to His disciples in John 15:3 tells them, *"ye are clean through the word which I have spoken to you"* and later in chapter 17:17 *"sanctify them by thy truth, thy word is truth."* In both cases, He presented the benefits that believers can draw from the Word and from the doctrines of Christ. The words of Christ received, purify the hearts and hence make them clean. Therefore, if the Word applied cleanses the heart, then the application of the same Word has to be of utmost importance and must be given first place in any ministry that is aimed at glorifying and pleasing God. This, therefore, means that the teaching of God's Word has an important place in the life of God's people. Its importance can be seen from Scripture in that it is (i) one of the spiritual gifts given by God to the church, (ii) one of the functions and duties required of the Pastor towards his flock and the church, and (iii) one of the major aspects of church life is evidenced in the New Testament church. The following three sections elaborate on this importance.

---

[37] Peter Oduor, "The Kenyan Church And The Gospel Of Prosperity", *Daily Nation*, Wednesday February, 13 2013, accessed September 12, 2019, https://www.nation.co.ke/lifestyle/dn2/The-Kenyan-church-and-the-gospel-of-prosperity/957860-1691986-fk8kt4/index.html.

Teaching is a Calling and a Gift[38] from God

"But now hath God set them members every one of them in the body, as it hath pleased him. ... And God hath set some in the church, first apostles, secondarily, prophets, thirdly teachers, after that miracles, then gifts of healings, helps, governments, diversities of tongues" (1 Cor. 12:18, 28).

The New Testament gives lists of spiritual gifts in four different epistles. These lists can be found in Romans 12, 1 Corinthians 12, Ephesians 4 and 1 Peter 4. According to Paul, these gifts are given *"for the perfecting of the saints, for the work of the ministry, for the edifying of the body of Christ"* (Eph. 4:11) and so as Peter points out, everyone is given a gift for its use in ministering to the church: *"As every man hath received the gift, even so minister the same one to another, as good stewards of the manifold grace of God"* (1 Pet. 4:10). Having seen the attributes of the Word of God as presented in 2 Timothy 3:16, it is clear to see the need for the gift of teaching. The Word of God that is inspired and profitable must be applied and taught. It must be proclaimed with clarity, it must be taught and explained systematically for God's people to be rooted and grounded in the truth and for God's people to be matured and established in the faith. The Great Commission included a call to teach those who would believe (Matt. 28:18-20).

In 1 Corinthians 12:18, the spiritual gifts are presented under the divine sovereignty and wisdom of God. Sovereignty[39] in that all gifts are given according to the counsel of God's will with God alone deciding what the gifts are and who are to be given which gift, as well as the place and order of the gifts and the purpose for which they are to accomplish. The divine wisdom of God is seen in that in the distribution of the gifts and their use by the men gifted, the unity and maturity of the whole body is built up with the gift benefiting the whole body. This means that teaching as a gift of the Spirit reflects God's will and pleasure and for the church to grow and mature, it has to appropriate what is provided for that purpose by the Head of the church who is Christ.

In 1 Corinthians 12:28, as the apostle sums up his argument thus far, he applies the picture of the body with its different members having different functions but contributing to the welfare and unity of the body to the church with the differing spiritual gifts bestowed her. He emphasizes the relationship between Christ and the church pointing out that the church is the body of Christ, and to this adds the relationship between the members one to another in 1 Corinthians 12:27. Verse 28 then presents a list of the gifts given by God, highlighting the order of the offices and placing teaching third in order after the office of the apostle and the prophet. These first three offices all deal with the Word of God, the distinction being their dealings with divine revelation in that the apostles and prophets proclaimed and taught the Word receiving it by the revelation of the Holy Spir-

---

[38] For the purpose of clarity, the definition adopted in understanding gifts in this section will be that given by James F. Stitzinger, "A spiritual gift, then, is any ability and accompanying spiritual ministry and effect that God, through Christ, enables a believer to use, or motivates him to use, for His glory, in the body of Christ, through the energizing work of the Spirit. God may grace the believer with a gift or gifts, or bring them to light, at salvation or later, but these abilities are only gifts when used for edification in the church. Today, as in biblical times, these enablings differ among churches according to the needs of the church and vary greatly as the needs vary." [James F. Stitzinger, *Spiritual Gifts: Definitions and Kinds*, The Masters Seminary Journal, 14/2 (Fall 2003), 161.]

[39] "The Gifts of the Spirit are under the control of the Spirit. He personally superintends them. They are operative and effective only when he makes them so. Thus the sovereignty of the Blessed Spirit is preserved, while the active agency of the possessor of the Gift is acknowledged. Those who preach without the consent of the Spirit, always find themselves beating the air. Many run before they are called. Paul possessed the general Gift of the ministry; yet it was kept under the direction of Holy Ghost." (Acts xiii. 2, 4; xvi. 6-10.) [Thos K. Doty, *The Two-fold Gift of the Holy Ghost* (Cleveland, Ohio: Christian Harvester Office, 1890), 203.

it, while teachers and pastors deal with the same Word of God and preach and teach it having received it by the illumination of the Holy Spirit who was promised to the disciples by Christ that when He comes He shall teach them (John 14:26; Luke 12:12). And as teacher, the Bible says that the Holy Ghost teaches all things (John 14:26 cf. 1 Cor. 2:13), reveals the things of Christ (John 16:14-15), and guides into all truth (John 16:13). And to this, Thomas Parry's explanation of the indwelling of the Holy Spirit will put the work of the Spirit in proper Biblical perspective when considering both the work of the Holy Spirit as a teacher and the gift of the Holy Spirit of teaching. Parry writes,

> The Holy Spirit does not dwell in the believer in the sense the mystics believe. As teacher and guide, the Spirit is not superior to the revealed Word of God. He does not supersede the Scriptures. When the apostle says, "Ye have an unction from the Holy One and ye know all things," and again, "The anointing which ye have received of Him abideth in you and ye need not that any man teach you," the scope of the meaning here does not go beyond the Scriptures. (5) The Holy Spirit does not work in believers collectively to add anything to the written Word with the view to guide the church. From this supposition came the Talmud to have greater authority than the original, inspired Scriptures. From a belief in the inward illumination of the Spirit in particular cases, oral teachings in the church of Rome came to have greater authority than the Bible. Hence, came Mohamed, Joseph Smith, and the vagaries of Carlstat. Hence, came the delusions of many Christians who are led to believe in many strange communications from the Lord, and who are led to do many things which are contrary to both common sense and the Word of God. The Spirit never speaks outside of the Scriptures.[40]

Teaching is Part of Pastoral Duty

"And he gave some, apostles; and some, prophets; and some, evangelists; and some, pastors and teachers" (Eph. 4:11). In Paul's list of spiritual gifts in Ephesians, Paul presents the church as the body of Christ and equipped by Christ its Head, who gives out differing gifts to different men. The picture presented is one in which the Head organizes the body and, in doing so, places gifted men in specific positions to accomplish His purpose and achieve His will for the church. In doing so, Christ gives pastors who are also teachers for the work of the ministry, the equipping and maturing of the saints, the building up of the church as His body so that being mature and grounded in the truth they may accomplish all His will.

The church, being a body, is made up of different parts, and being gifted with differing gifts, needs consistent and biblical teaching in order to maintain and build up the individual members as parts of the one body. The need to maintain and to build up the unity of the whole body toward accomplishing the purposes of God is placed upon those members of the body called to be pastors and teachers. In the New Testament the pastor's teaching role is consistently and continually highlighted and emphasized in relation to his shepherding role and his responsibilities to the church. Peter does so in 1 Peter 5:1-4, Paul does so in his address to the Ephesian elders in Acts 20, and again to Timothy and Titus in his Pastoral Epistles in 1 Timothy 3:1-8; 4:6; 5:17-18; 2 Timothy 2:2, 12-13; and Titus 1:5-9.

Teaching Is Part of the Church's Life and Commission

"Go ye therefore, and teach all nations, baptizing them in the name of the Father, and of the Son, and of the Holy Ghost: teaching them to observe all things whatsoever I

---

[40] Thomas Parry, *The Indwelling Spirit* (New York: Alliance Press Company, 1906), 23-24.

have commanded you: and, lo, I am with you always, even unto the end of the world." (Matt 28:20) The Great Commission has been by some, termed as the first commandment of the church, and as Jesus directed His disciples and gave them their mission, He commanded them to teach all nations. The principal intent of the disciples as they went forth was to make disciples of all nations. In the setting up of the Christian religion, teaching was to have a central part. Those who heard their preaching and believed, were to be baptized and to be taught to observe all things that the Lord had commanded. And in order to fulfil their roles, the apostles were given the promise of the Holy Spirit by Christ (John 14:25-26), as well as the example of Christ Himself to follow (John 13:12-17).

Teaching consequently took a central part in the life of the church during the New Testament period with the early church continuing *"steadfastly in the apostles' doctrine"* (Acts 2:41-42), and the apostles committing themselves to teaching the disciples even under unfavourable circumstances and persecutions (Acts 4:13-20; 5:25) and when the disciples were scattered abroad, they established the church upon the centrality of teaching (Acts 11:26). The apostle Paul introduced himself not only as an apostle, but also as a teacher (1 Tim 2:7; 2 Tim 1:11).

The importance of teaching is also seen in the apostolic injunctions to the church and to the young pastors of their time. Paul writing to Timothy commands him to pay attention to doctrine (1 Tim 4:12-16), to teach faithful men who in turn will be able to teach others (2 Tim 2:1-2), to instruct those who oppose themselves (2 Tim 2:22-26). Paul writing to Titus points out the pastoral duty to teach in Titus chapter 2 with what the pastor is to teach. James warns of the stricter standards required of teachers (Jas 3:1-2).

Biblical Terminology Related to Teaching

Teaching and learning abound in the Bible. Both in the Old and New Testaments, different words are used to present principles that relate to the giving and receiving of instructions or teachings. Teaching as presented in the Bible is a process that, first, involves God Himself through the person of the Holy Spirit and the instrumentality of the Holy Scriptures with the Holy Spirit being called teacher and the Scriptures referred to as teachings. Second, mature and qualified leaders act as teachers both in the home (where the persons tasked with the duty to teach are the parents) and in the church (where the persons tasked with the duty to teach are the pastors or teaching elders). Third, the members of the home and the church are engaged to both discover and act on God's will practically in their day-to-day lives. This engagement addresses both the mind and intellect as well as the heart and spirit of those being taught and is undertaken in all settings of life whether formally or informally. Finally, the learning settings and experiences are directed towards cultivating and maintaining a distinctly biblical and Christian worldview and lifestyle in those subjected to the teaching processes.

A consideration of the different terms and words used in Scripture that relate to the teaching process serve to give and develop the understanding of the role and place of teaching in the life of the church and Roy B. Zuck, in his article for *Bibliotheca Sacra*, discusses nine Hebrew words which relate to teaching, and in the conclusion observes,

> This study of nine Hebrew words for "teach" suggests several key principles for Christian education.
>
> 1. One who teaches must be first of all a learner--and an intense learner (cf. the Piel form of the verbs "to learn"). He cannot teach what he himself does not know. And conversely, intense learning should result in teaching.
>
> 2. The causative form of these Hebrew words indicates that Christian teaching is helping to learn (or causing to learn). Based on these nine Hebrew words, Christian

teaching is (a) making others familiar with divine truths, (b) giving discernment, (c) warning, (d) imparting knowledge, (e) correcting, (f) guiding, (g) training, (h) giving wisdom and insight, and (i) inculcating.

3. The Hiphil form may also show that teaching is helping pupils be what the teacher already is, and helping pupils know what the teacher already knows. In other words, a teacher cannot get his pupils to gain in discernment, knowledge, and insight if he himself does not possess that discernment, knowledge, and insight.

4. Christian teaching includes the imparting of biblical content. It is causing others to have a knowledge of and discernment in God's Word and ways.

5. Pupils learn as they are familiar with facts, open to correction, willing to be guided, interested in gaining insight, and anxious to grow in wisdom.

6. Learning spiritual truths is ultimately a matter between God and the pupil. In the final sense, only God is the Teacher.

7. Teaching that is lasting and effective must be done with diligence and ardor.

8. Teaching in the home may need to include a correcting of wrong conduct and/or wrong concepts (Prov. 31:1), and it should be done with enthusiasm, repetition, and purpose (Deut. 6:7).

9. Learning God's Word is to be of a transforming character. It is to help pupils be more obedient to the will and ways of God, so that they may do His will and thus glorify Him. What a high privilege then to be engaged in teaching others God's precious Word! To be effective in his teaching, every Bible teacher and Christian education worker should be a student of God's Word, and should pray with the psalmist: "Teach (ירה) me thy way, O Lord" (Ps. 27:11; 86:11), and "Teach (למד) me thy statutes" (Ps. 119:12, 26, 64, 68, 124, 135).[41]

From the above observations, what comes out is that teaching is a biblical principle, and that this principle as presented in the Bible as a continual process of helping others to learn or causing them to learn God's will, standards and ways in order to live godly lives. This (i) requires teachers who are acquainted with and have learned the things they are to teach, (ii) focuses on imparting biblical truth and content, (iii) requires God to work in the hearts and lives of the students, (iv) aims at transforming lives, cultivating obedience in the learners, and (v) is to be done at home and in the assemblies, constantly, diligently, repeatedly, systematically and with enthusiasm in order to be effective.

A survey of the terms used to imply teaching and the perspective they bring of teaching from the Bible shows the central place that teaching has in the lives of God's people. God Himself has taught His people, and requires His people to be taught as is seen by (i) the giving of instructions which they are to be acquainted with and follow, (ii) the sending forth of people with expressed commands to ensure that God's people know the Word of God, and (iii) the setting forth of institutions whose primary function will be that of teaching and training God's people.

The variety and extent of this biblical vocabulary make it clear that teaching is at the heart of God's plan for redemptive history. God as the ultimate teacher has mandated in Scripture that teaching occur in two primary contexts, both of which arise from his creative and redemptive acts. God delegates teaching to the family and the redeemed community. Both institutions explain his gracious initiative in redemption and urge loving, obedient response. God's gracious initiative places his

---

[41] Roy B. Zuck, "Hebrew Words For Teach.", *Pdfs.semanticscholar.org*, accessed February 6, 2018, https://pdfs.semanticscholar.org/fab9/d8817376b5059157812a4afd6a4314f28e88.pdf.

people in covenant relationship with him in which parents teach their children and spiritually gifted leaders of the people of God teach its members.[42]

From a survey of the Scriptures, some words which carry with them a teaching emphasis are as follows:

Teach

In the authorized version of the English Bible, a word search reveals that the word "teach" and its derivatives occur in 176 verses with the word "teach" occurring in 109 verses, "teacher" in six verses, "teachers" in fourteen verses, "teachest" in eight verses, "teacheth" in sixteen verses and teaching in twenty-five verses. The original language words of the above English words comprise ten Hebrew words in the Old Testament verses and twelve Greek words in the New Testament verses. Concerning the use of the word "teach" in the New Testament, The *Theological Dictionary of the New Testament* says, "Christian teaching, then, aims primarily to show from Scripture that Jesus is the promised Messiah. In this sense it is 'teaching about the Lord Jesus Christ' (Acts 8:31)."[43] Christianity is not a system of abstract principles, but practical ones—principles that can be lived out in daily life and practised under all of life's circumstances. As the chief end of man is to glorify God and enjoy Him forever, the Christian must, therefore, learn the principles of the Christian faith in order to be able to apply them correctly to the glory and praise of God in his daily life. Hall observes,

> But though reason would teach us to look for design in the creation of man, it could not teach us the whole design of the Creator. He alone can reveal this: and he has revealed it in his holy word, which was written under his own inspiration. By our reason thus enlightened and taught, we are to discover the end of man; that is the end for which he was created, and placed in this world.[44]

In this, Hall shows the insufficiency of human reason to find out God's designs and purposes pointing out that God in His infinite wisdom chose to reveal His design and purpose through Holy Scripture. This necessitates teaching in order to both discover the purpose for which man "was created, and placed in this world" as well as to know how he can fulfil and accomplish the purpose for which he was created in a manner acceptable to his Creator and Redeemer. The teaching motif as a biblical principle is one that is woven through the whole Bible. *The Popular and Critical Bible Encyclopaedia* points out that the "Torah is properly a text for teaching, and the teachers were the priests or Levites. In that early day, the judges who aided Moses were also teachers, hence he may have issued the toroth or teaching texts to the judge and to the Levite."[45] And as one reads through it, the constant repetitions in the text were teaching aids to help the people keep in mind their covenant with the LORD and His requirements for obedient living. The same Encyclopaedia points out that these repetitions are interwoven with "a multi-

---

[42] *Baker Theological Dictionary of the Bible*, Ed. Walter A. Elwell (Grand Rapids, Michigan: Baker Books, 1996), sv. Teach, Teacher.

[43] *Theological Dictionary of the New Testament,* ed. Gerhard Kittel and Gerhard Friedrich, trans. Geoffrey W. Bromiley (Grand Rapids, Michigan: William B. Eerdmans Publishing Company, 1985), sv. Didaskw.

[44] John Hall, *The Chief End of Man: An Exposition of the First Answer of the Shorter Catechism* (Philadelphia: Presbyterian Board of Publication, 1841), 19.

[45] *The Popular and Critical Bible Encyclopaedia and Scriptural Dictionary Fully Defining and Explaining All Religious Terms Including Biographical, Geographical, Historical, Archeological and Doctrinal themes, Vol. III*, Ed. by Samuel Fallows (Chicago: The Howard Severance Company, 1902), sv. Pentateuchal Objections.

tude of such commands as follows: 'These are the commandments, the statutes and the judgments which the Lord your God commanded to teach you,' 'Hear O Israel the Lord our God is one God,' 'Thou shalt love the Lord thy God,' 'Thou shalt not take His name in vain' and many others."[46] These serve to give the stamp of authority with which the teachings and injunctions are to be received and thus set forth the basis for God's people both receiving and responding to the teachings.

And as one studies the Old and New Testament texts and from them, the array of lexical facts, the teaching motif cannot be missed. Some Bible texts to help illustrate the biblical presentation of the teaching motif include:

Deuteronomy 4:1 (*lamadh*)

In considering what the Bible says concerning the place of teaching, Deuteronomy chapter 4 will give great insight. Deuteronomy is set in the context of transition, the wilderness wandering is coming to an end after forty years, the life of the man of God Moses is also coming to an end, the one to whom the Israelites had said at Sinai: *"Speak thou with us, and we will hear; but let not God speak with us lest we die"* (Exod 20:19). In this setting, Moses emphasizes the place of teaching in Deuteronomy 4. The word "teach" appears for the first time in this book of Deuteronomy in this chapter 4, and goes on to appear four times in this chapter: in verse 1 — *"I teach you"* (the "you" there refers to Israel as a nation); verse 5-8 — *"I have taught you"* (the purpose presented is that of a witness to the nations surrounding); verse 9-13 — *"teach them thy sons"* (presents a familial emphasis of teaching which ensures that all generations will get to know God); verse 14-19 refers the teaching back to the nation. John Calvin commenting on Deuteronomy chapter 4:1 says,

> Now, therefore, hearken, O Israel. He requires the people to be teachable, in order that they may learn to serve God; for the beginning of a good and upright life is to know what is pleasing to God. From hence, then, does Moses commence commanding them to be attentive in seeking direction from the Law; and then admonishing them to prove by their whole life that they have duly profited in the Law. The promise which is here inserted, only invites them to unreserved obedience through hope of the inheritance. The main point is, that they should neither add to nor diminish from the pure doctrine of the Law; and this cannot be the case, unless men first renounce their own personal feelings, and then shut their ears against all the imaginations of others. For non are to be accounted (true) disciples of the Law, but those who obtain their wisdom from it alone. It is, then, as if God commanded them to be content with His precepts; because in no other way would they keep His law, except by giving themselves wholly to its teaching. Hence, it follows, that they only obey God who depend on His authority alone; and that they only pay the Law its rightful honor, who receive nothing which is opposed to its natural meaning. The passage is a remarkable one, openly condemning whatsoever man's ingenuity may invent for the service of God.[47]

Teaching would form the basis of the nation's relationship to their God, and their response to His teachings would be measure of their faith in God and obedience to Him and as such indicative of their relationship to God. From what Calvin points out in his commentary, the following are noted: (i) God's people serve God after they have learned to know God and His will. (ii) The teachings and statutes of the Lord are the standard of

---

[46] *The Popular and Critical Bible Encyclopaedia and Scriptural Dictionary, Vol. III*, Ed. by Samuel Fallows, sv. Pentateuchal Objections.

[47] John Calvin, *Commentaries on the Bible (22 volume set)*, MyBible v. 4.7.0.

both faith and practice and as such they are not to be altered in any way by addition or subtraction, it is not to be subject to the imaginations of men. (iii) The measure of discipleship has to be the Word of God. And the one who gives himself over to the teachings of God and His Word, he is the one who would keep the Law of God and would be discipled indeed as Christ Himself asserted that he who keeps His Word, he is His disciple indeed.

The Hebrew word translated *"teach"* in Deuteronomy 4:1 is the Hebrew verb *lāmad*[48] which occurs eighty-six times in eighty verses. In the book of Deuteronomy alone, it is found in Deuteronomy 4:1, 5, 10, 14; 5:1, 31; 6:1; 11:19; 14:23; 17:19; 18:9; 20:18; 31:12, 13, 19, 22. It forms the major word used for teaching in the book. Only five verses rendered in English by the word *"teach"* in Deuteronomy are derived from a different Hebrew word (Deut 4:9; 6:7; 17:11; 24:8 and 33:10). *The Complete Word Study Old Testament*, in its lexical aids, says of the word *lāmad*,

> 3925 Lāmadh; to learn; to study; to be accustomed to; to teach, to instruct, train; to practice; to be taught, be trained. A derived form, *malmadh* (4451), was a goad for oxen. Through a yoke and a goad, Ephraim was taught like a cow (Hos 10:11). *Lāmadh* has both the idea of training and educating. Greek required two words, *manthano* (3129 NT), *"to learn"* and *didasko* (1321 NT), *"to teach"*, to achieve what the Hebrew does in one word *lāmadh*. All knowledge resides in the "fear of the Lord" (Deut 4:10; 14:23; 17:19; 31:12, 13). No one teaches Him or advises him (Is 40:14). He is the source of all truth.[49]

Apart from the book of Deuteronomy, the other book that has a repeated use of the word *lāmad* is the Psalms. The word occurs in twenty-seven verses in the Psalms. And of these, thirteen are found in Psalm 119.

It is instructive to study Psalm 119, the most concentrated use of lamad in the OT, where every verse deals in some way with the Word of God. In Psalm 119 we encounter the writer repeatedly crying out in prayer for God to teach him the Word (Ps. 119:12, 26, 64, 66, 68, 108, 124, 135, 171, cp David Ps. 25:4, 5). Beloved, we should daily do no less! And keep in mind that the writer of Psalm 119 clearly knew the Word and yet the cry of his heart was more teaching of the Word! Faith comes by hearing and hearing by the Word (Ro. 10:17). In natural revelation we can know

---

[48] This word is first used in the Hebrew Old Testament in Deut. 4:1: "… Hearken, O Israel, unto the statutes and unto the judgments, which I teach you.…" In Deut. 5:1 is used of learning God's laws: "Hear, O Israel, the statutes and judgments which I speak in your ears this day, that ye may learn them, and keep, and do them." A similar meaning occurs in Ps. 119:7. The word may be used of learning other things: works of the heathen (Ps. 106:35); wisdom (Prov. 30:3); and war (Mic. 4:3). About half the occurrences of are found in the books of Deuteronomy and Psalms, underlining the teaching emphasis found in these books. Judaism's traditional emphasis on teaching and thus preserving its faith clearly has its basis in the stress on teaching the faith found in the Old Testament, specifically Deut. 6:4-9. Following the Shema', the "watchword of Judaism" that declares that Yahweh is One (Deut. 6:4), is the "first great commandment" (Deut. 6:5; Mark 12:28-29). When Moses delivered the Law to his people, he said, "… The Lord commanded me at that time to teach you statutes and judgments …" (Deut. 4:14). [W. E. Vine, "Vine's Complete Expository Dictionary Of Old And New Testament Words. Ed. Merril F. Unger, William White Jr.", *Ultimatebiblereferencelibrary.com*, last modified 2019, accessed February 7, 2018, http://www.ultimatebiblereferencelibrary.com/Vines_Expositary_Dictionary.pdf. sv. Teach.]

[49] *The Complete Word Study Old Testament King James Version*, Gen. Ed., Warren Baker, (Chattanooga, Tennessee: AMG Publishers, 1994), 2329. The International Standard Bible Encyclopaedia says concerning the word *lamadh*, "As teaching is both a condition and an accomplishment of discipling, the word often means simply "to teach," "to inform" (2 Ch 17:7; Ps 71:17; Prov 5:13). The glory of teaching was its harmony with the will of God, its source in God's authority, and its purpose to secure spiritual obedience (Dt 4:5, 14; 31:12, 13). [*The International Standard Bible Encyclopaedia*, Gen. Ed., James Orr (Grand Rapids, Michigan: Wm. B. Eerdmans Publishing Co., 1955), sv. Teach, Teacher, Teaching.]

CHAPTER I: BIBLICAL BASIS FOR THE TEACHING MINISTRY OF THE CHURCH

about God, but in special revelation (Word) we can truly come to know God. Even now, let us all pause and cry out "LORD, teach us by Thy Spirit, Thy Word that we may know Thee more intimately. Amen" W Graham Scroggie adds this note—"The Psalmist is resolved to learn, and he repeatedly calls upon the LORD to teach him." This word occurs 9 times (Ps. 119:12, 26, 33, 64, 66, 68, 108, 124, 135); taught, twice (Ps. 119:102, 171); and teachers, once (Ps. 119:99). Two Hebrew words are used: yara, to point out, as if by aiming the finger, to inform, to instruct (Ps. 119:33, 102); and lāmad, meaning to goad, the rod being an Oriental incentive; this is the word used in all instances except in verses 33, 102. To learn is generally difficult, especially to learn obedience. Lāmad, is interesting for the fact that it implies suffering; it means to goad and so to teach, the rod being an Oriental incentive, and so, in Jdg. 8:16KJV, we read that Gideon taught (yada) the men of Succoth with thorns. See Ps. 51:13 ("Then I will teach transgressors Your ways").[50]

The relationship between God's people and their God is tied to their relationship with His Word, commandments and statutes. Wisbech on the vital importance of knowing and believing and obeying (by the Spirit) God's Holy Word writes,

Not only was Israel's life dependent on obedience to God's Word, but so was their victory over the enemy (Deut. 4:1b). Apart from faith and obedience, Israel couldn't enter the land and defeat the nations that were strongly entrenched there. How could the Lord go before His people and give them victory if they weren't following Him obediently? (Dt. 1:30) The ten spies who failed to grasp the power of God's promises led Israel into discouragement, defeat, and death because of their unbelief (Nu 13–14). "And this is the victory that has overcome the world—our faith" (1 John 5:4, NKJV); and that faith is generated by the Word (Rom. 10:17). Believers today must find their life and victory in God's Word. Unless we know what God commands, we can't obey Him; but if we know His commandments, believe them, and obey them, then His power goes to work in our lives. "And His commandments are not burdensome" (1 John 5:3-note). Obeying the Lord becomes a joyful privilege when you realize that His commandments are expressions of His love, assurances of His strength, invitations to His blessing, opportunities to grow and bring Him glory, and occasions to enjoy His love and fellowship as we seek to please Him. God's Word is the open door into the treasury of His grace.[51]

The relationship between God and His people is through obedience to commandments and statutes and judgments. Yet this obedience is only possible when God's children both learn and teach the commandments, statutes and judgments they are required to obey. Moses makes it clear in Deuteronomy that the commandments and statutes and judgments being taught and learned are practical and are to be done. This practical emphasis is seen by the use of the verb *"to do"* which is used ten times in conjunction with *lāmadh* in Deuteronomy 4:1, 5, 14; 5:1, 31; 6:1; 17:19; 18:9; 20:18 and 31:12). Out of these ten occurrences, the emphasis is positively obedience with the call being to practice and apply the teachings and lessons learned. In all the ten verses mentioned above, the verb *asah* which is translated *"to do"* is in nine occasions found in the Qal[52]

---

[50] "Ezra 7:10 Commentary | Precept Austin", *Precept Austin*, accessed March 30, 2017, http://www.preceptaustin.org/index.php/ezra_710.

[51] "Deuteronomy 4 Commentary | Precept Austin", *Precept Austin*, accessed February 6, 2018, http://www.preceptaustin.org/deuteronomy-4-commentary.

[52] "The Qal stem is the basic verbal stem in Hebrew language. Approximately two-thirds of the verbal forms in the Old Testament are in this stem. The Qal stem can be divided into two main classes: verbs that represent action (fientive) and verbs that describe a state of being (stative)." [*The Complete Word Study Old Testament King James Version*, 2282.]

Infinitive Construct[53] prefixed with the inseparable preposition *lamedh* which signifies purpose. This means that in nine out of the ten uses of the verb *"to do,"* it is presented as the purpose of the action of the main verb which stresses that the teaching and learning is to be aimed at doing. It is only in Deuteronomy 5:31 where the verb *"to do"* does not appear in the Qal Infinitive Construct, but rather in the Qal[54] Perfect[55] tense. The context of the verse presents the obedience and practising of the commandments of the LORD which Moses is to teach God's people as something that is to continue in the future as it is set as requirement even when they possess and dwell in the land of promise. The lessons were to be strictly drawn out of the law of the LORD and not of the customs, practices and ways of the nations whom they were displacing from the land. This is also seen in the two injunctions that they are not to follow the ways of the Canaanites: *"When thou art come into the land which the Lord thy God giveth thee, thou shalt not learn to do after the abominations of those nations"* (Deut 18:9); nor copy and do as practised by the Canaanites: *"But of cities of these people, which the LORD thy God doth give thee for an inheritance, thou shalt save alive nothing that breatheth: But thou shalt utterly destroy them; namely, the Hittites, and the Amorites, the Canaanites, and the Perizzites, the Hivites, and the Jebusites; as the LORD thy God hath commanded thee: that they teach you not to do after all their abominations, which they have done unto their gods; so should ye sin against the LORD your God"* (Deut 20:16-18). Commenting on these verses, the *Complete Word Study Old Testament* observes: "As the incident with the Moabites revealed (Num. 25:1-3), Israel was all to prone to adopt the idolatrous and inhuman practices of her neighbours. In fact, the inhabitants of Canaan that Israel did not destroy according to God's command are described as being "snares" to Israel (Ex. 23:33; 34:12; Deut. 7:16; 12:30)."[56] And following the ways of the Canaanites is sinning against the LORD.

The other aspect that comes out clearly in the use of the word *Lamedh* in Deuteronomy is the subject of or content of the teaching and learning. Six times the word *"statutes"* (*choq*)[57] and five times the word *"judgments"* (*Mishpat*)[58] are used with Deuter-

---

[53] "The Infinitive construct is a verbal noun that can fulfill the same function as the English infinitive or gerund. It can function in context as a noun or a verb. It can accept prefixed prepositions, the article, and pronominal suffixes. The infinitive construct can serve in any normal capacity: subject, predicate, object of a preposition, as the independent substantive in a construct phrase. Its most significant use is with prepositions, in particular with the prefixed prepositions .... With the prefixed prepositions *beth* and *kaph* it serves as a temporal marker denoting respectively and event occurring simultaneously with the action of the main verb and an event that follows the time of the main verb. With the inseparable preposition *lamedh* it may denote purpose, result, explanation, or an imminent event." [*The Complete Word Study Old Testament King James Version*, 2277.]

[54] "The Qal Perfect (qpf) indicates in the active voice, simple, perfective action, viewed as a whole." [*The Complete Word Study Old Testament King James Version*, 2283.]

[55] "The Perfect conjugation was traditionally thought to show the perfection or completeness of an action. The term perfective is the preferred description of this conjugation. The perfect depicts an event or situation as a whole, without any reflection on the duration of events or their completedness. Context determines whether the event is past, or future, or present, and when not in the present, how far into the past or future it is (near or far). It also determines whether the situation is viewed at its inception, in progress, or at its completion. It sometimes expresses resultant or persistent action: something that started in the past and has continued into the present or something that has started in the present and will continue into the future. It can also be used of the independent, future events, as is the case with some prophetic declarations of the future, often referred to as the prophetic perfect." [*The Complete Word Study Old Testament King James Version*, 2280.]

[56] *The Complete Word Study Old Testament King James Version*, 529.

[57] "This masc. Noun originates from *chaqaq* (2710). it is a statute, regulation, law, custom; decree; share, task, term, limit, boundary. The RSV. also translates it as "ordinance," "due," and "bound". An-

onomy 4:1, 5, 14; 5:31; and 6:1 having both *"statutes"* and *"judgment"* while Deuteronomy 17:19 having *"statutes."* In Deuteronomy 4:1, the two words are introduced by the preposition indicating motion towards: *"Now therefore hearken, O Israel, unto the statutes and unto the judgments, which I teach you, for to do them."* Thus we have both the practicality of the teaching presented in the purpose *"for to do them"* and the focus or direction of attention *"unto the statutes and unto the judgments."* In three of these verses is also another word, *Tsawah*,[59] which is translated "commanded" in Deuteronomy 4:5, 14 and 6:1. Thus Moses in Deuteronomy 4:5 affirms: *"Behold I have taught you statutes and judgments, even as the LORD my God commanded me, that ye should do so in the land whither ye go to possess it."* Teaching and the content taught was not a matter of choice, but, rather, of obedience. God requires obedience from His people. This is to be evidenced by His people doing what they have been taught. God also sets forth what is to be taught by giving statutes and judgments, and, as sovereign, commands His servants to teach. The teaching function of the priests of the Old Testament is seen right through to the post-exilic record as exemplified in Ezra 7:10: *"For Ezra prepared his heart to seek the law of the LORD, and to do it, and to teach in Israel statutes and judgments."*

Statues (02706) **and ordinances** (04941) – The scribes in the early years at the time of Ezra and before were so devoted to not putting an error in the Scriptures that they would copy the Scriptures with such fastidiousness it is beyond belief. Some scribes would write one letter, take a bath, change their clothes, get a new pen, write another letter, take a bath, change their clothes, get a pen, write another letter. They didn't get a lot done, but, what they got done was correct. There was a tremendous fastidiousness to the completion of the inerrant text and its preservation.

This comprehensive threefold designation—the Law of the Lord, statutes, and ordinances—indicates that he studied all facets of God's Word. Tradition says he was the founder of the Great Synagogue where the Old Testament canon was first recognized. A number of scholars feel Ezra is the author of Psalm 119 which deals with the Word of God in virtually all 176 verses.

In Nehemiah, we see an example of Ezra teaching the Word… And Ezra opened the book in the sight of all the people for he was standing above all the people; and when he opened it, all the people stood up (sign of reverence and humility). Then Ezra blessed the LORD the great God. And all the people answered, "Amen, Amen!" while lifting up their hands (A symbol of receiving God's blessing); then they bowed low and worshipped the LORD with their faces to the ground (in rever-

---

cient people often engraved their laws upon slabs of stone or metal and then displayed them in public places. However the root was not limited to these materials. These are precepts and rules which must be strictly obeyed." [*The Complete Word Study Old Testament King James Version*, 2317.]

[58] "Properly a verdict (whether favorable or unfavorable) which was pronounced judicially, a judgment, a sentence, a formal decree; justice, right, privilege; place of judgment; cause, suit; crime, guilt; law rule, ordinance, custom, manner; what is due. This is an extremely important word for the proper understanding of all government (human or divine). Unlike our modern democratic tripartite conception (legislative, executive, and judicial), the verbal root, *shaphat* (8199), from which the noun originates, refers to all functions of government, not merely the judicial process." [*The Complete Word Study Old Testament King James Version*, 2336.]

[59] "This root means to constitute, make firm, establish; to appoint anyone over anything (1 Sam 13:14; 25:30; 2 Sam 6:21; Neh. 5:21; 7:2); … It is the picture of a superior giving a verbal communication to a subordinate. The word includes the content of what was said (Gen. 12:20). Gen. 2:16 focused upon the action itself, where God set down the rule. God is not to be questioned regarding the work of His creative hands (Is. 45:11). His commands are unique, requiring an inner commitment, not mere external superficial obedience (Is. 29:13)." [*The Complete Word Study Old Testament King James Version*, 2358.]

ence, awe, and adoration). Also, Jeshua, Bani, Sherebiah, Jamin, Akkub, Shabbethai, Hodiah, Maaseiah, Kelita, Azariah, Jozabad, Hanan, Pelaiah, and the Levites, explained the law to the people while the people remained in their place. And they read from the book, from the law of God, translating to give the sense so that they understood the reading. (Nehemiah 8:5-8)

When one considers the role of Ezra (and those like him in our modern church), to be sure, every person is important to God and God's work; but, as **Dr. Lee Roberson** said "Everything rises and falls with leadership."

McConville has written — The model teacher in **Ezra** is a doer. And the doer can be no mere demonstrator. He must be what he would have his disciples be. (**Ed**: "Doer" not in the sense of "busyness" but in the sense of practising what he preaches.)

Every preacher should follow Ezra's example and be committed to the study of the Scriptures in a way that is consuming, careful, and comprehensive. Pastors must guard their hearts against the seemingly endless, mounting pressures placed on them to sacrifice the study of the Word of God upon the "altar" of their growing list of "priorities." The day the preacher ceases to diligently study God's Word, whether he realizes it or not, is the day he begins losing spiritual passion and power in his preaching.[60]

2 Chronicles 15:3 (*yarah*)

Another Hebrew word translated *"teach"* is the Hebrew verb *yarah*, a word that occurs eighty-four times in seventy-five verses. Concerning the meaning of the word *yarah* in its use, the *International Standard Bible Encyclopedia* (ISBE) states,

> *yarah* "to cast": The teaching idea from which the law was derived is expressed by a verb which means "to throw," "to cast as an arrow or lot." it is also used for thrusting the hand forth to point out or show clearly (Gen 46:28; Ex. 15:25). The original idea is easily changed into an educational conception, since the teacher puts forth new ideas and facts as a sower casts seeds into the ground. But the process of teaching was not considered external and mechanical but internal and vital (Ex. 35:34, 35; 2 Ch 6:27). The nominal form is the usual word for law, human and Divine general and specific (Dt 4:8; Ps 19:8; Prov 1:8).[61]

The idea presented by this word has an inclination to direction and the giving of it through instruction. This being the second most used word of the Old Testament Hebrew, translated to mean teaching and instruction, presents the importance placed on teaching in the relationship between God and His people.

The occurrences of this word include Exodus 4:12, 15; 24:12; Leviticus 10:11; 14:57; Deuteronomy 17:10, 11; among other verses. Most of the occurrences are found in the books of Exodus with eight verses, Job with nine verses, and the Psalms with twelve verses. Of these occurrences, six times the verse also refers to the *"way"* with all of these occurrences taken from the Psalms except one which is found in Isaiah. Five times the verses also refer to the word *"do"* and five times the verses also refer to the word *"law."* Its first occurrence is Genesis 31:51. In Exodus, it first occurs in 4:12.

---

[60] "Ezra 7:10 Commentary | Precept Austin", *Precept Austin*, accessed March 30, 2017, http://www.preceptaustin.org/index.php/ezra_710.

[61] *ISBE,* sv. Teach, Teacher, Teaching.

CHAPTER I: BIBLICAL BASIS FOR THE TEACHING MINISTRY OF THE CHURCH

In the Psalms, the word *yarah* is used in Psalm 11:2; 25:8, 12; 27:11; 32:8; 45:4; 64:4, 7; 86:11; 119:33, 102. Of the occurrences in the Psalms, it is translated as *"shoot"* in 11:2 and 64:4, 7 while it is rendered as *"teach"* in the remaining verses.

2 Chronicles 15 records the reforms of Asa king of Judah. The chapter begins with a word of exhortation sent by the LORD through the prophet, to encourage and strengthen the hands of Asa to continue in the path of reforms with promise of reward (vs. 1-7). This is then followed by Asa's response and reformation. In the midst of the encouragement of Asa is the verse which reads: *"Now for a long season, Israel hath been without the true God and without a teaching priest, and without law."* The declension of Judah is herein linked to the absence of "a teaching priest." The duty of the priests and Levites to instruct and teach is presented in the Old Testament in Deuteronomy 24:8 in which the priests and the Levites were to instruct and guide the children of Israel according to the Lord's commandments on matters of everyday life. The word *yarah* and the word *kohen* appear together in six verses: Deuteronomy 24:8, 2 Kings 12:2, 17:27, 28; 2 Chronicles 15:3 and Micah 3:11. These verses when considered bring out the link between the life of the people of God to the teaching duties of the priests. Such that when there was declension, it was due to lack of teaching by the priests, or lack of faithfulness in teaching by the priests as is in the case of Micah 3:11. Commenting on Micah 3:11, Barker notes that,

> The **priests** made their teaching ministry a source of gain. It was their duty to teach the law and decide controversies (Lev. 10:11; Deut 17:9, 11), not to enrich themselves beyond their tithes by charging extra for their services. And the false **prophets** sold their oracles or divinations, divorcing what should have been a spiritual ministry from ethics, morality, and integrity (Micah 3:5). "The love of money is a root of all kinds of evil" (1 Tim 6:10).[62]

The case of priests doing their duties for personal gain is always tied to declension in the Old Testament, for example the case of the sons of Eli. The declension due to the sons of Eli neglect of their duties as well as their selfish abuse of the privileges of the office they held and the failure of their father Eli to warn and correct them, finally ended with the destruction of Shiloh. B. Dale notes,

> The best things when corrupted become the worst. It is thus with official positions such as were held by the priests of old. Their positions were a hereditary right, and their duties consisted largely of a prescribed routine of services. It was required, however, that their personal character should accord with their sacred work (Malachi 2:7); and their influence was great for good or evil. Whilst they reflected in their character and conduct the moral condition of the times, they also contributed in no small degree to produce it. The sons of Eli employed their high office not for the welfare of men and the glory of God, but. For their own selfish and corrupt purposes, and afford an example of "great and instructive wickedness."[63]

The priests were to set the standards for life both by their conduct and their teachings. Thus, when the priests fail, the nation also fails.[64] The opposite also holds true as

---

[62] "Micah 3 Commentary | Precept Austin", *Precept Austin*, accessed March 30, 2017, http://www.preceptaustin.org/micah_3_commentary.

[63] B. Dale, "1 Samuel 2 Pulpit Homiletics Commentary, Rejoicing in the Lord", *Bible Hub*, accessed February 19, 2018, http://biblehub.com/ commentaries/homiletics/1_samuel/2.htm.

[64] Though it is true that the leaders are responsible for the decay when they lead the flock astray, Harry Ironside gives great inside for the flock in relation to the corruption of leaders. In His commentary on Micah, he notes that "The who should have known judgment, and who were raised up of God to rule the nation in righteousness, were the very ones who were leading the masses astray. Often has it been so in history of the church, as well as of Israel. Therefore the need to test all that is taught or practised, by the only infalli-

seen in the case of the of Jehoash and his reforms, the Bible in 2 Kings 12:2, records that: *"And Jehoash did that which was right in the sight of the LORD all his days wherein Jehoiada the priest instructed him"* tying the reforms of the King to the instruction and guidance of the priest Jehoiada. Commenting on 2 Kings 12:1-3, Orr observes,

> The reign of Joash began with bright hopes, showed for a while excellent promise, yet ended ingloriously. To explain this we may consider –
>
> 1. He had a pious education. As a child he was brought up by his aunt Jehosheba, who, with her husband the high priest, would instil into his mind the principles of true godliness. In his strict seclusion he was kept free from sights of vice. Like Timothy, he would be taught from a child to know the things that make wise unto salvation (2 Timothy 3:15). To have an early training of this kind is an inestimable advantage.
>
> 2. He had a good counsellor. The early education of our own Queen Victoria was carefully conducted with a view to the royal office she was afterwards to fill. It would not be otherwise with young Joash. Jehoiada would carefully impress upon his mind the principles of good government, and, after his coronation, this holy man continued to be his guide and counsellor. So it is said, "Jehoash did that which was right in the sight of the Lord all his days wherein Jehoiada the priest instructed him." It is a happy thing when a king is willing to receive counsel from older and wiser heads than his own (cf. 1 Kings 12:6-11).
>
> 3. He had an excellent opportunity. Joash started with every advantage for reigning well. The people were animated with hatred of idolatry from the experience they had had of it in Athaliah's reign; they were enthusiastic in their return to the worship of Jehovah; they had inaugurated the restoration of the line of David by a new covenant with God, and by zealous acts of reform. The tide was with Joash, if he had shown strength of character sufficient to avail himself of it.[65]

The example thus highlights the importance of the teaching and instructing duty of the priesthood in the Old Testament. 2 Kings 12:2 when considered together with 2 Chronicles 15:3 shows in two different periods and under two different kings, yet the expectation of the priests' ministry was the same: teaching.

> No teaching priest; i.e. the priests they had either no knowledge of the true God, of his character and requirements, and so could not teach the People; or, if they did, they were satisfied with the mere performance of their altar duties, without caring for the spiritual welfare of the people. If the first, they were disqualified for being priests by reason of their ignorance (Malachi 2:7); if the second, they were chargeable with indolence (Malachi 1:6) or hypocrisy (Nehemiah 9:34), or both. If, under the old covenant, priests were required to instruct the people in the tenets and precepts of religion, much more is it incumbent on Christian pastors to be also teachers (Ephesian 4:11). A ministry that does not preach or teach ipso facto stands condemned.[66]

---

ble rule, the unerring Word of God. If Christians are content to be styled "the laity," and leave their spiritual interests in the hands of their guides, they have themselves to blame if they are led in wrong paths. Each is responsible to exercise himself unto godliness, and to try the things that differ. [Harry A. Ironside, *Notes on the Minor Prophets*, (Neptune, New Jersey: Loizeaux Brothers Inc., 1909), 229.]

[65] J. Orr, "2 Kings 12 *Pulpit Homiletics Commentary,* A Mixed Character," *Bible Hub*, accessed 19 February 2018, http://biblehub.com/ commentaries/homiletics/2_kings/12.htm.

[66] "Pulpit Homiletics Commentary", *Bible Hub*, accessed February 19, 2018, http://biblehub.com/ commentaries/ homiletics/2_chronicles/15.htm.

2 Timothy 2:2 (*didasko*)

This is the most extensively used word in the New Testament appearing ninety-nine times in ninety-one verses. Of these verses, fifty-eight verses occur in the Gospels, out of which the main emphasis is the teaching ministry of Jesus Christ with only eleven verses not having Jesus as the subject of the verb. The Father is presented as teaching Jesus in John 8:28; John the Baptist as having taught his disciples to pray in Luke 11:1; the Holy Ghost as teaching in John 14:26 and Luke 12:12; the apostles as rehearsing to Jesus what they had taught when they were sent forth by Christ in Mark 6:30; as well as the Great Commission which has an emphatic teaching aspect in Matthew 28:20. Apart from these verses, there are five verses which present the understanding that men taught men in John 5:19; Matthew 15:9; 28:15 and 7:7. And thus the impression given by the Gospels is one in which teaching plays an important role in the life of God's people as they relate to Him. And with respect to the ministry of Christ, as Horne rightly observes, "We get the unavoidable impression that Jesus was repeatedly involved in teaching situations and that in each of these some method or methods were used."[67]

When considering the rest of the New Testament, it is the Acts of the Apostles that has the bulk of the occurrences of the word with a total of seventeen verses, while of the Pauline Epistles, Romans, Colossians, 1 Timothy, and Hebrews have the most occurrence with the word being used in three verses each. In 1 Timothy, the word occurs in 1 Timothy 2:12; 4:11; and 6:2 all of which stress teaching as a pastoral mandate, with Paul calling on Timothy to teach. In Colossians, the occurrence of the word is presented as the tool by which the minister accomplishes the purpose of the pastoral ministry. In Colossians 1:28, Paul states: *"Whom we preach, warning every man, and teaching every man in all wisdom; that we may present every man perfect in Christ Jesus."* Teaching also presents the standards by which the outcome of a sound pastoral teaching ministry is to be measured, whereby the maturity of the believers is seen in their continuing and abiding in the teachings they have received and producing the fruit of the teachings received as Colossians 2:7 states: *"Rooted and built up in him, and stablished in the faith, as ye have been taught, abounding therein with thanksgiving."* And finally the place of teaching is seen in the mutual duty of believers towards one another as in Colossians 3:16 where Paul writes: *"Let the word of Christ dwell in you richly in all wisdom; teaching and admonishing one another in psalms and hymns and spiritual songs, singing with grace in your hearts to the Lord."*

When considering the verses in which the word appears in the Acts of the Apostles, what comes out clearly is the fact that teaching had a central place in the life of the apostolic church with Acts 1:1 pointing out that the record of the life and work of Christ included teaching: *"The former treatise have I made, O Theophilus, of all that Jesus began both to do and teach."* This verse presented Jesus as a teacher and His ministry as mainly a teaching ministry. The Book of Acts also highlights that the relation between the apostles and disciples to the world was one that reflected the teaching that the church received and practised with Acts 4:2 pointing out that the Jewish leaders took offence that the apostles *"taught the people, and preached through Jesus the resurrection from the dead."* Thus, they tried to deter the apostles from teaching by commanding them *"not to speak at all nor teach in the name of Jesus"* (Acts 4:18). Acts 11:26: *"And when he had found him, he brought him unto Antioch. And it came to pass, that a whole year they assembled themselves with the church, and taught much people. And the disciples were called Christians first in Antioch."* This verse presents the establishment of the church at Antioch on the foundation of teachings as well as the term *"Christians"* was a

---

[67] Herman Harrell Horne, *Jesus the Master Teacher* (New York: Association Press, 1920), 3.

product of consistent teaching over a period of time. This foundation would be by Paul spread to the uttermost parts of the world through his missionary journeys in which preaching and teaching would be central as seen in the missionary accounts (Acts 18:11, 25; 28:31) and in the testimony both of Paul himself and those who witnessed his ministry (Acts 20:20; 21:21, 28).

In considering 2 Timothy 2:2, Simpson observes,

> The injunction to strengthen himself in the Lord and stand fast in His grace was peculiarly timely under his lieutenant's load of vexing cares and sombre tidings. Only thus could he withstand in the evil day and, having done all, still stand. It seems to be hinted that he too might be summoned to tread the same pathway as his preceptor; so it behoves him to commit the divine verities consigned to his charge to faithful trustees to hand on the holy doctrine to others. The torch of heavenly light must be transmitted unquenched from one generation to another, and Timothy must count himself an intermediary between apostolic and later ages. Two reflections emerge from this passage worth pondering.
>
> (1) An era of inspired teaching and apostolic surveillance, in itself exceptional, is to be followed by an era of diffusion and consolidation of a more normal type.
>
> (2) The Church is contemplated as a permanent institution, not to be superseded either by a cataclysm of calamities or a Second Advent suspending its operations ere they could mature. The 'blessed hope' did not foreshorten the tract of future time, in Paul's view of it, to an interstitial span. An expanse of human history was yet to be unrolled before the conclusive finish put a period to its annals. Cf. 11 Thes. ii. 2.[68]

The method ordained by which the "torch of heavenly light must be transmitted unquenched from one generation to another" is that of the generation to which the light is given take up the responsibility of taking heed unto the truth committed to them and pass it on by their word through teaching and their life through their unwavering commitment to practice what they have been taught.

Doctrine

Concerning the definition of the word "doctrine," the *Dictionary of the Bible* states,

> **Doctrine**, etymologically regarded, signifies the work of a doctor or teacher, from *doceo*, to teach; hence it denotes sometimes the act of teaching, sometimes the substance or matter of that which is taught. It may also be theoretical or practical, refer, that is, to either truth or duty — that which is to be believed, or that which is to be done.[69]

The definition presents the word "doctrine" in two lights, the first being teaching that is imparted, the emphasis being the act of teaching, while the second being the body of divinity or the compilation of teachings into a system that forms the basis for life and practice. This presents the biblical understanding of Doctrine to be both a matter of learning and of practice having to do with what must be known, and how that which is known governs life and must be translated into action. "The intimate relation between doctrine and practice, between right thoughts and right action, is fully and constantly

---

[68] E. K. Simpson, *The Pastoral Epistles: the Greek Texts with Introduction and Commentary* (London: The Tyndale Press, 1954), 130-31.

[69] *A Dictionary of the Bible Dealing with its Language, Literature, and Contents Including the Biblical Theology*, ed. by James Hastings (Edinburgh: T&T Clark, 1898), sv. Doctrine.

CHAPTER I: BIBLICAL BASIS FOR THE TEACHING MINISTRY OF THE CHURCH

recognized in Scripture. The warnings against false doctrine and its evil effects are numerous (1 Ti 1^{10} 4^{1}, Tit 2^{1}, He 13^{9}, 2 Jn^{9} etc.)."[70]

A word search in the authorized version of the English Bible reveals that the word *"doctrine"* and its derivatives occur in fifty-six verses with the word *"doctrine"* occurring in fifty-one verses, and *"doctrines"* in five verses. The original language words of these English words comprise of three Hebrew words in the Old Testament verses and three Greek words in the New Testament verses. It is however interesting to note that the English word *"doctrine"* occurs mainly in the New Testament with only six out of the fifty-one occurrences being drawn from the English Old Testament. Of the Hebrew words translated *"doctrine,"* lehkakh occurs nine times with six occurrences being in the book of Proverbs and translated *"learning"* four times (Prov 1:5; 9:9; 16:21, 23) and rendered *"doctrine"* only once (Prov 4:2). In the New Testament, the word *didaskalia*, occurs in twenty-one verses with nineteen of the occurrences rendered by the English word *"doctrine."* Of these appearances, three verses have both the words *didasko* and *didaskalia*. (Matt 15:9; Mark 7:7 and Rom 12:7). In the New Testament the Greek word occurs in a total of fifteen verses in the Pastoral Epistles (1 Tim 1:10; 4:1, 6, 13, 16; 5:17; 6:1, 3; 2 Tim 3:10, 14; 4:3; Tit 1:9; 2:1, 7, 10) making it a ministerial or pastoral word. Outside the Pastoral Epistles, two verses are noteworthy when considering the use of the word *didaskalia*. They are Romans 12:7 and Ephesians 4:14, which both relate to practical Christianity and the life of the church. Both verses also are set in a context which presents spiritual gifts given to the church and are drawn from the "practical side" of the respective epistles. The one verse emphasizing the place of teaching in the life of the church as a gift given to the body whereby different members having been given gifts *"according as God hath dealt to every man the measure of faith"* and that through the diversity of the gifts, the unity of the body in Christ be realized through the exercise of the gifts such that *"we, being many, are one body in Christ"* thus impressing the duty of each member of the body,[71] that by conscious exercise of the gifts given *"according to the grace that is given"* to live and work in relation to the rest of the body in such a manner that they both build the body of Christ and approve that which is good acceptable and perfect will of God. The other verse on the other hand emphasizes the place of teaching in the life of the church from the understanding that there is the presence of many false and hurtful doctrines, and in order to counter this, God through Christ has given gifts to men with some being *"apostles; and some prophets; and some, evangelists; and some, pastors and teachers."* These gifts not only have an edifying function in the church, but also a protective function which comes out very clearly in verse 14. Thus, doctrine has both an edifying role and a protective role in the church and a church devoid of doctrine is deprived both of avenue for growth and edification as well as protection against *"every wind of doctrine by the sleight of men, and cunning craftiness whereby they lie in wait to deceive."*[72]

---

[70] Ibid.

[71] Ian Paisley in his exposition of Romans points out that Rom. 12:4-8 deals with individual responsibility to the body. He says, "These verses deal without personal ecclesiastical responsibility or our individual responsibility in the church. We are all members of Christ's one body, but we have not all the same office. There is a blessed unity in membership but a bountiful diversity in office. It is our individual responsibility in the church to exercise our gift and magnify our office. Paul lists seven offices (seven is one of the perfect numbers, in scripture); the office of the prophet, i.e. the preacher or teller-forth; minister; teacher; exhorter; giver; ruler and dispenser, and exhorts those specially gifted to occupy these several offices to fulfil in God's will their respective duties. He stresses our individual responsibility in the church." [Ian R. K. Paisley, *An Exposition of the Epistle to the Romans* (Belfast: Ambassador Productions LTD., 1996), 167-68.]

[72] "Between the full maturity aimed at and our present state is the period of growth; and Christ appointed the ministry to bring the church to that end, in order that we should be no longer children but make

Another Greek word for *"doctrine"* in the New Testament is *didache* which occurs thirty times in twenty-nine verses. In the New Testament it is mainly used with reference to the substance or matter that was taught. In the Gospels, it occurs in Matthew 7:28; 16:12; 22:23; Mark 1:22, 27; 4:2; 11:18; 12:38; Luke 4:32; John 7:16, 17; 18:19. All of the references in the gospels point directly to the teachings and instructions given by Jesus. In the rest of the New Testament beginning at Acts, the word *didache* has been used to refer to the teachings and instructions of the apostles (Acts 2:42; 5:28; 17:19). It is also referred to as the doctrine of the Lord (Acts 13:12) and is what the church is to hold on to and to be governed and directed by as they obey[73] the teachings delivered to them (Rom 6:17; 16:17)[74]. In reference to pastoral ministry, doctrine is presented as that which governs the preaching and teaching ministry of the pastor (2 Tim 4:2; Tit 1:9).

In our modern churchgoing generation, the word *doctrine* often bears a scholarly, academic stigma. Most western Christians would not say that they are into *doctrine*. However, most would probably say they are into *truth*. This dichotomy is an unbiblical one. Doctrine is simply the ordering of truth, and the way that Biblical truths fit together as sound doctrine matters much more to the health and vibrancy of our hearts than we probably realize.

Another unbiblical dichotomy we often make is between *the teaching of sound doctrine* and *the pastoral ministry*. When we think of a pastor, counsellor, or mentor, we mostly think of someone with a heart of compassion who can guide us through the storms of life by coming alongside of us and encouraging us. While this is an important quality of pastors and mentors, we must realize that the Bible primarily emphasizes something deeper than mere affirmation and "you can do it, there's hope" encouragement as critical for pastoring and discipleship.

The biblical mark of a good pastor or mentor is godly lifestyle and character (1 Timothy 3:1-13) and the ability to teach sound doctrine (Titus 1:5-9). Yet as spiritual fathers, mentors, pastors, and leaders we've often sidelined the teaching of *sound doctrine* as the means to leading others into godly lifestyle and character. Words of affirmation and acts of compassion are important, yet they must flow out

---

constant progress. This intermediate design is expressed negatively in this verse, and affirmatively in the 15th and 16th. We are not to continue children, ver. 13, but constantly to advance toward maturity, ver. 15, 16. The characteristic of children here presented is their instability, and their liability to be deceived and led astray. The former is expressed by comparing them to a ship without a rudder, tossed to and fro by the waves, and driven about by every wind." [Charles Hodge, *A Commentary on Ephesians* (Edinburgh: Banner of Truth Trust, 1964), 169-70.]

[73] "'obeyed from the heart', v. 17. the Greek preposition translated here by "from" is literally "out of". We obey out of the heart, not out of the head. Salvation is a heart work not a head work. "Believe in thine heart" "from the heart man believeth" (Rom 10:9, 10). The word "obey" means "to hearken submissively unto." It has the thought of submission to irresistible authority. It is used of the obedience of the winds and waves (Matt 8:27), of the unclean spirits (Mark 1:27) and of the tree (Luke 17:6)." [Paisley, *An Exposition of the Epistle to the Romans*, 96.]

[74] "Paul blows a final trumpet blast of warning. Certain men are to be marked men to the church. They are to be labelled and then scrupulously separated from (lit. turn away from). Avoid never means associate! These men to be avoided cause divisions contrary to the doctrines which Paul has set forth in this epistle. Rejectors of the doctrines of the gospel we are to reject. They are not servants of the Saviour but servants of their own stomachs. To them the stipend is all important. They are deceivers, the progeny of that old serpent the devil who deceiveth the nations. By their good words (lit. kind speaking) and fair speeches (lit. praise) they ensnare the innocent. Obedience is demanded to this scriptural exhortation, "for he that knoweth to do good and doeth it not IT IS SIN." [Paisley, *An Exposition of the Epistle to the Romans*, 191.]

of a heart and mind ordered in the truth of God's word. Human words cannot save a soul, but God's words can.[75]

The pastoral ministry is a doctrinal ministry and therefore the absence of doctrine from the pastoral ministry corrupts the ministry and leaves the church weak, beggarly and defenceless. Hawkins further observes,

> The apex of sound doctrine is the person and work of Jesus Christ. His identity, life, and work is the main thrust of the New Testament. This makes the study of doctrine *personal and relational*, not a dry, sterile theological exercise. The neglecting of the "word of Christ" is perhaps the main reason for our pastoral crisis in the church today. Neutrality about Jesus, His identity, His work, and His return has a disastrous effect on the heart. ... A lack of concern for sound doctrine about Christ is nothing less than a concrete decision to unrestrainedly partake in the wine of delusion until one exists in a moral and spiritual drunken stupor. We can not be neutral, nor can we neglect the truth about Christ in our discipleship and pastoral ministry. The apostle John makes it clear that we should not even have fellowship with ones who do not abide in the *doctrine of Christ*, because they do not have God.[76]

The important place doctrine has in the body of Christ is not only seen by the injunctions and examples presented in the Bible concerning doctrine, but also in the warnings presented as to the presence of diverse doctrines that are false, strange, pervasive and corrupting of which the whole body of Christ has a duty to resist, shun and expose (Heb 13:9; 2 John 9-10; Rev 2:14-15, 24).

Pastor

A word search in the Authorized Version of the English Bible reveals that the words *"pastor"* or *"pastors"* occur only in two books, one in the Old Testament and one in the New Testament. In the Old Testament it is the prophet Jeremiah who uses the term *"pastor"* or *"pastors"* in Jeremiah 2:8; 3:15; 10:21; 12:10; 17:16; 22:22; 23:21 and 23:22, while in the New Testament the apostle Paul uses the term *"pastors"* only once in Ephesians 4:11. But the Greek and Hebrew words used give a different picture. The Greek word translated *"pastors"* in Ephesians 4:11 (ποιμήν) appears seventeen times in the New Testament in Matthew 9:36; 25:32; 26:31; Mark 6:34; 14:27; Luke 2:8, 15, 18, 20; John 10:2, 11, 12, 14 16; Ephesians 4:11; Hebrews 13:20; and 1 Peter 2:25. Concerning its use in the New Testament, the *Dictionary of the Apostolic Church* notes,

> **Pastor.** - Eph 4^{11} is the only passage in the NT in which 'pastor' occurs, although its Greek equivalent, ποιμήν, is frequent; everywhere else ποιμήν is rendered 'shepherd.' This exceptional translation is justified, because here only is ποιμήν used of some kind of Christian minister. It is used of Christ as 'the great shepherd of the sheep' (He 13^{20} from LXX of Is 63^{11}), as 'the Shepherd and Bishop of your souls' (1 Pe 2^{25}) and as the 'chief Shepherd' (1 Pe 5^4) — expressions suggested by Himself (J 10:11. ^{14}). But the metaphor is obvious, and is frequent from Homer onwards. The cognate verb ποιμαίνειν is used of tending Christian flocks; in Christ's charge to St. Peter (Jn 21^{16}), in st. Peter's charge to his 'fellow-elders' (1 Pe 5^2), and in St. Paul's charge at Miletus to the elders of the Church at Ephesus (Ac 20^{28}). In Eph 4^{11}, while 'apostles' and 'prophets' and 'evangelists' have each a separate article, 'pastors and teachers' are coupled by a common article, and probably form only one

---

[75] Joshua Hawkins, "Doctrine And The Pastoral Ministry", *Joshua Hawkins*, accessed February 21, 2018, http://www.joshuahawkins.com/resources/articles/2011/07/doctrine-and-pastoral-ministry.

[76] Ibid.

group, distinguished by being attached to particular congregations, whereas 'apostles,' 'prophets,' and 'evangelists' were itinerant preachers and missionaries. But 'pastors' and 'teachers' were not convertible terms; almost all 'pastors' would be 'teachers' but not all 'teachers' were 'pastors.'[77]

The Hebrew word translated *"pastor"* or *"pastors"* eight times in Jeremiah appears 173 times in 144 verses in the Old Testament. In its use in the Old Testament, the word has been used to mean literally a keeper or feeder of the sheep with the first occurrence of the word being in Genesis 4:2 referring to Abel as a *"keeper of sheep."* It is also rendered *"herdmen"* as in Genesis 13:7, 8; 26:20. It is this motif that is transferred to the minister of God's people and rendered the figurative meaning to the minister of a congregation which also in figurative language became referred to as a flock.

The frequent use of the word "shepherd" to indicate a spiritual overseer is familiar to Bible readers (Ps 23:1; 80:1; Eccl 12:11; Isa 40:4; 63:14; Jer 31:10; Ezk 34:23; 37:24; Jn 21:15-17; Eph 4:11; 1 Pet 5:1-4). We still use the term "pastor," lit. "a shepherd." leaders in temporal affairs were also called shepherds (Gen 47:17; Isa 44:28; 63:11). "Sheep without a shepherd" typified individuals or nations who had forgotten Jeh (Nu27:17; 1 K 22:17; 2 Ch 18:16; Ezk 34:5, 8; Zech 10:2; Mt 9:36; Mk 6:34).[78]

In the Psalms, the word occurs eight times presenting God as the Shepherd of Israel with the first occurrence being Psalm 23:1 in which David refers to the LORD as his shepherd. The other verses include Psalm 28:9; 37:3; 49:14; 78:71; 80:1 and 13. The Hebrew word appears thirteen times in the book of Zechariah which also form the last appearances of the word in the English Old Testament. The verses include 10:2. 3; 11:3, 4, 5, 7, 8, 9, 15, 16; and 13:7. The references to the Shepherd in Zechariah are mainly figurative with the flock referring to God's people and the shepherd referring to their leaders (10:2, 3; 11:5, 15) and to the Messiah (11:16; 13:7).

In the Old Testament, the word *"shepherd"* when in reference to leaders, both political (princes, kings) and spiritual (prophets, priests), distinguished them from the flock (children of Israel) by their responsibility to God as they ministered and served the people. In the New Testament, the leadership offices as a class that was passed on based on lineage (as in the office of the king and the priest) is replaced by the doctrine of the priesthood of believers, and as the church is a spiritual body with members from every nation and tribe and tongue, the shepherd motif could no longer be applicable to political or civil leaders, but rather became applicable to spiritual leaders stationed in geographical stations ministering to God's people. Schenck observes,

> The pastor, while closely related to several other offices mentioned in the Scriptures, is to be carefully distinguished from them. The priests of the Old Testament offered sacrifices for the sins of the people. The Great High Priest, our Blessed Lord, has offered Himself, the perfect sacrifice, and no further priest or sacrifice is needed. The pastor is in no sense a priest, other than as all believers are priests to offer the sacrifice of thanksgiving to God. The prophets of the Old Testament were preachers of righteousness to the people or nation; the pastors are preachers of righteousness, but to special churches, though some with rich gifts reach beyond the special church to the nation and the world. However, the prophets had also the power of prediction, and the most gifted pastor can claim no such power. The pastor is also distinguished from the apostles, who were sent forth as witnesses of the res-

---

[77] *Dictionary of the Apostolic Church*, ed. by James Hastings (New York: Charles Scribner's Sons, 1918), sv. Pastor.

[78] *ISBE* sv. Shepherd.

CHAPTER I: BIBLICAL BASIS FOR THE TEACHING MINISTRY OF THE CHURCH

urrection of Christ; from the evangelists, who preached the Gospel, but were not in charge of any particular church; from the elders, who ruled in a particular church but were not preachers of the Word; and from the deacons, who ministered specially in temporal matters. The pastor is also distinguished in our day from missionaries sent forth to organize churches in heathen lands; from ministers of the Word serving the Church, in various positions, but not in charge of a particular church; and from licentiates, those who are licensed to preach, and are candidates for the pastoral office, but who have not yet been called to particular churches.[79]

The pastoral ministry is thus tied to local churches in which the pastor ministers to as Chapell observes,

> By pastors, we mean stationed preachers who oversee, instruct, and build up the churches over which they are set. Each of these three departments of work is so important and imperative that it is difficult to give any one of them a secondary place. If the church is, on the one hand, to be called out of every nation under heaven, and on the other hand, to be brought to the stature of the fullness of Christ (Ephesians 4:13) and presented as a chaste virgin to Christ (II Corinthians 11 : 2), a glorious church, not having spot or wrinkle or any such thing (Ephesians 5 : 27), no part of the ministry can be set in the background.[80]

The pastor is thus thought of in relation to his duty and charge to the flock under his care. To them, his main duty as presented by the testimony of Scripture is preaching and teaching.

> The true preacher of the gospel is, however, a herald of the eternal purposes of God, going before the coming of the king, proclaiming his coming, and offering pardon to those who are in rebellion against him. Such a herald must, therefore, first of all, receive his commission and proclamation from God himself (Jonah 3:2; Ezekiel 3:17). His ministry is not a business or enterprise which he voluntarily takes up, but a work to which he has been called (Galatians 1:1, 11, 12, 15, 16). He is therefore a servant as regards the Lord, to whom he must be strictly subservient.[81]

As heralds and servants who are strictly subservient to their Lord, their need to know what the master says concerning the means lawful in the accomplishing of the duty assigned is paramount. The pastor must not only be sure of his calling, his mission and his message, he must also ascertain what methods the Master blesses and enjoins in the fulfilment of the calling and mission. As Beck observes,

> As we do not find in Scripture an abstract system of faith and morals, as little do we find in it a practical code of rules or a course of practice without rules; it gives for our instruction precepts and examples in living and concrete unity; that is to say, it gives us, on the one hand, express directions how the office of teacher or the ministry of God's word and the care of souls is to be discharged; on the other hand, statements as to how this was done in the most varied relationships of human life by those in whom dwelt the Divine Spirit. We have thus in Scripture a directory for pastoral work and a collection of examples combined. It not only gives us very suggestive and clearly-defined rules from the mouth of the most gifted and approved labourers in the field of Christian instruction, but it also introduces us directly into

---

[79] Ferdinand S. Schenck, *Modern Practical Theology: a Manual of Homiletics, Liturgics, Poimenics, Archagics, Pedagogy, Sociology and the English Bible* (New York: Funk & Wagnals Company, 1903), 103-104.

[80] F. L. Chapell, *Biblical and Practical Theology* (Philadelphia: Harriet Chapell, 1901), 132.

[81] Ibid., 118.

their sphere of labour, bringing before us in the midst of their operations those who were the originators and founders of the work which is assigned to ourselves, those who were its ablest promoters and most intimately acquainted with its spirit and aim.[82]

The church then finds new motif in the imagery of the body of Christ in which each member has a part to play, according to the giftings from the sovereign God with Christ being the Head. Thus, the pastor as a member of the body gifted for the special duty is presented as one who teaches the body as seen in Ephesians 4:11. Paul in Ephesians 4 presents why Christ gave gifts for men in verses 11-16 and that is for the work of furnishing, equipping and completing the saints for the work of the ministry, for the building up, confirming and encouraging the body of Christ. And to this effect, teaching finds a place in the church in every age. Van Oosterzee observes,

Unquestionably all believers are called to labour for each other's edification, and together to be one priesthood of the Lord. It is indeed the highest ideal of the New Testament that all its children should be taught of God, and consecrated to Him in truth. But, on the other hand, the words, "every man in his own order," do not less retain their force; and as God is a God of order, so is there a diversity of gifts and operations of the Holy Spirit. To some, who would leave all for His sake, the Lord assigns their own home as field of labour; and from the safer pursuit of the task of instructor, on the part of the unqualified, the Apostle with earnestness and wisdom dissuades. Moreover, though all are called in certain respect to be prophets and priests, not all are as yet qualified for the fulfilment of this vocation. The design of the office of pastor and teacher is that of bringing them thereto; and in this sense one may say that the ultimate aim of the ministry of the Gospel is attained when it has rendered itself superfluous.[83]

Biblical Examples on Teaching

When considering the Bible and its emphasis on teaching, it can be noted that the Bible asserts that teaching is to be conducted in (i) the family, (ii) the assembly, (iii) the preparation or mentoring of servants and (iv) discipling (proselytizing) converts.

Injunctions for Teaching in the Family
(Biblical Basis for Catechism)

From a consideration of the Old Testament, the injunctions to teach emphasizes teaching in the home are found in Leviticus 10:11; Deuteronomy 4:10, 6:7, 11:19, and 31:19. The injunction to teach the children comes out clearly with the focus of the teaching being their relationship to God. God's people are required to lay His Word to their heart and to make sure that they diligently teach their children. This is being enforced with the imagery of frontlets, tassels and signposts on doors. A brief consideration of some passages on the teaching of children indicates:

The word *"catechism"* occurs eight times in the New Testament in Luke 1:4; Acts 18:25; 21:21, 24; 1 Corinthians 14:19; and Galatians 6:6. The word though has become synonymous with the instruction of children, its use in the New Testament is in reference to indoctrination and instruction of believers as is seen in the verses in which the word is used.

---

[82] J. T. Beck, *Pastoral Theology of the New Testament,* Tr., James A. M'Clymont and Thomas Nicol (Edinburgh: T & T Clark, 1885), 2.

[83] J. J. Van Oosterzee, *Practical Theology, a Manual for Theological Students*, Trans. by Maurice J. Evans (London: Hodder & Stoughton, 1878), 21.

Deuteronomy 6:1-9 (*Shanan*)

The word *"shaman"* occurs nine times in the Hebrew Old Testament and carries with it the sense of sharpening through inculcation. It occurs only in four books: Deuteronomy (two times); Psalms (five times); Proverbs (once); and Isaiah (once). The first time it occurs is in the great text of Deuteronomy 6. It is there translated by the words *"teach them diligently"* and goes on to specify that the diligence is envisioned in the opportunities seized for teaching. The emphasis that comes out is that of every opportunity. This first occurrence is also the only figurative use of the word with the rest of the occurrences being literally translated with the words *"sharp"* used four times, *"whet"* used twice, *"sharpen"* and *"prick"* used once each.

The teaching or catechizing is not to be abstract, but is specific with the objectives and the course to be taught clearly set forth. In Deuteronomy 6, what is to be taught is set forth clearly in verse 4 and 5 which has become famously known as the summary of religion or creed of Israel. Thus, catechism cannot be separated from doctrine and thus must be creedal instruction. The other aspect that also comes out clearly from the context of Deuteronomy 6 is the practical aspect. What is to be taught is not only doctrinal, but also practical duty expected of man. Man cannot respond to God outside of knowledge of God, and when one knows God, that knowledge begets duty and man is measured by his performance of the duty. Thus, catechism from the Old Testament passage presents the means for propagating, maintaining and practising religion in both the heart (through the doctrines taught and embraced) and the house (through the duties observed and statutes kept). From the injunctions, it can be seen that the religion of Israel and the devotion to God are to be strengthened if the religion and the righteousness God required was to be propagated in the family unit. That this inculcation of the children is to have a practical bearing on the life of the nation is reflected in the following verse in which the Lord through Moses enjoins: *"and thou shalt bind them for a sign upon thine hand, and they shall be as frontlets between thine eyes."* These words are repeated in Deuteronomy 11:18. The context of verse 18 also brings with it the idea of instructing and teaching or training children at every opportunity available in the things of God as seen in verse 19. The motif of binding teachings also comes out in the book of Proverbs especially in the first nine chapters as can be seen in Proverbs 3:3; 6:21; and 7:3 where the stress is the continual regard, retention, and application of the commands and precepts received. The picture presented of an ornament *"about thy neck"* is that of a visible sign to all those who see and a constant reminder and identifier. This seems to be drawn from the injunctions in Deuteronomy 6 and 11 (which form the only occurrences of the Hebrew word *qashar* translated *"bind"* which occur in Deuteronomy 6:8 and 11:18). The benefit of religious instruction and catechisation is realized when the Word of God is (as expressed in the Proverbs) bound *"continually upon thy heart."* Its benefits come out clearly in that when the Word of God is bound to the heart, it keeps men from sin as in Psalm 119:9-11; it gives direction and guidance when followed as in Proverbs 6:20-22. It must be to the man of God his very life as in Proverbs 7:2.

The possession of the promised land and the prosperity of God's people in it, from the human responsibility aspect, hinged on the religion (and its practices) of Israel. This is also seen in the conditional statement of Deuteronomy 11:13-14 where the Bible says, *"And it shall come to pass, if ye shall hearken diligently unto my commandments which I command you this day, to love the LORD your God and to serve him with all your heart and with all your soul, that I will give you the rain of your land in his due season...."* Since the heart is the seat man's life (Prov 4:23), and the relationship to God has to permeate man's life, it follows that indoctrination is the only way to strengthen man's relationship to God and as such every opportunity available has to be seized for this great work. When the heart is filled with the Word of God, the eyes will focus on things above, the feet will not turn to the left or the right away from the ways of God, and the tongue will sing of the praises of God and the man will love the LORD God with all his heart and mind and soul and strength.

Galatians 6:6 (*katecheo*)

In the New Testament, the word for inculcation and indoctrination which also is rendered in English as *"instruct"* occurs eight times in seven verses and is used not in the indoctrination of children as seen in the verses taken from Deuteronomy, but rather is used in reference to Apollos in Acts 18:25, of Theophilus in Luke 1:4; of the Jews in Romans 2:18. This introduces another aspect of the use of catechism which clarifies why the Old Testament emphasizes the training of children. In the Old Testament context, Moses was speaking with the children of Israel who had witnessed the works of God and heard the commandments of God. They knew God's ordinances and requirements. Their children would be those who did not know or understand and thus they had to be indoctrinated. In the New Testament, the usages seen have the same bearing, that those who would be part of the family of God have to be indoctrinated with the words, works and standards of God. Hence, catechism is not just for training children, but is a system for making those who do not know the ways and words and works of God to know and understand, for in knowing, there can then be obeying.

Galatians 6:6 (which also forms the final occurrence of the Greek word from which the English "catechize" is drawn from) is set in the context of Christian duties towards self and others and exhortation towards the maintaining of the purity and purpose of the body of Christ through correction and restoration, through personal diligence and commitment and mutual support. Christians are called to be generous in the support of ministers as they minister to them. The aspect of ministry presented is that of teaching and learning with the Greek word used being *katecheo*. This word appears two times in Galatians 6:6: *"Let him that is taught in the word communicate to him that teacheth, in all good things."* From this, the Christian ministry comes out as a teaching ministry with the relations being set between *"him that is taught"* and *"him that teacheth"* with the subject, focus and curriculum of teaching being *"the word."* The Bible is clear even in other parts that ministers are to *"preach the word,"* *"declare the whole counsel of God,"* *"give attendance reading, to exhortation, to doctrine,"* and to *"take heed unto thyself and unto the doctrine."* And by doing this, the ministers ensure that (i) the flock stand by faith and the ministers are not lords who *"have dominion over your faith, but are helpers of your joy,"* and (ii) the faith of believers *"should not stand in the wisdom of men, but in the power of God."*

Injunctions for Teaching in the Assembly
(Biblical Basis for Church Indoctrination)

Paul in writing to the Philippians in chapter 2:5 says to them, *"Let this mind be in you, which was also in Christ Jesus,"* and while writing to the Romans in chapter 12:2, that they *"be not conformed to this world"* but rather be transformed to the extent that they *"may prove what is that good, and acceptable, and perfect will of God."* James on the other hand in chapter 1:22 calls on the believers to be *"doers of the word, and not hearers only"* and for the believers to be doers of the word, they have to first *"receiving with meekness the engrafted word"* (Jas 1:21) and James also goes on to call them to *"shew out of a good conversation his works with meekness of wisdom."* (Jas 3:13). Peter also exhorts believers in 1 Peter 2:2 to *"desire the sincere milk of the word, that ye may grow thereby"* and concludes his second epistle with the call to *"grow in grace and in the knowledge of our Lord Jesus Christ,"* (2 Pet 3:18) having noted that there are some things written which are *"hard to be understood, which they that are unlearned and unstable wrest as they do other scriptures."* (2 Pet 3:16) These and other like portions present the Christian faith, life and conduct as something that is to characterize all believers in all ages and is arrived at by learning which is to be constant, continuous, and following regeneration.

Acts 11:26 – Teaching as a Means of Christian Growth

It is interesting that the term "Christian" replaced the term "disciple" (Acts 11:26) which makes the two terms synonymous. The picture given of the church at Antioch in Acts 11 is that of an assembly that met regularly for a whole year, and an assembly that in its meetings over the stated period received continuous and systematic teaching. In the assembly, there was ordered structure with (i) the church at Jerusalem sending Barnabas to go as far as Antioch (Acts 11:22) and (ii) Barnabas upon reaching Antioch did the ministry of encouraging believers to *"cleave unto the Lord"* (Acts 11:23) and reaching out to those who had not yet believed such that *"many were added unto the Lord"* (Acts 11:24) and (iii) with Paul and Barnabas being the ones who *"taught much people"* at the church in Antioch. This account not only presents the order within the church pointing out that, right from the beginning, there was order within church leadership, with Paul and Barnabas being leaders at the church in Antioch, but also that the responsibility of leadership in the church in that early stage included and emphasized teaching.[84] At the meetings throughout the year, what the text highlights is that teaching was conducted and that the teaching effected in the believers Christ-likeness which led them to be called Christians.

> Even nature itself "is vindicating the need and the advantage of teachers and pastors and examples." "They assembled themselves with the Church, and taught much people." It was not all evangelization, nor all missionary journeys, even in the earliest days of Christianity. And this is more remarkable in the light of an example, when we remember that the good work at Antioch had sprung up of what in brief might be called "self-sown seed." Those of the dispersion whose hearts burned within them had been, under the Spirit, the beginning of the work. And it was on account of the proportions to which their work had grown, and the fame of it that travelled to Jerusalem, that Barnabas had been sent to visit Antioch. The flock only need to be hungry to look for a shepherd, and the hungry flock do not fail to look up to the shepherd that feeds it.[85]

The place of teaching at the church in Antioch is further emphasized by the account of Acts 13:1 where the scripture records: *"Now there were in the church that was at Antioch certain prophets and teachers ...."* The believers were called disciples meaning learners or pupils; they met regularly for a period of a whole year, and there were teachers teaching them over that period. Their Christian endeavour and life were aimed

---

[84] "The two men taught much people, which fact indicates the wide extent of their operations; their labors, however, are not to be viewed precisely as those of missionaries, but rather as those of teachers (διδάσκειν), who guided the converts in acquiring a knowledge of the truth, and conducted them onward in the Christian life and walk. It should, besides, be noticed that this διδάσκειν, in the proper sense of the word, is here, for the first time, mentioned in connection with Paul, (although Barnabas is also undoubtedly included), whereas in 4:2, 18; 5:25, 28, 42; comp. 2:42, it is represented as exclusively the act of the apostles." [John Peter Lange, "Acts 11 Lange Commentary On The Holy Scriptures", *Bible Hub*, accessed March 8, 2018, http://biblehub.com/commentaries/lange/acts/11.htm.]

[85] P.C. Barker, An Early Co-pastorate, *Pulpit Homiletics Commentary*, accessed 8 March 2018, http://biblehub.com/commentaries/homiletics/acts/11.htm.

at pleasing their Lord and Master; and in order to glorify Christ by their life, they engaged in teaching and learning. As they studied and learned, they were not ashamed to own their Lord, and as they declared His name through word and deed, the testimony of their life and conduct gave rise to the name that has come to be accepted and used throughout the world: "Christians." It is interesting to note that the Greek word translated *"disciple" (mathetes)* occurs only in the Gospels and Acts in 252 verses, with the word being used mainly in the Gospels (only thirty occurrences are in the Acts).

1 Corinthians 12:28 – Teaching as a Gift of the Holy Spirit

Outside the book of Acts, the place of teaching in the life of the church or assembly is seen in the presentation of teaching as one of the gifts given to the church. Both 1 Corinthians 12:28[86] and Romans 12:7[87] lists teaching as a gift of the Holy Spirit given to the church and is to be exercised by the believers given the gift for the benefit and edification of the whole church.

In 1 Corinthians 14:19 Paul again speaking in the context of a gathered assembly of believers says, *"Yet in the church I had rather speak five words with my understanding, that by my voice I might teach others also, than ten thousand words in an unknown tongue."* 1 Corinthians 14 addresses the problem of spiritual gifts in the church at Corinth with Paul correcting the wrong perceptions that had led to the abuse of the gifts by the immature believers at Corinth. In the context of verse 19, Paul gives directions for use in public church gatherings which include directions for practices that will edify and build up the church against those that will not. He then goes on to use himself as an example to place emphasis on the directions he has given. The apostle presents Christian worship and fellowship as something not for selfish gain or aggrandizement. Neither are the spiritual gifts for such purposes but rather they are for the accomplishing of the purposes of Christ which centre on the edification of the whole body.[88] The church as a body has the individual members related to one another and related to Christ. This common relation breeds common dependence, and hence the goal and purpose is to do things

---

[86] "The office of teacher is the most universal, and the most lasting, and embraces in itself, in part, professorships of the higher and lower schools, wherein the teachers themselves are trained, and, partly, the office of pastor in the churches. Their position ought even at this day to give evidence of its divine character, in the true spiritual qualification and fidelity they exhibit, and in their simple obedience to the divine call, not running unless sent." [Lange, "Commentary on the Holy Scriptures", *Bible Hub* accessed 8 March 2018, http://biblehub.com/commentaries/lange/1_corinthians/12.htm.]

[87] "The gift of prophecy. 1. In what does it consist? 2. What purpose should it serve? Comp. 1 Cor. 14:3 (Romans 12:7). —Has any one an office, let him wait on his office. This is said, first of all, of the special care of the poor (διακονία); but then it applies to every office (Romans 12:7).—What belongs to waiting on our teaching? 1. The appropriation of the material for teaching. 2. Observation of the proper mode of teaching (method). 3. The consecration of our own persons (Romans 12:7).—We should give with simplicity—that is: 1. From an unselfish heart; 2. With a single eye (Matt. 6:22); 3. With a pure hand (Romans 12:8)." [Lange, "Commentary on the Holy Scriptures", *Bible Hub* accessed on 8 March 2018, http://biblehub.com/commentaries/lange/romans/12.htm.]

[88] "Dr. Wilson points out the following facts. 1. These gifts are not essential to our salvation. 2. They are not the product of our reasoning powers or the human intellect. 3. They are not instituted to promote any private end or ambition. 4. Unlike salvation, they serve a purpose and for a time seem to be withdrawn. 5. Human learning or gifts cannot take the place of these gifts of the Spirit. 6. These gifts seem to appear in a more or less degree in great revivals. A certain writer said that these gifts were accommodative gifts given on certain occasions and for a purpose and were given severally as the Father wills. They were not given to all believers; not constant with those who receive them. No one received them all, and they were not essential to salvation. Note: The subject of Spiritual Gifts is discussed only in Paul's letter to the Church of Corinth." [G. W. Ridout, *Spiritual Gifts Including The Gift of Tongues: A Consideration of the Gifts of the Spirit and Particularly the Gift of Tongues* (Kansas City, Missouri: Nazarene Publishing House, nd), 3-4.]

CHAPTER I: BIBLICAL BASIS FOR THE TEACHING MINISTRY OF THE CHURCH

that benefit the whole body. Teachers are placed in the body to labour and work in building the body through the ministry of the Word and of doctrine. According to the order in 1 Corinthians 12:28,[89] they are placed third after Apostles (which office no longer exists with the passing on of John the last of the twelve apostles) and prophets (which office had the aspect of foretelling — which aspect also no longer exists with the completion of the canon of Scripture given the injunctions against addition or subtraction; and forthtelling which is an aspect of the pastoral ministry of preaching or declaring the Word of God. Thus, this means that the office of the prophet is that office practised by the pastors in their preaching and proclaiming ministry). This would then show that teaching has a central place in the edification of the church.

1 Samuel 12:23 – Teaching as a Safeguard against Sinning

In the account given in 1 Samuel 12:16-25, Samuel addresses the nation of Israel to convince them of their sin in desiring a king (like the other nations) with a sign from God of His displeasure (seen in the thunder and rain). And when the people were frightened by the signs, he encourages them not to despair, reminding them of God's faithfulness to His covenant and word (1 Sam 12:22) and cautions them against continuing in rebellion and turning aside from following and worshipping God (1 Sam 12:20-21). Finally, he comforts them in verse 23 with a personal assurance that he would continue to care for them. In his concern and care, Samuel says, *"Moreover as for me, God forbid that I should sin against the LORD in ceasing to pray for you: but I will teach you the good and the right way."* The assurance was based on the people's request in verse. 19 that Samuel prays for them. The answer and promise he gives to them is that he will not cease to pray for them, and that he will teach them. He assures them of his prayers for them and his instructing them in the good and right way.[90] This reveals that practical re-

---

[89] Apostles are set in the first place or rank, because they were called to their office by the Lord Jesus Christ himself; they had immediate personal knowledge of his life and character and teachings; and they were the actual founders and practical rulers and referees of the Church. Next come the "prophets," who were not persons merely endowed with the power of foretelling future events, but persons to whom direct revelations and communications from God came, and so were empowered to enlighten the Church upon the mysteries of the faith and upon the claims of duty. Compare the older Jewish prophets as directly inspired teachers. Then "teachers," regarded as those with ordinary powers of intellect, and the natural gifts of instructing others, who educated and trained the Church in Christian doctrine. After that "miracles," or the power of working miracles. This is set on a new and lower range, perhaps, because only exercised occasionally, and so not comparing with the more regular and orderly arrangements for the Church's culture. "Miracles" are distinguished from "gifts of healings," which we are to suppose were traceable to personal power on nervous systems, of which there seem to be modern instances. "Helps" may refer to such minor services as succouring the needy, tending the sick, etc. What the apostle meant by "governments" is very difficult to decide. Stanley thinks that reference is intended to the faculty otherwise known as "discerning of spirits." The word used, however, means "guiding the helm of affairs," and reference may be to those officers who managed, or ruled, the temporal affairs of the Church, and answered, in some measure, to the elders, or rulers, of the synagogue. "Tongues" St. Paul puts last; for, from other passages, we know that he did not greatly value the mere power to express Christian feeling in ecstatic and incomprehensible language, or in some foreign and unknown tongue. He thought that it could bear a very feeble relation to the Church's edification unless it were properly interpreted. [R. Tuck, "The Order of the Offices in the Christian Church, Pulpit Commentary Homiletics", *Bible Hub*, accessed 8 March 2018, http://biblehub.com/commentaries/homiletics/1_corinthians/12.htm.]

[90] "By the solemn asseveration "far be it," he points to the importance which he himself attributes to his intercession for the people. The word "sin" indicates his obligation before the Lord to intercede; to neglect this would be a sin against the Lord; for, as mediator between God and the people, he must enter the Lord's presence in whatever concerned them, for weal or for woe. Comp. his work of prayer in chs. 7, 8. The "not ceasing" indicates his persistency in intercession.—Along with this priestly mediation Samuel promises also his constant prophetic watch-care, which consists in "showing the good and right way," that is, the way of God. The predicates "good and right" show that moral conduct is referred to, and that according to the will

ligion and personal godliness have to be impressed upon the people before they can practice and live it out in their lives. Teaching is the avenue by which the impression is made and hence as judge and prophet over the people, he still would perform that obligation even in the light of the people having requested and obtained a king like the other nations (which thing had evidently displeased the LORD).

> Unspeakably the greatest effect ever produced by one personality on the human race has been exerted by the man Christ Jesus. The widest, deepest, and most beneficial influence has issued from him; and he began that mighty movement, which has outlasted many governments, and shows no symptom of weakness or decay, by the very instruments or weapons which were named and used by the prophet Samuel, viz., prayer and instruction. Jesus prayed; Jesus taught. ... The weapons by which he overcame were these — he prayed, and so prevailed with God; he taught, and so prevailed with men. In the same manner he continues to animate and strengthen the Church. He makes continual intercession in heaven; and by the abiding of his words and the living guidance of his Spirit he gives continual instruction on earth. In the very beginning of the Church the apostles showed their deep appreciation of this truth, and refused to be drawn aside from that way of highest usefulness which their Master had shown to them. They would concentrate their energies on moral and spiritual work. "We will give ourselves to the word of God and to prayer." Paul was of the same mind in his apostolate. He relied on weapons "not carnal, but mighty through God." He foresaw, and it is evident from the writings of Peter and John that they too in old age foreboded, evil days, as Samuel did in his declining years; but those apostles knew no better course to recommend to the faithful than that which Samuel followed — to pray always, and to teach sound doctrine. ... Samuel was a priest, and lived in a dispensation of religion which gave great scope for ritual. But we are left to assume that the rites prescribed through Moses were observed at this period. We hear wonderfully little about them. Samuel was intent on teaching that "to obey is better than sacrifice, and to hearken than the fat of rams." How weak and puerile to lay the stress of our religion on the observance of ritual, or the performances of a priesthood! The way to make and keep a people Christian is not to sing masses for them, or multiply altar ceremonies and celebrations, but to pray, and to "teach the good and the right way," of obedience to conscience and to God. Whoso would serve his own generation well, let him pray, and let him by example, and persuasive speech or writing, preach righteousness. These are the good man's weapons, and these through God are mighty. Mischief may go on, as Saul went on to distress the people of God; but prayer and teaching quietly counteract the mischief, and prepare the way for a revival of piety and the reign of the "King of kings and Lord of lords."[91]

Ezra 7:10, 25 – Teaching as a Means of Effecting Obedience

After the Babylonian Captivity, the Jews returned to Jerusalem as was foretold by the prophets. In their return, there was a need of both rebuilding Jerusalem as a city and a religious centre and the need for rebuilding the society and the nation as a people of God. For these functions God raised up different men to accomplish different duties at various

---

and law of the Lord (so Ps. 25:4). The instruction is to be given to king as well as people." [Lange, "Commentary on the Holy Scriptures", *Bible Hub*, accessed 8 March 2018, http://biblehub.com/ commentaries/lange/1_samuel/12.htm.]

[91] D. Fraser, "The Good Man's Weapons, Pulpit Commentary Homiletics", *Bible Hub*, accessed 8 March 2018, http://biblehub.com/ commentaries/homiletics/1_samuel/12.htm.

times. But one thread that runs through all the functions, endeavours and duties that were undertaken during the post-exilic period is that of teaching. This is best exemplified in Ezra 7:10 and 25. The civil, social and religious are not divorced from the spiritual. As they built the city and the temple, they had to build the people in the Word and in the knowledge of the LORD and His laws, His judgments and His statutes. In order to accomplish this vital and central task, Ezra the Scribe is chosen and his character and pedigree outlined in chapter 7. Concerning his character, his zeal and religious devotion are pointed out in verse 10. His learning[92] is seen in him being a scribe and a ready one at that. His piety is seen in his preparedness to seek the law of the LORD. His commitment and zeal[93] is seen in both seeking and doing the Law of the LORD. From the description given, his life and business seems to be centred around the Law of the LORD as the verse states: *"For Ezra had prepared his heart to seek the law of the LORD, and to do it, and to teach in Israel statutes and judgments."* As a teacher of the law, Ezra not only shows learning, zeal, and commitment, he also shows himself as an example because he was (i) a teacher who practised what he taught, for before he taught, he did; (ii) a teacher who was fixed and focused as seen in the preparations of his heart which were fixed on the law of the LORD; and finally, (iii) a teacher who had a burden for his people for he had set himself *"to teach in Israel"* showing that he had given himself for the profit of all, and for the edification of the whole body of God's people.

> To reform the congregation when it has fallen away to the world is impossible without a faithfully preserved and unfalsified word of God, which is their heavenly archetype; or rather ever holds before them anew the eternal norm, according to which they are to be fashioned. Even in Jerusalem, even in the most immediate vicinity of the temple, the congregation, when they neglected and forgot the law of God, might fall into a condition in which a reformation was pressingly necessary. And even in the distance, even in Babylon, Ezra, because he was a true student of the Scripture, might be called to be the reformer.[94]

And as Ezra set forth to teach in all Israel, he not only had the authority from God drawn by his devotion and relation to God through the law, he also has the gracious commission of the king of Persia, a commission which mandated him to set in Judah such as would judge and govern the people according to the laws of the LORD. This commission further strengthens the centrality and importance of knowing the law for the establishment of the nation. In the commission again it is noted that teaching has a great and important part in accomplishing the task that Ezra set out to do in Israel. Verse 25 reads, *"And thou, Ezra, after the wisdom of thy God, that is in thine hand, set magistrates and judges, which may judge all the people that are beyond the river, all such as know the laws of thy God; and teach ye them that know them not."*

---

[92] For Ezra had prepared his heart to seek the law of the Lord.... To attain to the knowledge of it, that he might be master of it, and expert in it, and know what was not to be done, and what to be done; he had set his heart upon this, bent his studies this way, and taken a great deal of pains in searching into it, in reading of it, and meditating on it: [John Gill, "Exposition of the Whole Bible", *Bible Hub*, accessed 8 March 2018, http://biblehub.com/commentaries/gill/ezra/7.htm.

[93] "And to do it; he was not only concerned to get the theory of it, but to put it in practice, to exercise himself in it, that it might be habitual to him; and the rather, as his view and intentions were not merely for the sake of himself, but to teach in Israel statutes and judgments: and therefore it was not only necessary that he should have a large and competent knowledge of the laws, moral, ceremonial, and civil, but that he should act according to them himself, that so by his example, as well as by his instructions, he might teach the people." [Ibid.]

[94] Lange, "Commentary on the Holy Scriptures", *Bible Hub*, accessed 8 March 2018, http://biblehub.com/commentaries/ lange/ezra/7.htm.

THE REFORMATION EZRA WROUGHT. He went up on a twofold errand. His own object was to teach the people "the words of the commandment of the Lord, and of his statutes to Israel." Disobedience of these had always been the crying sin of the nation, and had entailed on it its woes (Ezra 9:7); the new favour God had extended to them would be forfeited if they disregarded his laws (Ezra 9:14). And the disobedience that would provoke God might be through ignorance as well as through presumption. A nation perishes through ignorance; the violation of the Divine order brings social disorganisation and rain, it needs not that the violation be wilful. … He was also commissioned to set magistrates and judges over the people charged with the administration of Jewish law, and he was empowered to execute it (Ezra 7:25, 26). Artaxerxes knew that the law of the Lord was more than a mere ritual, that it prescribed social customs and regulated the life of the people, and he sympathised with Nehemiah's desire to re-establish its rule.[95]

Injunctions for Teaching and Mentoring Ministers (Biblical Basis for Pastoral Training)

It is sometimes said that the first preachers of the gospel were illiterate men — and in a certain sense this may be true; but it is true, in a more important sense, that they were very extraordinarily educated and furnished men. They had been trained for several years under the personal ministry of the Saviour. They had followed him in his journeyings, witnessed his example, and listened, not only to his public preaching, but to his more private lessons of instruction.[96]

Pond in the above quote presents the apostles of Christ as ministers who, though considered unlearned by the standards of their time, were not sent untrained and unprepared. They were sent after having been mentored, trained and prepared by Christ Himself. In considering injunctions for the training of men for the work of the ministry, the example of Christ in calling and training His disciples is seen in Mark's summary statement of the ministry of Christ in Mark 3:13-14: *"And he goeth up into a mountain and calleth unto him whom he would: and they came unto him. And he ordained twelve, that they should be with him, and that he might send them forth to preach."* From this one can see the calling of the apostles. In their calling, the sequence of their training is presented by the text. The sequence is as follows:

(i) The sovereignty of Christ in the choice of the twelve as seen in the phrase *"calleth unto him whom he would."* Christ is the one who chose and called those He desired, and He called them primarily *"unto himself."* The guiding principle was the same one as that which guided the creation of everything. In Revelation 4:11 *"for thy pleasure"*, in Colossians 1:16 *"for him"*, in Isaiah 43:7 *"for my glory"*, and Ephesians 2:10 *"created in Christ Jesus unto good works, which God hath before ordained that we should walk in them."*

(ii) Obedience to the call of Christ as presented by the phrase *"and they came unto him."* Men who are to be prepared for the ministry are to submit themselves to the training and to the instruction of their teachers. For the apostles, this began by heeding the call and coming to Christ when He called.

(iii) The separation from other pursuits to attend to Christ and His teaching as presented in the phrase *"that they should be with him."* Before they could go and proclaim the Gospel and the doctrine of Christ, they had first to be witnesses of the same

---

[95] A Mackennal, "Ezra and His Mission, Pulpit Commentary Homiletics", *Bible Hub*, accessed on 8 March 2018, http://biblehub.com/ commentaries/homiletics/ezra/7.htm.

[96] Pond, *Lectures on Pastoral Theology*, 23.

CHAPTER I: BIBLICAL BASIS FOR THE TEACHING MINISTRY OF THE CHURCH

Gospel and doctrine. They would later in proclaiming the Gospel testify that *"we have not followed cunningly devised fables when we made known to you the power and coming of our Lord Jesus Christ, but were eyewitnesses of his majesty"* (2 Pet 1:16) and again *"that which was from the beginning, which we have heard, which we have seen with our eyes, which we have looked upon, and our hands have handles, of the Word of life"* (1 John 1:1).

(iv) The end to which they were set apart for Christ as seen in the words *"that he might send them forth to preach."* The intent of their training is dealt with at the end of the sequence. Why were they called to Christ? Why would Christ spend time with them and through His life, ministry and words prepare them? The intent is that they might be able to go forth to preach. This intent Christ achieved with His disciples and is seen in His Commission to them to *"go ye into the world and preach the Gospel to every creature,"* (Mark 16:15) as well as in His charge to them to *"wait for the promise of the Father"* (Acts 1:4) in Jerusalem after which they would be *"witnesses unto me both in Jerusalem and in all Judaea, and in Samaria, and unto the uttermost part of the earth."* (Acts 1:8)

After Christ, there is also the example of the apostles and more specifically, Paul, who when giving his personal testimony in his epistle to the Galatians points out that his apostleship or call was *"not of men, neither by man, but by Jesus Christ and God the Father who raised him from the dead"* (Gal 1:1) and that his gospel also was not of men neither by man, but rather that after his call and conversion, he *"conferred not with flesh and blood: neither went I up to Jerusalem to them which were apostles before me; but I went into Arabia and returned to Damascus"* (Gal 1:17). This attests to the sovereign choice and pleasure of Christ in the call. But although Paul did not confer with flesh and blood, Paul does say in the same epistle that he did go up to Jerusalem *"by revelation and communicated unto them that gospel which I preach among the Gentiles"* (Gal 2:2) and received recognition of his apostolic ministry and gospel from the apostles and elders in Jerusalem, such that *"James, Cephas and John who seemed to be pillars, perceived the grace that was given unto me"* (Gal 2:9). Just as Christ called the apostles and prepared them for the work of the ministry, it is clearly evident from Paul's testimony that Christ also called Paul and prepared him before sending him out to preach to the Gentiles. This testimony was confirmed by the recognition given to him by the apostles and the church. The church accepted the ministry of Paul by their response when *"they had heard only, that he which persecuted us in times past now preacheth the faith which once he destroyed. And they glorified God in me."* (Gal 1:23-24). The apostles accepted Paul by their association with him and Barnabas when *"they gave to me and Barnabas the right hands of fellowship; that we should go unto the heathen, and they unto the circumcision."* (Gal 2:9). And also from the testimony of the church at Antioch at the beginning of the first missionary journey in which after a time of praying and fasting, the Holy Spirit testified of *"the work whereunto I have called them."* (Acts 13:2)

The example of the apostles, therefore, instead of pleading for an illiterate ministry, speaks volumes in behalf of a thorough preparatory education. The successors of these early preachers were many of them among the most learned men of their times. Without doubt, they were the most learned that could be obtained, who possessed the other requisite qualifications. The writings of Clement, Ignatius, and Polycarp in the first age after the apostles; of Irenaeus and Justin in the second and of Tertullian, Origen; and Cyprian in the third, are imperishable memorials, not only of their devotedness and diligence, but also of their general and professional learning. The necessity for an educated ministry was never greater than at the present time.[97]

Pastoral training is aimed at preparation, and preparation is mandatory for the work of the Gospel as both Scripture and history will testify of. The cares of the church in the context of the times are not to be approached and tackled without sufficient preparation. The testimony of Paul in Galatians gives guidelines in understanding how the ministry is verified. In his testimony, Paul shows that both for his apostleship and the Gospel he preaches were verified by their source (origin) and fruit (integrity). He shows that he is a true apostle and that the Gospel he preaches is the right gospel because his calling and the Gospel are (i) divine in origin since Paul received authority from God alone, and (ii) authentic and true since the integrity of both his apostleship and gospel is seen in the confirmation by the apostles at Jerusalem and the hand of fellowship extended to him.

Later in his pastoral epistles, Paul goes on to issue injunctions to both Timothy and Titus as pastors in ministry. The injunctions given to them include injunctions to train men for the ministry as well as place men who have been trained in positions of ministry thus establishing the place and need for training in the work of the ministry. Peter Masters points out,

> A Gospel church is, among other things, a college. This is not said to promote false intellectualism, which gives rise to 'theoretical' believers lacking real character, love and service. Nevertheless, a true church is a place where people love to hear the Word unfolded, its wonders researched and displayed, and the words and plan of God expounded.
>
> We call it a 'college' because this suggests a settled scheme of learning pursued to a high standard and culminating in some form of qualification. In reality, the ideal church will have very little atmosphere and feel of a college, and will certainly not have assignments, examinations and diplomas. However, the teaching elder will have a clear ambition to include, over time, all the counsel of God in his teaching plan. And the people of the church will be conscious that they are pursuing a grand course in divine knowledge and will revel in the topics, subjects and themes being set before them.[98]

Training for pastors and church workers thus becomes mandatory and is not to be considered as something optional that gives the one who has it an added advantage or an edge over his peers when seeking for a position in church ministry. Apart from acquainting one with the content, context and rigours of ministry, training also has a valuable maturation aspect in addition to the equipping one. With regard to the value of maturity, Paul points out to Timothy: *"These things command and teach. Let no man despise thy youth; but be thou and example of the believers, in word, in conversation, in charity, in spirit, in faith, in purity."* (1 Tim 4:12). And also: *"Take heed unto thyself and unto the doctrine; continue in them: for in doing this thou shalt both save thyself and them that hear thee."* (1 Tim 4:16). To Titus, Paul adds: *"In all things shewing thyself a pattern of good works: in doctrine shewing uncorruptness, gravity, sincerity."* (Tit 2:7). The responsibilities that lie on the pastor by virtue of the nature and requirements of the pastoral ministry demand that one who enters the office be equipped for that office. Pond in his *Lectures on Pastoral Theology* observes,

---

[97] Pond, *Lectures on Pastoral Theology*, 23.

[98] Peter Masters, *Do We Have a Policy? Paul's Ten Point Policy for Church Health and Growth* (London: The Wakeman Trust, 2002), 44.

He undertakes the charge of souls, and places himself in a situation where their salvation or destruction will depend, very materially, on his teaching, his example, and on the manner in which he shall discharge the various duties of his trust. If he is spiritual, skillful, earnest, faithful, he may hope both to save himself and them that hear him. But if he is palpably the opposite of this,—a blind leader of the blind,—both will undoubtedly be destroyed together. Such is the actual situation of every pastor, and such the circumstances into which every young man brings himself, when he assumes the pastoral relation.[99]

---

[99] Pond, *Lectures on Pastoral Theology*, 42.

CHAPTER II

HISTORICAL EXAMPLES OF SOUND TEACHING MINISTRY

"For enquire, I pray thee, of the former age, and prepare thyself to the search of their fathers: (for we are but of yesterday, and know nothing, because our days upon earth are a shadow:) shall not they teach thee, and tell thee, and utter words out of their heart?" (Job 8:8-10).

The passage above is part of Bildad's first speech to Job. Although Bildad's assessment and view of Job is wrong, he gives a very pertinent principle in these verses. The principle is that no individual man is the repository of knowledge, and everyone can learn from both the past and from those of the past. Knowledge attained from both past events and the lives of preceding generations form wisdom for those living in the present. Bildad challenges Job to study the past and from his study find lessons that he can apply to his present circumstances, thus implying that history with its examples profitably instructs the present.

History is valuable for one's learning since in the records of the past form a collection that gives tangible and practical perspective for those in the present to study. History provides a wider view to those who study and know it, adding to their experience a treasure trove of the experiences of countless others who lived, thought and did various things in the past amidst varied challenges and opportunities.

Church history therefore will show the present generation how past generations lived, what they did with their opportunities, how they responded to their challenges, how they dealt with theological and practical errors of their times, and from these lessons, the present generation can draw principles by which to understand the church of their own times, find wisdom with which to tackle the challenges of their day, and gain courage from learning how God has sustained the church through the numerous trials as well as how God raised and used men in difficult times.

Church history is also a vivid teaching tool that cultivates understanding when one applies himself diligently in learning from it. The psalmist said, *"We have heard with our ears, O God, our fathers have told us, what work thou didst in their days, in the times of old"* (Psalm 44:1). Thus, similarly, the church's past as recorded in history becomes a treasure chest full of gems that not only reveal the hand of God in providence, but also clarifies the dealings and ways of God as one learns from the errors, mistakes and successes of the past. Since the faith was once and for all delivered unto the saints, and since all believers share a common salvation, church history becomes a shared heritage, and as such provides vital lessons for, as well as practical examples and guidance to, the present. Just as those running the race run with patience learning from the great cloud of witnesses who ran before us, so also, the pastoral ministry can benefit greatly from looking at those who applied themselves in the same ministry in times past.

History of itself is as vast as the years that are past. And in considering historical examples of sound teaching ministry, only a small sampling is possible and will be sufficient to relate and emphasize the point. And as Protestantism and the church are greatly a product or counter-product of the great Protestant Reformation of the 16th century, the examples drawn and samples taken will be from the Reformation and Post-Reformation eras. Four examples will be cited each addressing one area of the pastoral ministry. These areas are (1) Catechism — Teaching in the home (2) Theology — Teaching in the church (3) Training — Teaching of the Bible college and (4) Discipleship — Teaching in missions.

CHAPTER II: HISTORICAL EXAMPLES OF SOUND TEACHING MINISTRY

IN the Home — Richard Baxter at Kidderminster, England

Introduction

"Of how great importance the wise and holy education of children is, to the saving of their souls, and the comfort of their parents, and the good of church and state, and the happiness of the world, I have partly told you before; but no man is able fully to express. And how great that calamity is, which the world is fallen into through the neglect of that duty, no heart can conceive; but they that think what a case the heathen, infidel, and ungodly nations are in, and how rare true piety is grown, and how many millions must lie in hell for ever, will know so much of this inhuman negligence, as to abhor it."[100]

The above quotation, on the importance and neglect of the duty of the instructing and the teaching of children, are the words of Richard Baxter who in practical pastoral theology is best known for the use of the catechism in his pastoral visitations and teaching in the families and who emphasized the catechism of members. For fourteen years he enjoyed a very fruitful ministry at Kidderminster, which led to his writing *The Reformed Pastor*.

In this age when emphasis is placed on experiences and on "revivals" with the modern-day "apostles and prophets" highly elevating "signs and wonders" as the key to reviving the church, encouraging the saints to holy living, and winning of souls to Christ, and with many employing modern-day psychological methods for church growth, there is a vital need to revisit and learn from the life and ministry of Richard Baxter. His ministry had a great effect on his parish and tremendous impact upon the people of Kidderminster. He was in his own way a reformer, a man who, through his commitment and dedication to his Lord, his call and to the flock committed to his charge, by the use of his gifts in preaching and persuasion reformed the pastoral ministry in his time.

In the exercise of his pastoral duties in Kidderminster, Baxter introduced house groups to discuss the sermon as well as the use of catechism effectively during his pastoral visitation. This enabled him to cultivate and promote true piety in the lives of every person in the Kidderminster area. Unlike many today, Baxter in his ministry did not seek for supernatural or fantastic means to "grow the church" but rather he sought biblical means and thus chose catechisation. Many today seek revivals, but sadly they fail to see that the God-ordained means of growing the church and maintaining spirituality among the saints is through the ministry of the Word and thus catechisation and teaching. Ursinus highlights catechism as a system of instruction and in "the whole economy or service of the church that it was instituted by God Himself and has always been practised in the church."[101] In the practice and use of the catechism, the church has over the ages designed a system that is set to address and reach all who are in its membership. Ursinus further points out that "classes should be instructed in the doctrine of salvation according to their capacity; the adults by the public voice of the ministry, and the children by being catechised in the family and school."[102]

---

[100] Richard Baxter, "The Duties of Parents for their Children", in *A Christian Directory: or a Body of Practical Divinity and Cases of Conscience in five volumes,* Vol. III (London: Richard Edwards, 1825), 175.

[101] Zacharias Ursinus, *The Commentary of Zacharias Ursinus on the Heidelberg Catechism*, translated from the original Latin by G. W. Williard (Cincinnati: T. P. Bucher Publisher, 1851), 11.

[102] Ibid., 12.

Right from the Old Testament times, God's design was that Scripture truths be faithfully passed down from one generation to the next both publicly (through preaching and teaching) and privately (through catechisation in the homes). This was both to ensure knowledge of and obedience to God's Word which is essential for growth in holiness, and at the same time prevent spiritual complacency and apostasy. If God's people would follow God's ordained method, they would be constantly in fellowship with God and thus have no need for God to intervene through revivals.

As it respects the institution designed for the instruction of adults, the case is clear and admits of no doubt. Touching the catechisation of children in the Jewish church, the Old Testament abounds in many explicit commands. In the 12th and 13th chapters of Exodus, God commands the Jews to give particular instruction to their children and families in relation to the institution and benefits of the Passover.

Catechization of children was diligently attended to not only in the Old Testament times but also in the times of the apostles. This is evident from the example of Timothy, of whom it is said that he knew the Holy Scriptures from infancy. Thus, from Scripture one can see so much concerning the origin and practice of catechization in the church.

As one looks through the pages of history, this principle of catechizing is visibly present and as far as the essential principles adhered to in the various periods of church history are in accordance with the Scriptural injunctions, those principles remain relevant for Christians in all ages including the churches today. It is with this in mind that the life and ministry of Richard Baxter is chosen to glean examples, principles and lessons for the church today concerning "the example of a sound family teaching ministry in pastoral ministry."

About the Man Richard Baxter

On 12 November 1615, Richard was born to Beatrice Adeney and Richard Baxter in Rowton in the County of Shropshire, England.[103] This period was a significant one historically for the English nation as Morgan notes, "The year after he was born William Shakespeare died, and twelve years before his birth Thomas Cartwright, the great puritan leader of Elizabeth's reign had died."[104] Both Shakespeare and Cartwright had great impact on England. The effect of Cartwright's death on English Puritanism is described thus, "The great Elizabethan Puritan courtiers had long since passed away, and the prevailing tendency at Court was to support the Episcopal party."[105] The Episcopal Party was that branch of the Anglican Church that was inclined towards the Latin ceremonies. Therefore, with an inclination toward ceremonies, formalism crept back in and with it secularism. The church was desired to be under the crown, and as a state church, to include all by virtue of birth or citizenship.[106]

---

[103] On the twelfth day of November, 1615, Richard Baxter was born at Eaton Constantine, a village in Shropshire, between the Severn and the Wrekin Hill. His father was a country gentleman, who had lessened his estate by gambling. Abandoning that vice before the birth of his son, he was compelled to husband what remained of it with scrupulous care. He listened to the inner voice which never deceives, and he resolved on other ways and better deeds. [John H. Davies, *The Life of Richard Baxter of Kidderminster* (London: W. Kent and Co., 1887), 6.]

[104] Irvonwy Morgan, *The Nonconformity of Richard Baxter* (London: The Epworth Press, 1946), 37.

[105] Ibid.

[106] On the accession of Charles I. two opposing currents moved English thought. On the one hand, the Hampton Court conference had revived in some of the Anglican clergy more or less sympathy with

CHAPTER II: HISTORICAL EXAMPLES OF SOUND TEACHING MINISTRY

Baxter grew up at this time of religious shift. The impact this shift had on the young Richard Baxter as he grew can be seen from his own testimonies. For example, he says concerning his confirmation,

> When I was a schoolboy, about fifteen years of age, the bishop coming into the country, many went to him to be confirmed; we that were boys each went out to see the bishop among the rest, not knowing anything of the meaning of the business. When we came thither, we met about thirty or forty in all, of our own stature and temper, that had come to be bishoped, as it was then called. The bishop examined us, not at all in one article of faith, but in a churchyard; in haste we were set in a rank, and he passed hastily over us, laying his hands on our heads, and saying a few words, which neither I nor any that I spoke with understood, so hastily were they uttered, and a very short prayer recited, and there was an end. But whether we were Christians or infidels, or knew so much as that there was a God, the bishop little knew nor inquired. And yet he was esteemed one of the best bishops in England. And though the canons require that the curate or minister send a certificate that the children have learned the catechism, there was no such thing done, but we ran of our own accord to see the bishop only, and almost all the rest of the country had not this much; this was the old careless practice of this excellent duty of confirmation.[107]

This formal ceremonialism that was reflected by the "careless practice" of the bishop to confirm boys that were not yet instructed in the Word or taught the catechism was not limited to the church. It pervaded even the education of that time. Those who taught did so for hire as Davis points out,

> Richard Baxter's early education was conducted under bad auspices. The curates of the village were successively his instructors, and of them he retained no good impressions. He long had reason to remember one of them, who had been clerk to a lawyer, but by dissipation he lost his employment, and entered into holy orders "for a morsel of bread."[108]

The men who were to be a light in a dark world were men who had not seen the light. But, by the hand of providence, Baxter was brought up under the tutelage of "a clergyman of character and ability, whose theological library consisted of a Greek Testament, Augustine's 'De Civitate Dei,' and Bishop Andrewes' 'Sermons.'"[109] Although the tutors under whom he studied taught him little, Baxter's personal study and labour profited him through the access he had to the books and libraries of his tutors. Such "careless practice" that was characteristic of public ministry at that time stood in stark contrast with his experience at home. His father who had changed his ways shortly before the birth of Baxter, grew in conviction of the importance God's Word "chiefly through the instrumentality of reading the Scriptures."[110] And as such, it is the Scriptures

---

the ceremonial of the Latin Church, and had produced an increasing aversion to the particularist doctrines of the French and Swiss Reformers; which they regarded as limiting the extent of the Divine mercy, and as denying to a great degree the free-agency and responsibility of man. Some of them desired to subordinate the Church to the State, and thus to make the king supreme in both; so that he should not only bear the august title, "Defender of the Faith," which the most despotic of the Tudors had received from the Pope; but that he should be acknowledged to have both the Divine right to rule, and to determine for his subjects the standard of truth and belief. [Davies, *The Life of Richard Baxter of Kidderminster*, 3.]

[107] Davies, *The Life of Richard Baxter of Kidderminster*, 7.

[108] Ibid., 8.

[109] Ibid., 9.

[110] Baxter, *Autobiography* (Christian Focus Publications: Ross-shire, 1998), 7.

that would set the stage for Baxter's own conversion. His memory of his youth at their home with his father is one that separated them from others as well as brought them into the knowledge of the Word. Davies writes,

> We could not, on the Lord's Day, either read a chapter, or pray, or sing a psalm, or catechise or instruct a servant, but with the noise of the pipe and tabor, and the shoutings in the streets continually in our ears. Even among a tractable people we were the common scorn of all the rabble in the streets, and called Puritans, precisians, and hypocrites, because we rather chose to read the Scriptures than to do as they did, though there was no savour of Nonconformity in our family.[111]

The memories of his childhood were memories of acquaintance with the Scriptures in a neighbourhood that was entangled by the pleasures of this world. His childhood teachings at home concerning the Lord's Day did develop in him strong convictions but did not free him from addictions that had snared him. The publication of "The Book of Sports"[112] did affect life at their home. Not only did it misrepresent them in the community as puritans whilst Baxter's testimony is that "there was no savour of Nonconformity in our family", it also distracted him from the study of the Word and prayer. Baxter stated, "Many times my mind was inclined to be among them, and sometimes I broke loose from conscience, and joined with them; and the more I did it the more I was inclined to it."[113] Baxter places his conversion at the age of fifteen while reading *Bunny's Resolutions*. He observed,

> In reading this book, it pleased God to awaken my soul, and show me the folly of sinning, and the misery of the wicked, and the inexpressible weight of things eternal, and the necessity of resolving on a holy life, more than I was ever acquainted with before.[114]

After Baxter's regeneration, the change in his life was evident. Within four years after his personal surrender to Christ, he was ordained (in 1641) and appointed to the church at Kidderminster, England.[115] In his appointment to Kidderminster, God's leading and intervention in the direction in Baxter's life was visibly seen when the people of Kidderminster drew up a petition against their minister whom they considered unfit for the ministry. Baxter was unanimously chosen for the post but his time at Kidderminster

---

[111] Davies, *The Life of Richard Baxter of Kidderminster*, 16.

[112] Baxter says: "I cannot forget that in my youth, in those late times, when we lost some of our conformable godly teachers for not publicly reading the 'Book of Sports' and dancing on the Lord's Day, one of my father's own* tenants was the town piper, hired by the year, for many years together, and the place of the dancing assembly was not a hundred yards from our door." [Davies, *The Life of Richard Baxter of Kidderminster*, 15-16.]

[113] Baxter, *Autobiography*, 9-10.

[114] Ibid., 11.

[115] "When he had reached his eighteenth year, Mr. Wickstead prevailed on him to relinquish his studies, and seek his fortune at court. He accordingly went to Whitehall, with a recommendation to Sir Henry Herbert, then Master of the Revels, by whom he was kindly received. But after a month's attendance, finding the kind of life which he must there live, little to his taste, and still feeling a strong inclination to the holy ministry, he returned home, and resumed his studies with great diligence; until at the instance of Sir Richard Foley, he was made teacher of the free school at Dudley. While in this situation he had the opportunity of perusing several practical treatises, by which means he was brought to a deep sense of religion. This seems to have been kept up by the ill state of health in which he then was; for he had the impression, that he should live not more than a year. Feeling now a strong desire to be useful in the conversion of sinners, he resolved to enter on the ministry, and applied to Dr. Thornborough, Bishop of Worcester, for ordination." [*The Life of the Rev. Richard Baxter, abridged from Orme's Life of Baxter* (Philadelphia: Presbyterian Board of Publication, 1840), 6-7.]

CHAPTER II: HISTORICAL EXAMPLES OF SOUND TEACHING MINISTRY

was not without controversy. Morgan cites that "the people [were] raging mad at him for preaching the doctrine of original sin, which they interpreted as meaning that God hated and loathed infants!"[116]

The Pastoral Practice of Richard Baxter

This is the area in which Baxter is immensely appreciated. His practical theology sets an example for the minister of God. As a preacher and minister of God's Word, Baxter was wholly given to the task committed to his charge by his Lord. He served his Master as well as the Master's flock under him, preaching and writing with the spiritual good of his flock in mind. Orme observes,

> The account which Mr. Baxter gives of the means and reasons of his success, deserves the attention of every pastor. The people to whom he came had not previously grown hard under the faithful preaching of the gospel. They had never before enjoyed an awakening ministry; but only a few formal, cold sermons. ... Baxter found also, that his having a good report among the people, as an honest and sincere man who really sought their good, was of unspeakable advantage in promoting the success of his ministry. If the people of the place had suspected the purity and benevolence of his motives; if they had believed him to be erroneous, scandalous, worldly or covetous, his ministry would have been hindered. A bishop must have a good report with those who are without.[117]

It is therefore not strange when the first topic in his classic work *The Reformed Pastor* is the life of the pastor. Half of the pastoral ministry is the life and testimony the pastor has and the character the pastor shows both to the flock and to those without. Baxter's character was exemplary, but so was his industry. With regard to his efforts, Baxter laboured more than other men in his day. Orme recounts of Baxter's efforts,

> On the Lord's day, there was no disorder to be seen in the streets; and as one passed along, he might hear a hundred families singing psalms, or engaged in repeating sermons. When Baxter first came to Kidderminster, there might, perhaps be found one family in a street, who worshipped God: when he left the place, there were some whole streets in which there could not be found a single family in which the worship of God was not maintained. Even in those houses which were the worst, such as taverns and ale-houses, there were commonly found one or more, who feared God, and called upon his name. Such as conducted themselves scandalously were excommunicated; and of six hundred communicants, there were not twelve of whose piety he did not entertain a good hope.[118]

Such was the fruit of his ministry during his time at Kidderminster. The man whose character and effort are sampled in the above results that reformed and transformed Kidderminster did also lay out his thoughts and admonitions for the pastoral ministry and for the work of a pastor in his wonderfully penned out work *The Reformed Pastor*. In this work, which is written for the purpose of encouraging and instructing fellow-workers on his methods of catechisation and practical pastoral ministry, Baxter showed his enthusiasm and devotion, which so characterized his life and ministry. He divided the work into three sections beginning with views on the minister's oversight of himself and the oversight of his calling and ending with a section on the common ministerial sins: of pride, of negligence, and of the sin of "a worldly temporizing policy" that makes a minis-

---

[116] Morgan, The *Nonconformity of Richard Baxter*, 40.

[117] *The Life of the Rev. Richard Baxter, abridged from Orme's Life of Baxter*, 26-28.

[118] Ibid., 24-25.

ter afraid to speak his mind. In line with the Puritan position of piety, Baxter held to the high calling of preaching, chastising many ministers and churches for its neglect and admonishing those who preach, declaring that: "A practical doctrine must be practically preached. We must study as hard how to live well, as how to preach well."[119] Baxter appealed to the great need of the people for a well-reasoned faith and a personal relationship with Jesus Christ. It is this drive that gave Baxter his power in his writings as well as by his example. He states,

> We must labour to be acquainted, not only with the persons, but with the state of all our people, with their inclinations and conversations; what are the sins of which they are most in danger, and what duties they are most apt to neglect, and what temptations they are most liable to; for if we know not their temperament or disease, we are not likely to prove successful physicians... Doth not a careful shepherd look after every sheep? and a good schoolmaster after every individual scholar? and a good physician after every particular patient? and a good commander after every individual soldier? Why then should not the shepherds, the teachers, the physicians, the guides of the churches of Christ, take heed to every individual member of their charge?[120]

Richard Baxter was to his flock a teacher, counsellor, and physician to their souls. To his fellow ministers, he implored saying, "Brethren, I earnestly beseech you, in the name of God, and for the sake of your people's souls, that you will not slightly slumber over this work, but do it vigorously, and with all your might; and make it your great and serious business."[121] Thus, the pastoral practice of Richard Baxter reveals a man earnest and zealous towards his Master, faithful and serious towards his duties yet compassionate and committed over the souls of men committed to his charge.

Biblical Principles for Contemporary Application from Richard Baxter's Ministry

Baxter's ministry was drawn from biblical injunctions and commands and in his ministry. He exhibited the necessity and wisdom in guiding his flock into recognizing and fulfilling their God-given responsibilities. This is seen in empowering parents in their parental responsibility in teaching children in family context in accordance to Deuteronomy 6:6-9.

According to Deuteronomy, the parents (especially the fathers) incorporate firstly the faithful obedience and faithfulness to the law and subsequently carry out their responsibility to instil in the minds and hearts of their children similar attitudes and faith to obey and revere God and His Word. Baxter writes,

> You cannot sincerely dedicate yourselves to God, but you must dedicate to him all that is yours, and in your power; and therefore your children, as far as they are in your power. And as nature hath taught you your power and your duty to enter them in their infancy into any covenant with man, which is certainly for their good; (and if they refuse the conditions when they come to age, they forfeit the benefit;) so nature teacheth you much more to oblige them to God for their far greater good, in case he will admit them into covenant with him.[122]

---

[119] *The Life of the Rev. Richard Baxter, abridged from Orme's Life of Baxter*, 64.

[120] Ibid., 91.

[121] Ibid., 46.

[122] Baxter, "The Duties of Parents for their Children", *A Christian Directory*, 176.

CHAPTER II: HISTORICAL EXAMPLES OF SOUND TEACHING MINISTRY

This is probably a lesson he learned from his experience under his father's instruction and example. He thus exhorted that care and diligence are to be used and no efforts spared in order to instruct the children. This instruction should be systematic and should begin as soon as the child is capable of grasping the instruction. The basis and foundation of this instruction has invariably to be Scriptural and the parent must strive to ensure that the child not only gets to know the commandments of God but also gets to serve, fear and worship Him. Baxter says,

> As soon as they are capable, teach them what a covenant they are in, and what are the benefits, and what the conditions, that their souls may gladly consent to it when they understand it; and you may bring them seriously to renew their covenant with God in their own persons. But the whole order of teaching both children and servants, I shall give you after by itself; and therefore shall here pass by all that, except that which is to be done more by your familiar converse, than by more solemn teaching.[123]

The failure of the religious system during Baxter's upbringing would have had the disastrous effects he feared and pointed out in his address to parents and would lead to children forfeiting the benefits of relationship with God had it not been for the grace of God and the piety in their home under the instruction of his father. Thus, his sentiments emphasize the parental responsibility and their primacy in the instruction of children in the things of God. Similar sentiments are expressed by Matthew Henry who also when commenting on Deuteronomy 6:7 writes,

> Those that love the Lord God themselves should do what they can to engage the affections of their children to him, and so to preserve the entail of religion in their families from being cut off. Thou shalt whet them diligently upon thy children, so some read it; frequently repeat these things to them, try all ways of instilling them into their minds, and making them pierce into their hearts; as, in whetting a knife, it is turned first on this side, then on that. "Be careful and exact in teaching thy children; and aim, as by whetting, to sharpen them, and put an edge upon them."[124]

Such parental responsibility requires of the parents' diligence for them to continually teach their children and carefulness in teaching for them to ensure the exactness of the content taught. To this effect, Baxter points out that this instruction has to be done regularly and with the right spirit, being careful not to plant the seed of rebellion in the children. The parents' duties in instructing the children include warning and pointing out the dangers as well as exhorting and encouraging them to pursue righteousness. Baxter writes,

> Tell them oft familiarly and lovingly of the excellency of obedience, and how it pleaseth God, and what need they have of government, and how unfit they are to govern themselves, and how dangerous it is to children to have their own wills; speak often with great disgrace of self-willedness and stubbornness, and tell others in their hearing what hath befallen self-willed children.[125]

The right balance in executing such solemn and divine duties will undoubtedly produce eternal fruit by the grace of God. Weakness or laxity in performance of this parental duty and irregularity or imbalance in the executing of it brings with it dangers, and thus, call for pastoral assistance in giving direction and guidance to families in order to

---

[123] Ibid, 176-177.

[124] Matthew Henry and Thomas Scott, *Commentary on the Whole Bible* [CD-ROM], October 2004.

[125] Baxter, "The Duties of Parents for their Children", 177.

ensure that parental instruction does not lead to rebellion. To this effect, Baxter exhorted parents to spare no efforts in ensuring that the children remember the words of God in every way and keep them. This requires a great deal of diligent attention and commitment on the part of the parent, a commitment that the Word of God clearly teaches and requires of parents. Baxter exhorts,

> Labour much to possess their hearts with the fear of God, and a reverence of the Holy Scriptures; and then whatsoever duty you command them, or whatsoever sin you forbid them, show them some plain and urgent texts of Scripture for it; and cause them to learn them and oft repeat them; that, so they may find reason and divine authority in your commands; till their obedience begin to be rational and divine, it will be but formal and hypocritical.[126]

In order for parents to be able to do thus they have to rightly understand the meaning of those holy ordinances and commandments which they are to impart to their children. For this, Baxter endeavoured both publicly and privately to teach and guide families to fulfil the duties expected of them. His continual availing of himself for family visitations and the opening of his house for those who would seek help opened the church to the advantages of what was expected of them and Baxter not only emphasized the reliance on Scripture in education but pointed out the result of such an approach upon those who pursued it. He said,

> It is conscience that must watch them in private, when you see them not; and conscience is God's officer and not yours; and will say nothing to them, till it speak in the name of God. This is the way to bring the heart itself into subjection; and also to reconcile them to all your commands, when they see that they are first the commands of God (of which more anon).[127]

How then was the conscience of the church to be awakened? Baxter pointed out and highlighted the impact the Word of God would have and indeed did have in the lives of the people when catechism was faithfully carried out not only on the children but to the whole family at large.

> 'Make them read those texts of Scripture which condemn their sin, and then those which command you to correct them. As for example, if lying be their sin, turn them first to Prov. 12:22, "Lying lips are abomination to the Lord, but they that deal truly are his delight." And 13:5, "A righteous man hateth lying." John 8:44, "Ye are of your father the devil, -- when be speaketh a lie, he speaketh of his own; for he is a liar, and the father of it." Rev. 22:15, "For without are dogs -- and whosoever loveth and maketh a lie." And next turn him to Prov. 13:24, "He that spareth his rod, hateth his son; but he that loveth him chasteneth him betimes." Prov. 29:15, "The rod and reproof give wisdom; but a child left to himself bringeth his mother to shame." Prov. 22:15, "Foolishness is bound in the heart of a child; but the rod of correction shall drive it far from him." Prov. 23:13, 14, "Withhold not correction from the child; for if thou beatest him with the rod, he shall not die; thou shalt beat him with the rod, and shalt deliver his soul from hell." Prov. 18:18, "Chasten thy son while there is hope, and let not thy soul spare for his crying." Ask him whether he would have you by sparing him, to disobey God, and hate him, and destroy his soul. And when his reason is convinced of the reasonableness of correcting him, it will be the more successful.[128]

---

[126] Ibid., 178.

[127] Ibid.

[128] Ibid., 188.

CHAPTER II: HISTORICAL EXAMPLES OF SOUND TEACHING MINISTRY

The Word of God is alive, quick and powerful, yet in the lives of the children it is to be exemplified. The Word is to be shown as practical, not abstract. For this, the parents' example is to support and supplement the Word. Baxter notes,

> Let your own example teach your children that holiness, and heavenliness, and blamelessness of tongue and life, which you desire them and to learn and practise. The example of parents is most powerful with children, both for good and evil. If they see you live in the fear of God, it will do much to persuade them, that it is the most necessary and excellent course of life, and that they must do so too; and if they see you live a carnal, voluptuous, and ungodly life, and hear you curse or swear, or talk filthily or railingly, it will greatly imbolden them to imitate you. If you speak never so well to them, they will sooner believe your bad lives, than your good words.[129]

It is clear that the focus of all teaching as far as Baxter was concerned was to be scriptural, and he showed how sufficient Scripture is in transforming the lives of the people and reaching any aspect of their lives that required transformation or edification. Thus, on this basis Baxter carried out systematic pastoral preaching, teaching and counselling (following the apostle's pattern) *"publickly, and from house to house"* (Acts 20:20). As he visited them in their own houses, he could know their personal cases and thus the state of their souls. He thus could instruct them privately and personally one by one taking every opportunity to instil biblical truths to them, and to enrich them with a larger knowledge of the Word of God, while at the same time expressing his affection, zeal and sharing in their lives' joys and sorrows. Edward Donnelly writes,

> He made no division, such as is now common, between preaching and pastoral work, for he understood what Paul meant when he reminded the Ephesians that he had taught them 'publicly and from house to house.' The task is one — the same truth communicated to the same people for the same end — the glory of God through their salvation or condemnation. Perhaps this is where Baxter may prove most serviceable to the ministers of today –in the forging of a strong link between pulpit and pastorate.[130]

Like Paul, Baxter did not esteem his public ministry as all that was required of him. He did not only occupy his time with the mechanics of public preaching, focusing only on the pulpit ministry, neither did he use this as an excuse for being detached from the lives of his congregation and not visiting them from house to house. Paul identified with his flock and did so with lowliness of heart and perseverance of love. Baxter in the same spirit spent his time and strength among his flock attending to them and to their spiritual well-being. Barnes noting Paul's example writes,

> (1) That Paul's example is a warrant and an implied injunction for family visitation by a pastor. ...
>
> (2) The design for which ministers should visit should be a religious design. Paul did not visit for mere ceremony; for idle gossip, or chit-chat; or to converse on the news or politics of the day. His aim was to show the way of salvation, and to teach in private what he taught in public.
>
> (3) How much of this is to be done is, of course, to be left to the discretion of every minister. Paul, in private visiting, did not neglect public instruction. ...

---

[129]Ibid., 189.

[130]Edward Donnelly, *Richard Baxter – A Corrective for Reformed Preachers* [Reprinted from The Banner of Truth Magazine, no. 166-167, Jul-Aug 1977, with permission], accessed 13 August 2004, http://www.puritansermons.com/baxter/baxter15.htm.

(4) If it is his duty to visit, it is the duty of is people to receive him as becomes an ambassador of Christ. They should be willing to listen to his instructions; to treat him with kindness, and to aid his endeavours in bringing a family under the influence of religion. [131]

How sorely this spirit is lacking in the church today. Both the minister and the flock have failed for many a minister would not care to visit their flock and when and if they do visit it is for mere ceremony, idle gossip and chit chat. The flock on the other hand, cumbered by much weariness of worldly pursuits has long forgotten their responsibility to receive the minister as an ambassador of Christ and be willing to listen to his instructions and have resorted to giving excuses. The preacher has lost the passion for preaching and ushering souls into God's kingdom and the flock has lost the hunger and thirst for righteousness. Both, as it were, go through the motions of "playing church" yet each expects that by some supernatural intervention God would grow their church.

Baxter in his ministry expected conversions from his preaching, and exhorted all ministers to have the same hope. He said, "If your hearts be not set on the end of your labours, and you long not to see the conversion and edification of your hearers, and do not study and preach in hope, you are not likely to see much success."[132]

How preachers and ministers need to learn this lesson. God's sovereignty is not to be used to hide a cloak of indifference on the part of the ministers. The Bible enjoins all ministers to *"study to shew thyself approved unto God"* (2 Timothy 2:2) thus ministers should be given to the study of God's Word. But the Bible also commands the saint to *"compel them to come in"* (Luke 14:23) and it is this longing for souls not only to come in but also for those who have come in to grow in grace and knowledge of the Lord and Saviour Jesus Christ that drove Baxter to the homes of his people and to the work of family and personal catechizing. His zeal was transmitted to his people and in turn they too realized their responsibility of receiving the minister of the Gospel and also of listening and learning from the Word of God. His earnestness drove him to the people and their homes and also drove the people to him and to open both their homes and their lives to the Word of God. It made him a diligent pastor and made his flock practising Christians.

Baxter's close and personal dealing with his people made them take his preaching seriously and Christianity practically. Preaching that is not enforced by close personal dealing, according to Baxter, is not taken seriously. He says,

> They will give you leave to preach against their sins, and to talk as much as you will for godliness in the pulpit, if you will but let them alone afterwards, and be friendly and merry with them when you have done, and talk as they do, and live as they, and be indifferent with them in your conversation. For they take the pulpit to be a stage; a place where preachers must show themselves and play their parts; where you have liberty for an hour to say what you list; and what you say they regard not, if you show them not, by saying it personally to their faces, that you were in good earnest and did indeed mean them.[133]

---

[131] Albert Barnes, *Barnes' Notes on the New Testament: complete in one volume* (Michigan: Kregel Publications, 1962), 499.

[132] Baxter, *Reformed Pastor*, 121.

[133] Baxter, *Reformed Pastor*, 85

CHAPTER II: HISTORICAL EXAMPLES OF SOUND TEACHING MINISTRY

From the Pulpit — John Calvin in Geneva, Switzerland

Introduction

Were I to go over the faults of ecclesiastical government in detail, I should never have done. I will, therefore, only point to some grosser sort, which cannot be disguised. And, first, the pastoral office itself, as instituted by Christ, has long been in desuetude. His object in appointing Bishops and Pastors, or whatever the name be by which they are called, certainly was, as Paul declares, that they might edify the Church with sound doctrine. According to this view, no man is a true pastor of the Church who does not perform the office of teaching. But, in the present day, almost all those who have the name of pastors have left that work to others. Scarcely one in a hundred of the Bishops will be found who ever mounts the pulpit in order to teach. And no wonder; for bishoprics have degenerated into secular principalities. Pastors of inferior rank, again, either think that they fulfil their office by frivolous performances altogether alien from the command of Christ, or, after the example of the Bishops, throw even this part of the duty on the shoulders of others.[134]

In a country where there is a great proliferation of false teachings and the number of men and women taking upon themselves the office of pastor who do not perform the office of teaching, or when they teach present the doctrines of men instead of the Word of God, there is need to revisit the teaching ministry of the church and the centrality of the preaching and teaching ministry from the pulpit. In order to do this, John Calvin and his ministry at Geneva is chosen to set the example for a sound church teaching program for the church today. The vital need to consider and learn from the life of John Calvin can be seen in both the lack of proper theological teaching and the strong disdain for it in today's church. The disdain for doctrine in today's church is attested by the presence of non-denominational churches, and the popularity of claim that doctrine divides. This rise can be seen and measured in the rise of the no creed but Christ and by a look at the many inter-faith and interdenominational endeavours. It is clearly heard in the messages of men who after taking upon themselves the office and role of the pastor, fill the pulpits with humanism, secularism and psychology. Pastors, after rejecting the authority of the Word, are left to appeal to the authority of men and to feed the flock with husks devoid of any theological bearing. This in turn makes for very worldly, secular and materialistic followers who think that material gain equals godliness.

John Calvin was born in a very tumultuous time in Europe. It was in 1509 that Henry VIII married Catherine in England and it is also in 1509 that, in Germany, Martin Luther becomes Baccalaureus Biblicus. A few years later Martin Luther would post his ninety-five theses on indulgences. Calvin's early life would be one of education. This education would see the young Calvin sent to Paris at the age of fourteen years.[135] This education would expose the young Calvin to the goings on in Europe and also make him acquainted with the Church Fathers.[136] From one "addicted to the superstitions of the Pa-

---

[134]Calvin, *The Necessity of Reforming the Church*, 11-12.

[135]Wendel in his book, *Calvin, the origins and development of his religious thought* writes, "After having followed the courses of the college of the Capettes in his native town, Calvin was sent to Paris to continue his studies. This was in 1523, when he was just fourteen years old." [Francois Wendel, *Calvin, the Origins and Development of his Religious Thought,* translated by Philip Mairet (New York: Harper & Row Publishers, 1963), 17.]

[136]To this, Wendel writes "a little after Calvin's arrival, the celebrated nominalist theologian John Mair, or Major, resumed his position on the teaching staff of Montaigu; it is likely that he, too, exercised a deeper influence upon the future reformer than is generally admitted. Since John Mair published, in 1529, a commentary upon the four Gospels in which he sought to defend the Roman teaching against the innovations

pacy,"[137] John Calvin after conversion became a minister of the Gospel, a reformer, pastor, educator, theologian and writer of materials, one who through his writings would help pastors in generations after him to become able ministers of the Word, rightly dividing the Word of Truth and able to instruct and convince and give a reason in defence of the faith and hope in Christ. It is with this in mind that the life and ministry of John Calvin at Geneva is chosen to glean examples, principles and lessons for the church today concerning the example of a sound church teaching in pastoral ministry.

About the Man John Calvin

John Calvin was born on July 10, 1509 in Noyon, France and raised in a Roman Catholic family. The local bishop employed Calvin's father as an administrator in the town's cathedral.[138] The father, in turn, wanted John to become a priest and at the age of fourteen Calvin went to Paris to study at the College de Marche in preparation for university study.[139] His studies consisted of seven subjects: grammar, rhetoric, logic, arithmetic, geometry, astronomy, and music. Toward the end of 1523 Calvin transferred to the more famous College Montaigu.[140] At the time of his arrival at Paris, the new theological teachings of individuals like Luther and Jacques Lefevre d'Etaples were spreading throughout Paris, and by the hand of providence, this brought Calvin into contact with the Reformation. Menzies observes that "when Calvin came to Paris, a Protestantism of a kind already existed in France. King Francis I and his sister, Margaret of Navarre, were

---

of Wycliffe, Huss and Luther, it is not improbable that he had previously made this the subject of one of his courses which Calvin may have attended, and which would have made him aware of certain Lutheran theses from that time. 9 In any case, John Mair gave him direct knowledge of the Sentences of Peter Lombard and of the Occamist interpretation that he put upon them. It was at Montaigu, lastly, that he seems to have made contact with the Fathers of the Church and notably with St Augustine, which would explain the precocious knowledge of them that he showed in his earliest publications." [Ibid., 19.]

[137] Wendel, *Calvin*, 37.

[138] Wendel writes that "In 1481 Gerard had become one of the town's registrars; later on, he added to this responsibility, probably not very onerous, those of solicitor to the episcopal offices, of fiscal agent, of secretary to the bishop and, lastly, of procurator of the cathedral Chapter. By 1498 he had been admitted to the status of a citizen. About the same time., he married a young bourgeoise, Jeanne Lefranc, who bore him four sons, Charles, Jean, Antoine and Francois, and two daughters, Marie and another whose name is unknown." (Wendel, *Calvin*, 16-17.)

[139] Concerning Calvin's study here, L. Plenning writes, "'WHAT do you know?' asked Cordier. And overcoming his bashfulness, Calvin replied: 'Nothing that I do not think to learn better from you!' Never could Calvin have been more fortunate; Cordier was the ideal of a teacher: learned, acute, full of patience, the originator of a new pedagogy. He had his own way of looking at things, and said that more could be done by gentleness and love, than by the whip and harsh words. A strange and singular assertion at a period when the scholars, if they did not learn, were thrashed like dogs. He tried to implant in their youthful hearts the love of God; they should be imbued with the spirit of Christ; he longed to write the sacred name of the Saviour in their hearts with ineffaceable letters, and went on the hypothesis, that the fear of the Lord is the beginning of wisdom. From this excellent master, Calvin learned the elegant Latin that awakened the admiration of his enemies, and that vigorous, temperate, and lucid French with which he exercised such powerful influence over the French nation. [L. Plenning, *Life and Times of Calvin*, translated by B. S. Berrington, (London: Kegan, Paul, Trench, Trubner & Co., LTD, 1912), 24.]

[140] From Cordier College, Calvin went to Montague College. It was a leap over a precipice. Cordier represented progress, spring, gentleness; Montague, winter, the old method, the strictest conservatism and the whip. The whip was the commonest means in resort to make young men learn; more than once the rectors of the University impressed seriously upon the minds of the teachers the necessity of thrashing their pupils well; ... When Calvin went to this college, the gloomy, fanatical Noel Beda was at the head of the institution. ... It was a hard school this, that Calvin had to go through, but he went through it with heroic courage. His mind was polished; he became the first in his class, and here learned the art of debating, after Cordier had taught him the art of writing. [Ibid., 25-26.]

in sympathy with the new movement, and did what they could to protect its preachers."[141] But the progress of the French Reformation at this time was short-lived, as the favour that the reform-minded preachers had turned into "hostility and persecution when the King met with misfortune and was forced to feel the need of conciliating the Papacy."[142] This hostility and persecution targeted both the reform-minded preachers and their works, and the college of Montaigu being in the forefront of championing for "strong measures against the Lutherans and their books."[143] Thus, Calvin and the students of the college at that time must have known the goings-on and the efforts of their principal. Menzies writes,

> When the fires of martyrdom broke out in various places through the country, the students at Paris could not but hear of it, and the students of the College of Montaigu especially must have known that their Principal, Noel Beda, was foremost in urging the King to strong measures against the Lutherans and their books. The New Testament of Le Fevre, published in 1523, and the Old Testament of 1528 were a special mark for Catholic persecuting zeal. All this Calvin must have heard of in his College; but of his views and feelings at the time he tells us nothing.[144]

That Calvin was closely tied to the Roman Church can be in part drawn from his testimony which he gives in his preface to his commentary on the Psalms where he says concerning himself and the "conflicts which the Lord has exercised" on him,

> My conditions no doubt, is much inferior to his, and it is unnecessary for me to stay to show this. But as he was taken from the sheepfold, and elevated to the rank of supreme authority; so God having taken me from my originally obscure and humble condition, has reckoned me worthy of being invested with the honorable office of a preacher and minister of the gospel. When I was as yet a very little boy, my father had destined me for the study of theology. But afterwards when he considered that the legal profession commonly raised those who followed it to wealth this prospect induced him suddenly to change his purpose. Thus it came to pass, that I was withdrawn from the study of philosophy, and was put to the study of law. To this pursuit I endeavored faithfully to apply myself in obedience to the will of my father; but God, by the secret guidance of his providence, at length gave a different direction to my course. And first, since I was too **obstinately devoted to the superstitions of Popery to be easily extricated** from so profound an abyss of mire, God by a sudden conversion subdued and brought my mind to a teachable frame, which **was more hardened in such matters than might have been expected** [emphasis added] from one at my early period of life Having thus received some taste and knowledge of true godliness I was immediately inflamed with so intense a desire to make progress therein, that although I did not altogether leave off other studies, I yet pursued them with less ardor. I was quite surprised to find that before a year had elapsed, all who had any desire after purer doctrine were continually coming to me to learn, although I myself was as yet but a mere novice and tyro.[145]

---

[141] Allan Menzies, *A Study of Calvin, and Other Papers* (London: Macmillan and Co., 1918), 134.

[142] Menzies, *A Study of Calvin, and Other Papers*, 134.

[143] Ibid.

[144] Ibid.

[145] John Calvin, *Commentary on the Psalms Volume 1* (Grand Rapids, Michigan: Christian Classics Ethereal Library, 1999), 21-22.

The providence of God, beginning with his father's motives and the change of course from Theology to Law, coupled together with the friendships Calvin developed with individuals like Melchior Wolmar of Rothweil[146] and Olivetanus[147] who were reform-minded eventually led to Calvin switching to the Reformed faith and fleeing Paris. Plenning details his flight from Noyon[148] to Paris which "could not hold Calvin; he longed for a quieter place, and already saw the dark clouds gathering, which would obscure the light of France's sun,"[149] and on to Poitiers where the reformer "unfurled the flag of the Cross"[150] and from there to Strasbourg where he did not stay for long because he "feared that the clerical trend in this new Jerusalem might work unfavourably upon the wavering character of his friend, Du Tilly."[151] He proceeded on to Basel in search of "quietness of his study,"[152] and finally arrived in Geneva when his "object had been to reach Strasbourg by way of Lorraine, but the roads were full of soldiers, for a new war had broken out between the French King and the German Emperor, and the traveller had taken a circuitous route to the south, in order to reach Strasbourg via Geneva."[153] While in Geneva, his friend Du Tilly who was by then at Geneva, made known to William Farel about the presence of Calvin. Farel went to see Calvin at the inn and invited him to stay. Farel ended up threatening Calvin with God's anger if Calvin refused to stay. Plenning writes,

> But Farel, who never gave up, was not going to give up this time either. He expressed undisguisedly his bitter contempt for the servants of Christ who shrank from the strife; he reminded him of Jonah, who had the temerity to disobey the Lord's command, and for his disobedience was cast into the sea. His short form grew taller; that angular, ugly, sunburnt face with that bristly hair and that red beard was lit up with the glow of a holy zeal. Like a prophet, he stood before Calvin, and fixing his flaming eyes upon the young man, he cried out with his voice of thunder: "You think of nothing but rest; you trouble yourself about nothing else than your studies. Well then, in the name of the Almighty I tell you, that unless you give ear to His call, your plans He will not bless. May God curse your rest do you hear what

---

[146] Menzies says of him that he was "a Humanist and a Protestant in all but name, who boarded students in his house and taught the Greek language. At his instigation, Calvin began to learn Greek." (Menzies, *A Study of Calvin,* 136.)

[147] Plenning writes of Olivenatus that he was "a Picardian; a son of Noyon and relative of Calvin. And whilst this defender of the truth was destined to become the heroic missionary of the Waldensian Alps, he guided Calvin into the path that was to lead to the highest seat in the most remarkable Republic ever known in profane history." (Plenning, *Life and Times of Calvin,* 42.)

[148] Where Plenning writes that, "He had gone to Noyon to renounce his clerical appointments; his chaplaincy and the pastorship at Pont l'Eveque which had been offered him some time before. He was now twenty-five years of age; the period at which one has either to serve the Church in reality or give up the emoluments connected with it. He felt in his heart compelled to come to the latter decision certainly a strange feeling to Marx, the apostle of historical materialism, who thought he could explain all the impulses of the soul by the materialistic key. There at Noyon he was confined in the prison, on account of an unseemly uproar caused in the church on the day before Trinity Sunday. That tumult was, no doubt, a device, or at least a pretext, to get hold of the dangerous heretic; for a week Calvin was in prison and then discharged." (Plenning, *Life and Times of Calvin,* 94.)

[149] Ibid., 95.

[150] Ibid.

[151] Ibid., 102.

[152] Ibid.

[153] Ibid., 119.

I say? May God curse your studies, if in such urgent need you dare hold back and refuse to give help and support!" Calvin had found his man; he bowed his head; henceforth his life was to be bound up with that of Geneva!154

This marked the beginning of Calvin's relationship with Geneva and his pastoral ministry. The relationship would see him chased from, and again called to, Geneva all because of his theological convictions and pastoral duties. It is also in this city that he would die after years filled with teaching, preaching, organizing the church and writing.

The Pastoral Practice of John Calvin

John Calvin was the greatest genius of the Reformation. ... Calvin was the genius because: 1. He was the great *theologian* of the Reformation. He sprang into fame at the early age of twenty-six, when he published his "Institutes of Theology," which was the greatest dogmatic work of the Reformation. 2. He was also the greatest *exegete* of the Reformation, — "the prince of commentators," as Spurgeon calls him. His careful, ripe judgment, his spiritual insight, his acute perception and his practical tact make his commentaries valuable even today. 3. He was the greatest teacher of *ethics* (or morality) in the Reformation. None of the early Lutherans compared with him in this subject, and Calvin was here the greatest among the Reformed. 4. And, finally, Calvin was the great *Church organizer* of the Reformation. Compared with him, Luther did little to organize the Church; he left the princes do that.155

This is the description of John Calvin the reformer. He is identified as having excelled in different aspects and areas of the pastoral ministry in his time. Calvin has a fair measure of those who support him and those who condemn him. What can be learned from him as a pastor from his practices at Geneva? A glimpse of his pastoral endeavours can be drawn from his extensive writings, of which many are subject of theological studies and debates in academic circles, but were never intended to be confined to the walls and halls of academia. Concerning Calvin, James Good notes,

It is strange that Calvin, who was so theoretic and logical, should also excel in such practical matters as Church organization. It reveals the universal character of his mind, which is one of the characteristics of genius. The great fault that has been found with Calvin has been his lack of heart, his intellectuality. He has been charged with being cold as an icicle. But that judgment is now being revised. Since his letters have been published, they reveal that, while Calvin was a man of very large head, he also had a very large heart; and Calvin is growing in the estimation of the world, as was shown in the recent 400th anniversary of his birth in 1909. Calvin would seem to be more of a builder-up of Churches already founded than a missionary, yet he had a true missionary spirit.156

So what can be drawn from *The Institutes* and from other writings of Calvin to show his pastoral practice? It is to be noted first as has been seen in his life that his road to the pastoral ministry was one of divine providence, since by intent, Calvin seems to have been pursuing reclusion as he fled France rather than seeking a flock to pastor. His aim seemed to have been to find a place to give himself peacefully to his studies and writings, yet even after being pastor he never stopped writing. Rather the pastoral ministry and duties seem to have shaped the direction of his scholarship and writings. This is

---

[154] Ibid., 121-122.

[155] James I. Good, *Famous Reformers of the Reformed and Presbyterian Churches: a Mission Study Manual on the Reformation* (Philadelphia: Heidelberg Press, 1916), 61.

[156] Good, *Famous Reformers of the Reformed and Presbyterian Churches*, 62.

clear in his extensive commentaries on the Bible, the catechism for the church at Geneva, and his Ecclesiastical Ordinances as well as Regulations for the villages. Concerning his catechism, the translator's preface notes,

> The careful revisions which the work thus underwent, and the translations of it not entrusted to other hands, as was usually done, but executed by Calvin himself, bespeak the importance which he attached to it, and naturally lead us to inquire what there is in a Catechism, considered in itself, and what there is in this Catechism in particular, to justify the anxious care which appears to have been bestowed upon it?[157]

The catechism as a pastoral tool is one that teaches theology by the use of questions and answers. The personal care that Calvin took in writing as well as in the subsequent revisions and editions of the catechism show the importance he attached to it as well as his pastoral emphasis in his ministry. It is worthy to note that Calvin placed upon himself the task of personally revising the catechism in 1541 for the French and 1545 for the Latin after they had been in use since they were first written in 1536 and 1538 respectively. In his preface to the catechism, Calvin saw the catechism as a tool that would enhance and maintain the unity of the faith and wrote,

> Seeing it becomes us to endeavour by all means that unity of faith, which is so highly commended by Paul, shine forth among us, to this end chiefly ought the formal profession of faith which accompanies our common baptism to have reference. Hence, it were to be wished, not only that a perpetual consent in the doctrine of piety should appear among all, but also that one Catechism were common to all the Churches.[158]

This unity of the faith is to be founded and built upon the common doctrine, and thus the catechism was designed as a doctrinal tool to be used by the pastor to enhance and maintain the unity of the faith. According to Calvin,

> Each Church shall have its own Catechism, we should not strive too keenly to prevent this; provided, however, that the variety in the mode of teaching is such, that we are all directed to one Christ, in whose truth being united together, we may grow up into one body and one spirit, and with the same mouth also proclaim whatever belongs to the sum of faith.[159]

The importance of the catechism to Calvin is not only seen in the above quotation, which exhorts the use of the catechism in the church as a document that teaches the sum of the faith and, as such, the basis for unity of the body, but is also seen in his exhortations which point to the lasting effects of the use of the catechism as a pastoral and doctrinal tool. Calvin said,

> Catechists not intent on this end, besides fatally injuring the Church, by sowing the materials of dissension in religion, also introduce an impious profanation of baptism. For where can any longer be the utility of baptism unless this remains as its foundation — that we all agree in one faith?[160]

---

[157] John Calvin, *Calvin's Tracts containing Treatises on the Sacraments, Catechism of the Church of Geneva, Forms of Prayer and Confession of Faith vol. II*, Trans. by Henry Beveridge (Edinburgh: Calvin Translation Society, 1849), vii.

[158] Ibid., 34.

[159] Calvin, *Calvin's Tracts*, 34

[160] Ibid.

CHAPTER II: HISTORICAL EXAMPLES OF SOUND TEACHING MINISTRY

To Calvin, a departure from the catechism of the church would be the beginning of error and dissension in religion. The catechism when properly used in the instruction of the members and especially those who would be baptized and enjoined into the church as a body promotes the unity of the faith. As a standard set of questions and answers, it would promote a standard set of instruction to all who would read and be instructed of it. Such is the importance of the catechism as a doctrinal and pastoral tool in Calvin's view. He further warned,

> Those who publish Catechisms ought to be the more carefully on their guard, lest, by producing anything rashly, they may not for the present only, but in regard to posterity also, do grievous harm to piety, and inflict a deadly wound on the Church.[161]

In penning his catechism, the danger of schism and disunity in the church seems to be of a great concern to him, and he rightly points out in his dedication to the care that needs to be taken for the flock when publishing materials for the church. Thus, his intent is clear: he was writing for the church with the intent of all agreeing in one faith. Volmer includes in his volume a letter that Calvin wrote to Bullinger in which Calvin's desire for the unity of preachers and of the church is plainly set forth. Volmer points out that it was Calvin's desire to "consolidate Protestantism."[162] But this unity must not be an ecumenical pursuit devoid of any doctrinal basis as that which is popularly propagated in this age, but rather it must be a unity that is both biblical and doctrinal. The unity of the faith can have no other basis than this. Volmer goes to note,

> It is refreshing to listen to some of Calvin's beautiful sentiments in favor of church union. In a letter to Bullinger, March 12, 1540, he writes: "What, dear Bullinger, should more anxiously occupy us in our letters, than the endeavor to keep up brotherly friendship among us by all possible means. It is important for the whole church that all should keep together to whom the Lord has committed the affairs in His church. It is, therefore, our duty to cherish a true friendship for all preachers of the Word, and to keep the churches at peace with each other. As far as in me lies, I will always labor to do so. I wish that something might occur which would afford me the opportunity of discussing the whole matter with you in a friendly manner, face to face. I have never been able to treat this matter with you by word of mouth. I beseech you, or rather conjure you, dear Bullinger, to let us wholly refrain from all hate and all strife, and even from all appearance of offense. Do not think that I have any doubt of your resolution. It is the peculiarity of love, that even when there is hope there is yet much of anxiety. Farewell, learned and pious man."[163]

This desire is not in no way to be mistaken for compromise or be seen to be an attempt to put aside doctrine, since in another letter in 1552, Calvin clearly pens the place of doctrine in unifying the church of Christ. In this letter which he wrote in response to an invitation to meet for the purpose of drawing up a consensus creed for the reformed churches, Calvin is recorded to have written,

> As nothing tends more injuriously to the separation of the churches than heresies and disputes respecting the doctrines of religion, **so nothing tends more effectually to unite the Churches of God, and more powerfully to defend the fold of Christ than the pure teaching of the Gospel and harmony of doctrine.** [Empha-

---

[161] Ibid.

[162] Philip Volmer, *John Calvin: Theologian, Preacher, Educator, Statesman* (Philadelphia: Heidelberg Press, 1909), 143.

[163] Ibid.

sis added.] Wherefore I have often wished, and still continue to do so, that learned and godly men, who are eminent for erudition and judgment, might meet together, and, comparing their respective opinions, might handle all the heads of ecclesiastical doctrine, and hand down to posterity, under the weight of their authority, some work not only upon the subjects themselves, but upon the forms of expressing them. Our adversaries are now holding their councils at Trent, for the establishment of their errors; and shall we neglect to call together a godly synod, for the refutation of error, and for restoring and propagating the truth?[164]

It is clear from Calvin's writings that the life of the church, the unity of the faith and the defence and protection of the flock are intrinsically tied to the doctrines taught to them. The modern thought that doctrine divides and is to be avoided at all ecumenical gatherings is weakening and destroying the church. Calvin advocated for learned and godly men to come together and discuss their doctrinal positions as well as hand down to the flock and posterity the tenets of the faith and the refutations of the errors done in their times. What Calvin desired for the reformed churches to do in unison, he did not refrain from doing in person. He states that plainly in the dedication of his catechism where he points out:

But if this is so necessary in the present day, what shall our feelings be concerning posterity, about which I am so anxious, that I scarcely dare to think? Unless God miraculously send help from heaven, I cannot avoid seeing that the world is threatened with the extremity of barbarism. I wish our children may not shortly feel, that this has been rather a true prophecy than a conjecture. The more, therefore, must we labour to gather together, by our writings, whatever remains of the Church shall continue, or even emerge, after our death. Writings of a different class will show what were our views on all subjects in religion, but the agreement which our churches had in. doctrine cannot be seen with clearer evidence than from catechisms. For therein will appear, not only what one man or other once taught, but with what rudiments learned and unlearned alike amongst us, were constantly imbued from childhood, all the faithful holding them as their formal symbol of Christian communion. This was indeed my principal reason for publishing this Catechism.[165]

Pastoral labour and endeavour have to be doctrinal. The pastor's preaching, teaching and writing must propagate doctrine. The basic teaching text that will supplement the Bible, according to Calvin, is the catechism in which the rudiments can be learned and unlearned alike. The catechism is not to be confined to a specific age group within the church but rather is to be used by all. Doctrine is for the church, and it is to be presented to all irrespective of their academic qualifications as the doctrine to which the church holds to is their formal symbol of Christian communion and as such the church must endeavour both to make sure it propagates biblical doctrines and ensures that all in communion are imbued from childhood with the same doctrines and hold on to them faithfully. Thus, the pastoral duty to cultivate true piety of life and heart (both of faith and practice) in those to whom he ministers seems to be the driving force in Calvin's pen.

To Calvin, doctrine was the means to uniting the church, preserving it from error, establishing it amidst the onslaught of the enemies both known and unknown. Thus, the church which seeks to stand must take a doctrinal stand, the pastor who wishes to leave for posterity a church faithful and true, free from the defilements of the present wicked

---

[164] Volmer, *John Calvin: Theologian, Preacher, Educator, Statesman*, 143-144.

[165] Calvin, *Calvin's Tracts*, 36.

and adulterous generation must set forth clearly, regularly and boldly doctrinal standards supported by and based on Scripture. This is the message of Calvin's most famous letter on the importance of church union. Volmer writes,

> In April, 1552, the former wrote his famous letter on the importance of church union in reply to Cranmer's letter, in which he says "In the present distracted state: of the church, you suppose that no better means can be employed than that pious, sensible men, brought up in the school of God, should unite in setting forth a common confession of Christian doctrine. Satan seeks by manifold wiles to extinguish the light of the Gospel. The dogs in the pay of the Pope cease not to bark, that they may drown the voices of those who preach the word of truth. Such is the madness, such the impiety which everywhere prevails, that religion can hardly any longer be protected from daily mockery. Nor is this state of feeling confined to the people alone. Still more lamentable to say, it is extending among the clergy. But the Lord Himself will communicate to us the unity of the true faith, in some wonderful manner, and by means altogether unknown to us."[166]

Calvin's concern to Cranmer remains a true concern even in this age. The drowning of the voices preaching the Word of truth is coming from more quarters than before, the proliferation of cults and heresies and hostility to Biblical Christianity and its doctrines is on the rise and its effects is reaching unprecedented levels. The attacks on the Bible take varied forms, and those who hold on to its words regarded as intolerant and heretics and divisive by those who have embraced the current ecumenical spirit. This is what forms the order of the day in this age. Does this mean that every pastor is to be confined to his own church and face these challenges alone? Or does it mean that the pastor's efforts are to be limited to his congregation alone? As dark as the days were prior to the revival of the sixteenth century Reformation, and as great as the opposition was during the Reformation, so was the extent and influence of the Reformers. It was extended beyond their churches and regions. Volmer points out how the extent of his effort and the influence of them extended to the church beyond Geneva. When noting the labours of Calvin during the last nine years of his life, Volmer writes,

> He preached two or three times a week, lectured every third day, presided in the consistory on Thursdays, and fulfilled the other duties of his pastoral office. His pen was unceasingly busy, writing new books, revising old ones, conducting the extensive correspondence, a selection of which in his published works fills twelve large volumes, taking part in the controversies of the time, chief of which were the Sacramentarian Controversies with the Lutherans. His body was in Geneva but his heart was in the church of God everywhere.[167]

Calvin's pen opened the whole world to him; it complemented his pastoral ministry and opened new doors for the propagation of the doctrines of faith. His writing ministry did not in any way diminish his pastoral duties, rather it enhanced them. From Volmer's description, Calvin's pen was theological and at times controversial as he wrote concerning the controversies of his time. Volmer notes,

> His theological writings, especially his Institutes and the famous commentaries on the Old and New Testaments, gained for him a renown as an accomplished author, both as to matter and style. Among his correspondents were kings, nobles, and persons of highest positions in all countries; his advice was sought in matters small and great. His name was a familiar one in courts and conclaves. His letters were prized

---

[166]Volmer, *John Calvin: Theologian, Preacher, Educator Statesman*, 144-145.

[167]Volmer, *John Calvin: Theologian, Preacher, Educator Statesman*, 71.

as literary treasures as well as for the worth of their contents. Not a church was in difficulty, hardly a martyr went to the stake, but received from him some message of guidance or consolation. Geneva became an asylum for the persecuted like no other city, and numbers of persons of rank, learning and piety, found refuge within its walls. ...

There is scarcely one of his letters in which he does not recur to his ideal of the "Church under the Cross" growing before God in proportion to her sufferings. Noticeable among his letters are the two beautiful epistles "To the Believers of France," in June and November, 1559. "Doubt not," he writes, "even if the wicked had exhausted all their cruelty, that there shall be one drop of blood which shall not tend to increase the number of believers."[168]

Another aspect of Calvin's pastoral practice was seen in his homiletics. In this aspect, Calvin's concern focused on the content and message being delivered as well as the method of delivery. Calvin's concern for the pulpit during his time is recorded by Volmer in a letter that Calvin wrote to Lord Somerset in which Calvin decried the state of the preachers in Lord Somerset's regions. Volmer writes,

The people must be taught in such a manner, that they may be inwardly convinced and made to feel the truth of what the Apostle says, that the Word of God 'is a two-edged sword.' I say this to your Highness because there is too little of living preaching in your kingdom, sermons there being mostly read or recited. I understand well enough what obliges you to adopt this habit. There are few good, useful preachers, such as you wish to have; and you fear that levity and foolish imaginations might be the consequence, as is often the case, of the introduction of a new system.[169]

Calvin not only points out the sorry state of affairs, but also addresses them by giving standards that ought to be aspired to and practised. The preaching ministry is unlike any other form of public speaking or oration as the intent is that men be convinced and convicted of the truth of God's Word. This is to be done through the instrumentality of preaching. Preaching is not just about the skills and gifts of the preacher since the Word of God is living and powerful, a two-edged sword, and since it is the Gospel that is the power of God unto salvation to everyone who believes. Preaching has to do with the person of the preacher and the content of his preaching as well as the mechanics he uses. If it is not biblical, irrespective of how gripping and pleasant to hear, it is not to be considered preaching. To this effect Calvin wrote,

But all this must yield to the command of Christ which orders the preaching of the Gospel. And this preaching must not be dead, but living, for doctrine, for correction, for edification. So that when a Christian enters the church, he may be moved to penitence, and be inwardly convinced. The preachers ought not to wish to shine in the ornaments of rhetoric, but the spirit of God should be echoed by their voices."[170]

Calvin's pastoral concern was not only seen in his letters and books which extended his concern to the church everywhere, but also in his sermons and his concern for the pulpit during his time. His pastoral concern for the pulpit ministry emphasized that preaching is not for formality, it has to breathe life into those who are brought under it. The truth of the Scripture has to be impressed upon the hearers of the word, and as such, Calvin not only broke off with what was the system and tradition of his period, but ad-

---

[168] Ibid., 71-72.

[169] Volmer, *John Calvin: Theologian, Preacher, Educator Statesman*, 123.

[170] Ibid., 124.

dressed the weakness of the practices of his time in his letters as well as echoed the spirit of God by his voice. Volmer writes again concerning Calvin's own homiletic practice,

> Calvin broke loose from the system of the pericopes of the church year and used free texts. Some of his extant sermons are based on four texts. His sermons in the form in which we have them are rather short. It is said that he rarely preached longer than half an hour. ... Calvin's sermons which have come to us were taken down by students. One of his hearers writes: "Calvin being asthmatic and speaking very deliberately, it is easy to write down all that he says." But for this remark, the style of the sermons would lead us to suppose that they had been spoken with great fire, rapidity and force. It is even said that he often broke off, and made long pauses, to give the hearers time to consider his remarks. Although not naturally eloquent himself, he appreciated the power of eloquence. "You must take care," he says, "as far as possible, to have good trumpets, such as may penetrate deepest into the heart."[171]

Whether it is in his pastoral methods, pastoral concerns or writings, John Calvin was of clear mind as to the place of doctrine in establishing the church especially in view of the tumultuous times seen in the opposition faced by the church. Even in his "Institutes of Christian Religion," considered his greatest writings, the preface points to its pastoral nature in that its aim was not that of purely academic pursuits, but practical. It was aimed at the instruction of the believers and later due to the rising opposition, a defence of the faith to the king as he states in his preface where he writes,

> Sire, — When I first engaged in this work, nothing was farther from my thoughts than to write what should afterwards be presented to your Majesty. My intention was only to furnish a kind of rudiments, by which those who feel some interest in religion might be trained to true godliness. And I toiled at the task chiefly for the sake of my countrymen the French, multitudes of whom I perceived to be hungering and thirsting after Christ, while very few seemed to have been duly imbued with even a slender knowledge of him. That this was the object which I had in view is apparent from the work itself, which is written in a simple and elementary form adapted for instruction. But when I perceived that the fury of certain bad men had risen to such a height in your realm, that there was no place in it for sound doctrine, I thought it might be of service if I were in the same work both to give instruction to my countrymen, and also lay before your Majesty a Confession, from which you may learn what the doctrine is that so inflames the rage of those madmen who are this day, with fire and sword, troubling your kingdom. For I fear not to declare, that what I have here given may be regarded as a summary of the very doctrine which, they vociferate, ought to be punished with confiscation, exile, imprisonment, and flames, as well as exterminated by land and sea.[172]

Thus, *The Institutes* (which has become known as a great theological treatise) was to Calvin an expression of his "pastoral world-view," his attempt to furnish the believers with those things which are most surely believed amongst those that are born again in plain language. A confession of sound doctrine was his aim, what was clear in his mind concerning God and man, what was supported by Scripture and what was most certainly to be preached to the ends of the world and proclaimed from the rooftops was what he penned down. Conviction out of consistent study of Scripture alone, assurance out of the inward working of the Spirit of God gave rise in him what he endeavoured to write for all to read and be convinced. What was intended for the church, for the born

---

[171] Volmer, *John Calvin: Theologian, Preacher, Educator Statesman*, 124.

[172] John Calvin, *Institutes of the Christian Religion*, Trans. by, Henry Beveridge (Edinburgh: The Calvin Translation Society, 1845), 3-4.

again believers, ought not be left on the shelves of libraries or left to be discussed just within the halls of academia!

Biblical Principles for Contemporary Application from the Ministry of John Calvin

John Calvin's ministry manifests an understanding and knowledge of biblical injunctions as well as a desire, zeal, and commitment to God and His Word and to the people of God of his time. This knowledge, understanding, desire and commitment is reflected in his principles and practices as seen in his life and ministry. He exhibited a commitment to the Holy Scriptures as the basis for his life and ministry and guided his flock with wisdom drawn from the Scriptures. Henry Beveridge in his Introductory Notice in the translation of *The Institutes of The Christian Religion* writes,

> This, however, was not his only labour. At the request of a friend, (apparently Louis du Tillet, canon of Angouleme,) he wrote what Beza calls "*Breves Admonitiones Christianas,*" — Brief Christian Admonitions, to be read in the neighbouring congregations, with the view of gradually alluring them to the knowledge of the truth. None of these Christian Admonitions are now extant, but they are deserving of particular notice here, as having, not improbably, suggested the idea, perhaps formed the ground-work, of The Christian Institutes.[173]

Calvin's desire was to explain and make clear the Scriptures and that through the Scriptures, the Christians are to know what they believe, and to worship and serve God on the basis of Scriptural knowledge. From his preface, Calvin shows that he was not interested in just explaining the truth, or writing literary treatises that merely expressed his understanding of the truth, but rather that his desire and goal both in his study and writing was the worship and service of God. Thomas Norton in his preface as translator writes,

> Good Reader, here is now offered you, the fourth time printed in English, M. Calvin's book of the Institution of Christian Religion; a book of great labour to the author, and of great profit to the Church of God. M. Calvin first wrote it when he was a young man, a book of small volume, and since that season he hath at sundry times published it with new increases, still protesting at every edition himself to be one of those *qui scribendo proficient, et proficiendo scribunty which with their writing do grow in profiting, and with their profiting do proceed in writing.*[174]

The Word of God is alive, quick and powerful, and as such, the pastoral ministry is relevant only as it deals with the study and proclamation of the Word. Paul instructed Timothy to give himself wholly to the reading of the Word and through it at length to show himself profitable by it to those who would attend to his ministry (1 Tim 4:12-16). This exhortation probably finds in the life of Calvin its applications when one reads Norton's testimony of Calvin's endeavour in the writing of the Institutes. In writing, he grew, and in growth, he wrote. The Institutes thus is a testimony to the growth of Calvin as he profited from the Word and as such further highlights the importance and place of doctrinal clarity and teaching in the pastoral ministry. Calvin himself in his prefatory address to the king wrote,

> Sire, — When I first engaged in this work, nothing was farther from my thoughts than to write what should afterwards be presented to your Majesty. My intention was only to furnish a kind of rudiments, by which those who feel some interest in religion might be trained to true godliness. And I toiled at the task chiefly for the

---

[173] Calvin, *The Institutes*, vi-vii.

[174] Calvin, *The Institutes*, cxi.

sake of my countrymen the French, multitudes of whom I perceived to be hungering and thirsting after Christ, while very few seemed to have been duly imbued with even a slender knowledge of him. That this was the object which I had in view is apparent from the work itself, which is written in a simple and elementary form adapted for instruction. [175]

For John Calvin, furnishing "rudiments" by which men "might be trained" and through which they may be guided into "true godliness" was the objective and concern for his countrymen. This was the driving force behind his great work. A concern and focus that is severely lacking in this age, yet direly needed in the pulpit. *The Institutes* is thus, first and foremost, a pastoral work, intended for the salvation, edification and growth of those who would read them that they be instructed in the doctrines penned therein. Paul instructed Timothy to teach and instruct the believers of his time in doctrine that would strengthen them in the faith, and that would provide them with the wisdom that would keep them from the seduction of the world in their age. Similarly, Calvin studied hard and searched the same Scriptures and from them drew out and expounded with great clarity the same truths. In this age, ministers must teach and command the same things, and by their life's testimony exemplify what they have been taught and received being drawn from and confirmed by the Scriptures. As a pastor, piety or godliness was Calvin's primary and only concern and his aim was writing what his countrymen could use to the profiting of their souls in the practice of their devotions, worship and service to God and not personal fame or glory. Beveridge records an incident that Calvin notes when he visited Basel,

> While Calvin is living at Basle, a perfect stranger, a work is published bearing his name on the title-page. Every one is in raptures with it; all are loud in Calvin's praise. Calvin maintains his incognito. He sees the popularity of his work, and doubtless rejoices in it, but he never opens his mouth to say to anyone, "I am Calvin." Assuming these to be the facts, was it anything more than a simple unvarnished statement of the truth when Calvin said, "Personal fame could not be my object in the publication. I was a perfect stranger. Nobody in the place knew who I was, and I left the place shortly after without having told it. They all knew from the title-page that John Calvin was the author, but none of them knew that I was that John Calvin;" or, in the very words which he has himself employed, "nemo illic sciverit me authorem esse" — "nobody there knew that I was the author."[176]

In the light of his accomplishments and achievements, a true minister of the Word does not get carried away and be lifted up in pride. The more he accomplishes, the more he immerses himself in the study of the Word. Through the study of the Word he gains much and grows in grace and in the knowledge of Christ, and as he grows, he accomplishes much more in the work of the ministry. This is the picture presented of Calvin through the above-mentioned event. Much of Calvin's pastoral work was at Geneva, and it is there that he helped developed Protestantism or what is popularly known as Reformed Theology. This was developed both through his practice and writings. Calvin developed a religion that was biblical both in belief and practice. Unique aspects that he developed and that distinguished his work at Geneva are seen in (i) Worship and Sacraments, (ii) Preaching, (iii) Visitation and Relations to the Society, and (iv) Discipline and Church Government and Order. In giving an overview of the achievements of Calvin as a pastor at Geneva, Thomas Smyth writes,

---

[175] Calvin, *The Institutes*, 3.

[176] Calvin, *The Institutes*, xiv.

Calvin was a member of the sovereign council of Geneva, and took a great part in the deliberations as a politician and legislator. **He corrected the civil code** of his adopted country. **He corresponded with Protestants throughout Europe** both on religious subjects and on state affairs, for all availed themselves of his experience in difficult matters. **He wrote innumerable letters of encouragement** and consolation to those who were persecuted, imprisoned, condemned to death for the gospel's sake. **He was a constant preacher**, delivering public discourses every day in the week, and on Sunday preaching twice. **He was professor of theology**, and delivered three lectures a week. **He was president of consistory**, and addressed remonstrances or pronounced other ecclesiastical sentences against delinquent church-members. **He was the head of the pastors**, and every Friday, in an assembly called the congregation, he pronounced before them a long discourse on the duties of the evangelical ministry. **His door was constantly open to refugees** from France, England, Poland, Germany and Italy, who flocked to Geneva, and **he organized for these exiled Protestants special parishes**. His correspondence, commentaries, controversial writings, etc., would form annually, during the period of thirty-one years, between two and three octavo volumes, and yet he did not reach the age of fifty-five. **When laid aside by disease from preaching he dictated numberless letters**, revised for the last time his Christian Institutes, almost rewrote his commentary on Isaiah, frequently observing that "nothing was so painful to him as his present idle life." And when urged by his friends to forbear he would reply, **"Would you have my Lord to find me idle when he cometh?"** [Emphasis added.] "Oh, the power of Christian faith and of the human will! Calvin did all these things —he did more than twenty eminent doctors, and he had feeble health, a frail body and died at the age of fifty-five years."[177]

Calvin's activity reflects his devotion, zeal and commitment to God, the ministry and his fellow men. A study of his pattern in ministry and his efforts in all the areas he engaged himself for the service of God presents an invaluable treasure for the pastor who would commit himself wholly to the work of his Lord. Consideration of his life, writings and works presents him as a pastor and reformer of the church at Geneva. And as a pastor, Calvin organized the church in its structure, doctrine, practices, and thus set up a pattern for pastors in all ages. From the pattern, the chief principle that can be drawn for contemporary application is the primacy of preaching. From the primacy of biblical and doctrinal preaching, the church would go on to be ordered in all other aspects of its life and practice. As a pastor, Calvin extolled the preaching of the Bible and stressed its primacy in the life of the church. The purpose of preaching the Word was to instruct life and effect obedience from the hearers. To Calvin, "the principal enemies of the Gospel" would then be those who would attend to hear the preaching of the Word, but would not submit themselves in obedience to practise the Word preached. Concerning Calvin's preaching, Beza writes,

> When Calvin came back, in 1541, from Strasburg to Geneva, in consequence of the Council's revocation of their own sentence of exile, he thus addressed his auditory: "If you desire to have me for your pastor, correct the disorder of your lives. If you have with sincerity recalled me from my exile, banish the crimes and debaucheries which prevail among you. I certainly cannot behold, without the most painful displeasure, within your walls, discipline trodden under foot, and crimes committed with impunity. I cannot possibly live in a place so grossly immoral. Vicious souls are too filthy to receive the purity of the Gospel, and the spiritual warship which I

---

[177]Thomas Smyth, *Calvin Defended: a Memoir of the Life, Character and Principles of John Calvin* (Philadelphia: Presbyterian Board of Publication, 1909), 28-29.

CHAPTER II: HISTORICAL EXAMPLES OF SOUND TEACHING MINISTRY

preach to you. A life stained with sin is too contrary to Jesus Christ to be tolerated. I consider the principal enemies of the Gospel to be, not the pontiff of Rome, nor heretics, nor seducers, nor tyrants, but such bad Christians; because the former exert their rage out of the church, while drunkenness, luxury, perjury, blasphemy, impurity, adultery, and other abominable vices overthrow my doctrine, and expose it defenceless to the rage of our enemies.[178]

This view instructed his personal efforts and labours in the pulpit. If the principal enemies are the wilful and disobedient hearers, then the assumption has to be that the preachers on their part were not only apt to teach, but also faithful in their preaching and teaching, and that their Gospel was unadulterated and biblical if it was expected to shape the lives of the hearers. Calvin thus approached his preaching with a systematic and orderly exposition of Scripture from one passage to the next that was rarely interrupted. Beza writes,

In every fortnight he preached one whole week; thrice every week he delivered lectures; on the Thursdays he presided in the meetings of the Presbytery; on the Fridays he collated and expounded the Holy Scriptures to what we term the congregation. He was engaged in illustrating many of the sacred books by commentaries of very uncommon learning; on some occasions he was employed in answering the adversaries of religion, and at other times wrote to correspondents from every part of Europe concerning subjects of great importance. Every attentive reader of his numerous productions will be astonished to find one weak little man able to accomplish so many and such great labours.[179]

Calvin evidently had a preaching program and pattern which afforded him the most of the opportunities that presented themselves in Geneva. Paul in writing to Timothy exhorted him to *"preach the word; be in season, out of season; reprove, rebuke, exhort with all long-suffering and doctrine"* (1 Tim 4:2). In this, Paul expressed the chief pastoral business. The minister is first and foremost a preacher. With preaching as his chief business, the minister is to do it with all earnestness and at all opportunities. In order to effectively accomplish this, it is necessary for the pastor to have a regular and orderly schedule, as is evidenced in Calvin's practice. The preacher's high calling to preach necessitates the need both to interpret the Word of God to the people, and to exemplify those truths he preached as well as impressing upon his hearers to enlist their obedience. This at times is not easy work as Beza notes from Calvin's life,

To return to Calvin's domestic disputes, —when his whole time was employed in proving that the gospel he preached was not a mere speculative doctrine, but consisted in a pious Christian life, he necessarily incurred the enmity of those, who had proclaimed war not only against all piety and virtue, but even against their very country.[180]

The task of impressing obedience upon hearers at times incurs the ire and enmity of many. But the pastor must perform his duties with tact and wisdom irrespective of the conditions. The oppositions Calvin faced were not a few, Beza notes of two significant occasions in which Calvin took a pastoral stand under difficult conditions, yet with wisdom and tact the mouths of gainsayers were stopped. One of the occasions involved the Carmelite monk from Paris named Jerome Bolsec, who when in Geneva attempted to

---

[178] Theodore Beza, *The Life of John Calvin*, translated by Francis Sibson (Philadeliphia: J. Wm S. Martien, 1836), 25-26.

[179] Beza, *The Life of John Calvin*, 27.

[180] Beza, *The Life of John Calvin*, 41.

bring confusion to the church by undermining the doctrine of predestination. Beza describes the incident in detail pointing out the attack on the doctrine and the response to the attack by Calvin. Beza writes,

> Being held in no repute among learned physicians, he aimed to establish his credit as a divine, by beginning to prate something privately concerning the falsehood and absurdity of predestination, and afterwards in the church. Calvin at first was content with refuting him, and used mild remonstrance, but afterwards, by private conversation, our reformer endeavoured to correct his errors.

But Bolsec refusing to heed the admonitions and corrections of Calvin and persisting in his errors took to the church's pulpit on an occasion in which he thought Calvin was absent though Calvin was only delayed. Calvin arrived late (and sat at the back of the church) just as Bolsec was preaching and "openly dared to support free will, and the foreknowledge of works, for the purpose of subverting the decree of eternal predestination."[181] Beza goes on to account of how Calvin proceeded to respond to the errors propagated immediately upon Bolsec's completing his address and, with so much force, put to silence the opponent of the faith. Beza writes,

> When the discourse of the monk was finished, Calvin suddenly appeared, and though he evidently spoke without premeditation, displayed on this occasion, as much as on any other, his great talents in controversy. Calvin indeed confuted his opponent with so much force, adduced so many passages from Scripture, so many quotations in particular from St. Augustin, and, finally, so many, and such weighty arguments, that all, except the monk himself, with his shameless front, blushed exceedingly for the daring assailant. He was seized by a magistrate in the congregation, who was empowered for that purpose, dismissed the assembly, and committed to prison as a seditious offender.[182]

The second incident was one which involved boldness and resolve in the exercise of church discipline to one Servetus Bertelier who due to his "abandoned impudence" had been put away from the Lord's Table. But Servertus, attempting to undermine the authority of the church, went to the Senate to have his sentence overturned, which thing he succeeded in achieving, though this was done inadvisedly. Beza points out that "Bertelier secretly obtained letters abrogating his sentence, and confirmed by the seal of the state, from the senate, which did not at that time direct its attention to the careful investigation of this subject."[183] Calvin seemed to be caught between a rock and a hard place, being forced either to undermine the authority of the senate by disregarding the letters Servetus had obtained, or to undermine the authority of the Presbytery and setting a precedence that might overturn its ability to enforce church discipline. Indeed, Beza points out that there were those who expected one of these two outcomes when he writes,

> Perrin, and his faction, expected that Calvin would either disobey the orders of the senate, and thus sink under popular tumult, or, if he obeyed them, all the authority of the presbytery, and with it all the powerful restraints upon the wicked, would, without difficulty, be afterwards broken for ever.[184]

---

[181] Ibid.

[182] Beza, *The Life of John Calvin*, 52.

[183] Ibid., 56.

[184] Ibid.

CHAPTER II: HISTORICAL EXAMPLES OF SOUND TEACHING MINISTRY

But it was not to be so, for Calvin approached and addressed the apparent dilemma with such resolve and wisdom that left no room for his opponents either to undermine him as a person or his ministry in Geneva. Beza writes,

> But Calvin, having received notice of this resolution only two days before the administration of the supper, as usual, in September, uttered, during the sermon, with uplifted hands, and in a solemn tone, many severe denunciations against the profaners of mysteries, whose sacred character he described and "for my own; part," said he, (after the example of Chrysostom,) "I will rather suffer myself to be slain, than allow this hand to stretch forth the sacred things of the Lord to those who are lawfully condemned as despisers of God." This voice, wonderful to state, produced such an effect, even upon his unbridled enemies, that Perrin immediately gave secret orders to Bertelier, not to present himself at the table, and the sacred mysteries were celebrated with a surprisingly profound silence, and under a solemn awe, as if the Deity himself had been visible among them. But, after dinner, in the course of his explaining that remarkable passage in the Acts of the Apostles, where Paul bids farewell to the church of Ephesus, Calvin protested that he was not the man who either himself knew anything about resisting magistrates, or taught others to do so, and exhorted, at considerable length, the people to persevere in the doctrine which they had heard.[185]

Calvin's pastoral oversight of the flock was with immediate zeal and scriptural arguments. Despite the oppositions and controversies faced, he never flinched in his pastoral responsibility to preach the Word even during the controversy with Servetus when he was placed in a position to choose between obeying God and obeying the senate. According to Calvin the church stands by obedience to the Word and, from his example, the doctrines of the Bible are practical and ought to be adhered to under all circumstances. The fervent preaching of the Word of God and the resolute obedience to the Word preached are what distinguish the church. The church needs pastors committed to Christ and his Word, resolute in their adherence to the injunctions and examples of Scripture and uncompromising in their stand for God and His Word even in the face of opposition and challenges.

The church today needs shepherds who would be committed to her, and to the Scriptures, and to her Lord! Shepherds who have mastered the Scriptures, yet continue to search them day and night and whose profit appears to all men. How the church needs men who would be bold and courageous, resolute and firm in their belief, their preaching and teaching, their defending of the scriptures against all forms of errors and attacks. The church needs pastors who are both scriptural and doctrinal like John Calvin.

In the Missions Field — William Carey in India

Introduction

In an age of great confusion, misunderstanding and neglect of the "Great Commission" and missionary endeavour, where humanistic and social methods and emphases have become the focus in the attempt to reach the unreached on the one hand, and on the other hand, where power evangelism with its counterfeit signs and wonders is touted to be the method by which the world will be saved, there is the need to reconsider the pastoral and practical theology of William Carey in his endeavour to revive the church of his time to the work of missions as well as his personal endeavours as a missionary. The prevailing thought generally regard missions as the work of some and not all believers.

---

[185] Beza, *The Life of John Calvin*, 56-57.

Some consider themselves unable and ill-equipped for the work of missions and therefore excuse themselves in one way or another from obeying the Great Commission and from missionary endeavours. There is a need to study the life and efforts of William Carey, commonly considered the "father of modern missions." Others, on the other hand, have claimed that there is a need for the restoration of the apostolic office with its power and authority for successful missionary endeavours, and some have even gone ahead to claim for themselves this power and authority and have then gone forth deceiving many, establishing a form of Christianity that is neither biblical nor Christlike. The correct and biblical understanding of the church's place and work in missions has been the challenge of many ages as can be seen in Carey's famous "Enquiry" where Carey writes,

> It seems as if many thought the commission was sufficiently put in execution by what the apostles and others have done; that we have enough to do to attend to the salvation of our own countrymen; and that, if God intends the salvation of the Heathen, he will some way or other bring them to the gospel, or the gospel to them. It is thus that multitudes sit at ease, and give themselves no concern about the far greater part of their fellow-sinners, who to this day, are lost in ignorance and idolatry. There seems also to be an opinion existing in the minds of some, that because the apostles were extraordinary officers, and have no proper successors, and because many things which were right for them to do, would be utterly unwarrantable for us, therefore it may not be immediately binding on us to execute the commission, though it was so upon them.[186]

The prevailing thought in this age especially in this writer's context is not much different from that which prevailed in Carey's time. Popular thought has compartmentalized the work of missions and evangelism, separating it from the work of the pastor and limiting it in some circles to "Western" or "affluent" countries as mission-sending and other countries as receiving. In Carey's age, the thought was that God would do it Himself without the church because of the perceived difficulties and obstacles; but in this age, the thought has been God would use others who are well off, more learned, without "us" to reach out because of perceived difficulties and shortcomings.

About the Man

WILLIAM CAREY'S life-work falls into two distinct periods: the English period when, almost singlehanded, he faced and overcame the prevailing indifference and hostility to missionary effort, thought out a well-developed scheme, published his amazing "Enquiry," and in the end almost compelled timid and hesitating men to form a Society for the evangelization of the world; and the Indian period, during which he put his ideas into practice, developing almost every form of missionary agency, translating the Scriptures into numerous languages, founding a splendid Christian college, and winning the confidence of one Governor-General after another. From being a simple shoemaker and village preacher, this man became so skilled a linguist that at the age of forty he was appointed Professor of Bengali, Sanskrit, and Marathi in the Governor-General's college in Calcutta a post he filled with distinction for thirty years.[187]

---

[186]William Carey, *An Enquiry into the Obligations of Christians to Use Means for the Conversion of the Heathens; in Which the Religious State of the Different Nations of the World, the Success of Former Undertakings, and the Practicability of Further Undertakings are Considered* (London: Button and Son, Paternostor-Row, 1818), 8-9.

[187]F. Deaville Walker, *William Carey, Missionary Pioneer and Statesman* (London: Student Christian Movement, 1926), 5.

CHAPTER II: HISTORICAL EXAMPLES OF SOUND TEACHING MINISTRY

The above are the opening words in the preface of Deaville's book on William Carey, the "Father of Modern Missions." The Indian period of William Carey's life highlights his missionary work and his efforts in ensuring that the Scriptures were translated into the language that could be understood by the natives of India and has had much attention over the years. The English period, on the other hand, highlights his pastoral endeavours and character and the preparations he made in changing the perspective and understanding of his generation towards the work of missions and the duty towards the Great Commission.

William Carey was born in a small village called Paulerspury, in Northampton, England on August 17, 1761, the firstborn child of Edmund and Elizabeth Carey, weavers by profession.[188] Growing up, William was introduced to the Scriptures and showed an aptness for learning as Deaville notes,

> Edmund and Elizabeth attended church with scrupulous regularity, and took their children with them. At home, they possessed a Bible, and they used it. Bibles were not numerous in the villages in those days, for the British and Foreign Bible Society had not been thought of, and Scriptures were expensive for humble folk. "From my infancy I was accustomed to read the Scriptures," wrote William Carey in after years. ... "When William was in his sixth year," she wrote, "he discovered a great aptness for learning. I have often heard my mother speak of one circumstance she had remarked with pleasure in him even before he was six years old. She has heard him in the night, when the family were asleep, casting accompts."[189]

Like Timothy who from a youth had known the Scriptures which were able to make him wise unto salvation, William Carey was instructed in the matters of religion at home and his hunger for knowledge, delight in books and determination in completing anything he ever began characterized William Carey's life as he grew up. This was observed by those who saw him as Deaville points out,

> His father adds this comment: "He was always attentive to learning when a boy, and was a very good arithmetician." Again we learn from Polly that: He was from childhood intent in the pursuit of knowledge. Whatever he began, he finished; difficulties never seemed to discourage his mind; and as he grew up this thirst for knowledge increased.[190]

---

[188] Ibid., 11.

In the book Memoirs of William Carey, by Eustace Carey, there is record of Carey's memory of his family in which is written, "Of my family I know nothing more than that my grandfather, who I have learned was born at Yelvertoft was master of the school which my father now superintends. He died while my father was very young, and left two sons; Peter who was a gardener, and Edmund, my father, who was put apprentice to a weaver, which business he followed until I was about six years of age when he was nominated master of the small free school in which his father died." [Eustace Carey, *Memoir of William Carey D.D. Late Missionary to Bengal; Professor of Oriental Language in the College of Fort William Calcutta* (London: Jackson and Walford, 1836), 6.]

[189] Deaville Walker, *William Carey*, 16.

Morrison in his Biography of Carey notes that, "He seems to have been a diligent scholar even from childhood. His mother often used to tell with fond pride how she had heard him, before he was six years, old, working at his sums in the night when the rest were asleep. Long after he had attained to fame his father wrote of him, in the formal language of an old schoolmaster: 'He was always attentive to learning when a boy, and was a very good arithmetician.'" [J. H. Morrison, *William Carey, Cobbler and Pioneer* (London: Hodder and Stoughton, n.d.), 10.]

[190] Walker, *William Carey*, 18.

Such discipline and determination would in his ministerial endeavour help him stick to the task at hand amidst difficulties both when pushing for the involvement of the church in the work of missions and also later in the midst of the difficulties faced in India. Apart from personal discipline, growing up as the school master's son brought with it some advantages for the young Carey. The piety at home as well as living in the schoolhouse, though laying the foundation for his encounter with Christ, did not bring him into salvation. In one of his letters, Carey points out,

> My education was that which is generally esteemed good in country villages, and my father being schoolmaster, I had many advantages which other children of my age had not. In the first fourteen years of my life I had many advantages of a religious nature, but was wholly unacquainted with the scheme of salvation by Christ. During this time I had many stirrings of mind occasioned by my being obliged to read books of a religious character; and having been accustomed from my infancy to read the Scriptures, I had a considerable acquaintance therewith, especially with the historical parts. I also have no doubt but the constant reading of the Psalms, Lessons &c in the parish church, which I was obliged to attend regularly, tended to furnish my mind with a general scripture knowledge.[191]

The lesson from Carey's childhood experiences seems to be that given in Proverbs 22:6, *"Train up a child in the way he should go and when he is old, he will not depart from it."* Though he was not acquainted with the doctrines of grace in his childhood days, the seed of the Word was already sown through the repeated and regular reading of the Scriptures and the lessons learnt from the church he attended. It was not until later in life that he came into salvation and that after some painful circumstances in his youth. Circumstances did not permit him to engage in agricultural pursuits, but rather led him to be apprenticed to a shoemaker at Hackleton, an occupation which he later embraced and of which he was never ashamed.

> Of real experimental religion I scarcely had anything till I was fourteen years of age; nor was the formal attendance upon outward ceremonies to which I was compelled, the matter of my choice. I chose to read books of science, history, voyages &c., more than any others. Novels and plays always disgusted me, and I avoided them as much as I did books of religion, and perhaps from the same motive. I was better pleased with romances; and this circumstance made me read Bunyan's Pilgrim's Progress with eagerness, though to no purpose. …
>
> A very painful disease paved the way for my being brought under the gospel sound. From about seven years of age, I was afflicted with a very painful cutaneous disease, which, though it scarce ever appeared in the form of eruption, yet made the sun's rays insupportable for me. This unfitted me for earning my living by labour in the field, or elsewhere out of doors. My parents were poor, unable to do much for me; but being much affected with my situation, they with great difficulty put me apprentice to a shoemaker in Hackleton.[192]

God's providential hand and leading would later lead Carey, albeit through an unfortunate turn of events in the form of a disease which unfitted him from earning a living outdoors, to the setting in which he would come into contact with the Gospel as an apprentice. It is during his time as an apprentice and the interactions with both his fellow apprentice and his master that he resolved to attend three churches in a day. These interactions would stir up an interest in religion which had been previously lacking, and being

---

[191] Carey, *Memoir of William Carey*, 7.

[192] Ibid, 7-8.

CHAPTER II: HISTORICAL EXAMPLES OF SOUND TEACHING MINISTRY

in the company of a "strict churchman" and the "son of a dissenter" would lead him to a consciousness of his ways and his need for Christ through the many disputes they engaged in. His account of this as recorded by Eustace states,

> My master was a strict churchman, and, what I thought, a very moral man. ... A fellow-servant was the son of a dissenter; and though not at that time under religious impressions, yet frequently engaged with me in disputes upon religious subjects, in which my master frequently joined. I was a churchman; had read Jeremy Taylor's Sermons, Spinker's Sick Man Visited, and other books; and had always looked upon dissenters with contempt. I had, moreover, a share of pride sufficient for a thousand times my knowledge: I therefore always scorned to have the worst in an argument, and the last word was assuredly mine. I also made up in positive assertion what was wanting in argument, and generally came off with triumph. But I was often convinced afterwards that, though I had the last word, my antagonist had the better of the argument, and on that account felt a growing uneasiness, and stings of conscience gradually increasing. The frequent comments of my master upon certain parts of my conduct, and other such causes, increased my uneasiness. I wanted something, but had no idea that nothing but an entire change of heart could do me good. ...
>
> As my uneasiness increased, my fellow-servant who was about this time brought under serious concern for his soul became more importunate with me. I was furnished by him now and then with a religious book, and my opinions insensibly underwent a change, so that I relished evangelical sentiments more and more, and my inward uneasiness increased.
>
> Under these circumstances I resolved to attend regularly three churches in the day, and go to a prayer-meeting at the dissenting place of worship in the evening, not doubting but this would produce ease of mind and make me acceptable to God.[193]

William Carey came to salvation, and he left the Church of England on February 10th, 1779 after which began proper the "English Period" of his life's work. As a cobbler, he was a skilful and honest workman[194] and as a student, he was diligent and relentless[195] such that neither his occupation as a "journeyman" nor the financial difficulties he had prevented him from learning. He could read the Bible in Latin, Greek, Hebrew, Dutch, French and English.[196] Carey was baptized in October 1783, about three years after he preached his first sermon (1780) and about one year after he joined the Baptist church at

---

[193] Ibid, 9-10.

[194] Morrison records Carey's testimony of himself as a worker that, "I was accounted a very good workman, and recollect Mr. Old keeping a pair of shoes which I had made in his shop as a model of good workmanship.'" [Morrison, *William Carey*, 13.]

[195] "Whatever may have been his ability at the cobbler's bench, Carey was essentially a student, and he pursued the path of learning with extraordinary doggedness. If genius be, as has been said, f an infinite capacity for taking pains,' then Carey had genius in the highest degree. His sister says 'Whatever he began he finished, difficulties never seemed to discourage his mind, and, as he grew up, his thirst for knowledge still increased.' 'I can plod,' was his own verdict upon his life's work. 'I can persevere in any definite pursuit. To this I owe everything.' In this spirit the poor cobbler lad snatched eagerly at every morsel of knowledge that came within his reach." [Ibid., 14.]

[196] "He had an extraordinary aptitude for languages. Latin he had made acquaintance with at the age of twelve, when he learnt his first grammar by heart. Hebrew he picked up by and by, with the aid of some neighbouring ministers. He puzzled over a Dutch book which he had found in an old woman's cottage till he made out the meaning of it, so that when some years afterwards his friend Mr. Ryland offered him a volume of Dutch sermons on condition that he could translate them, he took the book and returned in a short time with a translation of one of the sermons. In Somewhat similar fashion he acquired some knowledge of French." [Morrison, *William Carey*, 15.]

Olney, in which organization he afterwards would give his life to full-time ministry, and in which, after many hurdles and difficulties, it would lead to the formation of a "Society for the Evangelization of the World." The discipline and determination he had showed as a child, he showed in his new life and faith. He attended to the preaching he heard, and from them he began to form views that would transform the church and its perspective and approach to missions and world evangelization. In his Serampore letters, William Carey writes,

> The preaching of the Rev. Thomas Scott and other divines of the neighborhood led him to serious thoughts, and the perusal of a work by the Rev. Robert Hall, senior, convinced him that it was his duty to proclaim to others the Christ he had found for himself. Consequently, in the year 1780, when he was only nineteen, he made his appearance in one of the village pulpits, and preached his first sermon.[197]

The Pastoral Practice of William Carey

It is the English period in the life of William Carey that gives insight into the pastoral character and practice of William Carey. As a preacher, Carey was a man of zeal and commitment to his Lord. It is recorded of him that,

> At this time he was increasingly thoughtful, and very jealous for the Lord of Hosts. Like Gideon, he seemed for throwing down all the altars of Baal in one night. When he came home we used to wonder at the change. We knew that before he as rather inclined to persecute the faith he now seemed to wish to propagate. At first, perhaps, his zeal exceeded the bounds of prudence; but he felt the importance of things we were strangers to, and his natural disposition was to pursue earnestly what he undertook; so that it was not much to be wondered at, though we wondered at the change.[198]

His missionary zeal did not begin by reaching out to the heathen in distant lands, but rather in reaching out to kith and kin at home. At times his zeal exceeded the bounds of prudence, but Carey was always earnest in what was important to him. The zeal and earnestness was seen in his commitment to the preaching ministry, Carey gladly walked for twelve miles every Sunday to preach in a village about six miles away, a routine which he carried out for a period of three-and-a-half years.[199] In 1786, Carey moved with his family to Moulton where he was commissioned to pastor a Baptist church as well as to conduct a day school, for which he would receive "ten pounds a year from his people, and five guineas from a fund in London."[200] He continued to pastor and labour at Moulton though the income was not enough to support him and his family,[201] so he re-

---

[197] *Serampore Letters, being the unpublished correspondence of William Carey and others with John Williams*, ed. Leighton and Mornay Williams (London: G. P. Putnam's Sons, 1892), 5-6.

[198] Carey, *Memoir of William Carey*, 28.

[199] "Carey now began to preach with some acceptance, and by and by was invited to conduct a little meeting at Earls Barton, a village about six miles from Hackleton. This he continued to do for three and a half years, cheerfully trudging the twelve miles every Sunday. ... Soon after he began to go to Earls Barton, Carey, on the invitation of a few friends, came to preach in his native village. None of his own family went to hear him, but next morning a neighbour woman came in to congratulate his mother on having such a son. 'What!' exclaimed his mother, 'do you think he will be a preacher? 'Yes,' was the reply, 'and a great one too, I think, if spared.' From that time forward Carey conducted a monthly meeting at Paulers Pury in addition to preaching at Earls Barton." [Morrison, *William Carey*, 20-22.]

[200] Morrison, *William Carey*, 29-30.

[201] In the interval he had become a minister over a Baptist church, though his maintenance for a time was so inadequate, that he still needed to draw his support, in part, from manual toil. [Andrew Thomson, *Great Missionaries, a series of biographies* (London: T. Nelson and Sons, Paternoster Row, 1862), 219.]

turned to making and mending shoes to support the work and his family. This he did for about four years. During this period, the work of the ministry did not suffer due to the shoe mending work that he did, and unlike many who would pay more attention to their income-generating endeavours, Carey's commitment and zeal was still to the work of the ministry to the extent that the testimony given of him was that his shoemaking work suffered as a result of his ministerial duties. Morrison records an incident that reflects Carey's perspective of his life's work. He notes,

> Doubtless his zeal as a preacher must have told sadly against his work as a cobbler. A friend having expostulated with him for neglecting his business, 'Neglecting my business!' answered Carey. 'My business, sir, is to extend the kingdom of Christ. I only make and mend shoes to help pay expenses.' Which was perhaps hardly an adequate answer, coming from the father of a young family.[202]

Morrison goes on to relate how help for Carey and support for his ministry came from a Mr Thomas Gotch (who being a deacon in Fuller's church) volunteered to support William Carey so that he would give up shoemaking and focus on the pulpit ministry. Morrison writes,

> On making Carey's acquaintance, and hearing his gifts extolled by Fuller, Mr. Gotch said one day, 'Let me see, Mr. Carey: how much do you earn a week by your shoemaking?' 'About nine or ten shillings, sir,' replied Carey. 'Well, now,' said Mr. Gotch with a twinkle, 'I don't mean you to spoil any more of my leather. Get on as fast as you can with your Latin, Hebrew, and Greek, and I'll allow you from my private purse ten shillings a week.' Relieved by this generosity, Carey pursued his studies with renewed ardour.[203]

Carey gladly and promptly obliged and gave himself to the study and mastery of the original languages and Latin which in turn ensured that his profiting appeared unto all men as he gave himself to reading to exhortation and to the study of God's Word. On his use of the original languages, Morrison writes,

> In his preparation for the pulpit he was most conscientious and thorough, reading the selected passage in the original Greek or Hebrew, as well as in a Latin translation. His reputation as a preacher steadily grew, though some of the sterner Calvinists in the churches suspected him of heresy because he boldly proclaimed the freedom and universality of the Gospel.[204]

It was during these times, while reading Captain Cook's book on his travels, that reaching the unreached peoples began to burden him, and praying the Lord of the harvest to raise labourers into the great untouched portions of the world.[205] Carey began to share and preach about missions, boldly proclaiming a free and universal gospel for all men, which though not well-received, was not utterly rejected, and eventually gave birth

---

[202] Morrison, *William Carey*, 31-32

[203] Ibid, 32.

[204] Ibid, 33.

[205] Besides, a book he was reading was kindling his heart—the Voyages of Captain Cook., England's most humane and illustrious captain, who had thrice voyaged to the uttermost ends of the earth, and had unveiled countless coasts and isles and peoples, very romantic and intriguing, but wrapped in gross mental and spiritual darkness in their habitations of cruelty. Their ignorance and helplessness cried out to man and to God. Only the gospel of Jesus he was persuaded could deliver them from their cannibal debasements. Only His grace could develop their arrested intellectual and spiritual powers. They had shed the blood of England's noblest captain for lack of knowing the story of Christ's own shed blood. He felt that he must consecrate his life to their service, to go to them himself, if anywise possible, and to enlist on their behalf the care and prayers of a multitude of others. [S. Pearce Carey, *William Carey* (London: The Carey Press, 1942), 14.]

to a revival of religion movement. Carey pursued his thoughts not only in his preaching ministry, but also with his fellow ministers, repeatedly bringing up the matter at meetings irrespective of their response, and just as a little leaven when hid in dough works to leaven the whole lump, Carey's insistence began to work in the hearts of some men as pointed out by Andrew Thomson who writes,

> The thought which he had ventured to throw out in that meeting of ministers, fell into other hearts that received it with more sympathy than the venerable Mr. Ryland, and silently wrought in them like the leaven of the kingdom of heaven. Four years afterwards, a prayer-meeting of ministers was begun at Nottingham, for the revival of religion, and for the extending of the Redeemer s kingdom, at which were present, along with Carey, three men, who were great even among the good Robert Hall of Arnsby, Samuel Pearce of Birmingham, and Andrew Fuller of Ketiering. It was one of those quiet movements, which, bringing down the omnipotence of God to help the weakness of man, ultimately shape the destinies of nations. The growing missionary sentiment, which that prayer-meeting fostered and strengthened, took practical form at an ordination which occurred at Nottingham in June 1792.[206]

The missionary ideas of William Carey were clear in his convictions, but were challenged a lot by his peers. This did not deter Carey, who from his youth had cultivated a character of not giving up or leaving incomplete what he had started even in the face of difficulties. Casey records:

> At a meeting of ministers held at Northampton in 1786, Mr. Ryland, sen., having invited some of the younger men to propose a topic for discussion, Carey suggested, 'Whether the command given to the Apostles, to teach all nations, was not obligatory on all succeeding ministers to the end of the world, seeing that the accompanying promise was of equal extent.' This was too much for the venerable chairman, who broke out upon him, 'You are a miserable enthusiast for asking such a question. Certainly nothing can be done before another Pentecost, when an effusion of miraculous gifts, including the gift of tongues, will give effect to the commission of Christ as at first.' The rest sat silent, feeling, as Fuller says, 'If the Lord should open the windows of heaven, might this thing be.'[207]

Pearce Carey also records of the opposition Carey faced with regard to his passion, persistence and insistence on world evangelization. Pearce points out the withdrawal of some and the ridicule of others and their fronting the issue of language barrier as a great impediment. He writes,

> Few had the ears to hearken to his messages, and many withdrew themselves from his preaching, accounting him unsound. He would open his heart sometimes to his brother-ministers, and far into the night; but his thoughts were not their thoughts. Once a High-Calvinist veteran teased and snubbed him as "a miserable enthusiast," asking him, in the presence of his brother-ministers, whether he supposed he could ever preach in Arabic or Persian, in Hindustani or Bengali—little imagining that in the course of the years he was to acquire three of these very tongues, and to preach frequently in two of them, and with the last to become as familiar and happy as with the language of his birth.[208]

---

[206] Thomson, *Great Missionaries,* 219-220.

[207] Morrison, *William Carey,* 39.

[208] Carey, *William Carey,* 18-19.

CHAPTER II: HISTORICAL EXAMPLES OF SOUND TEACHING MINISTRY

When Carey could not respond to their objections in debate, he responded to them in writing. Carey put pen to paper and wrote down his views in what became his famous pamphlet: "An Enquiry into Obligations of Christians to use means for the Conversion of the Heathens ..." And it did not stop at that, for Carey was determined to have the other ministers as it were "hold the ropes as he went down into the pits"[209] Deaville writes,

> With that clear judgment that was always so conspicuous a trait, Carey saw that he must carry his ministerial brethren with him if he was to accomplish the purpose so dear to his heart. It was no light task to change their ultra-Calvinistic theories into missionary convictions, but he left no stone unturned, no argument unused to accomplish it. At several ministers' meetings between 1787 and 1790, this was his chief topic of conversation. Some of the older men thought it was a wild and impracticable scheme that he had got in his mind, and they gave him no encouragement. Undaunted, Carey tackled his fellow-ministers, one by one, till he had made some impression upon a few of them. At first he was alone. The leaders of the Church were against him, and he had no one to encourage him or with whom he could take counsel. With very little education, without status or influence, he had, humanly speaking, everything against him. An ordinary man would have yielded to the inevitable; a "miserable enthusiast" would have degenerated into an ill-tempered fanatic. Carey was neither, and he quietly applied himself to his task, confident in this that GOD HAD CALLED HIM.[210]

So in meeting after meeting Carey pressed on and stuck to his convictions about missions and the conversion of the heathens applying himself to win his brethren as well as prepare himself with conviction that God had called him to the missions field.[211] In 1792, at a ministerial gathering in Nottingham, Carey preached from Isaiah 54:2-3, in which he laid down his two general arguments, which have since become very well-known: "Expect great things from God: attempt great things for God." Many impressions have been made of this event. Percy Jones writes,

> THE ministers' meeting of 1892 came round. This time it was at Nottingham, and Carey the preacher. The "Inquiry" had been printed, and was on sale at the door.

---

[209] Andrew Thomson records concerning a private conversation Carey had that, "In private conference with his brethren, Carey formally laid himself on the missionary altar, saying to Pearce and Fuller, in those immortal words, "I will go down into the pit, if you will hold the ropes;" and so was formed the Baptist Missionary Society." [Thomson, *Great Missionaries*, 220-221.]

[210] Walker, *William Carey*, 64-65.

[211] Thus, it came about that meeting one day with Mr. Thomas Potts at Birmingham, the following conversation took place: "Mr Potts. "Pray, friend Carey, what is it you have got into your head about Missions? I understand you introduce the subject on all occasions." Carey. "Why, I think, Sir, it is highly important that something should be done for the heathen." Mr Potts. "But how can it be done, and who will do it?" Carey. "Why, if you ask who, I have made up my mind, if a few friends can be found who will send me out, and support me for twelve months after my arrival, I will engage to go wherever Providence shall open a door." Mr Potts. "But where would you go? Have you thought of that, friend Carey?" Carey. "Yes, I certainly have. Were I to follow my inclination, and had the means at command, the islands of the South Seas would be the scene of my labours, and I would commence at Otaheite. If any society will send me out, and land me there, allow me the means of subsistence for one year, I am ready and willing to go." Mr Potts. "Why, friend Carey, the thought is new, and the religious public are not prepared for such undertakings." Carey. "No I am aware of that; but I have written a piece on the state of the heathen world, which, if it were published, might probably awaken an interest on the subject." Mr Potts. "Why don't you publish it?" Carey. "For the best of all reasons. I have not the means." Mr Potts. " We will have it published by all means. I had rather bear the expense of printing it myself, than the public should be deprived of the opportunity of considering so important a subject." [Walker, *William Carey*, 66]

The two divisions of the sermon were the famous words that have ever since been the motto of the Baptist Missionary Society: "Expect great things from God, Attempt great things for God." If all the people had wept aloud it would not have been surprising, so clearly did Carey prove the great wrong Christians were doing in keeping the Good News to themselves and not preaching to the heathen. But they did not weep. They did not even wait. At the end they got up to go home as usual, just as if this sermon were no different from any other sermon. When Carey saw the people streaming out of the door, he hastened down from the pulpit, and seizing Andrew Fuller's hand, said: "Are we not going to do anything? Oh, Fuller, call them back! We dare not separate without doing something." Even now the ministers were afraid to venture, but Carey's pleading won over Fuller, so they decided that a plan should be prepared for the next meeting at Kettering four months later. Thus, it came to pass that at Kettering on October 2, 1792, twelve ministers and a student from Bristol College met in Widow Wallis's back parlour to consider this plan.[212]

Thus, the Baptist Missionary Society was born. The burden that had been placed upon the heart of one man had to be discharged, and by the importunity of Carey, the fire was beginning to catch. Carey would refer to himself as one who could plod, and that is what he had done in the grounds hardened by complacency and presumed difficulties. As regarding the Nottingham meeting, Deaville adds the following commentary:

> It is clear that at the Nottingham meeting Carey had a hard fight, and only secured the resolution by his importunate pleadings. By his dauntless perseverance and his deep convictions as to the course he proposed, he won where a less resolute man would inevitably have failed. And what did the resolution amount to? Probably it was little more than postponement a device to escape coming to a decision that day. Unable, on the one hand, to harden their hearts against Carey's arguments and pleadings, yet fearful of taking the action he proposed, they played for delay by the familiar expedient of referring the matter to their next meeting.[213]

Though fear and uncertainty prompted the whole group to delay, perhaps thinking that with time the matter would naturally die off, a smaller group took up the matter with urgency. Deaville goes on to describe how in "the evening a small group of twelve ministers, a student, and a layman met in the spacious dwelling of Widow Wallis a fine old Georgian house so noted for hospitality to preachers that it was commonly known among them as 'the Gospel Inn,'"[214] and how they deliberated on Carey's vision. As the fire was catching, the fears and doubts began to reduce, though they were still there. In the discussions, most of them seemed to suggest that the time was not right, but the resolute Carey won them over and carried the day. Deaville writes:

> But when hesitation and fear were about to triumph Carey made one more appeal. Pulling from his pocket a little volume entitled, Periodical Account of Moravian Missions, he cried, "If you had only read this and knew how these men overcame all obstacles for Christ's sake, you would go forward in faith!" There are moments when the faith of one man is contagious, and the strength of one becomes the strength of many. It was so in that little back parlour.[215]

---

[212]Percy H. Jones, *William Carey: The Pioneer of Missions to India* (London: Pickering & Inglis, n.d.), 56-57.

[213]Walker, *William Carey*, 95.

[214]Walker, *William Carey*, 95.

[215]Ibid.

CHAPTER II: HISTORICAL EXAMPLES OF SOUND TEACHING MINISTRY

As a result of his importunate pleadings in Nottingham, and a contagious faith, the meeting of October 1792, at a widow's home where twelve ministers were present, brought into realization the Baptist Missionary Society. From then on, funds were raised, Carey offered himself as the first missionary and providence would lead to the choosing of India.

Biblical Principles for Contemporary Application from William Carey's Ministry

If the principles for contemporary application that can be drawn from Richard Baxter's life be that of religion in the home and the use of catechisms, and from John Calvin's life be that of a doctrinal and didactic pulpit ministry, then the principle that can be taken from William Carey's life has to be that of reading, teaching and understanding of Scripture in the vernacular. William Carey's pastoral ministry manifests a clear emphasis placed on Scripture. His commitment in his pastoral and missionary endeavours was clearly that the Word of God be in the hands and hearts of the people he ministered to. During the English period, his personal labours and endeavour to understand the Scriptures and study the original languages as well as his efforts to convince his fellow ministers by Scripture of the need for missions and world evangelization exemplify this. During the Indian period, after a period of hardships and challenges, Carey came to the realization of the need for translation and education and immediately gave himself to the task of translating and printing at Serampore. This spirit was seen in the work he accomplished. Andrew Fraser writes,

> Self-denial was not the only mark of Carey's life. Thorough system enabled him to accomplish much work. Up at 5:45, reading a chapter in the Hebrew Bible, "private addresses to God," family prayers with the Bengali servants, reading Persian till tea, *translating Scriptures in Hindustani from Sanskrit*, teaching at the college from ten till two, correcting proof sheets of Bengali *translating of Jeremiah, translating Matthew into Sanskrit*, spending one hour with a pundit on Telinga, at seven collecting thoughts for a sermon, preaching at 7:30 to forty persons, *translating Bengali till eleven*, writing a letter home, reading a chapter from the Greek New Testament and commending himself to God as he lay down to sleep, is a sample of one day's work. **It would appear that Carey's chief work of life was to make translation of the Scriptures** [emphasis added] and it was his joy before the close of life to see "more than 213,000 volumes of the Divine Word, in forty different languages, issue from the Serampore press." But this was but a part of his life work.[216]

Such was the industry to which Carey routinely gave himself in Serampore. He had settled at Serampore after moving through a few places after he landed in Calcutta. Financial troubles moved him from Calcutta to Bandel, then back to Calcutta and then up the river to Malda. All this time, Carey went through pains and struggles which he bore patiently. At Malda, Carey took charge of the indigo factory at Mudnabati, an appointment of which he informed Fuller and the Mission Society. Morrison commenting says, "On receiving this appointment, Carey at once wrote home to Fuller, the society's secretary, intimating that he would no longer require financial support, but that he would still consider himself, in every other respect, the agent of the society."[217] Carey's commitment and zeal as well as his clear understanding of his call and purpose in respect to the ministry was not clouded by the prospect of taking charge of the indigo factory. So, Car-

---

[216] Andrew Fraser, *William Carey: The Missionary Spirit* (London: The Baptist Missionary Society, n.d), 30.

[217] Morrison, *William Carey*, 72.

ey was deeply pained when the Society's reply came back with a warning to him to be careful lest "the spirit of the missionary be swallowed up in the spirit of the merchant."[218] Carey's decision had not been out of the desire for money or personal gain and thus he responded to Fuller vindicating his decision and actions. He wrote,

> I should be very averse. It is a constant maxim with me that, if my conduct will not vindicate itself, it is not worth vindicating. ... I only say that, after my family's obtaining a bare allowance, my whole income (and some months much more) goes for the purposes of the Gospel. ... I am indeed poor and shall always be so till the bible is published in Bengali and Hindustani, and the people want no further instruction.[219]

And his conduct did vindicate itself as, true to his word, Carey pursued the translation of the Scriptures and the instruction of the people. His sustained commitment to the desire to ensure that every person could read the Bible in his own language drove him to great labours and efforts in the task set before him. And even after becoming a professor, Carey continued to sacrificially support the work of missions as Royer notes,

> About 1801 he was appointed professor of Sanskrit, Bengali and Marathi in Williams College, Calcutta, which position he held for thirty years. At first, he received £600 per year. In 1807 Brown University, U.S.A., conferred the degree of D.D. on him. His salary was increased to £1,200 per year, yet according to the arrangement with the missionaries, he lived on £40 and had £20 extra to enable him to appear in "decent apparel" at the college and government house, and the remaining £1,140 was turned into the mission treasury. He wrote articles on the natural history and botany of India for the Asiatic Society; he published the entire Bible in the Bengali in five volumes in 1809.[220]

Such sacrifice, commitment and drive are severely lacking yet direly needed today. The work of Christ received not only his finances, but also his personal efforts. Carey applied himself to preach the Gospel and this he did drawing his first congregation from the men that were under his charge at the factory. Through them, he acquired the language and even through the severest of adversity brought about by the illness of his wife and the death of his son, Carey plodded on finding consolation in God's presence and in His Word amidst these severe trials and never lost sight of his mission or hope in his God. Andrew Fraser writes of Carey's efforts and accomplishments,

> Carey's third method was the translation of the Scriptures. To that he gave himself from the very first. One of the things which most impressed him was the want of that Book which 'he had learned to regard as his most precious possession and his educational policy, as well as his unwearying efforts at translation of the Scriptures, was directed to enabling the people to study the revelation of God in their own tongue. I do not find myself free in this brief lecture to enter into details about this part of Carey's work; but I will give you one figure which will convey to you some idea of his wonderful labours in connection with translation. There were no less than thirty-four translations of the Bible, or parts of the Bible, made and edited at Serampore by Dr. Carey between 1801 and 1822; and there were six that were edited and printed only by Carey.[221]

---

[218]Morrison, *William Carey*, 73.

[219]Morrison, *William Carey*, 74.

[220]Galen B. Royer, *Christian Heroism in Heathen Lands*, (Elgin Illinois: Brethren Publishing House, 1914), 18.

[221]Fraser, *William Carey,* 33-34.

Such was the emphasis that he placed upon Scripture in the accomplishing of his task that it is said of Carey that "he carried the heathen world upon his heart"[222] and thus he would endeavour like Paul to commend them *"to God, and to the word of his grace"* (Acts 20:32) and therefore laboured to ensure that they had the Scriptures available in their own language. In Carey's missionary work, Fraser notes two governing principles. He says, "The one was that he should regard himself as the equal and companion of those to whom he preached the Gospel."[223] This principle led him not only to work towards the salvation of their souls, but also towards the betterment of their society. This he pursued mainly through the efforts for the abolition of the practice of Sattee. The second principle that Fraser draws from Carey was "the Pauline one, that he should not be burdensome to those to whom he was sent or even to the Church itself."[224] This is a principle that, as Fraser observes, should be embraced not by all missionaries only, but by all Christians alike. This second principle is one that permeated his work in the missions field and governed all of his human actions. Fraser further notes,

> To a man impelled by this desire there is nothing for it but to preach. "Though he preach the Gospel he has nothing to glory of; for necessity is laid upon him ; yea woe is unto him if he preach not the gospel." "Freely ye have received freely give" is not only a command. It is a principle of human action. His is not an estimable character who can freely receive without having the desire to give freely. It is natural response of a grateful heart to God to turn to the help of man ; for if we do not love men whom we have seen, how can we love God whom we have not seen?[225]

From the English period of his life, one great principle that can be drawn from the pastoral efforts of William Carey can be found in his endeavours to bring the fire of missions into the hearts of his fellow ministers, which endeavour when he was able to accomplish opened to him the great door to India. Laying hold of the promises of Christ and seeking to be obedient to the Great Commission, Carey based his claims on Scripture and constantly appealed to it. Andrew Fraser puts it thus:

> There is another great revelation that lies at the root of mission work it is the revelation of the: claim of Christ and of His commission as founded on that claim. The purpose of God concerning His Son is stated to be that He should be the "First born among many brethren." That purpose runs through the whole teaching of the Holy Scriptures. The Lord Jesus came to fulfil that purpose. The ultimate fulfilment of it was "the joy which was set before Him," for which "He endured the Cross and despised the shame."[226]

It is in the Great Commission that Carey saw not opportunity to send forth the Gospel both at home and abroad, but rather the opportunity to be obedient to Christ and be about the "Father's business." Just as the Great commission had influenced many before him, with its privileges and responsibilities, it influenced him as well. In his efforts, Carey had not in his mind that he would be the subject of future studies as the "Father of Modern Missions" or founder of a missionary society that would send many missionaries from England; or that he would be held in high regard as "Friend of India" or as a professor of languages in an oriental college. The thought that bore down on his mind was that of fulfilling the purposes of God concerning His Son! It is this desire that drove him

---

[222] Morrison, *William Carey*, 80.

[223] Fraser, *William Carey*, 34.

[224] Ibid., Fraser, *William Carey*, 35.

[225] Fraser, *William Carey*, 43-44.

[226] Ibid., 44.

to plead and plod and write and not rest until the work of missions was planted in the hearts of the ministers in England, and the burden was discharged with others catching the fire and vision and joining him in forming the Society. And even after that was accomplished, when the Society had been formed, he gave himself to go "down into the mines as the others held the ropes."

Such zeal and ardour, such commitment and sacrifice holding on to the claims and purposes of Christ and through them pursuing the cause of Christ. Indeed, he did expect great things and attempted great things. Fraser aptly sums it up thus:

> This is the commission, with its high privilege and grave responsibility, which influenced the heart of Paul, which influenced the heart of Carey, and which has influenced the hearts of all devoted missionaries in the history of the Church. The missionary spirit does not concern itself only with foreign missions or with home missions. It concerns itself with the claims of Christ, and takes the same broad view of these claims as the Lord Himself has taken. There are no departments in loyalty, no reservations in love. A man cannot say, "I believe in home missions, but do not believe in foreign missions," or "I will support foreign missions and let home missions alone." He will say, "I believe in the claims of Christ, and I desire to see Him reigning at home and abroad. I desire to see His world-wide purpose fulfilled." Loyalty to Christ, and the love for man which that loyalty produces, are not narrow nor circumscribed in their scope.[227]

In PASTORAL Training and Mentoring — John Brown of Haddington, Scotland

Introduction

The story of the Rev John Brown of Haddington is one of a boy who became a sheep herder after he was orphaned, but taught himself the original languages while herding sheep. He went on to become not only a minister of the Gospel at Haddington, but also a scholar, writer and a professor himself having not attended any theological college. The foreword of Robert Mackenzie's biography of Brown reads thus:

> "The shepherd boy from the braes of Abernethy, who had learned his Latin and his Greek while herding his sheep, surprising, by his ability to read St. John, the St. Andrews professor into the gift of a New Testament, becoming Burgher minister of Haddington, a patient pastor, passing rich on forty pounds a year,' a straight and strenuous preacher for God, a solid scholar amassing in an age of superficial knowledge stores of rare learning, a diligent professor, a quaint humorist, a tender father, potent in life and still more potent in the wealth of a name that has too richly blessed posterity ever to be willingly let die." A. M. FAIRBAIRN, D.D., LL.D.[228]

Brown became one of the most distinguished pastors of his time in Scotland. His diligent study of the Word is unmistakable and his wealth of knowledge and study though not recognized by many in his time has been a source of delight and enrichment of many in years to follow. In the preface to the same volume, Mackenzie writes concerning the labours of Brown,

> His early struggles read like a romance. Happily his unique gifts were quickly recognised in the new communion. While no University ranked him among its students, or recognised his services to religious literature, except a rising one in the new Republic across the seas toward the end of his days, he trod the path of a

---

[227] Fraser, *William Carey,* 46-47.

[228] Robert Mackenzie, *John Brown of Haddington* (London: Hodder and Stoughton, 1918), i.

scholar, and in the later years placed the fruits of his learning before the world. While Pastor and Professor, he single-handed produced a Dictionary of the Bible that held its own for a hundred years; and a Commentary of the Scriptures, which he happily entitled *A Self-interpreting Bible*, on which Charles Simeon nourished his soul with great delight, and which is still a living book in America.[229]

In a country where the number of men and women entering the ministry without proper instruction and in which churches and ministries increasingly have no spiritual supervision and mentoring, it is from this man that is the example for a sound teaching and mentoring program for the church today is drawn. The vital need to consider and learn from the life of Brown can be seen in the impact or rather the lack of it that the church has in this age. This can be measured by a look at the contemporary "Gospel Music Industry" with its music and lyrics which distort Bible History and Scripture's message, the increase of "Apostles and Prophets" who lack even a basic knowledge of what the Bible says and who instead of preaching the Word, force on people "new revelation" given to them directly from God, some of which contradict even the plain reading of Scripture.

Brown, though lacking in opportunity for formal university education, was an ardent student of the Scripture acquiring knowledge even of the original languages and when established as a minister of the Gospel provided the opportunity he lacked to others by instructing and teaching as well as writing materials that would help pastors to become able ministers of the Word, rightly dividing the Word of Truth and able to instruct and convince and give a reason in defence of the faith and hope in Christ. It is with this in mind that the life and ministry of Brown, a self-taught theologian, well versed in the Holy Scriptures as well as a prominent teacher of theology and a well published author who produced books that are held in high regard like his Bible dictionary and his study Bible (*The Self-Interpreter's Bible*), is chosen to glean examples, principles and lessons for the church today concerning the example of a sound pastoral training and mentoring program in pastoral ministry.

About the Man

Brown was born of poor Christian[230] parents in 1722 in the village of Carpow. His father was a basket weaver.[231] John was orphaned by the age of 11, but providence would have a different direction for his life other than poverty and ignorance. In the Centenary memorial of Brown, it is recorded thus:

He was born in 1722 in the village of Carpow, in Perthshire, of poor parents, his father being a weaver. The father died when the boy was about the eleventh year of

---

[229] Mackenzie, *John Brown of Haddington*, viii.

[230] In his memoirs, John Brown writes of the Providence of being born in a Christian home and of the Parental instruction in the Christian faith thus "The more I consider the dealings between God and my soul, I am the more amazed at his marvellous kindness to me, and at my ingratitude and rebellion against him. I reflect on it as a great mercy, that I was born in a family which took care of my Christian instruction, and in which I had the privilege of God's worship both morning and evening. This was the case in few families in that corner; and it was the more remarkable, considering that my father had not got any regular instruction in reading." [*Life and Remains of the Rev. John Brown, the late minister of the gospel at Haddington* (Aberdeen: John and Robert King, 1845), 9.]

[231] Robert Mackenzie writes, "In the days of Brown's father, small patches of ground were allotted to the workers on the farms, on which they grew flax, that was spun by the wives and daughters of their families. In the winter season, his father was one of the weavers of the place; in the summer he followed the salmon fishing, that is to-day and has always been, a profitable calling in the neighbourhood." [Mackenzie, *John Brown of Haddington,* 4.]

his age, and his mother dying soon after, he was left a poor orphan, and as he himself says, had nothing to depend upon but the Providence of God. The poverty of his parents did not permit them to continue him long at school, and the ordinary branches of reading, writing, and arithmetic, were all that they could afford to give him. One month at school, he says, and without his parents' allowance, he bestowed upon Latin. This appears to have been the whole literary education he received, so far as schools and universities were concerned.[232]

After being orphaned, Brown became a shepherd and it is during his time as a shepherd that is recorded a remarkable turn of events by providence that can only be attributed to the hand of God put him on the path to become one of the most prominent theologians of his time and in Scottish history. After the death of his parents, John was engaged as a shepherd boy and providence led him to a place near Abernethy where, beginning from the little literary education that he had received and building upon it, he went on to acquire great learning in the fields. In the "Centenary Memorial of Rev. John Brown," it is recorded,

> After his parents' death he was engaged as a shepherd lad, near Abernethy, and the story is told that after he had made some acquaintance with the Greek language, he was anxious to obtain a copy of the Greek New Testament, and having secured a substitute to take charge of his sheep, he walked all the way to St. Andrews to purchase the coveted volume. On entering the bookseller's shop, and asking for a Greek Testament, a gentleman present, one of the professors in St. Andrews University, surprised at such an unusual demand from a barefooted and unlettered-looking boy, said — 'My boy if you will read to me a verse of that book you seek, I will pay for it.' The book was produced, a passage was selected, and read with ease and intelligence, and it was honestly and triumphantly won.[233]

Such is the picture painted of the personal diligence and study of Brown. The spiritual care and nourishment he had received in his formative years at home under the care of his parents, and the foundations laid through their instruction in the ways of God coupled together with his thirst and hunger for the Word of God which would providentially be the key which turned around his world and pointed his future from a rough one, to one of service and ministry. Despite his life's circumstances, he directed his attention to the study of the Word of God. Brown himself in his memoirs recollects of the seed of the Word that was planted in his tender years. He records an incident that happened when he was eight years old as he attended a communion service in which the minister before administering the sacrament "spake of the commendation of Christ." He writes,

> About the eighth year of my age, I happened in a crowd to push into the church at Abernethy, on a sacrament Sabbath. Then it was common for all but intended communicants to be excluded. Before I was excluded, I heard one or two tables served by a minister, who spake much to the commendation of Christ: this in a sweet and delightful manner captivated my young affections, and has since made me think that children should never be kept out of the church on such occasions.[234]

In the same recollection, Brown goes on to talk about his delight and joy at learning by heart the catechisms even though the circumstances of life soon deprived him of an extensive formal education. Of this he writes,

---

[232] *Centenary Memorial of the Rev. John Brown of Haddington: A Family Record,* compiled by John Croumbie Brown (Edinburgh: Andrew Elliot, 1887), 20.

[233] *Centenary Memorial of the Rev. John Brown of Haddington,* 20-21.

[234] *Life and Remains of the Rev John Brown,* 9-10.

CHAPTER II: HISTORICAL EXAMPLES OF SOUND TEACHING MINISTRY

> My parents' circumstances were such, that they were not able to afford me any great length of time at school for reading, writing, and arithmetic. I had a particular delight in learning by heart the catechisms published by Vincent, Flavel, and the Westminster Assembly, and was much profited by them. One month at school, without my parents' allowance, I bestowed upon the Latin.[235]

One month's study of Latin, a thirst for knowledge, a delight in learning and a biblical foundation at home are all he had, but those are what led Brown to continued personal study through to his teenage years, though orphaned. Brown's testimony reflects the biblical principle presented in Proverbs 22:6. Concerning his salvation, Brown attributes it to the working of the Lord. He states,

> In the thirteenth and fourteenth years of my life, the Lord by his word, read and heard, did often strive with my soul for its good. The perusal of Alleine's "Alarm to the Unconverted" contributed, in some measure, to awaken my conscience, and to move my affections.[236]

He also points out the struggles, occasioned by his "corrupt mind," and how finally the Lord had His way. Brown describes his struggles to point out both his "legal covenanting with God" and his personal attempts to attain salvation by any means "rather than flee to Christ and trust his free grace alone." The influence of his readings also from various authors including Guthrie, Alleine, Rutherford, Gouge and others. Through his readings he confesses of the impressions which were made on his mind and the external change in his behaviour. The influence of the sermons he heard also had impact by the gracious work of the Holy Spirit in his life. He records,

> However, some of his hints, made worse by my corrupt mind, occasioned my legal covenanting with God. I made much the same use of that excellent book, Guthrie's "Trial of a saving Interest in Christ." Indeed, such was the bias of my heart under her convictions, that I was willing to do anything rather than flee to Christ, and trust to his free grace alone for my salvation. I had no small pleasure, about this time, in reading religious books, such as the Bible, "Rutherford's Letters," "Gouge's Directions how to walk with God," &c. By means of attention to these, I was led into some measure of tenderness in my external behaviour. The impressions which were made on my mind, by the sermons which I heard, and the books which I read, were on certain occasions very great, and sometimes continued for several days. Under these I was much given to prayer, but concealed all my religious exercises to the utmost of my power.[237]

These exercises and impressions were to be cut off for a period from his life when, after a period of frequent ailing, circumstances of life led him from the religious family he lived with into a secular family and a period which "was attended with much practical apostasy from the Lord."[238] He states of this period how "former attainments

---

[235] *Life and Remains of the Rev John Brown*, 10.

Robert Mackenzie commenting on the education of John Brown observes the mental discipline that the learning required. He writes, "He was not content with reading, but with "learning by heart" what he read. When one remembers what was read by this boy of eight or ten, the Catechisms of Vincent and Flavel, and the Larger Catechism of the Westminster Assembly, the mental grip must have early declared itself." [Mackenzie, *John Brown of Haddington*, 8.]

[236] *Life and Remains of the Rev. John Brown*, 10.

[237] *Life and Remains of the Rev. John Brown*, 10-11.

[238] Ibid., 11.

were lost, and religious exercises were often omitted."[239] But he was drawn out of this dark period again by the providential hand of God and led to Christ in his nineteenth year after another bout of fever. He writes,

> After many changes in the frame of my heart, Providence again afflicted me with a fever in the nineteenth year of my age: this in some degree awakened my concern about eternal salvation. After my recovery, I heard a sermon on John vi. 64, "There are some of you that believe not." This, though delivered by one that was reckoned a general preacher, pierced my conscience, as if almost every sentence had been directed to none but me; and it made me conclude myself one of the greatest unbelievers in the world. My soul was thrown into a sort of agony, and I was made to look on all my former experiences as effects of the common operations of the Holy Ghost. In this manner I viewed them for many years afterwards, till at last God showed me, that I was wrong in throwing aside all ray attainments, as having nothing really gracious in them. Next day I heard a sermon on Isa. liii. 4, "Surely he hath borne our griefs and carried our sorrows." This enlightened and melted my heart in a way that I had never before felt. I was made as a poor lost sinner, as the chief of sinners, to essay appropriating the Lord Jesus as having done all for me, and as wholly made over to me, in the gospel, as the free gift of God; and as my all-sufficient Saviour, answerable to all my folly, ignorance, guilt, filthiness, slavery, and misery. Through this, and other ordinances, the pleasure which I had enjoyed in some former years, was not only remarkably returned, but I attained far clearer views of the freedom of God's grace, and the exercise of taking hold of, and pleading the promises of the gospel.[240]

In addition to this, Mackenzie has another record, that of a contemporary of Brown, which was written and submitted, but received too late to be included in the first biography written. In the account is recorded the hand of providence at work in the life of the young Brown, that despite the circumstances of life that the young Brown found himself in, "as soon as he could do anything, Providence provided a friend for him in the neighbouring mountains to Abernethy in John Ogilvie a shepherd, venerable for age, and eminent for piety."[241] This friendship developed beyond the care of sheep. As Ogilvie could not read English, he engaged the young Brown to help him in the care of sheep so that he could read to him. Mackenzie writes thus:

> This worthy man, though intelligent and pious, was so destitute of education, as not to be able to read English. Knowing the narrow circumstances of your father's family, his serious disposition, his love of learning, his wonderful capacity, he was induced to engage him in his service, to help him with his sheep, particularly to tend his lambs, but chiefly to read to him.[242]

As this companionship developed, both of them profited much from it. Through the reading, both were edified as the elderly Ogilvie had the Word of God read

---

[239] Ibid.

[240] *Life and Remains of the Rev. John Brown,* 11-12.

[241] Mackenzie, *John Brown of Haddington,* 14.

[242] Ibid, 14.

In a previous section, Mackenzie explains that the elderly John Ogilvie had chosen and hired the young John Brown principally for the spiritual communings and fellowship they would have. He says that Ogilvie had "welcomed the service of the studious youth, not so much for herding his sheep as for his ability to read to him, and his delight in his spiritual communings." [Ibid., 13.]

CHAPTER II: HISTORICAL EXAMPLES OF SOUND TEACHING MINISTRY

to him, while the younger Brown progressed in his learning and "the wilderness and the solitary place was glad for them, and the desert rejoiced with joy and singing."[243]

The Pastoral Practice of John Brown

An excerpt from his address to students of theology, which was later published in the preface of his systematic theology, gives great insight into the practical theology and pastoral practice of Brown especially in the field of pastoral training and mentoring. Brown's focus in his address was a biblical ministry that rendered the minister mighty in Scriptures and sharp in thinking, able to relate what he reads and studies to what he is to do and hence if the mind was impressed with the things of God, then the ministry would flow with the things of God, becoming a ministry that would not only be biblical but also God honouring. The excerpt states in part,

> For my assistance in instructing you, this Compendious View of Natural and Revealed Religion was formed. To gratify a number of you, it is now published. Being formed, not to make you read, but <u>to make you think much</u>, it must now appear dry and meagre, as stripped of its additional remarks; and no doubt some of its expressions admit of a sense which I never intended. <u>To render you mighty in the Scriptures</u>, readily able to support the several articles of our holy religion by the self-evidencing and conscience-commanding testimony the things of the Holy Ghost, and accustomed to express texts are of God in his own language, multitudes of quoted, which I have laboured to lodge in ordinarily your memories. ... While I have been occupied in instructing you, your consciences must bear me witness, that my principal concern was <u>to impress your minds with the great things of God</u>. Now, when I am gradually stepping into the eternal state, to appear before the judgment-seat of Christ, permit me to beseech you, as you wish <u>to promote His honour, and the eternal salvation of your own and your hearers' souls</u>. [Emphasis added.][244]

The ministry of the pulpit is one that must flow from the knowledge of the Scriptures. All other things must be secondary and subordinated to this primary one. In his teaching ministry, his principal concern towards his students was that with minds saturated with the Word of God, they may be readily able to support the tenets of the faith once for all delivered to the saints by the use of Scripture which he endeavoured to make plain and clear to them. The same Scriptures that he had through much study and which he brings out most vividly in his letters and books is the centre of every God-honouring ministry. As Brown addressed his students in his late years, when he was "gradually stepping into the eternal state" and in light of the judgment seat of Christ before which every believer must appear to give account of the things done in the flesh, he laboured to impress upon the minds and memories of those who are beginning, preparing for and continuing in the ministry the need and importance of a ministry based on and guided by Scripture as evidenced through the knowledge and conduct of the minister.

In this age where little effort is put into acquiring a working knowledge of the original languages (in which institutions give excuses for replacing or removing it from the syllabus, or in which preachers and theological students give excuses for not knowing the original languages and for neglecting it after having learned it) and where emphasis is shifting from the writings and theologies of the Reformation and Puritan eras to a modern psychology-based and humanistic approach, there is much to be gleaned from the practices of Brown.

---

[243] Ibid 15.

[244] John Brown, *Address to Students of Divinity by Rev. John Brown, Late Minister of the Gospel in Haddington, Scotland* (np: nd), 101-102.

First, from his personal practice as a student of the Holy Scriptures. Mackenzie records concerning John's personal study,

> John Brown, with his scanty tools for acquiring knowledge, especially of languages, made such use of them as to display remarkable originality. The little Latin he had been taught, instead of being lost when life's hard school began, where in truth there seemed so little use for it, was carefully treasured, and added to, until the mastery of the language was well within his grasp. He borrowed books wherever he could find them. In the midday, when for two hours the labours ceased, he bounded off to the minister at Arngask, three to four miles away, Rev. J. Johnstone, or to his own minister at Abernethy, Rev. Alexander Moncrieff, who for a time, at least, was his friendly counsellor and helper. Moncrieff would set him studies that he imagined days would be required to overtake, but in a short time, Brown was at his door, with the work prescribed finished, and ready for more.[245]

The first distinguishing mark of a minister as a student of the Word has to be discipline and commitment. The apostolic injunction is *"study to shew thyself approved unto God a workman that needeth not to be ashamed, rightly dividing the word of truth"* (2 Tim 2:2). And in another place, it is an exhortation to *"give attendance to reading, to exhortation, to doctrine."* (1 Tim 4:12). The pastoral ministry is a teaching ministry that requires of the minister a continual commitment to study. And Brown, in his study, shows the principle that the minister's study is not primarily determined by the number or amount of tools available to him, but rather is determined by the disposition of the minister's heart and his commitment to the Word of God and his personal growth in it. His diligence in his studies would see Brown add Greek to his Latin, and Hebrew to both his Latin and Greek in such a remarkable way despite the little tools in his possession. He had invested in the pursuit of knowledge, and used the Latin he had to gain Greek, and Greek to gain Hebrew. These languages (which many in this age consider of little importance for the work of the ministry and which, in other cases, others struggle to memorize and master their basic rudiments) Brown mastered by commitment and determination. Mackenzie writes,

> But his browsing in Latin fields led him to seek the richer pasturage of Greek, and acquaintance with the very words of the New Testament. He was too modest to ask guidance in this more exclusive region. Latin then was common property; not so Greek; and he conceived a plan to reach his goal by himself, rather ingenious and entirely original. He took his Ovid, an old Latin grammar, and the names of the New Testament, especially the genealogies of the first chapter of Matthew, and the third chapter of Luke. The last he divined to be transcripts of the Greek, and to suggest the key to unlock the door between the two languages. "Reason told me," he argued, "that at least an unaccidented tongue could not much change names from what they were in the Greek." With these he made a discovery of the Greek characters, as true a discovery as Dr. Young's of the characters of the Rosetta stone, or Rawlinson's of the cuneiform letters. He compared the names and the letters verse by verse with the English. He treated the Greek as an expert uses a cypher, and bit by bit with wonderful patience and ingenuity, he learned the sound of the letters. Though only making guesses at the meaning, yet, by comparing it with the English, he was able to read the Greek. Then, having acquired so much Greek, he pushed on to Hebrew.[246]

---

[245] Mackenzie, *John Brown of Haddington,* 21-22.

[246] Mackenzie, *John Brown of Haddington,* 22.

CHAPTER II: HISTORICAL EXAMPLES OF SOUND TEACHING MINISTRY

The challenges and circumstances of life, as well as what he had been deprived of do not seem to bear weight or hinder him in his pursuit of knowledge. His endeavour, zeal, diligence, and commitment come out clearly. They give a glimpse to the disposition of his heart and what seems to come out is a hunger and thirst for the Word and a love and devotion to God. He who loves the Word would search the Scriptures, and as Daniel of old seeking to understand the things revealed to him in visions and dreams, Brown set himself continually to seek and study until he had unlocked the mysteries of the original languages. By study, seeking counsel and even developing ingenious methods devised by sober reasoning, he pursued knowledge and understanding of the scriptures. This is sorely lacking in this age in which people are contented to just parrot what they have heard from others and what sounds appealing to their ears, without searching the Scriptures diligently to see if those things are so. Many settle to surf the worldwide web without discernment (instead of searching the Scriptures) thus bringing into the church through the pulpit many a heresy poisoning the hearts of men. Many today want to be called ministers, pastors, professors, servants of God and yet shun the labours and rigours and study that is the portion of the pastor and servant of God. And when they seek study, they seek for that which is shallow and without substance, that which is easy and least demanding, that does not require one to exert himself and dig deep. Brown's zeal can be seen in the lengths he went to in order to find access to books and learning and counsel, yet doing all this without compromising his duties and labours. All his labouring was accomplished while he was still a shepherd before entering or taking upon himself the duties and responsibilities of the ministry. It is while he studied, and as he grew in his learning and knowledge of Latin, Greek and Hebrew that the Lord began to fix Brown's purpose upon the service of the Lord and the use of these gifts in the ministry of Christ. In his own words, Brown wrote,

> By means of my anxious pursuit of learning, as I could get any opportunity, I had, by the Lord's assistance, acquired some knowledge of the Latin, Greek, and Hebrew languages, and was beginning to fix my purpose to use it in the service of Christ, if He should open a regular door.[247]

The pastoral ministry of Brown was tied to his knowledge and study of the Holy Scriptures. Those who were learned, went to seminary to study of the ministry, but in Brown's case although he did not have much opportunity for formal academic pursuits in the seminaries of his time, his studies in the fields, his communion with the elderly John Ogilvie, and his extensive reading were indeed used of the Lord to prepare him for the work of the ministry. In the account above, Brown goes on to record the trials he faced from some ministry students who attributed John's knowledge of the original languages to the working of the Devil simply because he had covered more ground in his study than they had though they had the help of a professor.[248] Unfortunately the attack on the young Brown did hinder his entry into ministry for a period of time, but did not quench his desire both to study the Word and to use his gifts in the ministry of Christ. Mackenzie records,

> His irreproachable character, his manifest purity of motive and of life, alone warded off the slander and its dire possible consequences. Time brought its test; and in the

---

[247] Mackenzie, *John Brown of Haddington*, 28.

[248] "His marvellous acquaintance with Greek, in his circumstances, simply staggered a few young men in Abernethy who were studying for the ministry. The priggishness of youth, struggling with Professors' help to acquire the language, whetted their jealousy of this unkempt, untaught herd-boy, daring to sip the nectar of the gods. In conversation with William Moncrieff, son of the minister of Abernethy, William ventured to say, "I'm sure the devil has taught you some words." Brown laughed at the jest. But it turned out to be no jest; it was seriously meant." [Ibid., 27-28.]

end truth and sincerity prevailed. Moncrieff was as adamant to the last. Another year of disquiet had to be endured. Then on June 16th, 1746, the clean certificate of full membership in the Church was granted by the unanimous vote of the elders and deacons of Abernethy, Moncrieff dissenting, and refusing to sign it. Thus, after five years of persecution, his character was cleared. But the lash of the slander left its mark on the young spirit.[249]

That he would through the five years of hostility keep at his private studies and respond in writing to the charges to clear his name is a great testimony to the resolve and commitment he had for the church and for the work of God. And though he was cleared of the charges and granted membership to the church, the fact that he had no formal education was another hurdle that he had to overcome before entering the ministry. As he did not have means to attain the required university education for induction into the ministry, Brown took another available route, that of teaching at a school. Mackenzie writes,

> It was Brown's ambition to enter the ministry of the Church, but the means to obtain a university education were not available. The next step that was possible to take, he took, and became a schoolmaster. By his incessant self-culture, he was well equipped for the profession, which in .those days lay open to any one, without compulsory courses of training. He started at Gairney Bridge, two miles south of Kinross, where a monument stands today to commemorate the event of thirteen years earlier, when the Secession fathers met and founded their Church. As a teacher he was eminently successful. He drew scholars from a wide radius. With a passion for learning in his own soul, he communicated the fire of it to his pupils.[250]

Brown thus started off by teaching and as a schoolmaster, his dedication and influence led quite a number of his students into the ministry[251] and as teacher, he not only equipped others, but also grew himself. During his time as a teacher, events transpired which would grant him opportunity to enter into the full-time ministry. The reintroduction of the Burgess Oath split the synod and Brown sided with the Erskines on the issue. He continued to study and after acquiring what was required for divinity, he became licensed and chose to minister at Haddington. Mackenzie writes,

> But the ill fortune that befell the young cause was his opportunity. The "Associate" church required preachers. He offered himself, and was accepted. He continued his teaching for three years longer, until he had acquired a training in philosophy and divinity. Then the door to the ministry opened, and he passed within its portals.[252]

In the preface to the Self-Interpreting Bible, a memoir is included about Brown. That memoir reads in part,

> At twenty-five years of age he established himself at Gaisner Bridge, a village in the neighborhood of Kinross, and there laid the foundation of a school. ... The practical character of his teachings, the accuracy of his learning, the intimate experience which as a self-taught scholar he must have had of elementary difficulties and the best mode of solving them, and the conscientiousness and assiduity which always formed distinguishing features of his character, must have peculiarly qualified him

---

[249] Ibid, 44.

[250] Ibid., 59-60.

[251] After teaching for a time at Gairney Bridge, he crossed the Forth to Spittal, near Penicuik, Midlothian, where, he says, "I had a large school, and I hope was useful in training up, among others, several young men in the learned languages, who were afterwards eminent ministers of Jesus, as the late Archibald Hall of London and others." [Ibid, 64.]

[252] Ibid, 66.

for the discharge of his duties and laid a solid foundation for his general acceptance as an instructor of youth. He completed, when he was twenty-nine years of age, his preparatory course of study, and approved himself on trial before the Associated Presbytery of Edinburgh, and was licensed to preach by that body. He entered upon the sacred work with deep impressions of its solemnity and usefulness. [253]

The age by which he was accomplished as a self-taught scholar is remarkable, going on to be learned and proficient in Greek and Hebrew, and able to understand other languages like Arabic, Persian, Ethiopian, French, Spanish, Italian, Dutch and German. He also gave himself to study philosophy, natural history and civil law and went on to be elected by the Synod to the Chair of Divinity Professor after James Fisher and John Swanston. Brown not only distinguished himself as a Minister and Professor of Divinity but also as an author. Regarding his professorship, Mackenzie writes that while "the labours in the little square room in the manse of Haddington were being devoted to the Dictionary and other works, the eyes of his Church were being directed to the student pastor."[254]

Biblical Principles for Contemporary Application from John Brown's Ministry

If the principles learned from the ministry of John Calvin emphasized the need for a theological pulpit where the desire and endeavour is to make clear the Scriptures and through the Scriptures to teach all what they ought to believe and how to worship and serve God biblically, then from the life of Brown, the principles that can be drawn is the necessity of training and mentorship that produces for the ministry men who can explain and make clear the Scriptures. Men may be born with gifts such as those that have been seen in the persons considered in this section. Whether it is Richard Baxter, John Calvin, William Carey or John Brown, each was unique and endowed with gifts that are not common to all men. The Scriptures require that ministers be able to handle the Word of God effectively, to teach the truth with all of its implications, and to refute errors of all kinds. For such rigours, there is need for men to be equipped and prepared, not only by their unique giftedness but also by systematic and thorough training. Each of the men considered in this section not only had giftings, but also as a minister of the Gospel was made so by learning and training. Concerning Brown, Jerdan writes,

> In 1768 John Brown was appointed Professor of Divinity to his denomination, an office which he occupied with universal acceptance during the twenty years of his life that yet remained. No man in any Church was ever more thoroughly equipped for a chair in theology. He was a master in "the queen of the sciences," having amassed great stores of Puritan, Scottish, and Dutch divinity. He was well-read in universal history and general literature. The Holy Scriptures, in their original languages, were as familiar to him as his mother-tongue. He had also learned French, Dutch, German, Italian, and Spanish; together with Arabic, Syriac, Persic, and Ethiopic. He was, moreover, an eager student of the various departments of philosophy, as well as an expert in church history. Above all, he was a man of God, his heart being full of love to Christ, and of passionate yearnings for the salvation of his fellow-men.[255]

---

[253] *New Self-Interpreting Bible Library with commentaries, references, harmony of the Gospels, and the helps needed to understand and teach the text illustrated and explained in four volumes, Vol. I Genesis-Joshua* (New York: R. S. Peale and J. A. Hill, 1896), 14.

[254] Mackenzie, *John Brown of Haddington*, 127.

[255] Charles Jerdan, *Scottish Clerical Stories and Reminiscences* (Edinburgh: Oliphants LTD, 1920), 330-331.

Brown, though deprived of formal seminary training, had informal training through his personal endeavours. And after he entered the ministry gave himself diligently and continually to his study and also to the training of men. For about twenty years, Brown trained students for the ministry during the summer months in addition to the pastoral labours and ministerial work. His life and ministry clearly present the necessity of proper training for the work of the ministry. This is exemplified in his eagerness and commitment to his personal study and learning. Regarding his efforts to train men for the ministry, Mackenzie writes,

> ABOUT one hundred and eighty students in all passed through the Theological Institution of Haddington. Though in the five years which their training demanded, it was only ten months that really were spent under the immediate supervision of the Professor, the period left its deep impress upon them. A few turned out failures, and a few succumbed, like Michael Bruce, to the maladies that decimate our youth; but the vast majority entered the ministry, some going as missionaries to the New World, then opening its wonders to the nations of Europe.[256]

His address to students of divinity provides a rich mine of wealth for those who would enter into the ministry even today. In it he presents a biblical view of ministry giving counsel to ministers in preparation for the Gospel work.

> Ponder much, as before God, what proper furniture you have for the ministerial work, and labour to increase it. To him that hath shall be given. Has Jesus bestowed on you the Holy Ghost? What distinct knowledge have you of the mysteries of the kingdom? What aptness have you to teach, bringing out of the good treasure of your own heart things new and old What ability to make the deep mysteries of the Gospel plain to persons of weak capacities, and to represent things delightful or terrible in a proper and affecting manner? What proper quickness in conceiving divine things; and what rooted inclination to study them, as persons devoted to matters of infinite importance? What peculiar fitness have you for the pulpit, qualifying you, in a plain, serious, orderly, and earnest manner, to screw the truths of God into the consciences of your hearers? With what stock of self-experienced truths and texts of inspiration did, or do you enter on the ministerial work? [Emphasis added.] [257]

The questions which he puts forth for the student of divinity and Gospel to ponder are questions that illustrate his emphasis on the need of preparation for the Gospel ministry. It is from these questions that principles for contemporary application will be drawn. From the last question in the above question, it is clear that from Brown's perspective no man ought to enter into the ministry devoid of self-experienced truths and texts. This implies that preparation for the ministry, if it be thorough, ought to be more than academic pursuit. The one who is prepared should not only know the truths and texts, but should also experience them. It is said of Christ that *"he ordained twelve, that they should be with him, and that he might send them forth to preach"* (Mark 3:13). And when the apostles began their ministry at Jerusalem, it is recorded of them too that *"when they saw the boldness of Peter and John, and perceived that they were unlearned and ignorant men, they marvelled; and they took knowledge of them, that they had been with Jesus"* (Acts 4:13). Jesus Himself speaking to the disciples before His arrest and crucifixion said to them, *"and ye also shall bear witness, because ye have been with me from the beginning"* (John 15:27). In this Christ lays down the basis and ground for all effective ministry. The apostles were eye-witnesses and as such would not only relay

---

[256] Ibid., 143.

[257] John Brown, *A Compendious View of Natural and Revealed Religion in Seven Books* (Philadelphia: David Hogan, 1819), viii.

CHAPTER II: HISTORICAL EXAMPLES OF SOUND TEACHING MINISTRY

what they had seen and heard and what their hands had handled, they could also relate to their own message having had personal experience of being with Jesus.

The ministry of the Word is not an involuntary or a mechanical one in which the Holy Spirit uses the minister by excluding all personal influences or experiences. Rather, the minister under the guidance and leading of the Holy Spirit bears forth a personal witness that takes into account and makes use of the personal, historical and spiritual influences of the minister. Hence, Brown's question to consider with what stock one enters the ministry with. The truths being taught and preached ought to be, before all things, impressed upon the preacher's heart and embraced by the preacher before they can be given out to others. This is the understanding behind the question: "With what stock of self-experienced truths and texts of inspiration did, or do you enter on the ministerial work?" In explaining his questions, Brown goes on to write, "Thrice happy preacher, whose deeply-experienced heart is, next to his Bible, his principal note-book!"[258] To this effect, the address of Brown to his students contains many insights that balance the need of training with the person of the minister. Insights from which can be drawn biblical principles relevant for contemporary application today. The aim of training and mentoring ministers has to be seen as that; through the training, the ministers may be equipped for the work they are undertaking, the ministers may be informed and prepared to face the oppositions and defend the truth of the Gospel. And this Brown himself did so effectively that the testimony of David Hume concerning the ministry of Brown would be an apt place to conclude this section. It is recorded of Brown as follows:

> Neither in preaching nor in private conversation did he ever parade his learning. His pulpit prelections were always characterised by great simplicity, clearness, faithfulness, strenuousness, spirituality, and a moral earnestness which was often overpowering. David Hume the philosopher once heard him preach, and went away saying, "He speaks as if he were conscious that the Lord Jesus Christ stood at his elbow."[259]

Concluding Observations

William Bright in his book *Waymarks in Church History* presents an apt perspective with which the lessons of history ought to be viewed. Concerning the benefits of studying church history, he writes,

> And the actual direct benefits from these studies— do they not include a broader and <u>more vivid perception of a Divine order</u> carried on, as under "one increasing purpose," through all the ages between the call of the "friend of God" and the coming of God's own Son? Ought we not to gain some insight into that <u>mass of evidence at once for the truth and the power of Christ</u> which was necessarily unknown to the first believers; to learn what Christendom, after all deductions, can do in the way of witnessing for Christ; <u>how promises have been largely, though not as yet completely, fulfilled</u>; how <u>virtues neglected by Heathenism have got their rights</u>, and <u>vices long tolerated have been branded with due shame</u>; how the type of <u>character exhibited in the Gospels has been the permanent moral enrichment of humanity</u>; what a <u>stimulus to practical faith is to be found in the lives of eminent Christians</u>, ancient, mediaeval, modern; how the <u>significance of doctrine has thus become more apparent</u> [emphasis added], and the "*credo*" been felt to be more "worth living for and dying for"?[260]

---

[258] John Brown, *A Compendious View of Natural and Revealed Religion in Seven Books*, viii.

[259] Jerdan, *Scottish Clerical Stories and Reminiscences*, 329-330.

[260] William Bright, *Waymarks in Church History* (London: Longman, Green, & Co, 1894), 17.

Indeed, church history ought to present to its students (i) insight into God's divine order working through time, (ii) evidence of the power and the working of Christ through the ages, (iii) encouragement through the fulfilment of the promises and the Word of Christ in the different periods and circumstances, (iv) hope through the changes that faith has wrought both in establishing the truth of Christ and breaking the hold of vices in different cultures and (v) courage to press on and press through knowing that the Christian faith is practical under all circumstances through the lives of eminent Christian men of different ages and places.

What this section has shown is the importance of Bible teaching to the life and vitality of the church. Though the persons studied are taken from different places and times — Calvin from the 16th Century France (1509 – 1564), Baxter from the 17th Century England (1615 – 1691), Carey from the 18th Century England (1761 – 1834), and Brown from the 18th Century Scotland (1722 – 1854), yet the condition that the church of their time found itself in due to the lack of Bible-based and systematic teaching are strikingly similar. Declension of religion begins with the lack of proper, systematic and Bible-based teaching which in turn leads to ceremonial formalism as was the case of the condition of the church in the times of Calvin, Baxter, Carey and Brown. As they describe the state of religion in their times, though their experiences were different, they talk of the dead formalism of their age evidenced with different evidences from the bishop arbitrarily confirming the children he found outside the church compound during Baxter's time to church elders opposing Carey in his endeavours for missions to India. Each one's attempts and labours though done at different periods of history and to different groups of people, yet facing similar obstacles, challenges and problems from Brown being accused of knowing the original languages through the devil, to Calvin being accused and chased out of Geneva for his biblical stand.

William Bright in his book *Waymarks in Church History* under the topic "On the Study of Church History" points out the challenges facing religion during times of declension and what he points out rings true both for the times of the four considered persons above and the condition of the church in Kenya in this age. Bright says concerning the study of church history, "If the work of religion gets done, it is done with reverses, blunders, drawbacks. God's cause is compromised by the weaknesses or sins of His agents; great teachers use one-sided language, even saints at times act indefensibly."[261] The religion at the times of Calvin, Baxter, Carey, and Brown was in different ways compromised by the weaknesses, indifference and in other cases ignorance of those who were in ministry. Each one of the four persons considered in this chapter has in his account some description of an event that shaped his spiritual life, but sadly, the positive influence to religion in most cases was not drawn from the church establishment of their day. Carey and Baxter talk about the influence of their parents' piety and their family devotion when pastors did little from the pulpit. Brown talks of the providence that led him to a godly elder when orphaned.

Though the persons whose lives are considered here come from diverse backgrounds and times, their efforts in the revival of Biblical Christianity in the different areas of teaching they engaged in show the importance of and necessity for biblical teaching to the church in every age and in whatever challenge faced. Calvin was from France, brought up in a predominantly Roman Catholic background, while Carey and Baxter, though from England, lived at very different times under different circumstances. Baxter was raised in the Anglican church, while Carey joined the Baptist church. Brown on the other hand lived in Scotland at a time when there was a great divide in the Presbyterian

---

[261]Bright, *Waymarks in Church History* 10.

church. Yet despite such diversity, teaching stands out as the one consistent avenue used to restore biblical foundations, practices and testimony to the church.

> The Gospel has from the first been substantially one system. The object of its announcement has been from its first announcement in Eden, the same: — the salvation of men. All its true ministers have regarded this as the grand end of their mission. Their chief aim has ever been so to present the Gospel, that through their instrumentality sinners might be converted to God and built up in faith and holiness, and just so far as they have been successful in this, they have felt, that they were successful in their work. And I may add, that the qualities necessary to ministerial success have been in all ages essentially the same. All true ministers of Christ have felt, that a full and clear knowledge of the Gospel, a firm faith in its truths, and great diligence and prudence in proclaiming these, were indispensable to their success.[262]

The consideration of the lives of the men in this section, and many other men throughout the history of the church at different ages whose characters are such as these, emphasize both the place of teaching in the strengthening of the church and the assurance of the faithfulness of Christ to His promise to be with His Church both "till the end of the world" (Matthew 28:20) and "unto the uttermost parts of the earth." (Acts 1:8) Balikie rightly observes,

> While we are not better than our fathers, we are not practically in worse case; if unbelief is more aggressive or more thoroughgoing, we can yet see our own tokens in a revival of Christ-ward devotion, a drawing together, in aim and in spirit, of souls loyal to one Lord. We are not to "seek great things for ourselves," to demand that amount of visible success for the cause which would give us more sensible comfort; but to seek to lean on that "strength" which is never more truly "perfected" than in the weakness of those who wait upon Him.[263]

---

[262] George James, *The Field and the Men for it, an Address to the Divinity Students of Queens College Kingston at the Close of the Session 1859-60* (Montreal: John Lovell, 1860), 3.

[263] William Garden Balikie, *The Preachers of Scotland from the Sixth Century to the Nineteenth Century* (Edinburgh: T & T Clark, 1888), 16-17.

CHAPTER III

TEACHING AVENUES AVAILABLE FOR THE CHURCH TODAY

The church is in great danger as it presently learns from and imitates the world rather than turning to the Word and looking at its rich heritage for directions and examples in facing and reaching the world. This is exemplified in the conclusion given by Dickson Kagema in his article:

> Gospel hip-hop music plays a vital role of attracting many youths into the Church, hence an indispensable tool of evangelizing the youth in Kenya today. Due to globalization, we can no longer pretend that Kenya or even Africa as a whole is an Island. When it comes to evangelization, the Church in Kenya must wake up and employ all available avenues to enable her to reach to as many people as possible. So as to reach all people she must learn to contextualize the gospel of Christ to make it relevant and appealing to all races, ages, cultures, sexes, ideologies and philosophies. In this effort, she must not forget the youth who form a large population of Kenya's population. Gospel hip-hop music which is very appealing to the youth today can become a powerful tool of evangelization if properly utilized.[264]

From Kagema's conclusions, the thought that comes out clearly is that the end justifies the means and therefore the attractiveness and appeal of "Gospel hip-hop" among the youth in Kenya today justifies and warrants its use by the church as an avenue and tool for evangelism and outreach. Although, (i) the world is indeed becoming more secular and globalization has made a village of the world, and (ii) the church must wake up to the dangers around her and to her Gospel mandate, the end does not justify the means. This, therefore, does not mean that means and avenues by which the church is to perform her duties is to be determined by the world or to be conformed to it. The church's primary mandate is not to be attractive to any special interests of any particular group and be appealing to them, but rather to be obedient and faithful to her Lord and Saviour and to His Word. There has, therefore, to be a clear understanding of what constitutes acceptable means to the Lord before any attempts are made in the use of means to fulfil her call.

The church is not to look to the world for her mandate, or for her patterns and examples. She has a rich treasury in Scripture and history for that. The commands and injunctions from the Lord Himself, the pattern of the apostles and prophets of old, and the examples of exemplary men some of which have been highlighted in the previous chapter abound for the church to guide her understanding of means available, and give guidance to what is to be employed and what not to be employed. The church is not to conform to the world because Christians though in the world are not of the world. They are not to be controlled by the dictates of the world, they are to be dead to the world, dead to sin, crucifying the old man with his lusts and desires. As a people called out of the world, the church is to separate itself from worldliness.

Albert Barnes speaking on the Rule of Christianity in regard to conformity to the world rightly points out in great details six principles that the church is to use in determining the means available and acceptable and for the church to distinguish and separate herself from worldliness. These principles help the church to avoid the pitfall of using the end to justify the means. Barnes points out that the biblical principles are for all "those who belong to that original and peculiar community, which the Son of God came

---

[264] Dickson Nkonge Kagema, "The Use of Gospel Hip-hop as an Avenue of Evangelizing Youth in Kenya Today: A Practical Approach", *American International Journal of Contemporary Research*, accessed 12 March 2018, http://www.aijcrnet.com/journals/Vol_3_No_8_August_2013/19.pdf.

CHAPTER III: TEACHING AVENUES AVAILABLE FOR THE CHURCH TODAY

to establish"[265] and are thus to be applied to all church outreaches and programs. Barnes writes,

> You are not to regulate your feelings and views, your apparel and manner of living, your conversation and deportment, with a view of leading the world in their own ways of vanity, pleasure and ambition. You are not to seek to be distinguished in the manner in which they seek to be distinguished, and for which alone they live. The world is tending to a different destiny from the Christian. It matters little in what way they go; whether in the ball-room, the theatre, or any other scene of vice and sin, they are going to their own home, and it is a sad procession however gay or gorgeous, where a Christian moves at the head of a thoughtless throng that is sporting down to hell.[266]

The direction and destiny of the world is different from that of the church of Christ, and as such, the Christian cannot employ worldly means. Doing so is described above by Barnes as moving "at the head of a thoughtless throng that is sporting down to hell." The second principle pointed out by Barnes is that of discernment and the testing and trying of every spirit before approving anything. The ways and views of the church are different from the world and as such the Christian is not to embrace anything based on feelings or opinions, but rather it should be based on Scripture as Barnes says,

> You are not to regulate your opinions and feelings, and conduct, by the people of the world. You are not to approve of a thing because they approve of it; to do a thing because they do it; to love a thing because they love it; or to hate a thing because they hate it. You are not to inquire then, how they think or feel, or why they do it. They have their own views of these things, and you are to have yours — or rather you are to imbibe the views of the Son of God. With the feelings which the world has about the objects of life, a thousand things may be consistent, which would be repugnant to the laws of the kingdom of Christ.[267]

There are laws and principles that govern Christian life and work and thus the popular sentiments or views cannot be a governing principle for the church. The church, thus, in adopting avenues and looking for means by which it is to evangelize the world, is to turn to scriptural laws and principles. Christian temperance and testimony, seeking to please God and obey Him, prayerfulness, selflessness, and devotion to God is the only way to promoting the glory of God. Barnes adds, "The desire of obeying him to whom we are devoted, and of promoting his glory, will constitute a rule of action."[268] The third to the sixth principles presented by Barnes state in part,

> 3. If in any of your views and deportment, you coincide with the world, it will not be because they do it, but because it will be best. I know that this principle may be difficult to be understood, and may be abused. Still, it may be the correct principle in the case. Let me illustrate it. In many things, as I have remarked, you may coincide with the world. You are industrious. So are they. Your industry is not because the world requires it, but because it is best. It is required by the law of your religion. You are temperate, so may they be. You are temperate, not because this is the fashion of the world, but because your religion demands it. You are courteous, polite, kind. So may

---

[265] Albert Barnes, *The Rule of Christianity in Regard to Conformity to the World: A Sermon Delivered in the First Presbyterian Church in Philadelphia, March 4, 1833* (Philadelphia: Harrison Hall, 1833), 31.

[266] Barnes, *The Rule of Christianity in Regard to Conformity to the World*, 31.

[267] Ibid.

[268] Barnes, *The Rule of Christianity in Regard to Conformity to the World*, 31.

be, externally at least, the people of the world. In this you may coincide. But you are not thus because they are. You do not do it because they have originated it, or because they have the right to dictate its forms. You do it because it is the nature of your religion. It prompts to kindness, truth, courtesy, tenderness of feelings and character, mutual respect, civility. …

4. A fourth obvious principle in which Christians will apply the rule is that their views and feelings will not be prompted by a desire to elicit the applause, and approbation of the world. Your conduct will be regulated by a higher law. It is not to produce admiration, envy, rivalship, flattery, competition, that you live; it is not to be the subject of conversation, commendation, or praise, it is TO PLEASE God. If the kingdom of which you are a member stood alone; if the empires of this world were removed en masse to other abodes, your conduct would then be regulated by the Bible, and the will of God. So should it be now. This is one of the plainest applications of the rule. — And yet if honestly applied, what a sad invasion would it make in the Christian church. …

5. A fifth principle of the rule. It forbids all mingling with the world which is inconsistent with the great objects of the kingdom of Christ, or which will not in the whole tend to promote it. This principle seems also obvious. The desire of obeying him to whom we are devoted, and of promoting his glory, will constitute a rule of action. It is not needful to state what those objects are. They are known to all Christians. They may be summed up in a desire to become personally assimilated to Jesus Christ, and to bring our fellow men to the hope of the same Heaven. It demands of course the spirit of prayer, of seriousness, of self-denial; the faithful discharge of our duties in all the relations of life; a conscientious appropriation of our time, our influence, and our wealth; a faithful meeting of all the demands made on us as Christians and as men. God has given us enough to do and if we follow his will we shall not be oppressed with useless time, or afflicted with ennui.

6. A sixth principle of application of the rule. A Christian should have a spirit and temper above the things that influence his fellow-men. Though in the midst of these scenes, yet he may not be influenced by them. A man may have wealth, and it may be manifest that his affections are not supremely fixed on it. He may be surrounded by a thoughtless world, and yet be evidently living above it. Christianity produces a spirit that is elevated above these things; that draws its consolations and its principles of action from far different objects.[269]

The popular sentiments that spearhead the secularization of the church through syncretism and the compromise that is prevalent hinder the church in fulfilling its heavenly mandate. The church is losing its salt and dimming its light by appealing to the world and looking to the world for its basis and methods in outreach. The church is called to be separate, distinct and distinguished from the world. The church is to look up for its mandate and purpose and look out for its outreach. The church does not serve the Lord by imitating the world but rather does her Lord a great disservice in imitating the world. As Barnes pointed out in his second principle: "You are not to inquire then, how they think or feel, or why they do it." The reason is that the world has its own views on things and these views are different from that of the church. It is the nature of Christianity that should prompt the church in all her endeavours as she lives and witnesses in this world. In the light of the rules presented by Albert Barnes above, it is clear that the majority of the churches today have strayed and are lacking. This is evident in the church seeking to be conformed to the world, which thing the apostle Paul strictly forbids in his

---

[269] Barnes, *The Rule of Christianity in Regard to Conformity to the World*, 31-46.

epistle to the Romans in Romans 12:1-2. The danger of the trends that have been derived by the thoughts and imaginations of men who draw their inspiration from the world, which trends are increasing in popularity in this age, is aptly traced by Robert Barclay in the preface of his Catechism when he points out the form with which error enters and replaces truth. Man's devices are normally introduced initially as tools and aids in accomplishing the Christian mandate, but soon become equated to the truth and later replaces the truth. Barclay writes,

> Since first that great apostasy took place, in the hearts and heads of those who began, even in the apostles' days, to depart from the simplicity and purity of the gospel, as it was then delivered in its primitive splendor and integrity, innumerable have been the manifold inventions and traditions, the different and various notions and opinions, wherewith man (by giving way to the vain and airy imaginations of his own unstable mind) hath burthened the christian faith; so that indeed, first by adding these things, and afterwards by equalling them, if not exalting them above the truth, they have at last come to be substituted in the stead of it; so that in process of time truth came to be shut out of doors, and another thing placed in the room thereof, having a shew and name, but wanting the substance and thing itself.[270]

The hearts and minds of men, even the best of men with the best intentions at heart, still remains depraved; hence in seeking to fulfil the Gospel's mandate and in seeking to do God's will, the church has but only one source of inspiration, the Scriptures. The things that influence the world are not to be the things that influence the church, for as Barnes pointed out in his sixth principle: "Christianity produces a spirit that is elevated above these things; that draws its consolations and its principles of action from far different objects." The principles of Christianity are basically centred round two broad principles which ought to guide the church in all things. They are as pointed out by Barclay:

> First —That every principle and doctrine of the Christian faith, is, and ought to be, founded upon the scripture; and that whatsoever principles and doctrines are not only not contrary, but even not according thereto, ought to be denied as anti-Christian.
>
> Secondly —That the scriptures themselves are plain and easy to be understood; and that every private Christian and member of the church ought to read and peruse them, that they may know their faith and belief founded upon them, and receive them for that cause alone, and not because any church or assembly has compounded and recommended them; the choicest and most pure of which, they are obliged to look upon as fallible.[271]

The second principle logically follows the first in that the view of Scripture ultimately governs the relationship to Scripture. Thus the belief that "every principle and doctrine of the Christian faith, is, and ought to be, founded upon the scripture" ought to beget in every Christian and member of the church both the desire and the urge to "to read and peruse them, that they may know their faith and belief founded upon them." But the evident reality is contrary to this. The Scriptures are not read and thus not known and as a result the members of the church do not know their faith and belief. The mandate of the church is to be drawn directly from Scripture, the methods to be employed are also to be guided and controlled by scriptural principles and examples.

---

[270] Robert Barclay, *A Catechism and Confession of Faith: approved of and agreed unto by the General Assembly of the Patriarchs, Prophets, and Apostles, Christ Himself being the chief speaker in and among them* (Wilmington, Delaware: James Wilson, 1821), iii.

[271] Ibid., iv.

The church indeed has to wake up to her call and mandate, and the church has to employ all available avenues to fulfil her mandate as Dickson Kagema pointed out. But in fulfilling her mandate, and specifically with respect to her teaching mandate, there has to be a clarity first of all of what avenues are available for the church. Hence, the question begs, what are the avenues and methods available for the church to use in fulfilling her duty and calling? From the previous chapters, it has been made clear that teaching is a mandate of the church; hence in this section, avenues and methods for teaching that are available for the church to use are what will be considered for the church today.

In the Home

The home is the first and always should remain the most important factor in a child's education. This training should extend from the early years of childhood to manhood. The ancient Hebrews recognized the supreme importance of home instruction, and they earnestly tried to bring up their children in the fear and admonition of the Lord. When this ideal was earnestly adhered to, peace, joy, and prosperity crowned the people of Israel.[272]

The understanding and view of the family/home as an extension of the church is a biblical one and therefore the mandate of the church must extend to the family. The Old Testament abounds in injunctions that call for the propagation and teaching of piety within the home and thus the religion of Israel was one that found its place in the home. Charles Heathcote in his *Essentials of Religious Education* goes on to write,

> The home is the basic unit of society. It is such an important institution that great emphasis needs to be laid upon the instruction of Biblical truths therein. Alas, in too many of our homes the Bible! is a closed book and religious instruction is never given at all. No parent can expect the school and the church to give all the education the child needs.[273]

The neglect of the home and the family in the propagation of religious piety therefore undermines the effectiveness of the church and its ministry. The problem that Heathcote noted and lamented in the 1900s is still a problem in this age. The scripture clearly sets forth the home and family as one of the main places where instruction and teaching is to take place. From the Old Testament to the New Testament, evidence that piety in the home was deliberately cultivated is evident from injunctions given to parents to teach their children and from examples of those who were instructed at home in the ways of the Lord.

The Hebrew emphasis of the home as a centre of religious and spiritual instruction is unmistakable as the Bible commands: *"Gather me the people together and I will make them hear my words, that they may learn to fear me all the days that they shall live upon the earth, and that they may teach their children"* (Deut 4:10). The context in which this command is set is that of a rehearsal aimed at bringing to the mind of the people the providence of God and by this stirring up obedience and duty to God. In this context comes the charge to pay diligent and particular attention to the Word of the LORD. This attention is to be perpetual and so the process of learning and teaching is enjoined in verse 10. This teaching is to take place within the domestic setting with the parents teaching their household.

---

[272] Charles William Heathcote, *The Essentials of Religious Education* (Boston: Sherman, French & Company, 1916), 12.

[273] Heathcote, *The Essentials of Religious Education*, 12.

CHAPTER III: TEACHING AVENUES AVAILABLE FOR THE CHURCH TODAY

In another place, the command is given: *"And thou shalt teach them diligently unto thy children and shalt talk of them when thou sittest in thine house and when thou walkest by the way, and when thou liest down, and when thou risest up"* (Deut 6:7). The context in which this command is given is that of the religion and devotions of Israel with verses 4 and 5 presenting the creed of Israel. The context also contains the sum of the duty God requires of His people in relation to their LORD (verse 2, 13-17) and in relation to their fellow-men. All these requirements are perpetual, and they are to be perpetuated practically in the lives of the people through the avenue of teaching. This teaching is set to take place in the family.

The prescribed means for keeping religion and devotion and obedience to God alive is instruction in the home. The responsibility to accomplish this is laid upon the parents, and the methods implied require frequent repetition and constant indoctrination with the parents seizing every opportunity and trying every godly method to instil into the minds and hearts of their children the knowledge of God. The Law, ordinances and ways of the LORD are to be known and kept, as well as followed, and observed by everyone in the family for it is only by this means that the people of God can keep themselves from the temptations that would so easily ensnare them and separate themselves from the sins that would so easily corrupt and defile them.

For examples that present the place of teaching in the family, there is the plea of Manoah in Judges 13:8 where he asked, *"O my Lord, let the man of God which thou didst send come again unto us, and teach us what we shall do unto the child that shall be born."* And also there is the testimony of Abraham in Genesis 18:19 where the Lord says of Abraham: *"For I know him, that he will command his children and his household after him and they shall keep the way of the LORD to do justice and judgment; that the LORD may bring upon Abraham that which he hath spoken of him."* The responsibility of the parents to teach is further exemplified in the role of the society in dealing with stubborn children as set forth in Deuteronomy 21:18ff. The Bible points this out when it states in verse 18-19: *"If a man have a stubborn and rebellious son, which will not obey the voice of his father, or the voice of his mother, and that, when they have chastened him, will not hearken to them: then shall his father and his mother lay hold on him and bring him out unto the elders of his city, and unto the gate of his place."* The process set forth here presumes the responsibility of the parents to teach and instruct their children and thus places the role played by the elders of the city as secondary to the teaching role of the parents. The process also sets forth the bounds and limits of the responsibility of the parents as teaching by presenting a case where despite the teaching, the son still turns out rebellious and refuses to hearken.

The first nine chapters of the book of Proverbs are instructions to a young person represented by *"my son"* and with the duty and responsibility required of him as hearkening to the voice of the instruction of his father and his mother. This is seen in Proverbs 1:8 and 6:20 with the father setting himself forth as an example of one who had benefited from parental instruction in Proverbs 4:3.

The family, therefore, has a very important role in complementing the church in cultivating and maintaining the piety of its members and that this role was to include inculcation and teaching conducted in the homes. The family provides the primary platform for the practical working out of the faith for all its members. In making use of this platform to practise Christianity, the members of the family grow strong in faith, and as they mature in the faith, in turn the church is also strengthens. The ages in which the church knew this and embraced it evidences great maturity and piety in both the church assemblies as well as in the society. The *Directions of the General Assembly, concerning Secret and Private Worship* states,

Besides the publick Worshipping Congregations, mercifully established in this Land, in great purity; It is expedient and necessary that Secret Worship of each person alone, and Private worship of Families be pressed and set up: That with National Reformation, the profession and power of Godliness both Personal and Domestick be advanced.[274]

The General assembly then went on to give guidelines and directions in the setting up of private and family worship together with censures on those who would not. In their directions, both private and family worship are set as a necessity pointing out that it "is most necessary, that every one apart and by themselves be given to prayer and Meditation."[275] The child's duty to hearken and obey is hinged on the parents' duty to teach and set forth an example. Ambrose Isaac in his work "The Well-ordered Family" gives some insightful directives to the maintenance of a godly family which presents the balance between the duties of the parents and the children in the establishing and maintaining of a godly family. He writes,

> Now that we may comfortably carry on these family duties, observe we 1. Our entrance into them. 2. Our proceedings in them. For entrance, we must lay a good foundation in those that belong to this family.
>
> 1st. In the governor, whose duty it is, 1. To endeavour in a special manner for <u>knowledge in God's word</u>, and for <u>holiness of conversation</u>; this would tend much to the preservation of his authority, who otherwise will be slighted and disregarded. 2. To <u>marry in the Lord</u>, and then to <u>live chastely in wedlock</u>, that there may be a holy seed. 3. To <u>beware whom he admits dwelling with him</u>. See David's resolution herein. *Mine eyes shall be upon the faithful of the land, that they may dwell with me: he that walketh in a perfect way shall serve me; he that worketh deceit shall not dwell within my house; he that telleth lies shall not tarry in my sight.*
>
> 2nd. In the governed, whose duty it is both to <u>join together in the performance of family duties</u> with their governor, and to <u>submit to his government</u> [emphasis added]: – *my son, hear the instruction of thy father, and forsake not the law of thy mother; for they shall be an ornament of grace unto thy head, and chains about thy neck.*[276]

Isaac Ambrose, in his address, points out the need for teaching, the family as the primary place for such teaching, and the role of the members within the family for the teaching to be effective. An ill-balanced family proves difficult to manage and govern biblically, hence the need for a God-fearing and Bible-knowing head and governor as well as a family bond that is not one of unequal yoke, but one that is in the Lord. Dangerous and destructive teachings from outside can be stemmed by the carefulness in oversight exercised by the head of the family in the relations maintained by the members of the family as well as in those admitted into the family and home. This is sorely lacking in this present age. The pressures of the ever increasingly fast-paced world and the rapid urbanization are affecting the family especially by depriving it of time. With parents having to work long hours and some even juggling two or three jobs just to make

---

[274] *Directions of the General Assembly concerning Secret and Private Worship, and mutual edification, for cherishing Piety, for maintaining Unity, and avoiding Schism and Division. with an Act for observing these Directions, and for censuring such as use to neglect Family Worship. AND An act against such as withdraw themselves from the Publick Worship in their own Congregations* (Edinburgh: Evan Tyler, 1648), 5.

[275] Ibid.

[276] Isaac Ambrose, *Works of Isaac Ambrose, sometime minister of Garstang in Lancashire* (London: Caxton Press, nd), 125.

ends meet, and children having to leave early for school and stay up late learning and mastering their lessons. There is less and less time left for instruction by word and example. This has deprived the family, the church and the society of many benefits that piety would afford them. Christian parents ought to understand that they have a two-fold responsibility to the family. The world would seek to emphasize the physical over the spiritual responsibilities. But Scripture sets forth both in good balance. Ambrose points out the two duties of parents as follows:

> That which in general they owe to the whole family, is both to their bodies and souls.
>
> 1 To their bodies; concerning which, saith the apostle. *He that provideth not for his own, and especially for those of his own house, hath denied the faith, and is worse than an infidel.*
>
> 2. To their souls; concerning which, some duties they are to perform to the family, and some to require of the family.[277]

The care of the souls and the duties that accompany it, within the context of the family, is almost all but forgotten. The church has contributed in part to this by not presenting the biblical balance and thus keeping the families weak. Many who regularly attend churches and consider themselves Christians do not know what duties are required of families. Ambrose points out the duties of the parents to the promotion of piety in the family as follows:

> 1. To provide that they may live under the public ministry for otherwise how should they be brought into the sheepfold of Christ, if they hear not the voice of the Chief Shepherd speaking unto them by those whom he hath sent.
>
> 2. To oversee the ways of their families, that they serve God and as in all other duties, so especially in sanctifying the Sabbath to this the very words in the fourth commandment bind: all masters of families; *Remember thou, and thy son, and thy — daughter, and thy man-servant, and thy maid*: where the Lord speaks by name to the governors, as if he would make them overseers of this work of sanctifying of his Sabbaths.
>
> 3. To offer prayers and praises to the Lord, morning and evening. This was David's practice; *Evening, and morning, and at noon, will I pray, and cry aloud, and he shall hear my voice.*
>
> 4. To instruct their families privately in matters of religion, that they may not only profess, but feel the power of religion.[278]

The Christian parent is to be the teacher, leader and priest at home. As teacher, it is the parent's duty to ensure that the members of the family are brought under the sound of the Gospel and are instructed in the matters of faith and piety. As leader, it is the parent's duty to govern and guide the family, ensuring that their ways are pleasing to the Lord and that they serve the Lord and attend to every opportunity for public worship. As priest, it is the parent's duty to ensure that the religion of the home is vibrant and that all members are present and gathered at the set times for worship as well as that all members present at the family worship participate in offering prayers and praises to the Lord. As the parents or guardians governing the home fulfil these duties, they ensure that the ministry of the church is enhanced since the success and efficacy of the public ministry of the church is tied to the commitment of the family and especially the parents to the Word preached and taught in the church and in the family set up. This commitment, according to Ambrose, implies,

---

[277] Ambrose, *Works of Isaac Ambrose*, 126.

[278] Ibid, 126.

1. A familiar catechizing of them in the principles of religion. Thus were parents commanded of old. *Thou shalt teach these words diligently unto thy children, and shall talk of them when thou sittest in thine house, and when thou walkest by the way, and when thou liest down, and when thou risest up.*

2. A daily reading of scriptures in their hearing, directing them to mark and to make use of them: so Timothy was trained up by his parents, and that from his childhood.

3. A careful endeavouring that they profit by the public ministry: to this end, they must prepare them to hear the word, by considering God's ordinances, promises, and their own necessities. 2. They must remind them to look into the word for Christ, and for communion with Christ. 3. They must examine them after the ordinance, what they have learned, and what use they can make of it.[279]

The challenge this age faces is that parents do not have enough time to know their children and to direct them in the ways of the LORD, and children are deprived of seeing godly examples from their parents who are committed elsewhere in earthly pursuits. The rising popularity of boarding schools in Kenya has kept children away from home for up to twelve weeks at a time. All this is done in search of good grades that will be the key to a better future, a future which is pursued at all costs and many a times even at the sacrifice of the family and with it the avenues of teaching availed by family time. The church has been left as the only instructor in piety[280] and morals, yet its time severely restricted by its membership due to many other "commitments" and so the effectiveness of the church too has been severely hampered. The balance clearly presented in Scripture and in the creeds of the church is that of a joint and concerted effort both by the church and the home in the instruction of the children and in the spiritual growth of its members.

What is taught in the church must be followed up in the family. Religion is reflected in the home, not by chance but by deliberate and conscious effort in the family. Francis W. Harper points out the concerted effort of parents and church in instruction of children in the faith,

These are the words which the church puts into the mouth of her minister to say to the godparents about their godchildren as he stands beside the font, — "Chiefly ye shall provide that they may learn the Creed, the Lord's Prayer, and the Ten Commandments." No wonder when "the Creed contains all we need to believe, the Commandments all we need do, the Lord's Prayer all we need as for," — our faith, our works, our wants. With good right too, it is that the creed comes first, for in the Lord's Prayer we call upon God and in the Creed we believe in God; and it is written, *How shall they call upon Him in whom they have not believed?*[281]

Harper, quoting from the baptismal order in the Book of Common Prayer, shows that in the raising of godly children and teaching them what is necessary for faith and practice, there is need for avenues and means within the family context in which the

---

[279] Ambrose, *Works of Isaac Ambrose* 126.

[280] True piety is a principle which leads a man to honour God, in everything. It will have an influence upon him abroad, and at home; in society, and in solitude; upon common, as well as extraordinary occasions. It is this principle which leads a Christian to exercise a religious care over his family. And in this part of his conduct he shows, not only the devout state of his affections, but likewise the soundness of his judgment. Every wise man sees the necessity of having some plan of domestic government, in order to preserve his house from being a scene of confusion and misery. [James Bean, *Family Worship: a course of morning and evening prayers for everyday in the month to which is prefixed a discourse on family religion* (London: C. and J. Rivington, 1826), v.]

[281] Francis Whaley Harper, *Church Teaching for the Church's Children. An arrangement and exposition of the church catechism* (London: George Bell and Sons, 1877), 3.

Word is inculcated. "These are the duties that governors owe to families in respect of their souls; to correct them, catechize them, admonish them, call on them, read to them, pray for them."[282] Thus in the family context, the avenues that can be effectively used include (i) family worship and (ii) catechism.

Family Worship

James W. Alexander wrote in the preface to his book *Thoughts on Family Worship*,

> In a period when the world is every day making inroads into the church, it has especially invaded the household. Our church cannot compare with that of the seventeenth century in this regard. Along with Sabbath observance and catechizing of children, family worship has lost ground. There are many heads of families, communicants in our churches, and, according to a scarcely credible report, some ruling elders and deacons who maintain no stated daily service of God in their dwellings.[283]

This was a description of the 1800s and is taken from a book that was first published in 1847! And back in that time there was the worrying trend of the world making inroads into the church as families neglected the practice of spiritual things at home including family worship. The world gains ground in the church where family worship loses ground in the homes. How true this is of the present age. In many a Christian family, the plaque with the inscription "Christ is the Head of this family; the unseen guest at every meal; the silent listener at every conversation" can be found hanging on the wall. But in many of these homes, Christ is indeed kept silent, as no time is given to hear Him speak through the Word. He is often left unseen, as never do voices rise up in His praise! The home in which Christ is head should logically make time for Him and at every place in which Christ is a guest, logically, there should He find fellowship with those who have invited Him in. Thus every Christian home needs to have a family altar and a time for family worship. Where Christ is resident, He needs to have presidency! This means that every Christian home should be a house of prayer and the call to the head of the family should be,

> If in the family thou art the best.
> Pray oft, and be the mouth unto the rest;
> Whom God hath made the heads of families,
> He hath made priest to offer sacrifice.
> Daily let part of Holy Writ be read,
> Let, as the body, so the soul, be fed;
> For look, how many souls in thy house be,
> With just as many souls God trusteth thee.
> J. Weaver

Many a time, the witness of the church to the world is severely lacking and when one looks for the church's witness in the world one cannot find it; but rather what is evident is the presence of the world in the church! This more and more reflects the condition of the church today and the reason is that the family is the heart of society, and the home altar is the heart of the Christian family. Decay in the heart means decay in the life of society; and purity and vigour in the heart means strength and virtue in the life of the

---

[282] Ambrose, *Works of Isaac Ambrose*, 127.

[283] James W. Alexander, *Thoughts on Family Worship* (Morgan PA: Soli Deo Gloria Publications, 1998), v.

nation. The world has mastered the art of infiltrating the church through the Christian family. The way the church is going to stem the tide of worldliness is by restoring and strengthening religion and piety at home. One of the best avenues for doing this is through family worship!

The Basis for Family Worship

There are two institutions founded by God: the institution of marriage (family) and the institution of the church. The family is not only the heart of the society, but it is also the basic building block of the church. We read in the New Testament about the church that is in the house (Rom. 16:5; 1 Cor. 16:19; Col. 4:15; Phlm. 1:2). We also see the Gospel having a family focus when we see Cornelius and his family (Acts 10) as well as the Philippian jailer and his family receiving the Gospel (Acts 16). Thus, the church today needs to pay attention to build and strengthen families present in the church as this is what is reflected in the biblical pattern. In Ephesians 3:15, the church is described as *"the whole family,"* and this is the picture of fellowship the Bible presents. When we consider the place of the family in the church, we learn the following:

Commitment to God is a family issue – Joshua 24:15

The commitment of the church cannot go beyond the commitment of the individual members and since the individual members are also members in families, it can be implied that the commitment of the church cannot go beyond the commitment of the family. Joshua presents the father's position of authority when he asserts *"as for me"* (Josh. 24:15)! Family commitment begins with father's personal commitment. This inspires co-operation and participation from the family.

Family is the agency for strengthening the faith – 2 Timothy 1:5; 3:15

The passion and desire for the Lord and His work is planted in the family and the faith is developed in the church. What we find in the example of the faith of Timothy which first was in his grandmother and also in his mother. This presents the importance of the family in planting and propagating the faith.

Family is the agency for spreading the Gospel of the Kingdom – Proverbs 22:6

The family is the first school for every child born into this world, and thus the family is the best place to plant the Gospel seed. This means therefore that the family's place in the work of missions is a great one indeed. Not only is it a place where the children can be taught, but as a place of outreach it is a place that even friends, relatives, visitors and strangers can be ministered unto thus making the family a good agent for spreading the Gospel.

From the above, we see how the family as an institution fits into the church. But the question would be: how can the parents and the family at large be able to take full advantage of these opportunities and be a blessing to the church? How can the church equip and encourage the family to make use of the opportunities? The answer may be called the "family church" or in other words that are more common would be "family altar" or "family worship." This is presented in Deuteronomy 4:1-10 as God's desire of the family. This is what the church when working with the family needs to work at! Where the family church is strong and vibrant, there the faith grows, zeal burns and the Gospel spreads!

The Practice of Family Worship

The family altar may be said to be the first line of defence for the Christian church. It is the standard that can be raised to stem the tide of materialism, worldliness, idolatry, apostasy and every false "ism." The church can help the family by properly teaching the membership, by equipping them with materials like the Shorter Catechism, etc. and by supporting them through pastoral visitation in which the pastors can spend time with the family at the family altar. The practice of family worship is to reflect the nature of domestic religion in which worship is rendered to God by all members of a house. Thus, when considering the practice of family worship, we need to consider the role of the parents as well as the role of the children.

The role of the father in family worship – Job 1:1-5

J. W. Alexander observes concerning Job as priest of his household: "The service of Job on behalf of his children was a perpetual service; he "sent and sanctified them, and rose up early in the morning, and offered burnt-offerings according to the number of them all; thus did Job continually;" or, as it is in the Hebrew, 'all the days.'"[284]

From the example of Job, we can learn about the commitment that the father is to show in order for the family worship to be a rooted tradition and practice in the family. When one reads the first five verses of the book of Job, one notices the repeated reference to Job as a *"man"* (Job 1:1, 3) highlighting not only the maleness of Job as opposed to the female (a point which emphasizes the role of the father in the family) but also the humanity of Job in contrast to deity or divinity of any kind (a point which emphasizes that Job was human)! So what kind of man was Job? (i) He was a spiritual man, a man concerned with the things of God (Job 1:1, 5). (ii) He was a family man, a man who was head of his house and as head, was concerned about the spiritual welfare of his household (Job 1:2, 4-5). (ii) He was a busy and wealthy man, a man who had wealth and was aware of the condition of his property (Job 1:3). The commitment that Job had for the spiritual welfare of his family is reflected in his concern as well as his continual service on their behalf. The service that Job did as head and priest of his family was one that required.

(i) Time – Job *"rose up early in the morning"* (Job 1:5). Job gave the best hours to the service of the Lord and not his worst hours! The practice of family worship is often given no priority in many homes and prayers are often said when members of the household are tired and weary.

(ii) Resources — *"and offered burnt offerings according to the number of them all"* (Job 1:5). In order for a sacrifice of burnt offering to be made, preparation was required of (i) the wood for the fire that would burn the offering; (ii) the animal to be burnt as an offering (both in choosing of an appropriate animal and in the dressing of the animal)! Many would prefer to offer to the Lord that which does not cost them anything and would seek to worship without preparation.

---

[284] Alexander, *Thoughts on Family Worship* 4.

(iii) Dedication – *"Thus did Job continually"* (Job 1:5). Job was committed to the service that he did. Unlike many, he did not start with zeal and enthusiasm which would slowly fade with the passing of time. He kept at it and did it continually. Many a family worship has changed and waned with time and in homes where once the scripture was read, hymns sung and prayers made, now only an occasional prayer is heard!

The role of the children in family worship – 1 Timothy 5:4

For the family worship to be pleasing and acceptable to the Lord, it requires not only the godly leadership and commitment of the father but also the participation of the rest of the family. The scripture thus also points out the role of the children in family worship. Alexander observes,

> As prayer is the main part of all family worship, so the chief benefit to children is that they are the subjects of such prayer. As the great topic of the parent's heart is his offspring, so they will be his great burden at the throne of grace. ... The direct influence of family prayer is then to bring down the benediction of Almighty God upon the children of the house. ... Daily worship, in common, encourages children to acts of devotion. It reminds them, however giddy or care-less they may be, that God is to be adored.[285]

Paul writing to Timothy gives instructions by which Christian families within the church are to be directed. In this he highlights the duty of both the church and the family in relating to members of the congregation and in particular widows. It is in this context that we find insight into the role of the children in family worship. Paul says, *"let them learn first to show piety at home and to requite their parents: for that is good and acceptable before God"* (1 Timothy 5:4)

> He who is prayed for will know and feel that he is prayed for. Paths of duty will be indicated; dangers will be marked; sins will be arrayed before conscience; divine blessings will be set forth as infinitely desirable. By the same means, through God's blessing, incentives to piety will be reiterated, convictions deepened and the object of faith placed in open light. Where all this is done day by day, the heart of the child must experience some affection until it is steeled by habitual resistance. The daily regular and solemn reading of God's holy Word by a parent before his children is one of the most powerful agencies of a Christian life.[286]

Thus, to the children, the family altar is the place where they begin to please the Lord. There they learn:

(i) To show piety at home — "to act piously or reverently" toward God, one's country, magistrates, relations, and all to whom dutiful regard or reverence is due. It is at the family altar that morals are shaped and virtues are built and thus children should be at the family altar with open hearts and ready minds!

(ii) To requite their parents — "to repay them, as far as possible, for all their kindness. This debt can never be wholly repaid, but still a child should feel it a matter of sacred obligation to do as much toward it as possible."[287] Thus, from the family altar, the children are to learn the ways of the Lord and are to display obedience to the Lord!

---

[285] Alexander, *Thoughts on Family Worship* 34.

[286] Alexander, *Thoughts on Family Worship* 35.

[287] Albert Barnes, *Barnes' Notes on the Bible – 1 Timothy* [CD-ROM].

CHAPTER III: TEACHING AVENUES AVAILABLE FOR THE CHURCH TODAY

Practical Steps for a Family Worship Service

Finally, what are some practical tips that are to be considered both for the planning, practising and preserving the family worship? A profitable and God-honouring family worship requires planning as well as participation and cooperation from the whole family. The program may begin with singing in order to quieten the hearts and bring focus to those present at the family altar. The singing may be followed by a general prayer and then the reading of scripture and catechism. After the reading and expounding of scriptures, prayer requests may be taken after which prayer is made for the family and for all present at the altar. Some important points to note may be as follows:

(i) During singing, appropriate hymns should be chosen to encourage the participation of all present. For example, for families with young children, hymns with choruses would be preferable in order to give young children the time to sing as the choruses will be repeated. Family with older youths may add variety by encouraging special arrangements like solos or duets on certain portions of the hymns. Concerning the singing of hymns, "Good Mr. Philip Henry used to say that the singing of God's people at family worship was a way to hold forth godliness to such as pass by their windows, like Rahab's scarlet thread (Joshua 2:17)."[288]

(ii) During Scripture reading, variety in reading may be added by either reading responsively, or reading in turns. Narrative sections may be better for families with young children with lively reading made to capture the interest and attention of the children. Some time may be assigned on Sundays to reinforce the lessons learned from Sunday School and church service. Concerning the reading and explaining of Scriptures, "(h)ow far the portion of Scripture which is read shall be expounded must depend on the gifts of the officiating person and the circumstances and character of the family."

(iii) During prayer, focus should be made on the family and its needs in order to highlight the practicality of religion and the presence and providence of God in the family. Hence, special graces must be highlighted and answers to prayers pointed out with thanksgiving made for every good gift. Concerning the time and manner of prayer at the family altar, Annie Wilson highlights the following:

> This should be short. A very small child maybe taught to be reverent because "we are talking to God." The more closely the petitions follow Scripture phrases the better, for nowhere can anyone who is anxious to learn to pray gain more efficient help than in his Bible. ... Many families close with the Lord's prayer, the whole circle joining in it. This is well. The form of the Lord's prayer was given by one who knew every need of human nature, and it is very full and complete—answers for any age or occasion. Every child should learn it, for it literally teaches us how to pray and what to pray for.[289]

Considering the nature and benefit of family worship to the family, the following points about family worship should be noted:

1. It must be taken seriously and approached with gravity. There should be focus and dedication at the family altar. The time for family worship should not be shared with any distracting influences. All noise and disturbances should be shut out. Switch off phones, radios, television sets (not just mute the sound)! The time for family worship should not be rushed through or attended to with haste so that "we can move on to more

---

[288] Alexander, *Thoughts on Family Worship* 127.

[289] Annie E. Wilson, *The Family Altar, helps and suggestions for family worship* (Richmond VA: Presbyterian Committee of Publication, 1898), 7-8.

important things!" Many children raised in Christian homes have despised religion because the home religion was despised and insulted!

    2. It must be held consistently and kept regularly. There should be a set time for family worship which should be known to all members of the family. Its observance should not be subject to questions such as: "Will we have prayer now or tonight?" For its regulation, as much as possible, heads of the family must ensure that they plan their time to avail themselves at home in time for family worship. Late night visitation should be discouraged where family worship is done in the evenings; and sleeping in late discouraged where family worship is done in the mornings! No one in the family is to be excused from family worship and thus the time set should consider the participation of all members.

    3. It has to be regulated in its observation by the family. There should be not only a set time and place for family worship, but also a set program that can give some sense of normalcy and regulation. This is to ensure that *"all things be done decently and in order"* (1 Cor 14:40). In its regulation, the family worship has the following "essential steps":

1. Find a time convenient for all the family together. The after-dinner hour is usually the best.

2. Find a place where all the family can meet together for fifteen to thirty minutes.

3. Sing choruses and hymns let the father or mother lead. The songs of this COMPANION TO FAMILY WORSHIP are specially chosen for Family Worship.

4. Read God's Word everybody should have a Bible. We recommend the King James Version. Take turns to read, using daily reading helps.

5. Pray together one or all may pray, in turns. Father or mother should lead.[290]

Alexander also gives suggestions to the constituents of family worship saying,

The constituent parts of family worship, when fully observed, are, first, the reading of Scriptures; second, singing praise to God; and, third, prayer. And these may very properly follow each other in these orders. ... The length of the domestic worship is worthy of attention. It was the fault of our forefathers to make it insufferably long. This goes far to destroy all good influence on the young by creating weariness and disgust. ... Family prayer should be varied; otherwise the inevitable result will be formalism and tediousness. Indeed the snare into which we are most prone to fall in this service is that of sameness and routine. Daily changes in the condition of the family will infallibly work a corresponding change in the prayers if they are sincere.[291]

From the above statements, it is clear that family worship is to be regulated in the sense that there are elements that must needs be present for it to be called worship, yet there needs to be room for variations which would give the family worship life and vitality corresponding to the life of the family. Therefore, prayer, scripture reading and hymn singing are to be perpetually present and regulated, yet varied in order to maintain life and vitality. A sample family worship session which takes about twenty to thirty minutes and which include singing, praying, and reading of Scripture/Catechism may have duties distributed as follows:

---

[290] *Every Home A Godly Home* (Singapore: Tabernacle Books), 1.

[291] Alexander, *Thoughts on Family Worship*, 112, 114.

Family member in charge	Duty to perform	Description of details
Father	Scripture reading	• Choose portion to be read • Read passage or assign someone • Highlight and explain one or two verses • select and explain catechism section
Father	Family prayer	• Take charge of prayer time • appoint person to note requests • appoint persons to pray • explain importance of prayer to all
Mother	Hymn singing	• Choose songs to be sung • lead the singing of hymns • explain meaning of hard words
All members present	Participation	• Be present and punctual • accept roles assigned to them • participate with understanding and love for God and family.

Family worship has been shown to be a happy instrument for the promotion of piety in a household. A true Christian will desire that his children and dependents should be not merely safe, but eminently holy. Are you conscious of any such desires? In the absence of them can you persuade yourself that you are a child of God? Or feeling them, can you possibly endure a life without so much as one common prayer as a family? Have you no call for domestic thanksgiving? No daily mercies? No special deliverances? No long-continued exemptions from evil? It is monstrous that a Christian household should be absolutely dumb on these points. I scarcely know how it can be so. Some tribute of gratitude will surely burst forth, unawares and ascend to heaven from a sanctified dwelling.[292]

Catechism

There is an increasing drive to forsake the creeds and confessions with claims that creeds and confessions bind the conscience, stifle the growth of truth, and promote discord and strife. In addition, the modern "no creed but Christ, no book but Bible" that rose from the Stone Campbell movement of the early 19th Century which sought to return the church to "apostolic Christianity" has given rise to practice that rejects the study, memorization, affirming or pledging any form of written creeds and, with it, the use of the catechisms of the church. This has deprived the church of the second avenue that has been profitably used by God's people in different ages. As regards the place of the catechism in the life of the church, James Fisher, in *The Westminster's Shorter Catechism Explained*, notes,

---

[292] Alexander, *Thoughts on Family Worship* 140.

Nothing tends more to the advantage and well-being of the church, than sound standards of doctrine, worship, and government; because, as they are a strong bulwark against contrary errors and opinions, so they tend to <u>preserve truth in its purity, and the professors of it in unity and harmony among themselves</u>. On the other hand, there is nothing more galling to the adversaries of truth, than such public standards, because they are a very severe <u>check and curb upon their unbounded and licentious liberty</u> [emphasis added], being directly levelled against their erroneous schemes, and plainly discovering the harmonious chain of scripture truth, in opposition to them.[293]

Contrary to claims made by those who reject them, confessions, creeds and catechisms, were intended to (i) preserve the truth as well as the unity and harmony of the church, (ii) stem the propagation and growth of error by exposing it, and (iii) instructing the church in the knowledge of Scripture truth and church history since most of the church's confessions and creeds were written in response to errors and heresies that the church grappled with at different points of time. Thus, as Fisher notes above, they "tend more to the advantage of the church" and are a "strong bulwark against contrary errors and opinions." In addition to this, Fisher goes on to assert that the catechism is not an invention of the church as it draws its warrant from the Scripture. He writes,

The divine warrant for such composures, is abundantly clear from 2 Tim. 1. 13, where we read of the form of sound words wherein Paul instructed Timothy; and Heb. v. 12, of the first principles of the oracles of God and chap. vi. 1, of the principles of the doctrine of Christ, — Besides, there are several summaries, or compendious systems of divine truth, recorded in scripture; such as Exod. xx. 2—18; Matt. vi. 9—14; 1 Tim. iii. 16; and Tit. 2. 11 — 15, with many others, which are the examples, or patterns, upon which the Christian churches, both in ancient and latter times, have deduced, from the pure fountain of the word, the principal articles of their holy religion, as a test and standard of orthodoxy amongst them.[294]

The catechism as a tool for teaching, uses questions and answers to present the teachings of the Bible in a systematic, clear, easily memorizable and logical form to those instructed. The subject of the instruction given through the catechism is the "Fear of the LORD" as the Psalmist calls, *"Come, ye children, hearken unto me: I will teach you the fear of the LORD"* (Ps. 34:11). The catechism, through the use of questions, draws the attention of the children (*"Come, ye children, hearken unto me"*) and, through the answers given to the questions, instructs them (*"I will teach you the fear of the LORD"*). Starr Meade in introducing the book, "Training Hearts, Teaching Minds" points out another reason for the neglect of catechisms both in the church and more specifically in the home. He writes,

There is, however, another graver reason catechisms have fallen out of favor. It is that doctrinal instruction in general, for anyone and especially for children, has become unpopular. In an attempt to attract non believers, the church has occupied herself with providing things the world finds attractive. In doing so she has lost sight of her true purpose of being the pillar and support of the truth.

---

[293] James Fisher, *The Westminster's Shorter Catechism Explained, by way of questions and answers part I, by several ministers of the Gospel* (Philadelphia: Presbyterian Board of Publication, 1850), iii – iv.

[294] Fisher, *The Westminster's Shorter Catechism Explained,* iv.

CHAPTER III: TEACHING AVENUES AVAILABLE FOR THE CHURCH TODAY

From the pulpit, comfort, inspiration, and "spirituality" are acceptable; doctrine is not. In a misguided attempt to maintain unity at any cost, doctrinal teaching is shunned because "doctrine divides."[295]

This assessment was well illustrated in the introduction to this chapter where Dickson Nkonge Kagema's article titled, "The Use of Gospel Hip-hop as an Avenue of Evangelizing Youth in Kenya Today: A Practical Approach." It was used to show how the church indeed has lost her focus and her true purpose as she endeavours to be more appealing to the world, rather than pleasing to her Lord. As Paul rightly asserted, *"If I yet pleased men, I should not be the servant of Christ"* (Gal. 1:10b). The church ought to be of another spirit, not that of appealing and pleasing men, to the extent of altering the Word of God or omitting what is a divine duty and call, in order to gain favour, or receive the applause, or as in the case of Paul, reprieve and rest from rage and opposition, but, rather, the spirit of the church ought to be that of (i) commitment and faithfulness to her Lord and His Word, (ii) sincerity and purity of intentions in the discharge of the commission and call committed to it, and (iii) consistency and persistence in the use of means available and acceptable in the discharge of her true purpose. It is here where the use of the catechism finds value in the church's teaching mandate. In talking about the church's true purpose, Meade writes,

> The supreme test of a church, however, at least from the perspective of the New Testament writers, is this: Is the church the pillar and support of the truth? Is it thoroughly acquainted with the truth of the gospel as given in the Scriptures? Does it exalt God's Word, giving it the place of preeminence in all its worship and in all its activities? Does it defend the truth at whatever cost, proclaiming it without compromise in a world of confusion and falsehood? Does it call its people to *know* God's Word for the purpose of faithfully *living* by God's Word?[296]

The catechism, as an avenue for teaching, aids the church in ensuring that by a systematic course of instruction through questions and answers, the members of the church know the Word of God and live by it. Meade further observes that "the church's most critical task is to uphold and proclaim the truth as it was delivered to her by her Lord."[297] The catechism's questions and answers work towards accomplishing this by developing the children's religious and moral duty, fixing biblical truth to their memory by the repeated use of simple and direct questions and answers in plain language.

In his address to parents in the book "Lectures on the Catechism," James Abercombie describes the need for the catechism by decrying the peril of the neglect of children and youth in words that remain true and reflect the conditions of the family even in this age when he writes,

> The general and truly lamentable inattention of parents, with respect to the instruction of their children in religious knowledge, induces the present publication.
>
> It is indeed, a subject of very alarming and distressing observation to every serious, every real Christian, that the rising generation are so cruelly, so criminally neglected at home, as to their spiritual and eternal interests; and that in so high a degree, that it requires not the spirit of prophecy to foretell, that unless an immediate reformation of conduct towards them take place, they will be a generation of Infidels.

---

[295] Starr Meade, *Training Hearts, Teaching Minds: family devotions based on the Shorter Catechism* (Philipsburg New Jersey: P&R Publishing, 2000), 3.

[296] Meade, *Training Hearts, Teaching Minds:* , 1.

[297] Ibid.

This assertion is founded not merely, upon vague supposition, or groundless apprehension, but upon the irresistible conviction resulting from experience.[298]

He then goes on to describe how the declension of his time had been visible, and how it was directly linked to the neglect of the use of the catechism as a teaching tool, a tool that had been, until the time of neglect, a very basic and useful tool in the importing of biblical knowledge and, through the knowledge acquired, the strengthening of morality and religion through its instruction. He decries the ignorance of the principles of religion particularly among teenagers and charges the parents for it, saying, "Dreadful, cruel inattention! That in a Christian country, children, many of them youths of fifteen years, the offspring of parents calling themselves Christians, should, at that age, be as ignorant of the principles of the Christian religion,"[299] thus implying that during his time the catechism as a tool for instruction was used in the family and aimed at training children in the principles and doctrines of the Bible. Abercombie then goes on to write, "O, Parents, Sponsors, Guardians! Awake from your spiritual lethargy! Rouse yourselves from your infatuated devotion to worldly objects; your criminal, fatal indifference to the spiritual and eternal welfare of those whom Providence hath placed immediately under your authority and direction."[300]

The inattention of this age in the church, has extended from the family and the parents to the pulpit and the pastors. How many pastors in this day and age would, like Abercombie, claim a habit of examining their children and youth in the catechism of the denomination weekly? The inattention of the pulpit deepens the slumber and spiritual lethargy of the home. The worldly objects and pursuits of the age have multiplied a hundred fold or even more and the eternal welfare of the youth and children set at double jeopardy. This alone should be sufficient to convince one and sundry of the need to return to the catechism in the family. What then is the role and place of the catechism in the Christian education of the family? How should the pastor view and use the catechism in his pastoral ministry to the family? These questions can be answered in part by first answering the question 'what is catechism?' G. F. McClear states that a catechism "is a course of instruction by question and answer in the first principles, or elements, of any subject."[301] Meade adds,

> A catechism is simply and instructional guide. It is a handbook of questions and answers designed to teach principles of religion. To "catechize" children is to teach them to memorize the answers found in a catechism, so that when the catechism questions are asked, the children can reply with the correct responses. Because a good catechism is at the same time concise and thorough, when children have learned it well, their understanding of the basic doctrines of the Christian faith can be tested and found to be complete.[302]

As a course of instruction, the catechism is a teaching tool. As a course of instruction by question and answer, it aids memorization and as it focuses on elements and first principles, it emphasizes nurturing and grounding in the faith of the young both in

---

[298]James Abercombie, *Lectures on the Catechism, on confirmation, and the liturgy of the Protestant Episcopal Church; delivered to the students of that denomination in the Philadelphia Academy* (Philadelphia: Bradford and Inskeep, 1811), xiii.

[299]Ibid, xiv.

[300]Ibid.

[301]G. F. McClear, *A Class Book of the Catechism of the Church of England* (London & Cambridge: McMillan and Co., 1868), 1.

[302]Meade, *Training Hearts, Teaching Minds*, 2.

CHAPTER III: TEACHING AVENUES AVAILABLE FOR THE CHURCH TODAY

age and in faith. Many today have a reluctance to employ catechism in their churches and when they do, it is but a shallow formality lacking any meaning other than a church requirement mainly for new converts and adherents. The common misconception, which has become a popular concept, is that "if the Bible is preached, then there is no need for catechism for members." This has resulted in the side-lining of catechism and limited its use to follow up of new converts and baptismal candidates. The assumption is that catechism tends to produce mere intellectual assent. Churches thus fail or fall short in their attempt to produce true heart religion by depriving its membership of what systematic and regular catechism would offer.

The preaching of the Bible must necessarily be accompanied by catechism of the church. Concern for conversions, fervour and holy living should almost invariably stimulate and drive one's interest and commitment to learning individual truths of the Christian faith continually and systematically and this ought to necessitate the need for teaching doctrine in a full, systematic and coherent manner. Catechism offers an avenue for this and those who express antagonism against the use of catechism in inculcating precise doctrine, often in its place, elevate an experience oriented view of "spirituality" that has neither biblical nor historical basis for such claim. Both the Bible and history present catechisation as a legitimate tool for teaching God's Word systematically to the whole church.

During the Middle Ages (the Dark Ages), the Bible was taken away from the people, and Bible-based catechetical instruction languished. The church was in deep ignorance and superstition but with the emergence of the Reformation and the Bible returned to the people, catechisms re-emerged. In the introduction to *The Heidelberg Catechism*, it is recorded,

> The Reformation had been inaugurated but it; was established only by slow degrees. As in the individual heart there is first an instantaneous transition from death to life, and afterwards a progressive growth, so, in the religious experience of the young Protestant communities, there followed, when the decisive step had once been taken, an enlightening and strengthening process. Year by year they became better acquainted with the old-new faith which they had professed. One method especially their leaders adopted for their instruction. It was not altogether a new method. At an early period in the history of the Church, catechetical teaching had been imparted to the converts who had renounced heathenism and been baptized. But during the Middle Ages the duty had been neglected. When the Reformers set themselves to compose their Catechisms, in which by question and answer the cardinal doctrines of their creed were explained and enforced, they may not have done an absolutely original thing. But they revived a wholesome custom which had fallen almost universally into desuetude.[303]

That this practice and use of questions and answers as a means of instruction in the faith was not altogether a new method but rather was one that flowed from the biblical pattern of the children of Israel who were commanded to instruct their children in the ways of God. Whenever a child was to ask his father, *"What mean the testimonies, and the statutes, and the judgments, which the LORD our God hath commanded you?"* (Deut. 6:20), the father was to answer with a summary of the mighty works of God for the redemption of the people (Deut. 6:20-25). In the New Testament, the illustration is given of Apollos, who before meeting Aquila and Priscilla, had been instructed or literally "catechised" in the way of the Lord and was teaching with accuracy the things con-

---

[303] *The Heidelberg Catechism: the German text, with a revised translation and introduction* (London: Andrew Melrose, 1900), viii-ix.

cerning Lord, knowing only the baptism of John (Acts 18:25). Upon hearing Apollos speak in the synagogue, Aquila and Priscilla took him and instructed him more accurately in the way of the God after which Apollos continued his teaching greatly helping the church through his teaching and defence of the faith against the Jews (Acts 18:27-28).

Specific admonitions of Scripture such as *"Teach them diligently to thy children"* and *"talk of them when thou sittest in thine house, and when thou walkest by the way, and when thou liest down, and when thou risest up"* which were the instructions accompanying the second giving of the Law (Deut. 6) support the use of this method which included memorization of fundamental precepts. Thus, when organized logically, catechisms augment understanding and give enormous help in comprehending the sense of Scripture.

In Church history, the use of catechization as valid methods of biblical instruction for the whole church in the truths of Scripture can be traced long before its reintroduction and use during the Reformation. Concerning the place and use of the catechism in the family, Bonar writes that they were handbooks and manuals for instruction in doctrine. He observes,

> These hand-books were not regularly authorized; for the church had sanctioned only the three creeds; but on the basis of such summaries public and family instruction was carried on. As to the latter, Chrysostom thus writes, "Let the husband repeat to his wife the things which have been spoken in the church; let the wife learn, let the children attend, and let not the servants be forbidden from listening. Make thine house to be a church, for thou wilt have to answer for the salvation of thy children and thy servants."[304]

That catechisms were bases for both public and private instruction is clear from the quotation above. During the Reformation, the revival of religion renewed the efforts in instruction of the family and with it the writing of catechisms. The reformers wrote catechisms which they used to instruct those under their ministry. Bonar points out,

> But it was the Reformation that introduced catechizing in earnest; and, not till the example had been set by the Protestant churches, did Rome, in her Centreline catechism, tardily and reluctantly direct its efforts to the instruction of the young and ignorant. That these were merely out of rivalship, or to save appearances, is evident from the prolixity of the catechism, and its being locked up in the Latin tongue. ... But the Reformers began in thorough earnest to instruct the people. It was their duty, and it was their safety. Hence the numerous catechisms published in the sixteenth century.[305]

The spiritual condition of the people at the time of the Reformation necessitated the thorough and earnest instruction through the catechism. Concerning this Bonar quoting from Luther writes,

> The common people, wholly without any knowledge of Christian doctrine, particularly in the villages; and many pastors, alas! almost as incapable of teaching them; and yet they must all be called Christians, all be baptized, and all receive the holy sacrament, although they could not so much as repeat the Lord's Prayer, the Creed, or the Ten Commandments; they live blindly, like their cattle, or senseless swine; and now that the gospel has reached them, learn only so much of it as boldly to abuse its liberty. Therefore, I implore you, my dear brethren, who are parish pas-

---

[304]*Catechisms of the Scottish Reformation*, ed. by Horatius Bonar (London: James Nisbet and Co., 1866), xxi-xxii.

[305]Ibid., xxii.

tors, priests, or preachers, in the holy name of God, to apply to your duties with your whole hearts, and take pity on the people committed to your charge, and help to bring the Catechism home to their hearts especially to the young and, such as are blessed with no better gift I beseech to take these tablets and forms, and thus bring the people forward step by step.[306]

The present age needs the same imploring call to pastors to bring the catechism home to the hearts of their members and especially the young. Similar sentiments to those of Luther are recorded of Calvin as he wrote to Protector Somerset in 1548. Of this letter, Bonar quotes,

> Believe me, Monseigneur, the Church of God will never preserve itself without a Catechism, for it is like the seed to keep the good grain from dying out, and causing it to multiply from age to age. And therefore, if you desire to build an edifice which shall be of long duration, and which shall not soon fall into decay, make provision for the children being instructed in a good catechism, which may shew them briefly, and in language level to their tender age, wherein true Christianity consists. This Catechism will serve two purposes, to wit, as an introduction to the whole people, so that every one may profit from what shall be practised, and also to enable them to discern when any presumptuous person puts forward strange doctrine.[307]

Thus, not only does the catechism offer opportunity for instruction in the Word of God, but, it also enables them to discern between truth and error. Both Luther and Calvin placed high priority on instruction by catechetical method and considered the success of the Reformation as virtually dependent on the understanding and application of this process by Protestants. For example, Calvin says,

> Believe my Lord, that the Church of God shall never be conserved without catechism, for it is as the seed to be kept that the good grain perish not but that it may increase from age to age. Wherefore if you desire to build a work of continuance to endure long, and which should not shortly fall into decay, cause that the children in their young age be instructed in a good catechism.[308]

The use of the catechism continued well after the time of the reformers with Richard Baxter being an excellent example of the use of the catechism with all groups whether childhood, youth, or mature age and there seems to be a high regard of the catechism in the use of training and raising up of children even into modern history as reflected by Robert Barclay's illustration in the introduction of his book, *A Catechism and a Confession of Faith*, where he writes,

> CATECHISM "All the books the Lincoln cabin could boast, at that time, were the Bible, Catechism, and the copy of Dilworth's spelling book that Sarah and Abraham shared between them. This was a very small library even for a pioneer, hut it was good as far as it went. Any library that begins with the Bible begins well. The Catechism and spelling book were suitable companions for the Book of Books. 'The safeguards of our country are the Bible, Sabbath, and Public School;' and here they were in the Lincoln cabin, — elements of family and national growth."[309]

This presents a very strong case for the practical application of catechism in the development of morality, religion and piety in the home. The safeguards of the family and

---

[306] *Catechisms of the Scottish Reformation*, xxiv.

[307] *Catechisms of the Scottish Reformation*, xxvii.

[308] "History of Catechisms," accessed 13 August 2004, www.kfpc.org/January17/tsld012.htm.

[309] Barclay, *A Catechism and Confession of Faith*, i.

the nation are spiritual, as asserted by Barclay. This then further asserts that the elements of family and national growth ought to be spiritual too. The church thus, as the light of the world, has to ensure that these spiritual safeguards and elements of growth are planted deep in the hearts of its members hence the need for a continual and consistent use of the Scriptures and Catechism.

Upon perusal of the book on the life of Abraham Lincoln by William Thayer titled *The Pioneer Boy*, the influence of Lincoln's mother especially in catechizing Lincoln comes out clearly as having a great part in shaping the character of one of the greatest presidents of the USA. The following excerpt illustrates this well:

> The Ten Commandments were made an important matter in the Sabbath Lessons, and Abraham was drilled in repeating them. Four of them were particularly pressed upon his attention, viz.: (III.) "Thou shalt not take the name of the Lord thy God in vain; for the Lord will not hold him guiltless that taketh his name in vain.", (IV.) "Remember the Sabbath day to keep it holy." (V.) "Honor thy father and thy mother, that thy days may be long upon the land which the Lord thy God giveth thee.", (IX.) "Thou shalt not bear false witness against thy neighbor." Of the Third Commandment she would say, "It is God that speaks here. Never swear, my son." "I never do," said Abraham. "And I hope you never will." ... Another point, derived from the Ninth Commandment, upon which she laid much stress, was truthfulness. "Always speak the truth, my son." "I do tell the truth," was Abraham's usual reply, and he could say it without fear of being disputed. "I think you do; but it is well to think of the consequences if you don't." "What are the consequences?" "God's displeasure." "And be disgraced among men," added his father. "Nobody wants to see a liar about." "That is so," responded Mrs. Lincoln "and nobody will believe a liar when he tells the truth. But, after all, the anger of God is worse." "The Commandment don't say that God is angry with a liar," said Abraham. "But the Bible says so many times, or what is just the same. 'Lying lips are abomination to the Lord; but they that deal truly are his delight.' 'The king shall rejoice in God; every one that sweareth by him shall glory; but the mouth of them that speak lies shall be stopped.' 'A false witness shall not be unpunished, and he that speaketh lies shall perish.' 'The fearful and unbelieving, and the abominable, and murderers, and whoremongers, and sorcerers, and idolaters, and all liars, shall have their part in the lake which burneth with fire and brimstone; which is the second death.' Abraham almost trembled sometimes before the array of Scripture texts that his mother would bring to enforce a subject. She was very familiar with the Bible, and its authority was always appealed to as above on the sin of lying. "No; my children must never lie. Better be poor than be false. There is nothing worse than lying." "Ain't swearing worse?" asked Abraham, thinking that his mother made that appear the worst sin there was. "Both are bad enough, and God is displeased with both," answered his mother, "and that is enough for us to know."[310]

The picture presented from the extract is not only one of instruction through catechism, but it is also indicative of the joint effort of both parents as in the extract there is dialogue between the parents (both the father and the mother) and the child (Lincoln). It is remarkable that what is noted concerning the parents and especially the mother in the extract is "the array of Scripture texts that his mother would bring to enforce a subject." That the impression upon the boy in the family home was the knowledge of the Scripture

---

[310] William M. Thayer, *The Pioneer Boy, and How He Became President* (Boston: Walker Wise and Company, 1864), 54-58.

and their being related to practical issues and the questions and subjects discussed at home is one that should be impressed on every child raised in a Christian home.

Why is it Necessary to Introduce and Teach the Catechism in the Church?

Zacharias Ursinus provides the answer as follows:

1. Because it is *the command of God*: "Ye shall teach them to your children" etc. (Deut. 11. 19.)

2. Because of the divine glory *which demands that God be not only rightly known and worshipped by those of adult age, but also by children*, according as it is said, "Out of the mouth of babes and sucklings hast thou ordained strength." (Ps. 8. 2.)

3. *On account of our comfort and salvation*; for without a true knowledge of God and his Son Jesus Christ, no one that has attained to years of discretion and understanding can be saved, or have any sure comfort that he is accepted in the sight of God. Hence, it is said, "This is life eternal that they might know thee, the only true God, and Jesus Christ, whom thou hast sent," And again, "Without faith it is impossible to please God." (John 17. 3, Hei. 11. 6.) And not only so, but no one believes on him of whom he knows nothing, or has not heard; for, "How shall they believe in him of whom they have not heard?" "So then faith cometh by hearing, and hearing by the word of God." (Rom. 10. 14, 17.) It is necessary, therefore, for all those who will be saved, to lay hold of, and embrace the doctrine of Christ, which is the chief and fundamental doctrine of the gospel. But, in order that this may be done, *there must be instructions imparted to this effect and of necessity, some brief and simple form of doctrine, suited and adapted to the young, and such as are unlearned.*

4. *For the preservation of society and the church.* All past history proves that religion and the worship of God, the exercise and practice of piety, honesty, justice, and truth, are of the greatest importance to the well-being and perpetuation of the church and of the commonwealth. Hence, there is a necessity that we should be trained to the practice of these things from our earliest years; because the heart of man is depraved and evil from his youth; yea, such is the corruption of our nature, that unless we early commence the work of reformation and moral training, we too late apply a remedy when, through long delay, the evil principles and inclinations of the heart have become so strengthened and confirmed, as to bid defiance to the restraints we may then wish to impose upon them. If we are not correctly instructed in our childhood out of the sacred Scriptures concerning God and his will, and do not then commence the practice of piety, it is with great difficulty, if ever, we are drawn away from these errors which are, as it were, born in us, or which we have imbibed from, our youth, and that we are led to abandon the vices in which we have been brought up, and to which we have been accustomed. If, therefore, the church and state are to be preserved from degeneracy and final destruction, it is of the utmost importance that this depravity of our nature should, in due time, be met with proper restraints, and be subdued.

5. There is a necessity that all persons should *be made acquainted with the rule and standard according to which we are to judge and decide*, in relation to the various opinions and dogmas of men, that we may not be led into error, and be seduced thereby, according to the commandment which is given in relation to this subject, "Beware of false prophets." "Prove all things." "Try the spirits whether they are of God." (Matt. 7. 15, 1 Thess. 5. 21, 1 John 4. 1.) But the law and the Apostle's creed, which are the chief parts of the catechism, constitute the rule and standard accord-

ing to which we are to judge of the opinions of men, from which we may see the great importance of a familiar acquaintance with them.

6. *Those who have properly studied and learned the Catechism, are generally better prepared to understand and appreciate the sermons* which they hear from time to time, inasmuch as they can easily refer and reduce those things which they hear out of the word of God, to the different heads of the catechism to which they appropriately belong, whilst, on the other hand, those who have not enjoyed this preparatory training, hear sermons for the most part, with but little profit to themselves.

7. The importance of catechisation may be urged in view of its *peculiar adaptedness to those learners who are of weak and uncultivated minds*, who require instruction in a short, plain, and perspicuous manner, as we have it in the catechism, and would not, on account of their youth and weakness of capacity, be able to understand it, if presented in a lengthy and more difficult form.

8. It is also necessary, *for the purpose of distinguishing and separating the youths, and such as are unlearned, from schismatics and profane heathen*, which can most effectually be done by a judicious course of catechetical instruction.

Lastly. a knowledge of the catechism is especially important for *those who are to act as teachers, because they ought to have a more intimate acquaintance with the doctrine of the church than others, as well on account of their calling, that they may one day be able to instruct others*, as on account of the many facilities which they have for obtaining a knowledge of this doctrine, which it becomes them diligently to improve, that they may, like Timothy, become well acquainted with the Holy Scriptures, and "be good ministers of Jesus Christ, nourished up in the words of faith, and of a good doctrine, whereunto they have attained." (1. Tim. 4, 6.) To these considerations, which clearly show the importance of catechisation, we may add many others of great weight, especially with the great mass of mankind, such as the arguments which may be drawn from the end of our creation, and from the prolongation and preservation of our lives from childhood to youth, and from youth to manhood, etc. We might also speak of the excellency of the object of the doctrine of the catechism, which is the highest good, even God himself, and might show the effect of such a course of instruction, which is a knowledge of this highest good, and a participation therein, which is something vastly more important and desirable than all the treasures of this world. This is that pearl of great price hidden in the field of the church, concerning which Christ speaks in Matt. 13:44, and on account of which Christians in former times suffered martyrdom, with their little children. We may here refer to the example of Origen, of which we have an account in the sixth book and third chapter of the Ecclesiastical History of Eusebius. So the fourth book and sixteenth chapter of the history of Theodoret may be read to the same purpose. But if we are ignorant of the doctrine and glory of Christ, who from among us would be willing to suffer on their account? And how can it be otherwise but that we will be ignorant of these things, unless we are taught and instructed in them from our childhood? **A neglect of the catechism is, therefore, one of the chief causes why there are so many at the present day tossed about by every wind of doctrine, and why so many fall from Christ to Anti-Christ** [emphasis added].[311]

Ursinus presents here an excellent case for the necessity of the catechism as a teaching tool, that this writer thought it necessary to be included in its entirety. From his

---

[311] Zacharias Ursinus, *The Commentary of Zacharias Ursinus on the Heidelberg Catechism*, translated from the original Latin by G. W. Williard (Cincinnati: T. P. Bucher Publisher, 1851), 14-16.

exposition, Ursinus presents a biblical and historical case for the necessity to introduce and teach the catechism in church, but this case also includes the teaching of the catechism at home. In his biblical case, Ursinus first appeals to the Old Testament injunctions given for instruction and teaching which was to take place continually in the lives of God's people. This instruction was to be done mainly in the home setting. Second, Ursinus appeals to the command for the worship of God by all. God is presented in His covenant relationship and thus the duty and privilege of worship is to be accompanied by a right knowledge of the God being worshipped. God is thus to be worshipped in spirit and in truth necessitating the knowing and understanding of God in His attributes and in His requirements before worship can be done acceptably. Man must first know God aright before he can worship Him. While referring to New Testament verses, the connection between the knowledge of God and salvation is brought out to show the necessity of "some brief and simple form of doctrine" for salvation and the knowledge of God.

In his historical case, Ursinus first uses past history to support the biblical case in that the "exercise and practice of piety, honest, justice, and truth," have been tied to the knowledge of God and as such have been accomplished where teaching was a necessity and men were trained from their earliest years. Thus history presents a record of the preserving work of teaching and of the catechism in eras in which it was used to restrain and subdue the depraved passions and inclinations of the natural man. The catechism thus, apart from introducing men to the doctrines of salvation and the knowledge of God, also served to introduce and acquaint men with the rules and principles of morality, giving men a sense of direction in judging the opinions of other men and equipping them with a general understanding of the principles of doctrine placing them in a position to better understand the preached Word.

Ursinus then discusses the suitability of the catechism to exercise influence on the minds of men. The catechism being a system of questions and answers is adapted for use even with those of weak minds; and to those who would be teachers, it nourishes them up in the words of faith and the doctrines of Christ. The catechism thus serves a manifold purpose to those who are instructed in it. Its use is informative, preventive, instructive and, as such, becomes an important teaching tool and a protective safeguard for the family and the church.

The use of the catechism has a two-fold emphasis with one being in the home while the other in the church. Both in the home and in the church, the use of the catechism affirms the teachings and beliefs as well as establishes the learner in the doctrines and teachings through repetition, mainly through question and answers. To many in this age, religion has lost its meaning as churches have been turning a blind eye to the spiritual welfare of its membership whilst focusing on the pursuit of wealth. The extent of this problem is reflected in Meade's Introduction to the book *Training Hearts Teaching Minds* which says,

> For many of today's churchgoers, a pillar and support of truth is not necessarily what they seek when they look for a church. The first concern may be the warmth of the welcome, the style of the church's music, or the number of weekly activities from which to choose. Faithfulness to biblical doctrine is becoming increasingly rare as the first thing people seek in a church.[312]

Some out of ignorance have thought that the only option is to stop attending any church believing that it is optional in such situations and one can maintain the Christian faith without attending any church slipping into further error and going astray. The church has to return its focus to its purpose as "the pillar and ground of the truth" (1 Tim.

---

[312] Meade, *Training Hearts, Teaching Minds*, 1.

3:15) and instruct her people in the Word of God. The catechism is an avenue that can greatly help the church return to her purpose, and the role and place of the catechism as an avenue for teaching in the church can be clearly seen when one considers the church as the pillar and ground of the truth. The task of the church would thus be to uphold, maintain and propagate the truths of the Gospel as presented in Scripture. The catechism serves to provide a foundational guide to Scripture and doctrine. It provides (i) a teaching tool that is straight to the point with its form in question and answer form, and (ii) a handy manual that can be used with those who are young in age as well as young in faith.

The Practice of Catechism

Those of us who care about passing on the baton of historic Christian truth must awaken to the importance of faithfully imparting its doctrines to our children. We cannot depend on haphazard hit-or-miss Bible stories and memory verses, hoping that somehow our children will distil from them Christianity's important teachings. Rather, we must provide careful, systematic instruction in doctrine. Children need a grid through which to sift all that they see and hear. We must provide this for our children while they are still young. Doctrine cannot wait until children are teens, because adolescents are making major life decisions. The theological framework on which to base those decisions, the biblical worldview, must already be in place.[313]

The practice of catechism is to provide a sure, careful and systematic means for learning both the Scripture and Christian doctrine. This learning is centred in the church and home front. The home front places the practice upon the parent, especially the father. In the home, the catechism is to be used interactively with the parent instructing and the children learning. The parental role to teach principles of religion is a biblical one. The Bible assigns the teaching role to the parents and singles out the father for it. Right from the instructions given in Egypt as they prepared to leave during the institution of the Passover in Exodus 13:8 to the period of the conquest and division of the promised land under Joshua, the ordinances and religious practices were to be accompanied by teaching so that the children do not only become acquainted with the routines but also learn to understand and know God through the instructions. Even today children would learn by seeing and in some cases go through the motions without understanding. The parents, especially fathers, were tasked with the duty of ensuring that the children knew God and His acts by recounting to them the mighty acts of God which led to the ordinances which they were required to observe at set times. In Exodus 13:8, the Bible states, *"And thou shalt show thy son in that day, saying this is done because of that which the LORD did unto me when I came forth out of Egypt."* This clearly shows that the LORD requires that religion and devotion be based on the knowledge of God. This is because religion has to be man's grateful and loving response in honour to God who has done much in redeeming His people. Therefore, they were instructed to say, *"this is done because of that which the LORD did unto me"* (Exod. 13:8).

In the prophets, this theme recurs. The prophet Isaiah says that *"the father to the children shall make known thy truth. The LORD was ready to save me: therefore we will sing my songs to the stringed instruments all the days of our life in the house of the LORD"* (Isa. 38:19b-20). Another aspect rises from these verses that is presented by the clause *"the father to the children shall make known thy truth."* The making known of the truth implies that the teaching is not just about rote memorization, but rather has to include and aim at not only remembering, but also understanding. To this effect, Meade points out,

---

[313] Meade, *Training Hearts, Teaching Minds*, 6.

CHAPTER III: TEACHING AVENUES AVAILABLE FOR THE CHURCH TODAY

It is said that if we require our children to memorize by rote, they will only memorize meaningless sounds and words without understanding them. Certainly we do a disservice to our children if we insist that they memorize words they do not understand, while we fail to take time to discuss, teach, and explain the meanings to them. The solution, however, is not to discard memorization as a teaching method, but to faithfully supply meaning by discussing and explaining.[314]

Thus, the use of the catechism is to provide a balance between memorization and understanding. This is to be achieved through regular, constant and repeated sessions in which the parents read the Bible with their children and rehearse the catechism questions with them.

From the church front, the catechism focuses on the pastoral ministry in the local church. The catechism is therefore a tool that every pastor should have and make use of. Baxter used his catechism effectively during his visits to the homes of his parishioners "centering his visits on the instruction given in the Westminster Shorter Catechism."[315] Meade also observes,

Once, catechisms were used routinely. Church and family worked together to provide the most effective teaching possible for children growing up in Christian circles. Parents would work with their children at home, requiring them to memorize the answers to the catechism (and memorizing the answers themselves as well). Families would discuss together the meaning of the questions and answers. Pastors would preach on topics addressed in the catechism and would systematically visit each church family, asking the questions to see how well family members had learned the answers.[316]

This balance is desperately needed again and the church on her part, should not assume that the families represented in her congregation conducts regular teachings sessions but should ensure that they equip and enable the families to do so. And the families on their part, should not assume that the church will perform the role of teaching the children in its entirety in the Sunday School programs. The family heads should ensure that the home environment is suitable for spiritual growth and that family worship is part of the home life.

The home should also cooperate more earnestly with the church and give it better support and see that the children attend the sessions of the Sunday School regularly and faithfully. Too many parents think it is the duty of the pastor and Bible School teacher alone to see that their children attend church worship and the sessions of the Bible School. They frequently meet with the experience of a Bible School teacher who once visited a home to see that one of the daughters attended her Bible School class more regularly. The mother said that it was the duty of the teacher to see that the daughter attended regularly. We agree that it is the duty of pastors and teachers to see that the children come regularly, but it is not their whole nor first duty, for this rests upon the home.[317]

Here, the mutual and complementary roles of the pastor and elders, as well as the parents are necessary. But the primary point for instruction in catechism has to be the home as has been drawn from the biblical injunctions. Just as many parents have left the

---

[314] Meade, *Training Hearts, Teaching Minds*, 3.

[315] Meade, *Training Hearts, Teaching Minds*, 2.

[316] Ibid.

[317] Heathcote, *The Essentials of Religious Education*, 13.

education of their children to the schools and any perceived weakness in any subject is supplemented by extra tuition classes at tuition centres, many parents have excused themselves entirely from the spiritual instruction of their children assuming that the church with its regular and special programs and camps will cater for all spiritual needs of their children. Such assumptions are a major reason for the lack of spiritual instruction in the home. Church programs are to be supplements to the parental instruction at home, not vice versa.

Practical Steps in Catechism at Home

Finally, what are some practical tips for the planning, practising and instruction by catechism? Having considered a profitable and God-honouring family worship and what it requires, the catechism may be best set and included in the family worship schedule or may be set for a separate time which may require the participation of and co-operation from the whole family or set for a one-on-one time between the parent and the child. Some important points to note in using the catechism as a teaching tool in the home may include the following:

(i) Consistency: This focuses on the ability to keep at it. The catechism consists of a set number of questions and answers, but the goal is not to finish the course by going through all the questions once through. The catechism as a system of instruction is flexible in that it takes into consideration the ability of the child. Catechism should be taught at the level of the learner such that younger children are taught in smaller portions with more frequent repetitions.

> The nature of the content must be allowed to condition not only the form but the method of instruction. On the other hand, because instruction has to take into account the nature of the receiver, the mode of communication will be conditioned also by the mode of reception.[318]

Consistency in teaching also helps both the one teaching and the one learning to set a routine that creates a rhythm. Whether it is as simple as going over one question and its answer every day of the week fifteen minutes before bedtime or reciting the previously memorized answer before leaving for school, a routine creates a platform for easy interaction between the parent and the child and also helps instil discipline in the learning process.

(ii) Memorization and recitation: Children from a very young age learn to imitate what they hear and see. Thus, having a regular memory and recitation program for the family will help even the youngest to learn and memorize both the Word of God and the catechism. The first step when considering memory work and recitation is the choice of the portion to be memorized and the time to be assigned to the task. Once these are set, a recitation plan can then be drawn up which includes the initial reading, and it is to be carried on until the whole passage is memorized and can be recited by all. Periodical recitation of sections previously memorized serve to re-affirm what has been learned.

> An old maxim is, that repetition is the soul of instruction. Compayre says that it is one of the essential conditions for development of memory. Bain says that it "is the first law of memory. The process of fixing the impression occupies a certain length of time; either we must prolong the first shock, or renew it on several successive occasions." Do not be afraid then of using over and over again in your teaching

---

[318] *The School of Faith: the catechisms of the Reformed church*, translated and edited by Thomas F. Torrance (London: James Clarke & Co. LTD, 1959), xxi.

work those objects or symbols which will serve to recall — and hence to re-impress — certain truths or facts which have been presented to the scholar's mind.[319]

(iii) Application and comprehension: What is memorized and recited needs to be understood and practised. Although the goal in teaching the catechism is initially simple memorization, and since catechism is fixed and will be revisited and repeated at later times, explanations for application and comprehension can be graded over time. There is no need to explain every term and illustrate every truth all at once. Therefore, in seeking to make it practical, understandable and applicable, great wisdom needs to be exercised. Deciding on which words to define and what explanations to give will depend on the parent's knowledge of the catechism, its explanations, and the Scripture references given, as well as a knowledge of the children's understanding levels, habits, weaknesses, etc. Some words may be explained in the catechism, others by the scripture readings either in the questions and answers being memorized or in past or future questions and answers. Hence, it will be necessary that the parent teaches a particular catechism question and answer with the context of the whole catechism in mind. This will help in grading the applications given and the comprehension achieved allowing the children to grow in steps and also to relate the different sections of the catechism together even as they memorize the answers.

(iv) Variety and creativity: The catechism being set and fixed naturally will require repetition of areas previously covered. This may make it difficult to learn if enthusiasm is lost. One of the greatest hindrances to continual study and use of the catechism is boredom. Hence, creativity and variety need to be added to the memorization and recitation process. There are no limits to creativity and variety. From those who use songs and mnemonics to help memorization, to those who draw and add activities, many options are available and have worked in different settings. There is no hard and fast rule to this, except that whatever variety is added, the guiding principle must be a Scriptural one, and methods used must be God-honouring and which can cultivate godliness and piety. The Outline of Sunday School Teachers' Normal Course points out,

> a. The power of memory depends upon two things — the susceptibility of the brain tissues to receive impressions, and the attention which is given to the things which are to be remembered. …
>
> b. The greater the number of the senses brought into use in producing an impression on the mind, the deeper will be that impression, and hence the more easily reproduced by memory. It is usually considered that sight furnishes the most lasting memory images, but the muscular sense is of great importance. Children remember far better what they do, than what they see or hear.[320]

(v) Caution: The catechism is a system to aid understanding of biblical truths. It must not replace the Bible. This is a caution that every parent has to always bear in mind when using the catechism. Children are impressionable, and as they memorize the catechism, and as the parents recognize and reward their effort, the distinction on how to please God and be acceptable in His sight has to be clear to the parents and be made clear to the children. So the catechism has to be taught with great caution. Caution that the children do not equate their retention with conversion or their knowledge of the truths presented in the catechism questions and answers with a saving knowledge and faith in Christ. Parents must also exercise caution not to replace the Bible with the catechism, but rather the catechism is to accompany the Bible. Precedence has to be given to the Scrip-

---

[319] George William Pease, *The Sunday School Teachers' Normal Course* (New York: Fleming H. Revell Co., 1895), 135-136.

[320] Pease, *The Sunday School Teachers' Normal Course* 134-135.

ture alone. The goal of the catechism is to assist in growth in grace and knowledge of Jesus Christ. It must not be looked at as the actual growth in grace and in knowledge of Jesus Christ.

In the Church

The Great Commission given to the apostles in Matthew 28:18-20 outlines the intent of Christ towards the proclamation of the Gospel to the world. The emphasis that comes out of this commission is discipleship. This discipleship emphasis forms the basis of the church's teaching commission. The apostles were to endeavour in their efforts to make disciples of all nations. And from this command to make disciples, the church has an obligation to seek out and pursue teaching avenues available that may enable her to fulfil and accomplish her mandate as is directed in the Great Commission, which mandate involves the making of disciples of all nations, and the teaching of them to observe all things commanded by Christ. In his book *The Function of Teaching in Christianity*, Charles B. Williams observes,

> Again, when Jesus was about to leave the world he commissioned the Twelve (the nucleus of the church of the future) to "make disciples of all the nations, baptizing them into the name of the Father, and of the Son, and of the Holy Spirit: teaching them to observe all things whatsoever I commanded you" (Matt. 28: 10, 20). Jesus gave to the Twelve a commission, and that commission is that they teach the nations the truths of Christianity and to make the citizens of "the nations" "learners" of Christ and thus citizens of the kingdom of heaven. The verb "*matheeteuo*" means to "make a disciple, instruct." This verb is used only four times in the New Testament to refer to the process of making men pupils, or followers, of Christ.[321]

From Williams' observations on the Great Commission, it can be noted that Christianity has a standard set of truths or doctrines as well as a distinct lifestyle that are to be acquired by all through constant and gradual instruction and learning. Therefore, the place of discipleship and teaching in Christianity cannot be replaced or displaced.

The apostles were, thus, to be instructors and teachers as much as they were preachers who went forth preaching the Gospel. But for them to go forth preaching and teaching, they themselves had to be prepared and taught. This was done by Christ Himself as they followed and learnt from Christ during His public ministry. Having learnt, and having been prepared and equipped, they were finally commissioned to teach others also. Their duty, as they went into all the world and made disciples, was to teach all that Christ had commanded while the duty of the disciples who came under the ministry of the apostles was to learn to obey all that Christ had commanded. Thus, in considering the teaching and learning relationship of the church in the light of the Great Commission, the central focus is the commands of Christ with the teachers commanded to teach only what Christ had commanded while the learners to obey whatsoever Christ had commanded.

Presently, this Great Commission is, by many, seen as a purely missions or evangelistic commission. This has limited it to missionaries and missionary-sending churches vis-a-vis missions fields and stations. When rightly considered, the Great Commission must be seen as the church's mandate both to reach out and to teach all who are reached. The perspective that the Great Commission brings on the teaching life of the church is often lost as Morrison rightly points out,

> Christians often view Christ's final instructions to His followers — The Great Commission — as something fulfilled primarily by missionaries working on foreign

---

[321]Charles B. Williams, *The Function of Teaching in Christianity* (Nashville, Tennessee: Sunday School Board Southern Baptist Convention, 1912), 14-15.

CHAPTER III: TEACHING AVENUES AVAILABLE FOR THE CHURCH TODAY

soil and directed toward those who have never heard the Gospel. While missionary endeavour is certainly an essential element of His imperative to the church, it is not the only aspect of Christ's command. The Great Commission applies equally to the education and training by the local church of its own members. More specifically, as history demonstrates, if the church is not successful in fulfilling the Great Commission with its own youth, it has fumbled the ball, so to speak, in one of its primary areas of responsibility.[322]

Morrison's pointed challenge rightly emphasizes the pastoral responsibility of the Great Commission and the teaching emphasis of the local church in the Great Commission. The lack of emphasis on them even with the increase in missionary activity has been hurting the church in its growth and maturity. The Great Commission, thus, ought rather to be considered as a pastoral commission with every pastor and church leader considering it as his individual responsibility to teach the church if the church is to mature and be grounded and established in the faith. In his book *The Great Commission*, E. A. Kilbourne presents the Great Commission as one that is timeless: "Each generation of disciples has a debt to pay to its generation of unsaved people of whatever nation or colour."[323] He goes on to observe and point out that in history, the picture presented is one that is strewn with failures in the accomplishing of this mission. But despite the failures of the different generations of the past, "our individual responsibility has not lessened in the slightest degree, for the Great Commission has not been withdrawn or cancelled."[324] In most cases, failure to accomplish the mission of the church is occasioned by the spiritual immaturity of the particular church and this in part has to be due to the neglect of teaching in the local church. The neglect of the teaching emphasis of the Great Commission is the neglect of what Morrison rightly terms as "one of its primary areas of responsibility," namely that of "the education and training by the local church of its own members."

The Great Commission must thus be seen as a commission to and for the local church. It is a Pastoral Commission. As such, it gives specific instruction for the teaching of all in the church, sets the definition and limits of what is to be taught to all in the church, namely, the commands of Christ. Thus, all that is left for each successive generation to determine is the how of teaching. This is what this section of this paper seeks to draw attention to through the consideration of the teaching avenues available for the church as she accomplishes her Lord's commission.

The educational emphasis is a key one in the fulfilment of the Great Commission. The church has been vibrant and Christianity strong when the teaching of the Bible was central in its life, and the church has decayed and Christianity weakened whenever the Bible and its teaching was set aside and Christian education and training was replaced by any other thing. That is the testimony of history and it seems to be the danger facing the church in every generation.

The Great Commission is not just about making disciples, or winning the lost, it is also about teaching those won to Christ. Christianity begins with the new birth (com-

---

[322] John Morrison, *The Great Commission and Christian Education: a pointed challenge to Christian parents and church leaders*, accessed 27 August 2018, http://www.gcswarriors.org/about-us/christianeducationresources/The%20Great%20Commission%20and%20Christian%20Education%20by%20John%20Morrison.pd f.

[323] E. A. Kilbourne, *The Great Commission* (Tokyo, Japan: Oriental Missionary Society, 1913), 2.

[324] Ibid.

ing to Christ), but then extends to living for the glory of Christ hence the Great Commission must be seen as extending beyond evangelism and extending into Christian living. After winning disciples, there has to be teaching and maturing of the disciples. *"Teaching them to observe all things whatsoever I have commanded you"* (Matt. 28:20) presents a goal, and for this goal to be achieved there has to be the use of means and methods; hence, the place of considering what teaching avenues are available for use. What Christ expects of His church is obedience, i.e. obedience to *"all things whatsoever I have commanded you"* (Matt. 28:20).

Preaching the gospel and evangelizing the world is the first mission of the church, and since the apostolic commission, the church has been sending out preachers to evangelize the world. But the work of the preachers throughout the ages has encompassed more than evangelism. It has included teaching and discipling converts in the faith. Acts chapter 2 presents the life of the early church in summary form. After the conversion of many through the preaching of Peter, Acts 2:42-47 records what characterized the life of the church. The summary given presents the church life as one that was of steadfast attention, perseverance in continuance and carefulness to apostolic doctrines, to prayer and sacraments, and to fellowship and sharing.

The activities that the church was involved in were spiritual in nature and aimed at establishing the believers in the faith and in their relationship with Christ and with one another. These activities following conversion thus characterize the life of the Christian and of the church. Lange writes,

> The *doctrine* or *instruction* was the first instrumentality that was employed in the work of strengthening and establishing the new converts. The Christian Church is primarily a communion of faith, and hence essentially needs instruction, a knowledge of the truth, and the ministry of the word. Any attempt to edify without instruction and doctrine as the basis, is neither in accordance with the example and command of Jesus, nor with the practice and principles of the apostles, and is therefore unevangelical.[325]

It is interesting that Lange presents doctrine both as synonymous with instruction and as the "first instrumentality" in the maturing of believers especially since the thought that is popularly propagated today is that "love unites, doctrine divides." The church during the New Testament times as presented in the book of Acts was a doctrinal church, instructed and established in the apostles' doctrines such that Lange rightly concludes, "Any attempt to edify without instruction and doctrine as the basis, is neither in accordance with the example and command of Jesus, nor with the practice and principles of the apostles, and is therefore unevangelical."[326] Their focus on the Scripture was their safeguard against error. If one is to be wholly given and surrendered to God, if one's meat and drink is to be found in doing the Father's will, if one is to love the Lord his God with all his heart, soul and might, if one is to present his body a living sacrifice, holy and acceptable before God, then he has to continue steadfastly in the apostles' doctrines. The Word of God must have a prominent place in the life of the believer and of the church. Growth in faith is to be achieved through the instrumentality of the Word; hence the emphasis on teaching as their first instrumentality that is to be employed in the growing and maturing of believers. The church today is increasingly becoming unbiblical as it puts aside doctrine as dry and divisive.

---

[325] John Peter Lange, *Commentary on the Holy Scriptures: Critical, Doctrinal, and Homiletical*, accessed 27 August 2018, https://biblehub.com/commentaries/lange/acts/2.htm.

[326] Lange, *Commentary on the Holy Scriptures: Critical, Doctrinal, and Homiletical*, obtained from URL: https://biblehub.com/commentaries/lange/acts/2.htm.

CHAPTER III: TEACHING AVENUES AVAILABLE FOR THE CHURCH TODAY

The educational emphasis is further highlighted by the apostle Peter who, when writing his second epistle, talks about things that the believer needs to add to his faith in 2 Peter 1:5-11. In the list of Christian graces that are to be exercised, the grace of knowledge (2 Pet. 1:5) is included. The word *"knowledge"* occurs three times in the epistle, including in the theme verse (2 Pet. 3:18) which exhorts growth in grace and in knowledge of Jesus Christ. Thus, the mandate of the church must facilitate the growth in grace and in the knowledge of Christ of every believer and member of the church.

Paul too, while addressing the Ephesian elders, speaks about teaching the whole counsel of God and keeping nothing back that was profitable for the church, but rather teaching publicly and privately. He then charges the Ephesian elders, under whose charge the flock is committed, to do the same. He also exhorts his sons in the faith in the pastoral epistles on the necessity of teaching the church (Tit. 2:1-10) and of teaching men who would in turn minister to and teach others also (2 Tim. 2:1-2). Teaching ought to have a central part in the life of the church, both in the life of the members and in the work of the ministers as one studies the New Testament church. This teaching covered both faith and practice, and the curriculum and the subject which is to be taught is the Word of God as revealed in Scripture.

How the church is to work towards achieving what Christ expects of His church may vary within set limits. The variations may be due to the contexts under which the particular church lives and serves, but the limits set must be defined and confined by the content of Scripture and Christ's commands. Thus, the application of the means and avenues that will be suggested here (by which the mandate of the church is to be achieved) needs to take into account the context of the church. The methods and means employed in the development of Christian graces (which graces the Bible expects every Christian to be exercised in) is to be generally considered under the heading Christian Education.

The definition of Christian education that will be adopted by this writer in the discussion to follow is that which is given by Randolf Miller. He defines Christian education as "the effort to make available for our generation — children, young people, and adults — the accumulated treasures of Christian life and thought, in such a way that God in Christ may carry on his redemptive work in each human soul and in the common life of man."[327]

Thus, the methods and means to be discussed and to be considered are to be based on their ability to make available, and to bring to the life and thought of the church the accumulated treasures of Christian life and thought. These treasures are stored up in Scripture and in church history, and how it may be brought to a particular generation may vary. J. J. Hawes in his report to the Brunswick Baptist session highlights the necessity of Christian education in respect to its guiding of life as it unfolds, and in its relation to the Great Commission as follows:

> Can a man be educated without knowing God? Not to the highest degree. Can a man achieve greatness without a personal knowledge of God and His plan of salvation? No one can attain the highest degree in life except he become God's servant. Jesus taught that Greatness comes through service.
>
> Then, if we are to enjoy the best in life we need a christian education. In defining christian education one does not have to receive a diploma or degree from any school of our land, but to have learned from the school at the feet of Jesus. So we can readily see that a christian education is available to all where Christianity is known, and it is our duty to carry out God's command to "Go Ye Into All The

---

[327] Randolf Crump Miller, *Education for Christian Living*, 2nd ed. (Englewood Cliffs N.J.: Prentice Hall, 1963), 53-54.

World And Preach The Gospel To Every Creature, Teaching Them To Observe All Things Whatsoever I Have Commanded You."

Guiding life as it develops is an important matter. Christian education is that continuous learning of God's plan in life which consists of man's duty to God, to himself, and to his fellowman.[328]

From the above, it can be surmised that Christian education has to be a continual process of learning and growing in which one, by attending to the Word of God, is instructed both in the knowledge of God and of man, and through the knowledge gained, is also equipped for a life of service to God, and to his fellow-men. Such education is aimed at promoting right relationships with God and with others and should be made "available to all where Christianity is known," and therefore becomes the duty of the church.

Indeed, in various degrees and using varied methods, it is performed by all churches and in many places this role has come to be placed under what is popularly known as "The Christian Education Department" of the church. The Christian Education Department of the church[329] implements the church's education policies, evaluates the church's educational needs, and monitors the church's educational objectives. This is normally done through the selection of curriculum to be used, recruiting and training of the teaching personnel, and identifying the teaching needs and groups within the context of the church. The degree to which a particular church employs teaching avenues and methods is usually linked to the understanding and perspective held by the church with regard to Christian education. The most common avenue is that of the Church School commonly called the Sunday School.

The general misunderstanding of the Sunday school has contributed greatly to the weakness of Christian education in the church in this writer's context. This weakness is clearly seen in the general understanding, or rather misunderstanding, among most churches that associates the Sunday school ministry with teaching of small children. This has greatly hindered churches from the proper teaching of the whole counsel of God's Word to the whole congregation. In many cases, the children have their Sunday school and in it memorize Bible portions and learn Catechisms and Bible stories, but the rest of the congregation attend and spectate at church service where the pastor stands at the pulpit to preach and the "praise team" or choir sings. In many cases, there is little or no spiritual growth as whatever growth to be achieved is left to the individual's effort with little or no assistance from the church through its programs. This has severely hindered both spiritual growth and maturity as well as personal dedication and service to God. The result has been churches that are secular, people that are carnal, and a gospel that is social. The general picture of the church in Kenya today is one in which people go to church and call themselves Christians but do not know the doctrines of the Bible, people give verbal assent to biblical statements but their lives and practices are at variance to the statements they subscribe to, and consequently ecumenism, syncretism, charismatism are rampant because the church is very weak and spiritually ignorant. How should the

---

[328] J. J. Hawes, *Christian Education*, a report presented to the Brunswick Baptist Association at their 43rd Annual session as recorded in the *1941 Minutes of the Brunswick Baptist Association North Carolina*, 10.

[329] The Christian Education Department of the church in this writer's context is generally understood as that committee or commission of the church that is charged with planning, monitoring, overseeing and unifying the educational ministries of the church so that each person is taught, instructed, warned and corrected with all wisdom, doctrine and long-suffering to the end that each person may be presented complete in Christ (Col. 1:28). And in many local churches or denominations, it is mainly involved in and limited to Sunday School work.

CHAPTER III: TEACHING AVENUES AVAILABLE FOR THE CHURCH TODAY

church view Christian education and its teaching role? What avenues and methods are available for teaching in the church, that believers may be encouraged, strengthened and grow in faith? How can those who attend church, and subscribe to the Bible, know what they believe and what God says? These questions inform the Christian Education department of the church in its teaching role and duty, and in its developing avenues and methods of teaching, and thus through them forming the "how of teaching." Concerning the Christian Education department of the church, Pazmino writes, "Christian education is one of the church's ministries that seeks to encourage persons of all ages to choose life — the spiritual life found in Jesus Christ for the Christian church. ... Christian education entails sharing a knowledge of, and encouraging a response to God that results in life."[330]

The picture presented of Christian education by Pazmino above is one that is, first, necessary for all and thus should be directed towards all. The church must endeavour to reach and teach all persons within its congregation. Second, Christian education requires the use of means and avenues that work towards the strengthening and encouraging of the spiritual life found in Christ. Third, Christian education is graded to ensure that all who attend church continually and systematically grow in grace and in the knowledge of Jesus Christ, knowing what God says and what they ought both to believe and to do through the teachings. As a ministry that seeks to encourage and strengthen persons of all ages, the methods used may be varied to suit the persons or groups targeted and the growth area intended. As Christian education entails sharing knowledge and encouraging response, it would be clear that it would be a teaching ministry of the church.

The teaching avenues it presents to the members of the church must promote the following:

(i) Personal devotion to God and submission and commitment to His will as revealed in Scripture. Hence, Christian education must involve the reading and understanding of Scripture before any applications are made.

(ii) Personal development in grace and maturity in relation to God's revealed will and in relation to fellow-men. Hence, Christian education must involve drawing out and applying biblical and scriptural principles for daily use to aid the growth and maturity of the individual Christian.

(iii) Personal disposition that reflects godliness, holiness and blamelessness in daily duties and tasks of life. Hence, Christian education must involve the practice of piety on a daily basis and growth in Christ-likeness in which the members shine as light in the midst of a perverse and crooked generation, as well as holding fast the Word of life and living godly lives.

This is the perspective reflected in Paul's prayer for the Colossian Christians in Colossians 1:9-11, where Paul in expressing his desire for their spiritual growth and development prays that they may become Christians who are knowing and intelligent in the things of God (Col. 1:9). John Calvin in his commentary on Colossians 1:9 writes,

> The knowledge of the divine will, by which expression he sets aside all inventions of men, and all speculations that are at variance with the word of God. For his will is not to be sought anywhere else than in his word. He adds — in all wisdom; by which he intimates that the will of God, of which he had made mention, was the only rule of right knowledge. For if anyone is desirous simply to know those things which it has pleased God to reveal, that is the man who accurately knows what it is to be truly wise. ... For the animal man does not perceive the things that are of God.

---

[330] Robert W. Pazmino, *Foundational Issues in Christian Education: an Introduction in Evangelical Perspective* (Grand Rapids, Michigan: Baker Books, 1997), 24.

(1 Cor 2:14) So long as men are regulated by their own carnal perceptions, they have also their own wisdom, but it is of such a nature as is mere vanity, however much they may delight themselves in it.[331]

Calvin rightly observes the effect of man's natural disposition on the things that are of God, pointing out that the natural man, "animal man," cannot perceive spiritual things as they are spiritually discerned, and he cannot understand them. The knowledge of God, of His ways, and of His will must be directly linked to the knowledge of His Word. As the chief end of man is to glorify God and enjoy Him forever, the knowledge and understanding of our chief end is the best knowledge one can achieve and this is what the apostle prays for on behalf of the church and desires of them. It is as they increase in knowledge of God that their life's conduct changes to be more pleasing to God. Good knowledge when applied practically and daily results in good life. When what is known is good, but is not put into practice, there is no profit derived from that knowledge and understanding. But when there is knowledge and understanding, and it is correctly, systematically, gradually and consistently applied, then there is fruit that exemplifies the knowledge and understanding; hence Paul talks about walking *"worthy of the Lord unto all pleasing"* in Colossians 1:10.

Not only is the believer's knowledge linked to the Word, but so also is his relation and disposition. He becomes fruitful in every good work as he abides in Christ and Christ's Word abides in him. He becomes strengthened with might by God's Spirit in the inner man and becomes pleasing unto his Lord as God's Word abides in him. Thus, the wisdom of the church, the strength of the church, and the standing of the church are directly linked to the place the Word of God has in the church and consequently in the lives of the members of the church.

The programs that the church chooses to include must therefore be seen as tools and instruments towards achieving and promoting the desired ends and objectives. And as Paul chides the Corinthian church in 1 Corinthians 3, these tools (which may include persons, giftings, and means) are nothing of themselves and do not possess any inherent efficacy in themselves. The profiting that is to be derived and evidenced from the use and application of whatever tools used has to be understood as the work of God who gives the increase (1 Cor. 3:7). These programs which are summed up under the Christian Education ministry of the church, offer teaching avenues that are aimed at the spiritual growth and maturity of the church.

Before considering the teaching avenues available, there are a few things that need clarification. First, what does education entail? Pazmino highlights, "Education entails conscious planning, implementing, and evaluating of educational experiences. Intentionality in Christian education involves the effort to share biblical content, to grapple with its implications for life, and to suggest avenues for appropriate response."[332]

From Pazmino's description, Christian education has to be understood as that process of sharing of biblical content in a practical manner that makes the practice of the Christian faith possible. As such, Christian education includes all the processes from planning to implementation and practice of what is taught. Thus, Christian education is to be theocentric (God-centred) in all its steps and processes as its aim is the knowledge of God and His will for man.

---

[331] John Calvin, *Commentary on Philippians, Colossians and Thessalonians*, trans. By John Pringle, (Grand Rapids MI: Christian Classics Ethereal Library, n.d.), 122-123.

[332] Pazmino, *Foundational Issues in Christian Education* 22.

Second, what does it mean to grow in grace and in the knowledge of Christ? How does one grow in grace, and what helps and avenues are available for the church to aid this growth? To grow in grace is to mature in faith; hence Christian education also must have an anthropocentric (man-centred) approach. Pazmino writes,

> Education should have an impact upon people's lives and should enable them to grapple with the practical consequences of those truths studied or discerned. Therefore, the appeal to a strictly theoretical or academic agenda that addresses the mind divorced from the affections and actions cannot claim to be faithful to the biblical tradition.[333]

In this, he points out that education is not only God-centred, but must also be person-oriented. It is the person that has to grapple with the practical consequences of biblical truth, and it is the person that has to apply the biblical principles in his daily life and context. The process of spiritual growth and maturity has to be founded and based upon biblical truth, but it has also to be applied and implemented in the course of one's daily life. Therefore, Christian education must enable the student both to evaluate the issues of life based on the Word of God and to relate his life's experiences to biblical principles.

In order to achieve and promote personal devotion to God, personal development in grace as well as a personal disposition reflecting piety and godliness, the Christian Education programs of the church must: (i) centre and focus on the Word of God, (ii) be systematic and gradually focus on specific aspects of growth and developing it, (iii) use relevant teaching methods to communicate the Bible considering both the audience being communicated to and the context in which they live, (iv) ensure continuity and progression by constant recruitment and training for members both to grow and to participate in the training of others also, (v) relate to the students, thus making the lessons being learned both practical and applicable, and (vi) be flexible and regular to ensure that the schedule allows for regular and greatest attendance and participation.

In discussing the avenues available here, considerations made will have basically a two-fold focus: namely teaching avenues that aid (i) growth in grace and knowledge of Christ through the Sunday School ministry; and (ii) service to God and to fellow-men through the Bible college ministry.

---

[333] Ibid., 31.

Christian Education Department and the Teaching Avenues Available to Aid Growth in Grace and Knowledge of Christ

2 Peter 3:17-18 is a passage that is useful here. The context of the second epistle of Peter presents a picture that is closely reflective of the state that the church finds itself in this age. In 2 Peter 1, there stands out as an appeal to the authority of Scripture and is regarded as a classic text with regard to the inspiration of Scripture. In 2 Peter 2, there stands out a clear warning against false teachers and false prophets with their damnable heresies pointing out the effect their presence and teachings will have on the people. And in 2 Peter 3, Peter gives his theme verse in which he presents the place of teaching in spiritual growth and maturity. In this epistle, Peter presents keys to living in the last days and living with eternity's values in view. His theme is living a godly life in an ungodly world. In doing this, Peter shows his concern for the spiritual welfare of the church. He continually reminds them (2 Pet. 1:12-15; 3:2-4) to (a) know and remember their call (2 Pet. 1:10), (b) know and remember the times (2 Pet. 2:1; 20-22), and (c) know and remember their hope (2 Pet. 3:11-13). It is with this in view that 2 Peter 3:17-18 exhorts on how to care for, and build and maintain, the spiritual welfare of the church.

The context presents the importance of teaching for growth in grace and knowledge of Christ. It first presents what constitutes Scripture with Peter asserting that Paul's writings are Scripture, then goes on to state that Scripture can be hard to understand as is evidenced by many who have failed to understand it and have twisted it and misapplied it and finally leading to the danger and destruction that follows misinterpretation and misunderstanding of Scripture. It is then in this context that he turns to the believers and exhorts them to grow spiritually. In his exhortation to growth, he calls for watchfulness and carefulness towards teaching. His exhortation focuses on the following:

Spiritual awareness (2 Pet. 3:17)

In view of the nature of the last days and the false teachers that abound, the church and especially leaders must be on guard and always on the lookout and watch on behalf of the church because:

(i) error is active and it is easy to stray out of the right way. If not careful and watchful, one will be *"led away with the error of the wicked"* (2 Pet. 3:17b, cf. Gal. 2:13), and

(ii) falling away is real and it is possible to forsake one's steadfastness and to let go of what Christ has placed in one's hands and life in order to establish him in the faith and so *"fall from your own steadfastness"* (2 Pet. 3:17c, cf. Gal. 5:4).

Spiritual growth (2 Pet. 3:18)

Growth or increase implies being firmly rooted or attached just as branches which are to bear fruits need to be attached to the tree. How is the church to grow spiritually?

(i) Grow in grace: Christ is the Author of grace, and grace shapes our attitudes.

(ii) Grow in knowledge: Christ is the object of knowledge and knowledge guides and builds relationships. Knowledge also leads to maturity in Christian faith and practice.

Growth in grace and growth in knowledge go together, for when one grows in grace, he grows in knowledge too. 1 Peter 2:2; 1 Corinthians 3:1; and Ephesians 4:11-15

CHAPTER III: TEACHING AVENUES AVAILABLE FOR THE CHURCH TODAY

all point to what aids the believer's growth in grace and in knowledge of Christ, and from them can be drawn what the church's education programs should emphasize and include in order to aid growth. The programs that aid growth and maturity are here to be considered under the Sunday School ministry of the Christian Education department of the church.

What is the Sunday school? Various definitions have been fronted, but in this section, the one which will be considered and used is the detailed and broad description that is given by John H. Vincent who writes,

1. It is the mission of the Church of Jesus Christ to secure the regeneration and sanctification of men, making them "disciples," training them in Christian truth, experience, and service. The Church is the school of eternity, where immortal souls are taught, and thus prepared for the fellowship and service of heaven.

2. This blessed work of regeneration and culture is to be accomplished, under the agency of the Holy Spirit, through the ministry of the Christian home the pleadings, admonitions, and instructions of the pulpit; the meditations and divine communings of the closet; the discipline and experience of life; the inspiring service of the social meeting and last, though by no means least, through the diligent, prayerful study and teaching of the word of God in the school of the Church. Let us call this last the true Church-school, the Bible-school, the Bible- Service of the Christian Church.[334]

The Sunday school is the "school of the church" as presented by Vincent above, and would thus encompass every teaching opportunity provided by the church and through which the church puts forth, "its legitimate effort in its most inviting field of action,"[335] as stated by R. G. Pardee. In its consideration of the Sunday school as an avenue for teaching, this paper considers all teaching opportunities provided for the church membership both the regular and special teaching avenues put forth by the church for its membership to be part of the Sunday school though some of those opportunities may be held at different days other than on Sunday, and at different locations outside the church premises. Thus, the Sunday school is to be seen as encompassed in any teaching avenue of the church for its membership that provides: (i) a platform for learning which encourages interaction between the students and their teacher, (ii) a platform for graded and systematic learning of specified topics which can be set at varied depths, which may be designed to effectively meet specific needs, age or groups identified prior to the setting of the class, and (iii) a platform for fellowship in learning as well as developing and strengthening bonds and mutual faith of all those in the Sunday School class. This makes the Sunday School an effective and flexible teaching avenue.

The Sunday school must be organized for it to function smoothly and for it bear fruit that will glorify God. E. D. Jones in writing about the value of the Sunday school to the church, as one considers the role it has come to play, points out that as an avenue that is indiscriminately available for all, it teaches salvation, matures the Christian, and equips and encourages him for service. He states,

As an educator, it is, by no means an inferior one. Its doors are open for all, irrespective of age or condition; the children of the members of the church and congregation, the children at large, and the members of the church and congregation themselves. All, indeed, may come, and are welcome to labor, or to learn in this Bible-school of

---

[334] John, H. Vincent, *Sunday School Institutes and Normal Class* (New York: Carlton & Lanahan, 1872), 9.

[335] Franklin Eddy, *The Sabbath School Century: an authentic history of the rise and progress of Sabbath Schools for the past century. The work of Raikes, Fox, Pardee, Jacobs, Vincent, Eggleston, and many others* (Hamilton, Ohio: J. H. Long, Steam Book and Job Printer, 1882), 18-19.

the church. Here the Scriptures may be faithfully taught; here salvation is supplemented by Christian culture and training in those things which go to enlarge and strengthen the converted soul. The Sunday-school cannot be otherwise than a great power in the hands of the church when properly used.

The members received from its ranks prove, generally, the best and most efficient workers for Christ, and are able to take hold of any religious enterprise with greater zest, and bring to it greater wisdom and secure for it greater success than are those who enter at later periods of life, with habits and customs hard to be broken or modeled to the rule of Christ's law.[336]

Sadly though, some churches would give the least effort in helping to organize the Sunday School ministry. A teacher (irrespective of maturity and proficiency), and a place for the children to meet for their lessons (irrespective of its conduciveness to learning) would be all they are ready to offer. In many churches in Kenya, no considerations beyond the presence of a teacher (in most cases any young person willing to spend time with the children and occupy them) and a place to meet are made. Broadening the scope of the Sunday school to accommodate all groups within the church, or any other needs this essential ministry would have, is unheard-of and unknown.

The fundamental aim of having a Sunday school in most churches has been limited to the salvation of the children. This definitely is one of the primary aims and Erwin House rightly points out that "the object of the Sunday School is not only to bring the child to Christ, but to bring him *now*."[337] This function the Sunday school may do effectively as it (i) offers a conducive environment for the children to hear and learn about what Christ has done for them, in a language and manner which they can understand, (ii) trains Sunday school teachers to know how to present the gospel in a simple yet clear way to the children, and (iii) provides helps and aids such as pictures, gospels songs and scriptural verses, with which children can be led to confess Christ as their personal Saviour and begin to grow in the Christian way.

But this cannot be considered as the sole aim of the Sunday School. The Sunday School in its work should not be limited or confined to children. There must be more than that. The Sunday School must be the place where any person of any age can come to the saving knowledge of Jesus Christ, and the place where one who has come to know Christ can grow in grace and in knowledge of the Lord Jesus Christ irrespective of his age or condition of life. Jesse Lyman Hurlbut, on the aim of the Sunday School, states,

> The primary aims of the Sunday School are religious instruction, character-development and effective service. It is not to teach history, nor science, nor sociology, but religion; and not merely to impart a knowledge of religion to the intellect of its pupils, but, infinitely more important, to make religion an effective force in the life of the individual scholar. ... A true religious education, such as the Sunday School seeks to give, will include three main aims: (1) knowledge, (2) character, (3) service. There must be an intellectual grasping of the truth; a character built on the truth, out of faith in God, and the life of God inspiring the human soul; and service for God and humanity."[338]

---

[336] E. D. Jones, *Aids to Sunday School Workers* (Philadelphia: American Baptist Publication Society, 1870), 10.

[337] Erwin House, *The Sunday School Handbook: a companion for Pastors, Superintendents, Teachers, Senior Scholars and Parents* (Cincinnati: Hitchcock and Walden, 1868), 11.

[338] Jesse Lyman Hurlbut, *Organising and Building up the Sunday School* (New York: Eaton & Mains, 1990), 14-15.

CHAPTER III: TEACHING AVENUES AVAILABLE FOR THE CHURCH TODAY

Hurlburt rightly broadens the scope and aims of the Sunday school. The Sunday school imparts knowledge, aiming at salvation and spiritual growth of the soul. It trains the whole man, aiming to present him complete and perfect in Christ. It equips the believer and, through him, equips the body for service to God's glory. The Sunday School as a teaching avenue provides a platform for increase in one's (i) knowledge of the Word of God, (ii) wisdom for daily Christian living, and (iii) zeal to serve God and fellowmen. Hurlburt classified these three as knowledge, character and service. A limited understanding of the aims of the Sunday school has limited the work of the Sunday school. The limiting of the aims/goals and scope to one primary goal, that of the evangelization of children, has made the Sunday school to be considered by many as exclusively a children's ministry, and has limited the curriculum and lessons taught to reflect that focus alone. In extreme cases, even the catechism has been excluded from the Sunday School lessons.

A broader understanding like the one given by Hurlbut above will certainly broaden the scope both of those to be taught and subjects to be taught in the Sunday School and, with it, increase the effectiveness and opportunities of the Sunday School. True religious education can only be offered as guided by the Scripture and through it, biblical doctrines can be taught in the church. The Sunday School also helps to develop the character of its scholars and introduce them to effective service in the church. The Sunday School can help all to learn how to read the Bible, pray, give and even worship in a way that is acceptable and pleasing to the Lord. John Adams puts the opportunities for effective Sunday School teaching in good perspective when he points out,

> The object of the Sunday School teacher is not so much to impart knowledge as to mould character. His work is tested not so much by what his pupils know as by what they are. He seeks to impart a knowledge of sacred things, in order that this knowledge may develop in the right direction the nature of the pupil. If his work is to be successful, the teacher must know not only the subjects to be taught, but also the nature of the pupil. He must know not only his Bible but also his boy.[339]

Therefore, when a Sunday School adopts aims and objectives, and when its functions are guided by clear objectives, like those set by Adams above, the efficiency and effectiveness of the Sunday School is enhanced, and the progress of the teaching and instruction as well as its impact can be measured and evaluated to see whether it has met its purposes. The aims and objectives of the Sunday School can be determined from what Adams points out as (i) the knowledge of the Bible (relating to the subjects required and intended to be taught) and (ii) the development of the student (relating to the pupils in attendance and the lives required to be shaped and moulded). When these are fixed and established, the focus can then shift to the method and organization of the Sunday School. Hurlburt points out three essentials that may guide the method and organization of the work of the Sunday School:

> To attain its aim the Sunday School employs the teaching method.... The Sunday School is a *school* and the very word shows that its aim is instruction and character formation, and its method is that of teaching. For the work of a Sunday School the essentials are three: There must be the living teacher who is fitted to inspire, to instruct and to guide.... There must also be the scholar who is to be taught.... There must be a text-book in the hands of both the teacher and the pupil.[340]

---

[339] John Adams, *Primer on Teaching: with special reference to Sunday School work* (Edinburgh: T & T Clark, n.d.), 7.

[340] Hurlbut, *Organising and Building up the Sunday School*, 16-17.

The three essentials form the basis for the grading of the Sunday school. The Sunday School can be broken down and grouped depending on the following:

(i) Availability and "fittedness" of the teacher who is to instruct, inspire and guide the pupils. This implies that the Sunday school classes will be as effective as the teacher is able to impact the lives of his students through his word and example.

(ii) Classification or grouping of the scholars who are to attend to the set course of study. This implies that the effectiveness of a Sunday School class is greatly reduced when the students grouped together are not classified based on their spiritual needs and the lessons presented are not geared towards them with particular or defined emphasis and objectives (i.e. the lessons are generalized).

(iii) Identification and making available of a suitable curriculum that is drawn from, based on and governed by Scripture to be used by both the teacher and the students. This implies that the aims and intentions of the church in setting up a Sunday School class is to be effectively and consistently relayed to the teacher and students in the class through the curriculum and materials chosen to be used in the class.

In order for the church to have an effective Sunday School, these three essentials must be given serious consideration. Wade Crawford Barclay, in presenting the essentials for the work of the Sunday School, sees five essentials adding two more to the three essentials discussed above. He writes,

> When we think of the work of the Sunday school there are five chief factors which claim attention. These factors are the pupil: for whom the school was instituted and exists; the institution itself, the Sunday school, the school of the Church; the teachers through whom and by whom the work of the school is chiefly done; the lessons, the materials of religious education and; the principles and methods used by the teacher in making the lessons effective in the religious education of the pupil.[341]

Both Barclay and Hurlburt agree on three essentials, namely, the teacher, the scholar, and the textbook or lesson materials. Crawford includes the institution[342] (the Sunday School as the church school) and the teaching methods[343] as elements to be considered too. When evaluating the aims, objectives and purposes, the three essentials mentioned by both writers above have to be looked at closely. The church cannot hope to help its membership learn how to read and understand and believe the Bible without paying attention to them.

The Practice of the Sunday School

Charles B. Williams in his book *The Function of Teaching in Christianity* has an excellent section on ways the pastor can teach his people, in which he presents excellent tips on the Sunday school as a teaching platform for the pastor to teach and grow the church membership. In the section on "Some Ways the Pastor Can Teach the People," Williams addresses the Sunday school and its teaching role as supplementary and secondary to the pulpit ministry which forms the primary teaching and instructional tool for

---

[341] Wade Crawford Barclay, *First Standard Manual of Teacher Training* (New York: The Methodist Book Concern, 1912), ix.

[342] When presenting the institution as an essential, consideration is to be given to all who are involved with the Sunday school including even those who though may not be the ones teaching the class but are involved in the planning and implementing and evaluating of the class teaching functions, groupings and effectiveness.

[343] When considering the teaching methods as an essential, consideration is to be given to both the text of the curriculum and the methods of presenting the curriculum as well as all other issues related to the implementation of the curriculum.

CHAPTER III: TEACHING AVENUES AVAILABLE FOR THE CHURCH TODAY

pastoral ministry. The Sunday School offers manifold assistance and benefits to the church's teaching ministry which this writer will reproduce here in some length before commenting on it. Williams writes concerning "Some Ways the Pastor Can Teach the People,"

> But how must the pastor teach the people? Of course every sermon should be so filled with truth that it is the means of instructing the people in the teachings of the gospel as well as a force to inspire motives for the higher living of the principles of the gospel. But there are the five following ways in which especially the pastor may teach his people "the Word of God."
>
> 1. In expository preaching. Zwingli aroused Zurich to the work of the reformation by expounding to the people the gospel of Matthew, just as a teacher would do it. In a similar way many a modern pastor could arouse the people to religious thinking and spiritual living if he would give to the people skilful, attractive expositions of the books of the Bible. The world is hungry for truth. The preacher must master the books of the Bible and then give the people the truth by expository preaching. It must be conceded that this is the most difficult method of preaching from the preacher's view point. He must know the books of the Bible. But this is his business, and people need the truths of the Bible. The preacher is the divinely appointed man to teach the people. This he can effectively do by often preaching expository sermons.
>
> 2. By teaching a class in the Sunday School. Of course, it is well known that there are arguments for and against the pastor's teaching a class in the Sunday School. But the following arguments for this method of teaching the people far outweigh all the arguments against it: (1) Teaching a class in the Sunday School will necessarily make the pastor a better Bible student. If he teaches acceptably intelligent men or women from Sunday to Sunday, he will have to study the books of the Bible in a systematic way. (2) Teaching the Sunday School class will make the pastor a better preacher by giving him more and better material for his sermons. His systematic study in the preparation of Sunday School lessons will suggest to him new texts and furnish fresh material for sermons each week. (3) It will also make him a better preacher because of the personal contact with individuals in the Sunday School class. Although the pastor cannot teach all his flock in the Sunday School class/he will be able to teach enough of them to give him the personal point of view of the individual layman in his church. This will help him to adapt his pulpit message to the actual needs of his people. (4) It will make the pastor a better shepherd, because it will give him knowledge of the people's needs. The discussions in his Sunday School class will bring out many instances of personal need among the members of his flock where he can render service as the shepherd.
>
> 3. By teaching a class of Sunday School teachers. Every modern pastor should be so versed in pedagogy that he can in person conduct a Sunday School teachers' training class. If he cannot, or has not the time, he should arrange for some competent teacher to train a class of Sunday School teachers.
>
> 4. By organizing the young people of his church into Bible, mission, and social study classes. He should either teach these classes himself or have them taught by a competent teacher.
>
> 5. By organizing special study classes among his 'church members. Each pastor should have, at different times, special study classes, in Christian doctrines, on the fundamental principles of missions, on individual mission fields, on the mission of

the church to modern society, that is, its duties to working men, capitalists, neglected children, fallen women, etc., etc.[344]

Williams in his discussion above presents two teaching avenues available for the pastor for teaching the congregation. The avenues are the pulpit and the Sunday School. From these pastoral teaching tools, the following can be deduced:

(i) The pulpit as the pastor's primary teaching platform must be filled with truth and doctrine as well as inspire practical Christian living and for that the pastor must be expository, systematic and relevant in his preaching. For this, William points out that the pastor will require a thorough knowledge of the Bible when he says,

> The preacher must master the books of the Bible and then give the people the truth by expository preaching. It must be conceded that this is the most difficult method of preaching from the preacher's view point. He must know the books of the Bible. But this is his business, and people need the truths of the Bible.[345]

(ii) The Sunday school is the pastor's second teaching tool and as such the pastor is not to be exempt from taking and teaching a Sunday school class. In the third point in William's discussion above, the pastor has to have three perspectives in mind. The first perspective is a personal one, with the pastor seeing in his Sunday School class an avenue for personal growth as he interacts with his Bible and examines himself as he prepares to teach the Sunday School class. The second perspective is an inter-personal one with the pastor seeing in his Sunday School class an avenue for building relations with his congregation in a class setting. As he hears and responds to their questions during the class and lesson presentation, he understands them more with their challenges and assesses their world-view and perspective on the issues being taught to them and through this also he can develop the individuals for areas of ministry within the church. The third perspective is a pastoral one with the pastor seeing in his Sunday school an avenue for *"perfecting the saints for the work of the ministry"* (Eph. 4:12) and maturing them that they *"be no more children tossed to and fro with every wind of doctrine"* (Eph. 4:14) labouring and striving to *"present every man perfect in Christ Jesus."* (Col. 1:28). Thus, through the Sunday school class he is able to meet the needs of the members and the needs of the church as he teaches and provides opportunities for others to join him in the work of the ministry in different capacities according to the giftings identified and opportunities available.

From William's excerpt, three principles for the practice of the Sunday School can be drawn. These principles include exposition, preparation and participation, and they are as follows:

---

[344] Williams, *The Function of Teaching in Christianity*, 96-99.

[345] Ibid, 96-99.

CHAPTER III: TEACHING AVENUES AVAILABLE FOR THE CHURCH TODAY

1. Exposition (Acts 20:20, 27): The pastor's teaching avenues provide a platform for the skilful and relevant thought-provoking exposition of the books of the Bible with the Sunday School having the added opportunity of interactive teaching. This provides members with the understanding and knowledge of the Word of God book by book. For this, Williams points to the pastor's teaching functions and the church's need for teaching. Since the pastor is to preach and teach the whole counsel of God, expositional preaching and teaching becomes the primary method in conducting this business. The Sunday School offers additional opportunity for exposition that can be used to study books of the Bible chronologically, thematically, topically or theologically in a systematic and interactive manner.

2. Preparation (2 Tim. 4:2; 1 Tim. 4:13-16): The pastor by taking up a Sunday School class is personally profited by the preparation. His preparation draws him to give more attention to the reading of the texts and its doctrines so that he may exhort and instruct the class. For this Williams points to the pastor's study in preparation for teaching in the Sunday School class. Since the Sunday School is interactive, the pastor in teaching the class has to study diligently in order to understand and to relate the text to the particular class he is teaching and also to address it to the particular challenges and answer the questions that may arise from interaction with the class.

3. Participation (Heb. 10:24-26): The pastor by the use of the Sunday School class increases his inter-personal skills and strengthens the bonds he has with his members and among the members themselves. For this, Williams points out that the pastor conducting teacher training classes enables him to know and equip his co-labourers, as well as interact with them at different levels. In addition to this, the class divisions and organization reflect the pastor's knowledge of the church membership and its needs and offers opportunities for the different groups within the membership to be trained and to participate in the church's mission.

In regard to the practice of the Sunday School, despite the variations that may be seen in the implementation of the different programs due to the contexts, needs or groups within the particular church, considerations have to be given to two major aspects: the content and the organization of the Sunday School.

The Teaching (Content and Curriculum) of the Sunday School

The curriculum of the Sunday School ministry is very important. It is necessary that when the scholars gather every Sunday for their lessons, they are taught in the best way possible knowing that the teachings they get from the Sunday School will guide them in their spiritual lives, develop their character and enable them to know how to serve the Lord. Although the teachings and messages of the Sunday school can vary from catechism questions to crafts and games, the one and very important teaching in which all other teachings must follow is that of the Bible. A Sunday School teacher may teach without using pictorials, teaching aids or any other materials, but will not be able to teach without the use of the Bible. Concerning the Bible, J.C. Ryle said, "A thorough knowledge of the Bible is the foundation of all clear views of religion. He that is well-grounded in it will not generally be found a waverer, and carried about by every wind of new doctrine. Any system of training which does not make a knowledge of Scripture the first thing is unsafe and unsound."[346]

A church that wishes to see her members grounded on the right and true doctrines must see to it that the Bible is the main and fundamental book in its curriculum. Ryle continues to say,

---

[346] J. C. Ryle, *Training of Children* (Singapore: Christian Life Publishers, 1992), 12.

... and some are to be found in like manner who honour a catechism more than the Bible, or fill the minds of their children with miserable little story books, instead of the Scripture of truth. But if you love your children, let the simple Bible be everything in the training of their souls; and let all other books go down and take the second place.[347]

What Ryle says concerning the content of the Sunday School and its curriculum is applicable to all Sunday school classes irrespective of the age or nature of the group being taught. For the Bible to be taught effectively, accurately and practically through the Sunday School class, its lessons must be well outlined and prepared at an appropriate time. H. M. Hamill says concerning time in the teacher's preparation,

- Study Daily — Fifteen or twenty minutes of daily study of next Sunday's lesson is better than hours massed together upon a single day. ...
- Study when freshest — The evening hour, when body and mind are worn by the day's labours, is the least profitable for Bible study. ...
- Begin at once — Begin Sunday afternoon while heart and mind are warm with the lesson just taught. ...
- Form a Habit of study — The mind is as much a creature of habit as the body. It does its best work periodically.[348]

The Organisation (Time and Class Grouping) of the Sunday School

The Sunday School can be conducted before or after the worship service. Its duration can also vary from half an hour to one-and-half hours depending on the group being taught and the lesson being presented. This means that the church needs to do her arrangements as pertains to the time and programs. Should the teaching be done before the main worship service or after? The church's leadership needs to determine the suitable time for conducting a particular Sunday School class.

The age groupings and class groupings of the Sunday School class are varied and can be arrived at differently depending on the composition of the congregation being taught. The Sunday School can be set up for different classes either considered by age groupings, spiritual status, membership status, or any other variable status in the church's context that may need addressing and teaching. It is imperative that every church should be going through teachings in order for her members to be admonished in the Word of God regardless of one's age. There must be proper arrangement of teachings as pertains to different ages, groups and people. Paul addressed the teaching of the various groups in the church (Tit. 2:1-10). He advised Titus how to teach and what he was supposed to teach. The groups that were to be taught included old men, older women, younger women, younger men, and even slaves. No one was left out.

In the local church setting today, this may be done in different ways for example: (i) <u>Teachings as arranged according to ages:</u> 1-3 years old; 4-10 years old; 11-15 years old; and so on up to 90 years old depending on the members of the congregation. However, these ages must have their curriculum topics based on the needs of the church. (ii) <u>Teachings as arranged according to groups:</u> Toddlers, teens, youth, young adults, adults, seniors. (iii) <u>Teachings as arranged according to classes of people:</u> Youths who are in boarding schools, widows, single mothers/fathers, single ladies/men, young families, retirees etc. All these programmes can neither be done by the pastor alone nor done in only

---

[347]Ibid., 12-13.

[348]H. M. Hamill, *The Sunday School Teacher* (New York: Fleming H. Revell Company, 1901), 25.

CHAPTER III: TEACHING AVENUES AVAILABLE FOR THE CHURCH TODAY

one moment of time. It is an ongoing process that must continue until Christ comes, just as the Bible says, *"occupy till I come"* (Luke 19:13). The early church continued steadfastly in doctrine as the Bible says: *"And they continued steadfastly in the apostles' doctrine and fellowship, and in breaking of bread, and in prayers"* (Acts 2:42). And, *"But we will give ourselves continually to prayer, and to the ministry of the word"* (Acts 6:4).

When people are properly trained and grounded in God's Word, there are many benefits both to the individual person, to the church as a whole, to the society and to the nation. The teaching of God's Word sanctifies people's lives for the Bible says, *"Sanctify them through thy truth: thy word is truth.... Now ye are clean through the word which I have spoken unto you"* (John 17:17; 15:3). Moreover, the consistent teaching of God's Word makes a person wise unto salvation and to abide in the faith right from childhood to adulthood. Apostle Paul told Timothy that, *"And that from a child thou hast known the holy Scriptures, which are able to make thee wise unto salvation through faith which is in Christ Jesus"* (2 Tim. 3:15). This wisdom is not only unto salvation, but also gives a person the spiritual sensitivity to discern wrong teachings. If a person gets proper teaching from God's Word, he will not be gullible and will not be easily enticed by wrong teachings. The Bible says, *"Through thy precepts I get understanding: therefore I hate every false way"* (Ps. 119:104). Apostle Paul warned the Colossians that they must be on their watch, *"lest any man should beguile you with enticing words"* (Col. 2:4).

The church that receives proper teaching from God's Word is rooted and built up in Christ and is very stable in the faith. Such a church is able to shun unbiblical traditions and cultures that have crept into the church. The Bible says, *"As ye have therefore received Christ Jesus the Lord, so walk ye in him: Rooted and built up in him, and established in the faith, as ye have been taught, abounding therein with thanksgiving. Beware lest any man spoil you through philosophy and vain deceit, after the tradition of men, after the rudiments of the world, and not after Christ"* (Col. 2:6-8). Her members will be able to identify cults and reject cultic teachings and influences. They will also be able to properly explain and defend the faith in which they believe. The Bible says, *"But sanctify the Lord God in your hearts: and be ready always to give an answer to every man that asketh you a reason of the hope that is in you with meekness and fear"* (1 Pet. 3:15). The members of such a church will always be fruitful and ready and willing to witness and testify of that faith which they possess.

In addition to the regular Sunday school, there are other "special" Sunday school platforms that can be used to accomplish all that has been discussed in this section of the teaching avenues available that aid the spiritual maturity and growth of the church. These other platforms are here considered as special due to the time, frequencies, venues and teaching methods used and their impact on the life of the church. They form part of the church calendar of programs and are regular though they may not be as frequent as the regular Sunday school programs and the time assigned for them also differs from the time assigned for the regular Sunday school classes due to the nature of the teachings conducted and the venue and periods assigned for these avenues. They include:

Mid-week Bible Study and Home Fellowship Programs

These are conducted regularly and are usually set in the course of the week on days other than Sunday and the location also may be varied mainly being done outside the church in the homes of different members. In most churches, this is set on a rotational basis and groups determined either by their location (mainly determined by proximity to dwelling locations) or by availability (mainly determined by the time set for the meetings and which is most convenient to members).

Bible Camps, Church Camps and Conventions

These are teaching programs set in the church calendar that gathers specific groups or church family to an identified location for a set period to cover identified topics drawn from the Bible. These are set mainly during vacation time or for periods when the identified group is available to get away from their normal schedule of life and homes to gather together and "camp" at identified location for a time of teaching and instruction. This special Sunday School has been used effectively in many cases to also address contemporary issues facing the church and also for controversial issues that need clarification.

Vacation Bible Schools and Vacation Bible Training Programs

These are similar to the church camps and conventions. But, unlike camps that have the group gathered together at the set venue for the period of teaching and instruction set, Vacation Bible Schools and Bible Training Programs are conducted over the set period as a day or half-day program. This means that the group being taught gathers daily over the period set for the number of hours fixed with everyone leaving at the end of the day's program to their own homes and regather the following day for the set programs.

Christian Education Department and the Teaching Avenues Available to Aid in Serving God and Fellow-men

Hebrews 5:12-6:3

The book of Hebrews presents Christ to the believing Hebrews, urging them to believe, adhere to and persevere in the Christian faith. In order to do this, Paul highlights the excellency of Christ as Prophet, Priest and King. Hebrews 5:12-6:3 presents Paul's indictment of the weakness of his readers as he speaks concerning the priesthood of Christ. Hebrews 5:12 not only shows the nature of the weakness and condition of the people's spiritual state, it also shows the expectation and direction that their faith was to take in the course of their Christian walk and growth. *"For when for the time, ye ought to be teachers, ye have need that one teach you again which be the first principles of the oracles of God"* (Heb. 5:12). This charge shows an expectation of proficiency in the things of God. There is a time when one does not know the things of God and, as a babe in Christ, is fed with milk. But the milk of the Word is for the intent that they may grow thereby. This growth in grace and in knowledge of Jesus Christ brings the reasonable expectation that there will be a time when *"ye ought to be teachers"*! This expectation of proficiency not only points to spiritual growth but also service to God and to one's fellow men. The expectation to be teachers has the understanding of teaching fellow men. This expectation seems to be directed to all believers, but conditioned on (i) the good understanding and knowledge of the doctrines of the Bible and (ii) the maturity and good personal progress in the spiritual knowledge of the one who would become the teacher. Since the church as an institution draws and gets its teachers from among its membership, and as teaching is the means by which the doctrines of Christ are passed on from one generation to the next, incompetent and immature teachers who are ignorant of the Word do much harm to the church. Paul's indictment has been repeated over different periods in history by men who saw the sorry state that immaturity was putting the church in. Charles Reynolds Brown in his contribution to the book *Education for Christian Service* (put up by the faculty of the Divinity School of Yale University) said,

CHAPTER III: TEACHING AVENUES AVAILABLE FOR THE CHURCH TODAY

The inability of any minister to meet the deepest needs of mind and heart is a criticism which should sting him into an effective effort to make his preaching more adequate.

When we think of all the weak, inefficient preaching that is being perpetrated on a patient, trusting public, we marvel that the Christian religion has stood up under it without being annihilated. If our faith had not been divine in its origin and essence it would have collapsed long ago.[349]

Brown, looking at the state of the church under a weak preaching and teaching ministry, sees the divine nature of the Christian faith as its sustenance in dark and ignorant periods, but this does not absolve the church of its teaching duty. He points out also that the divinely appointed instrumentality by which the Christian faith is to be propagated, defended and explained is through preaching and teaching. The church must place a strong emphasis on its preaching and teaching ministry and must hold its ministers to the highest standards. The church falls into such a sorry state when its ministers are inadequate to their task. This sorry state seems to be more visible and widespread now than when the faculty of the Divinity School of Yale University took it upon themselves to address the issue of "Education for Christian Service." The church seems to have deteriorated from weak inefficient preaching to no preaching at all, and instead of preaching, many have turned to motivational speeches drawn from human psychology.

Paul in Hebrews 5:12 not only presented the expectation of proficiency in the things of God, but also pointed out the disappointment in the condition of the people of God. This disappointment was directly linked to the lack of proficiency in the things of God among God's people. The expectation was that with time they would become teachers in the things of God, but the sad reality was that they still *"have need that one teach you again which be the first principles of the oracles of God"* (Heb. 5:12). Scripture contains in it some things that are hard to be understood. But, though hard, they may be understood. Those who are mature and have their faculties exercised, and have teeth, may eat of the strong meat. The expectation is that through constant, consistent and continual application, one would go forward in Christian knowledge and maturity. But the sad disappointment is the forgetfulness and the weakness shown in the people whose maturity was expected.

Christian education, through the Sunday school, works at and has greatly aided the growth in knowledge and maturity of the believers. This same Christian education has a role to play in the expectations presented in the indictment of Hebrews 5:12 by preparing men and women to meet the expectation expected here. The expectation of having men and women who are mature in the faith and can aid in serving God and their fellow men is even greater than ever today because of the presence and increased popularity of those whom Brown refers to as "bunglers" who through the use of unsound notions, and false interpretations, have misled many and brought in confusion and "made it difficult" for those who would preach the Word faithfully. They have also perverted many young and impressionable men by their fame, and popularity, causing them to imitate and parrot popular sayings and to disdain exact and thorough knowledge and study of the scriptures. Brown writes,

There are hundreds of men preaching who are steadily pushing the thoughtful and discriminating, the robust and aspiring, the men of exact and thorough knowledge, farther and farther away from organized religion by their own method of presenting

---

[349]Charles Reynolds Brown, "The Training of a Minister", in *Education for Christian Service, by Members of the Faculty of the Divinity School of Yale University* (New Haven: Yale University Press, 1922), 9.

the Gospel. They are also loading young minds with false Biblical interpretations and with unsound ethical notions which will have to be unlearned later when the inevitable awakening comes, to the confusion and hurt of the young people who have been thus misled. Worse than all, those men are making it more difficult for other preachers who really can preach to secure a chance at the people whom they desire to reach and influence. These people have been already repelled by the discredit and reproach brought upon the work of preaching by those bunglers.[350]

To stem this tide, the church must turn to its teaching programs that prepare ministers for service since the work and cause of the "bunglers" are greatly abetted by weak, inefficient preaching and teaching.

After the indictment of Hebrews 5:12, in the context of Hebrews 5:12-14, Paul goes on to present a case for the need of maturity through teaching by first pointing out that the doctrines or teachings are at varied grades of difficulty using the imagery of milk for the first principles or basics, and strong meat for deeper teachings and showing that the milk is for the babes or young in faith while the strong meat is for the mature in faith. Thus, the teaching programs of the church that are to prepare men for the service of God need to be graded since the doctrines of the Bible are presented as varied in degrees of difficulty in understanding and reception. This ought to be done so that different doctrines can be effectively taught at the different grades or levels of training. The distinction between babes in Christ and the mature in Christ or those who have come of full age is testimony to this need since the babes are described as unskilled, while those who have come of full age have done so by reason of use and have exercised their senses to discern between good and evil.

It is those who have come of full age that are expected to grapple with the strong meat of the Word and it is they who are expected to be teachers. Herein begins the problem of this age as the ministry and pulpit in this age have been invaded by throngs who would be considered babes by the apostle. Worse still is the presence of some who do not know that they do not know and are obstinate in their ignorance. Brown concerning such writes,

> The man who does not know and does not know that he does not know and is not willing that anyone should tell him that he does not know, had better not enter the ministry he had better raise sweet potatoes. The real work of the world is not being done in these days by rule of thumb or by clever guesses on the part of kind-hearted people whose intentions are good. It is being done by men and women who know how because they took pains to learn how. In no calling is this more true than in the high and hard task of leading the minds and souls of men out of darkness into light, out from the bondage of evil into the freedom of righteousness.[351]

The nature of the task of teaching demands that those who endeavour to venture into the office be of certain calibre. Serving God and fellow-men is honourable and if any man desires the office of a bishop he desires a good work; yet this good work has standards which are mandatory. Paul talks about being apt to teach (1 Tim. 3:2; 2 Tim. 2:24) and about holding fast the faithful Word which one has been taught (Tit. 1:9). James 3:2 provides a caution that puts proper balance especially in regard to the teaching ministry while Hebrews 10:24-26; 13:7, 17 point to what aims or ends Christian service should be directed to. These help to give the biblical perspective for Christian service to God and fellow-men, and from them can be drawn what the church's educational pro-

---

[350] Brown, "The Training of a Minister", 9-10.

[351] Ibid, 11.

grams should emphasize in order to ensure those seeking to serve God and men are prepared and equipped for service.

The Sunday school would address the congregation and the teaching needs for the different groups and different levels present in the congregation. But still there remains one need that must be addressed, that of the kind of teachers that take it upon themselves to instruct others. This need according to this writer's view is to be addressed through a different avenue of Christian education, namely, that of the Bible school/college ministry of the Christian Education department of the church.

The Bible College

Just as with the Sunday school, the Bible school/college is another teaching avenue of the church that is misunderstood in this age. And just like the Sunday School, the misunderstanding has affected its effectiveness. With the Sunday School, it was the scope that had been limited: the focus being limited to children's ministry. For the Bible college, it is the purpose that has been lost with many in this age not seeing the need for training those who would serve and minister in God's church. The growth of the Gospel in the New Testament was accompanied by the training of those who would take the lead in the work of the Gospel and since the Great Commission focuses on the teaching responsibility of the church, the burden and responsibility for doing this has to be placed on the leaders who are charged with the spiritual growth of the church as they take the gospel of Jesus Christ to the whole world. Since the great commission involves discipleship, it thus calls for teaching programs in the churches. There ought to be teaching not only in growing and maturing believers, but also teaching in preparing those who would serve in the church, and lead, and those who would take the gospel to the whole world.

The example of the early church in the book of Acts also sets a biblical precedence for a teaching emphasis in the church's life as can be seen in Acts 2:41-42; 11:22-26; 15:35; 18:11; 20:20, 25-26. This biblical precedence in the Acts is further affirmed by the epistles where teaching is clearly presented and emphasizes as pastoral responsibility and is to be required in pastoral qualifications as the ability to teach (1 Tim. 3:2; 2 Tim. 2:24-26). Systematic teaching programs formed part of pastoral ministry in the New Testament with teaching being conducted privately from house to house as well as publicly (Acts 20:20). This should be the perspective with which one views the Bible college and its place in the church as a teaching avenue that aids service to God and to men. When this view is obscured by any other, the Bible college loses its purpose.

It is sad that to many the Bible college has lost its purpose. To some it is being considered as an academic institution one needs to go to get the necessary papers and accreditation in order to fulfil denominational prerequisites for ordained ministry required by churches. To others, it is seen as a man-made hindrance to the leading and guiding of the Spirit which emphasizes and focuses on man-made manuals to propagate the minds of men over the Word of God and is to be avoided by those who trust the Spirit to lead them and teach them. And then there are those who would limit the Bible college to formal class format that is commonly used in this age, then go on to claim that the first generation Christian church had little or no theological education and were men of average or below average intelligence and learning, yet were used mightily by God to spread the Gospel and plant churches.

Why should the Bible college be considered a purely academic institution that is to be shunned yet the very nature of the Gospel work and service of God demands that those who would enter the service be mature in faith, knowledgeable in the Word and competent in service? Why should the Bible college be considered only as a denominational prerequisite for ordained service which those seeking ordination should meet yet the Bible college teaches the Word which is alive and quick, sharper than any two-edged sword? Why should those who are called to other areas of service apart from the ordained ministry think they can serve without being equipped and trained? In all areas of service those who serve must do so according to the Word of God and those who minister in any capacity handle the things of God and His Word Why should there be those that think that all one needs is Christ's help and guidance through the Holy Spirit without any personal diligence or endeavour to study and understand Scripture yet Christ Himself was often referred to as teacher and the apostles considered as disciples or learners and were often taken to task about what they heard and saw while with Christ? Why should the Bible college be viewed as strictly formal and the training of men for service to God and their fellow-men not include mentorship and discipleship programs?

Though all these questions may not be adequately answered in this paper, and all these views may not be addressed in detail here, yet some consideration may be given to bring some clarity on this writer's view and perspective of the Bible college as a teaching avenue of the Christian Education department of the church to aid in the preparation of men and women for service to God and men. This consideration is premised on the understanding of teaching and what it is. Many have attempted to address the issue of teaching, but when considering the teaching role of the church, Seldon Roberts after a lengthy discussion gives an insightful summary which this writer agrees with and which would be the understanding adopted in this section. Roberts writes,

> We may now summarize our thought about teaching in the particular relationships in which we are to study it as church-school teachers. It is <u>the personal assistance</u> which a more mature and experienced person gives a younger or less-experienced person, to help him know and do the will of God in such a way as to realize his own best self through living, thinking, and working in a Christian way. <u>It requires</u> on the part of the teacher <u>the largest possible sympathy, patience, and purpose</u> to be helpful, and presupposes, as we shall see, on his part a <u>large knowledge of God</u> and his will, <u>a fine degree of skill</u> in understanding and helping people, and <u>the embodiment in his own character of those Christian virtues</u>, attitudes, and ways of acting which he seeks to help others attain. It necessitates upon the part of the learner cooperation and action in keeping with the way in which the teacher leads, a willingness to try, to endure, and to correct patiently errors and mistakes. While it is not supposed that any learner will be perfect at his first effort either in attitude or performance, it is necessary that he in time accept whole-heartedly the ideals involved, and press on until he has approximated the goal of Christian living. [Emphasis added.][352]

Roberts' summary puts the place of teaching and the need for teachers to be trained, prepared and equipped in good balance. This balance draws out not only the need for the Bible college as a teaching avenue, it also gives the direction of training that the Bible college should take. The misunderstanding of the purpose of the Bible college, the loss of direction and the lack of practical mentorship in many training centres today may be cleared by the balance presented by Roberts in his summary above.

Considering what teaching would demand from the one who is to teach, there can be no doubt that training must be necessary for any who would teach, and having considered teaching as an expectation for all in Hebrews 5:12, then training for all who would serve God and their fellow-men must surely be mandatory. The kind of training that is to be pursued has to be one that aids in accomplishing the desired end, which, according to

---

[352] Seldon L. Roberts, *Teaching in the Church School: a manual of principles and methods for church school teachers* (Philadelphia: The Judson Press, 1927), 13.

Roberts, is to help mature believers. This maturity is to be seen in and measured by an individual's (i) knowledge of and obedience to the will of God, and (ii) understanding of himself and the development of his own Christian life and conduct.

In order to do this successfully, Roberts says that, on the one hand, the teacher would be required to help through (1) his teaching of the Word, (2) his testimony and character reflecting the "virtues, attitudes and ways of acting which he seeks to help others attain,"[353] and (3) his attitude and relationship to his students as seen in his compassion, and passion towards them. And on the part of the student it would require (1) submission to instruction, (2) effort in application, (3) endurance through correction, and (4) commitment to the whole learning process. As the teacher is to be a mature Christian who assists the less matured to discern and obey the will of God, the Bible college has to be a place that matures and gives knowledge of the will of God that in turn can be used to help others mature.

As the teacher is to be one with "the largest possible sympathy, patience, and purpose to be helpful,"[354] the Bible college has to be the place where his compassion, sympathy, patience and purpose is stirred up, enlarged, and developed, so that it may be directed towards the students clearly and visibly so that the students may acquire and imitate the same. As the teacher is to be the one with "a large knowledge of God and his will, a fine degree of skill in understanding and helping people,"[355] the Bible college has to be the place where he who seeks to teach others grows in the knowledge of God and his will, and sharpens his understanding of men and the skills needed in helping people. And finally, as the teacher is to be the one with "the embodiment in his own character of those Christian virtues, attitudes, and ways of acting which he seeks to help others attain,"[356] then the Bible college must be the place where he who seeks to teach others develops, sharpens and shows those Christian attitudes that he must help others attain. Concerning teaching, Hovey and Gregory rightly note,

> No one can be competent to teach the Bible until he knows what the Bible contains. This knowledge must not only cover a general outline, but, to some extent, must embrace details. It is not enough to say that merely a devout spirit is required. The Bible addresses the intellect, as well as the heart, and we can acquire a knowledge of its contents by hard study only.[357]

Therefore, the Bible college must be seen not as an academic institution of the church, but rather also as a pastoral and practical institution where those who would be teachers grow and mature as teachers and those who would instruct others acquire, perfect, and affirm the knowledge and doctrines they would impart. Whether in an informal mentorship setting or in a formal classroom setting, the Bible college is the teaching avenue available for the church to aid those who would serve God and their fellow-men.

The need for the Bible College as a Teaching Avenue

The work and ministry of the Bible college is vital to the life and ministry of the church because it is through the Bible college that the church finds a platform to (i) pre-

---

[353] Ibid, 13.

[354] Ibid.

[355] Ibid.

[356] Ibid.

[357] Alvah Hovey and J. M. Gregory, *Normal Class Manual for Bible Teachers* (Philadelphia: The Bible and Publication Society, nd), 4-5.

pare ministers for the work of the ministry and through them, advance the work of the church and the Great Commission of Christ, and (ii) safeguard the church by teaching and warning the pastors and the students who enter its halls of the apostasy, false ecumenism, and other false "isms" that are gaining a wide acceptance and following day by day. From this two-fold platform of preparing and protecting, the need of the Bible college as a teaching avenue of the church can be urged upon all. Through an understanding of the present state of the church and the context in which it serves, the preparing and protecting needs can be considered and drawn up. When this is done, the need of the Bible college becomes clearer. The present state of the church and its context when considered reveals the following:

(i) There is an increasing proliferation of falsehood. Peter writing his second epistle warned of false teachers and the influx of false teachings. Wicked men are propagating their teachings at a very fast pace, be it through the print media, the radio, television, or internet. The church's safeguard is in its training and teaching programs. False teachers and cultic leaders spare no effort in equipping their followers and sending them forth to propagate their error and to lead more people astray and will continue to do so. The church has to raise up a standard against them, the church has to stem the tide, and this is to be done through the teaching avenue of the Bible college.

In 2 Timothy 3, what Paul says to Timothy seems to closely relate to this. In 2 Timothy 3:1-9, Paul warns against the error of the last days, then in 2 Timothy 3:10-17 he points to the standard that will stem the tide so that *"they shall proceed no further"* (2 Tim. 3:9) and which standard will ensure that *"their folly shall be manifest unto all men"* (2 Tim. 3:9). But what standard is he pointing to? It is the standard of his godly example and doctrine (2 Tim. 3:10-11), of *"the things which thou hast learned and hast been assured of knowing of whom thou hast learned them"* (2 Tim. 3:14), of the holy scriptures *"which are able to make you wise unto salvation"* (2 Tim. 3:15) and which are *"given by inspiration of God"* (2 Tim. 3:16) and which are *"profitable for doctrine, for reproof, for correction, for instruction in righteousness"* and which are able to furnish the man of God *"unto all good works"* (2 Tim. 3:16-17). This is the alternative the Bible college offers against the influence and teachings of the false teachers.

(ii) There is pressure from an increasingly secularized world. In his foreword to his work "Qualifying Men for Church Work," Gerrit Verkyul wrote,

> The deepest need of our world is Christian leadership. Beginning with the home, and touching every conceivable phase of life in each institution, organization, establishment and enterprise there is a call for men who plan, initiate and carry through with Christ a wholesome, benevolent program. None but men of Christian calibre are able to respond to our modern needs. This means that the Church must address herself to the qualifying of Christian workers, and it is with the conviction that such workers can be adequately qualified, even in face of the most severe demands, that these chapters have been written.[358]

The Christian influence and morality, as well as the Christian testimony and life, are the salt and light of the world. But because of the proliferation of falsehood and false teachings, morality is waning. With many in the church not knowing the Gospel or the Lord's standards and will for life and conduct, the salt of Christian influence and the light of Christian testimony are dimming outside the church. The secular activism that is rising and popular psychology that is being propagated are numbing the people's conscience against sin, and against God. Morality is giving way, and in its place relativism is

---

[358] Gerrit Verkuyl, *Qualifying Men for Church Work* (New York: Fleming H. Revell Company, 1927), 7.

CHAPTER III: TEACHING AVENUES AVAILABLE FOR THE CHURCH TODAY

rising. Absolutes are being done away with and the lack of proper, consistent, Bible-based teaching in the church is abetting this. The rise of strong-willed, theologically deficient but eloquent men to leadership positions in the church and to active service to God and fellow-men is slowly replacing the Lord's standards with worldly standards. The world is creeping into the church because the church is not preparing and teaching those who would be given opportunities to serve God and their fellow-men.

(iii) There is a persisting resistance to the Bible college. The growing anti-Bible-college sentiments (whether the formal classroom experience or the informal field-mentorship experience) is totally unbiblical and very dangerous for the church. An example is cited by Randy Frame in his online article titled "Is Seminary Education Always Necessary for Pastoral Ministry?" Randy goes on to narrate an incident that Craig Williford experienced when talking to a group of youth pastors. Randy writes,

> Craig Williford, former president of Denver Seminary, tells of a group of youth pastors that attended a meeting held at the school. During a question-and-answer period, Williford asked those in attendance how many planned to pursue graduate-level theological education. According to Williford, one brash youth pastor responded, "I do not need seminary. I pastor high school students. They need me to love them and teach them about life, so a seminary education is not necessary."
>
> Williford challenged the young man to consider the fact that Scripture is the best source for understanding life. The youth pastor agreed, but said that since the Bible moved him personally, he had no need of formal theological training.[359]

The increase in this kind of thinking is evidenced by the increasing number of "ministers" and "preachers" who have no biblical background and grounding whatsoever. The Bible strictly forbids novices in the pastoral ministry as can be seen in Paul's enumeration of the qualifications of the Bishop in 1 Timothy 3:6, yet many novices are in the pulpits. They have neither formal nor informal training and have for their confidence statements such as that recorded in the quotation above ignorantly claiming New Testament precedence that the apostles of Christ never attended any seminary or Bible college and were unlearned men, yet they turned their world upside down and filled it with the Gospel. Paul Van Buren writes,

> "Words may be given me", he writes. Paul did not speak from his own great knowledge and training. Paul did not speak from his own opinion or speculation. <u>Paul did not study for four years to come up with the gospel of grace</u>. Paul was infilled by the Spirit. Equipped, enabled and empowered to be the apostle to the Gentiles. He was given the revelation of the gospel of grace through the Spirit of God.
>
> We've gone crazy with education. Knowledge is great. All minds should be expanded to the best of our capacity but God is not dependent on our education. <u>We do not have to go off and be trained according to the methods of man before we can preach, teach and evangelize</u>. A pastor does not need letters after his name and neither do apostles, prophets, evangelists and teachers. <u>There is nothing wrong with Bible colleges but God doesn't require them</u> [emphasis added]. We need to have Paul's understanding of God's equipping.[360]

---

[359] Randy Frame, *Is Seminary Education Always Necessary for Pastoral Ministry? How formal education can help build the church*, accessed 17 September 2018, http://www.seminarygradschool.com/article/Is-Seminary-Education-Always-Necessary-for-Pastoral-Ministry%3F.

[360] Paul Van Buren, "An Uneducated Pastor", *Pastor Paul's Blog*, 23 November, 2012, accessed 17 September 2018, http://pastorpaulvbsblog.blogspot.com/2012/11/an-uneducated-pastor.html.

The common perspective that is presented by Van Buren in his article is reflected in the statement: "There is nothing wrong with Bible colleges but God doesn't require them." This stems from a common misconception and misunderstanding of the Bible college. It seems that to many people, the Bible college is not seen as a training institution and teaching avenue of the church, but as an academic institution that teaches the mechanics and methods of man for ministry. Therefore, though there will be an acknowledgement for the need to be trained and to be taught, yet there will still be an undermining of the Bible college. The questions that need to be asked are: "Must the Bible College and Training for ministry and service to God be different things?" and "What is it about the Bible College?" or "Why is it not to be considered as a teaching avenue for the training which everyone agrees is necessary?" Why should training be necessary but the Bible college not necessary? In the same article, Van Buren goes on to write,

<u>I would rather sit under the training of an uneducated former alcoholic</u>, saved by grace, empowered by the Holy Spirit than the best trained and educated seminary graduate. <u>The anointing of God is all that we need to serve him</u> to the full potential to which he has called us. Do not let anyone tell you any different. <u>God's training school is all you need</u> [emphasis added].

In this he presumes that there is a difference and a distinction between God's training school and the Bible college, and that the Bible college cannot be and is not God's training school. He also assumes that "the best trained and educated seminary graduate" is unsaved and is not empowered by the Holy Spirit. Training for the ministry should be the task of the Bible college. The assumption that training can be done elsewhere and should be conducted outside the Bible college is what seems to drive the thought that it is not "God's training school" and so the church does not need the Bible college. The handling God's Word requires skill, and this skill does not come naturally to man and so training is necessary and should be mandatory. In the New Testament there is clear indication that the skill required to handle God's Word was acquired and conveyed through training. This is acknowledged by all, but the Bible college will not be looked at as an avenue in which the skills needed are conveyed and acquired. Many would view the Bible college based on the credentials it offers. This is where in this writer's view, the issue has been separated and there has been the distinction made by many between "God's training school" and "the Bible college" is an unnecessary one that has distorted the view of many. The Bible college has to be the place where the church trains and equips its ministers.

(iv) There is a gradual departure from the precedence of the New Testament Church. A survey of the book of Acts reveals the place that teaching had in the spread, growth and establishment of the New Testament church. The first verse of Acts talks about the teaching work of Jesus and the context presents it as it will continue through the work that will be committed to the apostles through the Holy Ghost. In the Gospel, Christ is presented as *"a teacher come from God"* (John 3:2) and His life and ministry set the foundation for the church. Luke, in writing Acts, reminds Theophilus of the previous treatise (which is the Gospel of Luke) that it contains all that *"Jesus began both to do and teach"* (Acts 1:1), which work was to be continued by the apostles.

The life of the church under the apostles and their ministry is characterized by teaching since the Jewish leaders severally took issue with the apostles teaching in the name of Jesus (Acts 4:2, 18; 5:21, 25, 28, 42), and severally tried to silence the apostles. They ordered the apostles to stop preaching or teaching Christ and threatened them with punishment. The church also was established by teaching as evidenced and exemplified in the church at Antioch (Acts 11:26; 13:1; 15:35), and the missionary endeavours were accompanied by teaching (Acts 14:21; 16:21; 18:11, 25; 20:20; 28:31).

CHAPTER III: TEACHING AVENUES AVAILABLE FOR THE CHURCH TODAY

The apostles then went on to train and teach others and commit to them the ministry of the Gospel as is seen in Paul choosing and training Timothy. The example of Christ in the Gospels, and that of the Apostles in the Acts is not one of hiring pre-qualified or pre-trained men with the right credentials, but rather that of choosing, calling, discipling, and training men and women for the areas of service and ministry opportunities in the church.

There has been a gradual shift of focus from this over the years with discipling and training for service gradually decreasing in emphasis and focus by many. This fact is attested of by Dr. U. Obed Admi in his keynote address at the Africa Congress on Discipleship that was held in Nairobi in May 2017. Dr. Obed pointed out that the ecumenical efforts and meetings on world evangelization focused on "missions and the best strategies for carrying it out; evangelism and the tools for it; church growth and church planting; research, and more."[361] But he did not discuss discipleship though he tried in vain to raise the issue at the Global Congress on World Evangelization in Pretoria 1997 and the pre-Lausanne meeting in Cape-town 2009. In his address, Dr. Obed went on to describe the effects of increased evangelization without discipleship in Africa, attributing the description of the church in Africa as "one mile wide and one inch deep" as an outcome of the lack of discipleship focus. He says,

> But I was also concerned that in discussing the great commission, focus was limited to missions and the best strategies for carrying it out; evangelism and the tools for it; church growth and church planting; research, and more.
>
> I spoke to the then General Secretary of the AEA about my amazement that nothing was mentioned about discipleship as a vital component of the great commission. His answer was, "Who doesn't know what discipleship is?" I was embarrassed. But I left Pretoria wondering about what African church leaders really know regarding discipleship.
>
> In 2009, at the pre-Lausanne 2010 meeting in Cape Town, I again raised the issue in a break out session of African church leaders. Once again, it was obvious that discipleship did not seem to have a significant place in global and African church discussion on world evangelization.
>
> But then, the impact of a lack of focus and emphases on discipleship in Africa has become obvious. The continent's response to earlier world evangelization efforts yielded much harvest. Many souls were won to Christ and to the churches. Much church planting was done. To a fair-minded person, Africa excelled in the much that the global church emphasized in its pursuit of the great commission.
>
> But soon, some people began to describe Christianity in Africa as being "one mile wide and one inch deep." A number of times I heard some ministers use this statement in a derogatory manner. They spoke as if spiritual decline is native to Africa, or just to spite what God has been doing in Africa's pursuit in the mentioned dimensions of the great commission.[362]

The planting of churches gave rise to the need for ministers who would tend to the churches. The concern was thus getting someone to pastor the churches and as such, there was less concern whether people seeking to serve God are trained to do so and less

---

[361] U. Obed Admi, *Keynote Address Africa Congress on Discipleship*, electronic article accessed on 23 August 2019 available at URL: https://maniafrica.com/african-congress-on-discipleship-may-1-5-2017-karen-nairobi-kenya-keynote-address-by-dr-u-obed-admi/

[362] Ibid.

emphasis on the belief that handling God's Word biblically, accurately and correctly is important.

In some quarters, this has been replaced with what papers, credentials or, as Van Buren put it, "letters after his name" a person has. In other quarters, there is a total abandonment of training and a turning to a mystical approach that believes that the Holy Spirit will teach without any agency or instrumentality and that whatever such persons say, they say under the influence of the Holy Spirit. This has totally changed the perspective of ministry to the extent that churches on the one end will opt for advertising and hiring "the right candidates" in order to fill in the "vacant positions" while churches on the other end will unquestioningly follow and adhere to what their leaders say without the counsel of Scripture. In both cases, the churches would fill their pulpits with men sourced from outside determined by unbiblical standards rather than choosing to train and equip men and women in their membership in preparation for service within their church setting.

The practice of the Bible College as a Teaching Avenue

When the above four issues affecting the church today are considered soberly and biblically, the need of the Bible college as a teaching avenue in relation to Christian service and ministry as well as a teaching avenue in relation to safeguarding the church and stemming the tide that is ever rising against it becomes clear and the focus and purpose of the Bible college may be properly set. The practice of the Bible college should be drawn with the view and understanding of the believer's standing and relationship with God. The attacks as presented in the first three fronts threaten the standing and the relationship the Christian (and by extension the church) has with God. Christianity and the church, as an institution and as the body of Christ, is unique and distinct from all other societies and institutions of men. Its distinction is derived from the relationship of its members (both individually and collectively) to their Lord and Head hence what undermines the relationship is to be shunned and what strengthens the relationship is to be pursued, embraced and preserved. In describing this relationship, Lightfoot in his book *The Christian Ministry* rightly observes,

> The kingdom of Christ, not being a kingdom of this world, is not limited by the restrictions which fetter other societies, political or religions. It is in the fullest sense free, comprehensive, universal. It displays this character, not only in the acceptance of all comers who seek admission, irrespective of race or caste or sex, but also in the instruction and treatment of those who are already its members. It has no sacred days or seasons, no special sanctuaries, because every time and every place alike are holy. Above all, it has no sacerdotal system. It interposes no sacrificial tribe or class between God and man, by whose intervention alone God is reconciled and man forgiven. Each individual member holds personal communion with the Divine Head. To Him immediately he is responsible, and from Him directly he obtains pardon and draws strength.[363]

According to Lightfoot, the uniqueness of the church is seen in its nature which is spiritual unlike other societies and institutions which are physical. This is evidenced in its treatment of men as reflected in its admission into fellowship and development in the faith. As each individual member holds personal communion with the Lord and is immediately responsible to the Lord, each individual member ought to be (i) trained and informed in the knowledge of the Lord, His ways, His requirements, and His words; (ii) trained and enlightened in the areas of service of the Lord available and how

---

[363] J. B. Lightfoot, *The Christian Ministry* (New York: Thomas Whittaker, n.d.), 5-6.

the Lord is to be served acceptably; (iii) trained and equipped for living for His Lord in this world as well as for managing resources bestowed by the Lord for both personal use and the use of the church as an institution in the furtherance of the work of her Lord.

The life, growth, and fruitfulness of the church is intrinsically tied to the Word of God. This necessitates the training, equipping and teaching in the Word of God and informs the basis for the practice of the Bible college as a teaching avenue of the church. The practice of the Bible college has to be considered in its two-fold approach, first in the training of men for active and full-time Christian ministry and second in the training of believers in the knowledge of God and for Christian living.

Ephesians 4 presents an exhortation to Christian unity, covering what that unity entails in verses 3 to 6, and what gifts, means and methods to the propagating, maintaining and promoting of that unity in verses 7 to 16. It is in this context that the practice for the training of men for "active," "full-time" Christian Ministry can be derived. In the context, both the unity and the growth of the body are tied to the knowledge of the Son of God (Eph. 4:13), and thus pastors who are teachers must equip church members. Later in the chapter, Paul again exhorts the believers to pattern their lives not after the world but after Christ (Eph. 4:17-19) reminding them that the pattern they follow is one that they have *"so learned Christ"* (Eph. 4:20), hence affirming that believers must be equipped for Christian living. The training of ministers and the equipping of members are thus correlated and linked.

Training for Christian Ministry (Ephesians 4:11-16)

This first section focuses on ministers who are supposed to first *"take heed"* unto themselves, and after that then take heed *"to all the flock"* (Acts 20:28a). If they are to train and equip the members, then, they must first be trained and equipped themselves, therefore the question that is raised is: "How can the Bible college train men for Christian ministry?" As a practical and academic avenue, the Bible college can train men for Christian ministry through its practical training programs as well as its academic training programs.

Practical training programs of the Bible college will include discipleship, mentorship and internship. Discipleship, mentorship and internship is one way of preparing men for the ministry, especially the pastoral one. It should be the primary way by which the theological and practical, ecclesiological and pastoral, are caught and stoked within the church context. This form of practical training is easy to set up as what it requires is for the pastors to identify persons in whom they see the grace of God at work and place upon themselves the duty and commitment to train up such persons for the ministry by forming a relationship bond with them and then setting himself as an example to them as well as involving them in the work of ministry identified.

The biblical model given puts this as one of the primary duties of the Christian ministry as exemplified by Christ Himself, as He identified and called unto Him twelve men, and taught them doctrines, modelled to them holy living, and by sending them forth at different times to perform different duties, gave them opportunities to practically apply themselves to the pastoral ministry that He would later send them. The apostle Paul followed this model with his "sons in the faith" especially Timothy as can be traced beginning at Acts 16, and throughout Paul's ministry and evidenced in his epistles. From the examples of Christ and Paul, this model of teaching and training includes: (i) identifying men, (ii) calling the men into a teacher-student lifestyle relationship, (iii) committing self, talents, and time to teach and equip them for Christian life and ministry, (iv) trusting them to perform set tasks at set periods during the mentorship relationship and assigning them those tasks under instruction and supervision with corrections and lessons given when needful.

This form of training is essential as it provides ministerial experience during the training as the student is placed to serve under the oversight of experienced pastors. This not only gives the students ability to gain knowledge of the Bible and the doctrines and teachings of Christ, but also helps them to build wisdom, sharpen their gifts, and prepares them for ministerial responsibility in the context and setting of the church. The number of men entering the ministry without experience is increasing and many such men who enter with little or no experience, and with no mentors to guide and instruct them, fall into many dangers and make many mistakes.[364] From the burden of the pulpit ministry, to the care and concern of pastoral counselling. From the decency and order required of church administration to the planning, management and stewardship of church funds. The pastoral ministry is demanding, and apart from this, the challenges that come from opposition, hostility, false brethren and cults, and the pitfalls and snares that face the pastor and other Christian ministers by virtue of their calling, giftings and duties. Indeed, leading a church with all its various ministries, duties and responsibilities without any guidance or experience is the most perilous vocation any man can engage in and churches must provide teaching avenues in which gifts, calling, and character can be observed, tested, and developed.

Academic training programs of the Bible college must be biblical, pastoral and theological. Biblical, pastoral and theological training is the next way of preparing men for the work of the ministry. This second way should not be seen as divorced from the first one, but rather, the two should be together and pursued as one. In the ideal situation, every pastor mentoring or discipling someone must also train them academically. But practically this has not been the case. This is where the academic institutions, colleges and seminaries come in. They are there to ensure that men training for the ministry receive the best academic preparation. The church must therefore work with the institutions of theological training. In the ideal situation, every church must have its own academic institution, but since this has not been practically possible, each church must have a Bible college which she identifies with and where she sends her students for training. The church should monitor the progress and testimony of her students while in college, and the college should do the same when her students are on school break and return to their churches. The church should inform the college of how the student applies the teachings received at college and how the student is maturing in understanding, while the college at the same time should

---

[364] "Though Kenya is considered a Christian nation (Operation World says nearly 83 percent identify with the faith), ethnic cultural practices are frequently mixed with biblical truths, and the need for trained leaders in more than 80,000 congregations is massive. Chen, who teaches from a Reformed perspective at the Tenwek International School of Chaplaincy, said, "It didn't take us long to realize that the many hundreds of churches in rural Kenya love the name of Jesus but know very little of what the true gospel is. Almost every Sunday we were saddened and burdened by church services we attended. We heard either legalism or prosperity messages without any true message of grace. "Few pastors have any theological education; anyone can self-identify as a pastor without any qualifications in the local denomination here. Those who do have theological education still seem to view preaching as more akin to a motivational speech than to teaching the Word of God. ... Much of the focus is on how to obtain blessings from God, basically that if you follow the rules you will receive blessing." ... The Chens attend Imani Fellowship Africa Gospel Church at Bomet and gave pastor Willy Koskey two of the TGC-IO books. Koskey explained it's not only a challenge for untrained ministers to access theological materials; they lack the training to handle them. "It's like giving someone a gun to use without training," he said. Unfortunately, he said, some Christians assume theological training is unnecessary." [Elizabeth Roberts, "Faithfulness Among The Frauds In Kenya", *The Gospel Coalition*, last modified 2019, accessed August 22, 2019, https://www.thegospelcoalition.org/article/christianity-in-kenya-faithful-in-the-midst-of-frauds/]

inform the church of the conduct and relations of the student while on campus, how he performs assigned duties, how he responds to authority and how he relates to others, etc.

Academic training may take different forms depending on the nature of the program pursued and the students being trained. The more popular forms include the residential or full-time training, the in-service (or in-ministry) or part-time training, the extension or lay-men training and the correspondence or distance training. A good academic program should consider the following: (i) Instruction time — mostly in the classroom setting with lectures, notes, assignments, assessment and evaluation. (ii) Application time — offered in form of ministry opportunities through outreaches available to the college. In some colleges, this is done by including in the timetable times for ministerial activities like evangelism, schools ministries, hospital or prison ministries and outreach to different areas by invitation. (iii) Devotion time — offered through spiritual activities organized for the students while on campus like the morning chapel, prayer groups and counsellor/mentorship programs in which students are assisted to grow spiritually.

Training for Christian Stewardship and Church Leadership (Ephesians 4:17-28)

In this second section, focus is on the whole body of Christ and is to include *"all the flock"* (Acts 20:28a) which the ministers are to tend and feed and who are to be matured and equipped in the faith. The question that is addressed is: "How can the Bible college train and equip men for godly Christian living?" This question deals with the cultivating and building of Christian character and conduct that facilitates godly and profitable living and service and is thus to be made available to all believers. Special attention is to be given to those who have an interest in any responsibility and stewardship position within the church. If the church is to have worthy men serving in all areas that may enable the pastoral team to give themselves to the ministry of the word and prayer, then all willing believers are to be trained and prepared. Jeffrey Khoo rightly observes in "Role of the Bible College in Missions,"

> We must not forget another important role of the Bible College--the training of the "ordinary" Christian. The biblical and theological grounding of the Christian is crucial for the healthy and growth of the church. All Christian men and women should know their doctrines well. Moreover, the secrets for successful living are found in the Scriptures. To know the Bible and theology is the responsibility of all Christians. I am sure every child of God desires to please his Father in heaven. How to live a victorious Christian life for Christ? There is no shortcut. Every Christian needs to engage in an intensive, systematic study of God's Word (2 Tim. 2:15). [365]

The question then becomes "How can the Bible college train the 'ordinary' Christian for stewardship and leadership?" Education has to deal with finding out what is needed to know when one needs to know, and the earliest picture of equipping for service is presented in Exodus 31 in which God gave wisdom, understanding and skill to different men for the work that was set before the children of Israel. But it is not to all generations that God does as He did in Exodus 31, but men know how to work and do the will of God by learning, and understanding.

The apostle Paul in his missionary endeavours trained up leaders everywhere he went. At the end of the first missionary trip, the record given in scripture is that of churches organized with local leadership structures for growth. The growth of the gospel through the work of those who have come to a saving knowledge and relationship with Christ is clearly presented in the New Testament church. How then were the converts

---

[365] Jeffrey Khoo, "Role of the Bible College in Missions", *Frontlines in the Gospel Mission Fields* (Singapore: Maranatha BP Church, 2003), 71.

and disciples equipped for the winning of others? Ministry in the New Testament church is not presented as the work of a given class of believers but as that of all believers equally, with differing ministries and service based on differing giftings.

The modern minister is not sent to save a few souls here and there out of this present world and incorporate them into some religious sect for its particular aggrandizement. He is not sent to collect a choice array of monks and nuns standing quite apart from the domestic, the industrial and the political activities of the race in a detached and private sort of saintliness. He is sent to save men and women in this present world and to train them for intelligent, competent, conscientious action in saving the world itself as an object of divine interest and the subject of a divine redemption. He aims at the moral renewal and the spiritual strengthening of all those plain people who are to bear the heat and burden of a long, hard day as participating members in this intricate modern life. It is to equip him for this exacting duty that the Divinity School exists.[366]

Concluding Observations

The Christian Education department of the church is a vital part of the life and work of the church. This is because (i) the programs of the Christian Education department will form a large part of the church's work in the lives of its membership, (ii) the programs of the Christian Education department will require the participation and involvement of most of the people if not all within the church's membership, (iii) the activities of the Christian Education department will include the chief duties of the pastoral ministry and will require of the pastor not only to participate fully, but also to effectively organize, coordinate and prepare others for the different avenues for teaching and equipping availed by the Christian Education program.

As discussed above in this chapter, Christian education is an important part of a church's ministry from the biblical mandate, injunctions and examples drawn from the New Testament. (i) The Lord Jesus Christ in giving the Great Commission set it as an integral part of work and ministry of the apostles and through them the church (Matt. 28:19-20). (ii) The life of the early church presents a picture in which Bible teaching is central and is a core ministry with the apostles steadfastly teaching even under threatenings and persecutions (Acts 2:42, 5:42, etc.). (iii) The Gentile church and the expansion of Christianity was built on an active teaching ministry with the apostle Paul both teaching disciples (Acts 11:26, 18:11), and where churches were established, training men who would carry on the teaching function in the church and in his epistles exhorting teaching as a gift given to members of the body (Rom. 12:7; 1 Cor. 12:28, Eph. 4:11) and as a requirement for the pastoral ministry (1 Tim. 3:2, 2 Tim. 2:2).

The challenge facing the church today in regard to the discussions presented in this chapter is its approach to Christian education. Although almost every church conducts a Sunday school, and thus has some form of Christian education in the church, the lack of understanding and the lack of a teaching emphasis have made most of the church's effort to be weak.[367] In areas where there is a variety of teaching programs set,

---

[366] Brown, "The Training of a Minister", 15-16.

[367] "The programme of Sunday school is haphazardly introduced in many Church denominations in Africa. Due to lack of proper planning, professional implementation and inadequate supervision, Sunday schools are afflicted by a myriad of problems and challenges. Though Sunday schools play a useful role in the Church their attractiveness and effectiveness are marred by the manner in which they are conducted. ... In one Church it was found that 80% of the total Sunday school teachers were seventeen years old and below. Some Church denominations have done a good job by ensuring that Sunday school teachers are a mixture of young and grown-ups. There are many other Church denominations where Sunday schools are led by chil-

the effort bares little fruit due to the disjointed and uncoordinated approach churches have. Many of the church's programs and events when considered and evaluated seem to stand on its own rather than contribute towards one common vision and goal. Every program seems to operate "individually" and in some cases even in competition with other programs within the same church. In very few cases does one find the children's Sunday school supplementing the pulpit ministry or preparing its children for the youth ministry and later for full membership of the church. In some cases the proliferation of "Ministries" and "churches" rises from discord and friction that one given to lead a Sunday school class has with church leadership and sets out to start his own church with those who were attending his class breaking off with him. There has to be a clear understanding that the effectiveness and success of any Christian education program is to be measured and seen in its contribution to the unity, spiritual health and maturity of the whole church and so each individual program must endeavour to work together and in coordination with all other programs in the church. In order for this to happen, the following issues have to be addressed by the church:

Ignorance

Some churches do not have trained pastors or elders who are able to properly formulate their Christian education curriculum. Ignorant church members with ulterior motives may cause schisms within the church. And gullible church members follow them; hence becoming deceived and led astray. Paul gave this warning to the Ephesian elders: *"Take heed therefore unto yourselves, and to all the flock, over the which the Holy Ghost hath made you overseers, to feed the church of God, which he hath purchased with his own blood. For I know this, that after my departing shall grievous wolves enter in among you, not sparing the flock. Also of your own selves shall men arise, speaking perverse things, to draw away disciples after them. Therefore, watch, and remember, that by the space of three years I ceased not to warn every one night and day with tears"* (Acts 20:28-31).

People have misused the time that is for the teaching of the Word of God which will show them the way to live and glorify God by replacing it with other things, such as the so-called praise and worship, prolonged testimonies, interpretation of dreams, tongues speaking, etc. All these activities may consume about three to five hours of the service, after which there is no sermon, but just a portion of a verse read. Then follows a time of miracles, laying of hands, casting out demons, etc. The Lord's Day ends without any proper teaching of God's Word. People may be in church from 8 am to about 5 pm without any proper teaching of God's Word. Yet they claim to have been blessed. God laments the delusion of such people through the prophet Jeremiah: *"For my people have committed two evils; they have forsaken me the fountain of living waters, and hewed them out cisterns, broken cisterns, that can hold no water"* (Jer. 2:13).

---

dren and young people. There are also many other cases where there are very few Sunday school teachers. This has impacted towards compromising the quality of Christian nurture given. Training of Sunday school teachers is another problem facing Sunday schools in Africa. Some Church denominations have not created opportunities for training Sunday school teachers. ... In many Church denominations no deliberate efforts have been made to provide the basic facilities such as study rooms, seats, writing materials, blackboards, lesson books, teaching aids, registers and stationery. Lack or inadequacy of the above facilities has hampered the smooth running of Sunday schools." [Peter M. Mumo, "Sunday Schools as the Foundation of Christian Nurture and their Relevance for Theological Education in Africa", *Handbook of Theological Education in Africa*, ed. By Isabel Apawo Phiri, and Dietrich Werner, (Oxford: Regnium Books International, 2013), 798.]

Negligence

Apart from the lack of proper knowledge of Christian education ministry and the whole counsel of God's Word, there is also the issue of negligence which comes in many forms. The most common form mainly affects small churches where the pastor is all alone performing every activity to the different ages and groups in the church. Due to such a burden, the pastor may sometimes neglect to carry out the other teaching responsibilities and just concentrate on the worship service. There needs to be training and delegation of others to help him, and the pastor must go the extra mile of making arrangements on how different groups are to be taught in the church and ensure that the arranged teaching is being done faithfully.

Other forms of negligence stem from the view held of God's Word and its place in the life of the church. Many churches have substituted the time for teaching God's Word with unbiblical practices which are popular with the social gospel, the prosperity gospel, and charismatic movement. Examples include teaching people how to "plant a seed," giving time for testimonies by those who "planted" and gained double or triple, and giving time for those present to pledge, and through their pledges, show their faith that whatever needs they have requested will be answered. Prayer also is removed from the service and relegated to private sessions with the pastor in his special room where members go in one by one to be "prayed" for and be given "a word of prophecy" about his future life. These among other unnecessary activities take away the much needed time for the teaching of God's Word.

CHAPTER IV

THE CURRENT STATE OF BIBLE TEACHING IN THE CHURCH IN KENYA

"And they continued steadfastly in the apostles' doctrine" (Acts 2:42). The life of the New Testament church centred on the Word of God and right from the time of the Pentecost, they were drawn to the Word. What comes out clearly from the passage of Acts 2:42 is that the apostles (who were the church leaders of the New Testament church) taught the Scriptures and the believers submitted and gave themselves devotedly to the doctrines and teachings of the apostles. The passage of Acts 2:42-47 has by many been used as indicative of the early worship of the church with the essentials of the church's worship being drawn from what characterized the early church. As one considers the list, the areas of focus and devotion for the church are clearly drawn out. The Lord's blessing upon the church is clearly indicated by Acts 2:47 which says, *"... And the Lord added to the church daily such as should be saved."*

After considering the biblical and historical principles for teaching in the church, as well as the avenues available for the church to teach, the current state of Bible teaching in the church in Kenya is to be considered in this section. Bible teaching has to be understood as teaching that is based on the Bible. Considering the context of the Bible passage, lessons are drawn out and presented with the aim of building, protecting, and warning the body of Christ as well as exposing errors and dangers that face the church of Christ. Bible teaching is not to be understood as using a Bible passage to express one's own ideas irrespective of whether those ideas are good or bad. The Bible must set its own agenda and chart its own course and the Bible must speak for itself. This means that those who set out to teach the Bible must search the Scriptures, and study to show themselves approved unto God rightly dividing the Word of truth. For as 2 Peter 1:2 says, *"Knowing this first, that no prophecy of the scripture is of any private interpretation."* Bible teaching and preaching were the core of the New Testament church's life and must be the core of church life in every age. The Great Commission of the church has been stated as, and shown to be, a teaching commission in the previous sections of this thesis. Mark's rendering of the Great Commission presents it as a Gospel commission: *"Go ye into all the world and preach the gospel to every creature ... and they went forth and preached everywhere"* (Mark 16:15, 20a). Thus, the church's work has to be gospel work. George James while addressing students preparing for ministry said concerning the gospel,

> The Gospel has from the first been substantially one system. The object of its announcement has been from its first announcement in Eden, the same: — the salvation of men. All its true ministers have regarded this as the grand end of their mission. Their chief aim has ever been so to present the Gospel, that through their instrumentality sinners might be converted to God and built up in faith and holiness, and just so far as they have been successful in this, they have felt, that they were successful in their work. And I may add, that the qualities necessary to ministerial success have been in all ages essentially the same. All true ministers of Christ have felt, that a full and clear knowledge of the Gospel, a firm faith in its truths, and great diligence and prudence in proclaiming these, were indispensable to their success.[368]

---

[368] George James, *The Field and the Men for it, an address to the Divinity students of Queens College Kingston at the close of the session 1859-60* (Montreal: John Lovell, 1860), 3.

The above assertion affirms that the church possesses a yardstick by which it must measure its efforts and fruits by. As the Gospel has not changed, and as the gospel is the "grand end" of every minister's mission, it follows that qualities and requirements for success in the gospel ministry ought to be the same. Thus, as James puts it, "All true ministers of Christ have felt, that a full and clear knowledge of the Gospel, a firm faith in its truth, and a great diligence and prudence in proclaiming these, were indispensable to their success."[369] This is the testimony of history too. The church has seen revivals and declensions at different ages, and when measured against the Gospel yardstick, what is presented by James above stands true. Hence, when considering the state of Bible teaching in Kenya, there is a clear declension over the years due to the decline in Gospel focus among the churches. As Bible teaching gets replaced and displaced, the church sinks and strays further away from God. The attempts to grow the church without emphasizing Bible teaching weaken the church. The church is on the decline because Bible teaching is neglected.

Barry Voss in his article "Six Lessons Christians Must Learn from Church History" addresses the importance of Bible teaching. He points out that the Christian faith must be defended against false teaching in his second point, and that the church must be built on a biblical foundation in his fourth point. It is in his sixth point that he points out the problem that has caused declension throughout church history. On explaining how "man will always try to replace God with himself," he writes:

> As the world progressed in its knowledge of science and technology, liberalism invaded universities (which were Bible based at the time) and the Church. Many Christians began to try and reconcile modern thought with Biblical teaching and refused to accept the authority of God's Word alone on many issues. They believed that truth must pass the test of human reason. Consequently, universities abandoned the Bible and liberal theology in the Christian Church began to grow. Today it manifests itself in prosperity theology, acceptance of homosexuality, and other false teachings that go beyond or outside of Scripture. These are all an attempt to make God subject to our intellect rather than adhere to His teaching as found in His Holy Word.[370]

Departure from the Word of God is the caution given by the testimony of history. In this age, departure from the Word is on the rise and is propagated through the rise of the many false teachings "that go beyond or outside of Scripture."[371] The following section will deal with the factors that have contributed to the current state of Bible teaching in Kenya.

Challenges Facing the Church in Kenya

The Beginnings of Christianity in Kenya

Christianity in East Africa can be traced to the first contacts with traders in the 15th century. Stephen Morad writes,

> The first Christian contact with Kenya may have been as early as the fourth century when Ethiopian monks were reported to have visited the East African coast. How-

---

[369] James, *The Field and the Men for it*, 3.

[370] Barry Voss, "Six Lessons Christians Must Learn From Church History |", *Faithlifeministries.Net*, last modified 2019, accessed February 8, 2019, http://faithlifeministries.net/six-lessons-christians-must-learn-from-church-history/.

[371] Ibid.

CHAPTER IV: THE CURRENT STATE OF BIBLE TEACHING IN THE CHURCH IN KENYA

ever, powerful peoples, such as the Orma, prevented the expansion of Christianity from Ethiopia. Christianity's next contact with East Africa occurred as part of the Portuguese conquest of the Swahili culture on the coast. The Spanish and Portuguese had just completed the reconquest of the Iberian Peninsula from the Moors, so Christianity first confronted Islam in Kenya in the context of crusade and jihad. Nevertheless, sufficient peace was established between the foreign Christians and the local Muslims, so the first missionary work in Kenya occurred during the seventeenth century. In 1593 the viceroy of Goa sent six Augustinian monks to Mombasa, three priests to the Lamu archipelago, and one priest to Zanzibar. Five years later the Augustinians reported 600 converts in Mombasa and a House of Mercy that cared for the sick, disabled, and orphaned.[372]

There has been a general misconception that associates Christianity in East Africa with colonization in the 18th and 19th centuries. However, Morad shows that from the beginning, and through the European Expansion, many missionary societies and missions stations have been formed in East Africa. Their purpose was to preach the Word of God and convert Africans to Christianity. This purpose was approached using various methods and with varying results. In the Christian Religious Education textbook for Form 2, L Wanjie notes,

> The aim of all missionary societies and the individual missionaries was to preach the word of God and convert Africans to Christianity. But they came from different backgrounds and had different attitudes and ideas about their work. This meant that there was great variation in approaches and methods used in missionary work.[373]

Their methods and approaches were not without effect on the Africans whom they worked with. This is evident in the present state of Christendom in East Africa. Wanjie goes on to write,

> The missionaries had to face these new challenges throughout the period of colonial administration. Many missionaries also had a negative view of many aspects of African culture which they condemned without seeking to understand them first. They had definite views about how African Christians should behave although the same rigid standards of behaviour were not required of the European Christians. This and other issues of political aspirations of the Africans led some African Christians to start their own churches and schools. ... When the church came to Africa, there were problems as to what traditional African beliefs and religious practices could be incorporated in Christian worship. The fear of certain ritual practices connected with witchcraft and sorcery and misunderstanding of African values and cultural activities led many missionaries to condemn almost all aspects of African culture. They made their converts adopt the 'Western' way of life and worship. The African found the formal worship of the church lacking in the spontaneous character of traditional African worship. Christian worship was also unrelated to many issues of life. Many took part in such worship only when they had to while others wanted to integrate some aspects of their culture with the Christian life and worship. Impatience with the slow change in missionary policy in this and other areas of Christi-

---

[372] Stephen Morad, "The Beginnings Of Christianity In Kenya", *William Carey International University*, last modified 2019, accessed February 3, 2017, http://www.wciu.edu/docs/resources/Course10_readerGC2_C10R_Morad_Beginnings_of_Christianity_in_Kenya.pdf.

[373] L Wanjie, *God Meets Us: Christian Religious Education Form 2* (Nairobi: East African Educational Publishers, 1992), 44.

anity led some to leave the missionary churches and form their own churches. These are called Independent churches examples being the Akorino, Africa Israel Church Nineveh and Legio Maria of Africa.[374]

There has been a general perception that the coming to Africa of missionaries and explorers from the West before the colonizers was a deliberate move with the former being sent over to break the fallow ground so that the latter would have an easier task of colonizing the countries. This has caused some measure of difficulty for the church as Christianity has been in part seen as the colonizing of the mind and as a religion of the West.

The Constitutional Court last week ruled that children in mission or private schools are compelled to attend chapel services and observe religious policies at those institutions. If they are uncomfortable, they are free to transfer to other schools. What choice, really? What choice? Isn't there a choice of freedom of worship and religion in this country? Well here is my modest opinion on the Constitutional Court's ruling.

When the colonialists invaded this country at the end of the 20th century they had a well-orchestrated plot and that was to send their evangelical missionaries first so that they could take away the social and cultural fabric of the natives and replace those with their own supposedly Christian beliefs.

They stripped black people of their identity, their rituals and rites, their traditions and their sacraments and ceremonies. The result was that black people became so submissive and so stoic in their way of life that they abandoned that which bound them together. The blacks even got to the extent of fighting each other if one remained traditionalist while the other had been converted to so-called Christianity.

The strategy worked very well for the imperialists because when they eventually invaded our land with the Pioneer Column, the colonialists met very little resistance from the indigenous black people because the likes of missionaries such as Reverend John Smith Moffat and Charles Dunell Rudd had managed to make us believe that fight for our sovereignty or our cultural pedigree was against the will of God.[375]

From Madoda's statements above, we get a glimpse of the perspective that has been a thorn in the flesh of the Christian Church in Africa as well as the beginning of the conflict between African Culture with Christianity. This and such like views have created some measure of resistance against Biblical Christianity leading to the labelling of the biblical practices and world-view as Western especially on points of conflict with African Culture and thus facilitating the rise of "African" Christianity in East Africa. Today in many churches, African practices, customs and beliefs have been incorporated and such syncretism is accepted. This gave rise to a kind of religiosity in which Christianity is required to incorporate man-made religions and adopt cultures and practices that are unbiblical but which the proponents would seek to present as necessary as it is part of the African identity.

The Teaching of Christianity in the Kenyan School Curriculum

Another unique aspect that has affected Biblical Christianity in Kenya which continues to play a significant role is the incorporation of Christian Religious Education (CRE) in the school curriculum both in the Primary and Secondary schools and the

---

[374] Ibid., 46.

[375] Vukani Madoda, "Flag Continues To Follow Cross", *The Sunday Mail*, last modified 2019, accessed October 28, 2017, http://www.sundaymail.co.zw/flag-continues-to-follow-cross/.

teaching of Religious Education as part of the Humanities in teacher training colleges and universities. How CRE can affect Christianity in Kenya can be drawn from the objective of the CRE curriculum which states,

> The aim of the Diploma Christian Religious Education (C.R.E.) syllabus is to prepare a teacher who is competent in knowledge and pedagogical skills to handle the secondary C.R. E syllabus and have a good foundation for further education in religious studies. It also aims at making the teacher a role model to the learner developing the Christian character.
>
> The syllabus covers seven main areas namely; Introduction to religion and Philosophy, Traditional African Religions, Comparative Religion, Biblical Theology, Development of Christian Church in East Africa, Approaches to Contemporary Challenges and Pedagogical Skills. The approach adopted in this broad study is progressive in the sense that it brings out the unfolding pattern of God's revelation to human kind. The learner will use the Christian insights to critically analyse and evaluate the implications of the issues raised on his/her life and that of secondary school student.
>
> The syllabus emphasizes the use of both human and biblical experiences in the training of the teacher in order to make the teaching of C.R.E. relevant.
>
> The traditional African religions should be presented as a living experience and not as a phenomenon of the past. Emphasis should be on the positive aspect of the African heritage.
>
> The main themes of Christianity are supposed to be identified and emphasized as the learner goes through the Biblical Theology.
>
> This syllabus is objective based as every topic is handled according to specific objectives which are divided into knowledge, attitude and skill. It is for this reason that although the attitudinal objectives may not seem to have content directly linked to them, they are closely related to the content covered in each topic.[376]

The CRE curriculum is not aimed at spiritual growth and in its teaching tries to marry Christianity with the African traditional beliefs. For the church to leave its teaching programs to the schools, it is inevitable that Christianity is being mixed with traditional religious beliefs and practices. Many are led to believe that people who claim to be believers in Christianity can retain their traditional beliefs and practices because they are African and, as such, an African theology is in the making in the faith and practice of the African Christian. African Christians are made to understand, accept and practice the Christian faith in terms of what they already know and accept from their African beliefs. This combination of traditional religious beliefs and practices and influence of Christianity has given rise to a significant degree of syncretism in the church and has hindered spiritual growth. The syncretistic emphasis grew with the years, and the review panel went further than the 1968 panel. The panel wanted to emphasize practical issues that affect life, and thus shifted from Bible themes to life themes. Ngunju Alice and Wycliffe Amukowa note that,

> In respect to the teaching of CRE, in schools, a joint church panel was set up in 1968 to work on a syllabus which could be more relevant to the Kenyan situation. A committee of Catholics and Protestants from Kenya, Malawi, Tanzania, Uganda and Zambia under the title "Rubaga workshop" prepared a syllabus 223 Christian living

---

[376] Republic of Kenya, Ministry of Education Diploma Teacher Education Syllabus vol. III Humanities and Creative Subjects (Kenya: Kenya Institute of Education, 2008), 58.

today in 1970 with an aim of enabling students to grow towards responsible maturity. This syllabus emphasized life related themes.

The second CRE panel met in 1980 to review the syllabus developed after independence and the panelists observed that aims of CRE were biblical or Christian centred and that what the learner was taught was pre-determined and hence the learner had little say on what was taught. The panel therefore recommended that a new syllabus which would move from Bible themes to Life Themes developed. This prompted the syllabus Review report (1980) which was to emphasize on a more learner centred approach to teaching of CRE. At this period, the Government was working on an overhaul of the education system and restructured. This resulted to the Mackay report which placed CRE as compulsory subject in Form I and II and optional in form 3 and 4 in group IV Social sciences (Humanities) together with History and Geography (emphasis added).[377]

This shift in emphasis has made the pursuit of CRE in Kenyan schools to be a purely academic pursuit void of any spiritual focus. In replacing Bible themes with life themes, it replaced God with man. And being a compulsory subject in the first two years of secondary education means that Christian youth are exposed to this anthropocentric shift that in fact teaches humanism as Christianity. Coupled with the lack of a systematic preaching and teaching program in the church, all who do not know the tenets of the Christian faith are in danger of being led astray and deceived.

The Influence of Africa Traditional Culture and Promotion of an "African Theology"

The influence of the African traditional religions and the promotion of an African theology is seen most clearly in the proliferation of the signs and wonders movement and the rapid growth of the charismatic and deliverance churches. The African religious concept of material and physical prosperity as a sign of favour from the spirits is a common theme in these churches to an extent that salvation has taken a new dimension: that of physical deliverance from ills of life and is chiefly evidenced by ease in life.

Kenneth Enang, in his study of the understanding of salvation among the Annang people of Eastern Nigeria in 1979, identified that they understood salvation in the following ways. 1) Salvation means first deliverance. Statements from the church leaders during interviews include, "Salvation is deliverance from the power of evil principalities and the enclaves of human enemies"; "salvation is liberation of man from the powers of the demon", "the defeat of evil entities and the wicked plans of the enemy", "deliverance from the traps of evil beings", and "deliverance from ill health and misfortune". 2) Salvation is wholeness, being in peace — "where one is in unity with himself, with his neighbours, friends and God, he can say that he is in salvation". 3) Salvation is progress in life, "good health", "flourishing economic concerns" and "having children." [378]

Thus, the common presentation of salvation, especially in the Kenyan churches which emphasize deliverance, revolves around breaking generational curses, pulling

---

[377] Ngunju Alice Wambui and Wycliffe Amukowa, "Constraints Facing Teachers Of Christian Religious Education In Using Life Approach In Secondary Schools In Nairobi East District In Kenya", *Academic Journal of Interdisciplinary Studies* (2013), accessed February 18, 2017, https://www.researchgate.net/publication/271040628_Constraints_Facing_Teachers_of_Christian_Religious_Education_in_Using_Life_Approach_in_Secondary_Schools_in_Nairobi_East_District_in_Kenya.

[378] Chigor Chike, "The Doctrine Of Salvation Among African Christians | Fulcrum Anglican", *Fulcrum Anglican*, last modified 2019, accessed February 18, 2017, https://www.fulcrum-anglican.org.uk/articles/the-doctrine-of-salvation-among-african-christians/.

CHAPTER IV: THE CURRENT STATE OF BIBLE TEACHING IN THE CHURCH IN KENYA

down spiritual altars in family circles, and such like themes. The popularity and acceptance of such explains in part the popularity of the different shades of this kind of gospel preached and propagated in Kenyan towns and cities. The biblical understanding of salvation has been replaced by the syncretistic understanding which incorporates the African traditional view in interpreting the Bible. The emphasis of salvation is currently on physical deliverance, not spiritual redemption. Chike goes on to write,

> The Kenyan theologian John Mbiti has also noted that African Christians, especially those in the African Instituted churches, have broadened the understanding of salvation beyond simply the question of sin and soul (as the missionaries present it) to include a physical deliverance. On deliverance, Kofi Appiah-Kubi writes, "There is more than ample evidence to show that the main preoccupation of many African Christians is redemption from physical dilemmas or evil forces."[379]

From this perspective, salvation is evaluated by one's physical, economic and social well-being, and people are judged based on how they fare outwardly, how much they possess, how well they prosper in their endeavours and such like standards. Enang's research further points out,

> On material possessions, Cyril Okorocha's story about his encounter with a Nigerian business woman provides further evidence. He asked her whether she was saved:
>
> "O yes," she replied and then proceeded to narrate how in fifteen years in the long distance haulage business none of her vehicles had ever been involved in a road accident. Furthermore, she was very wealthy, had several houses in town and above all had two grandsons and a third was on the way.
>
> The emphasis on deliverance from distress in the present life and blessings in this world are, according to these studies, a common feature of the African understanding of salvation.[380]

These benefits, which define salvation physically, have no biblical warrant yet are widely accepted and used by one and sundry when they give their testimonies of their salvation experience or of the goodness and leading of God in their lives. In many services, when a person rises to share a testimony, it is more often than not an account of the changes in status of one's life socially or economically as in the example that Enang pointed out:

> Another Kenyan preacher, Apostle James Nganga, writing about his own conversion, stated: "When I was delivered my life changed. God started manifesting himself in different ways. He established my life. From a common beggar to a comfortable life." Very often, salvation is linked to its benefits. Adeboye writes, "The moment you give your life to Jesus Christ, God deposits a seed of greatness in you. From that moment he expects you to end up at the top." The predicament of the "unsaved" is the opposite: "While God's children are busy enjoying the blessings, the unsaved are suffering in the flood of destruction."[381]

The church in Kenya has taken a very strong humanistic emphasis that makes the happiness of man the aim of all things and that God exists only to make man happy both in this life and in the life to come. Salvation has become the key to attaining all the social and economic happiness one can get in this life and eternal life being a continuation of what one has begun to obtain and enjoy in this life. This, Enang shows when he quotes

---

[379] Chike, *The Doctrine of Salvation among African Christians*, obtained from URL: https://www.fulcrum-anglican.org.uk/articles/the-doctrine-of-salvation-among-african-christians/

[380] Ibid.

[381] Ibid.

from the Ugandan preacher pastor Robert Kayanja of the Miracle Centre Cathedral in Kampala, who said, "The Salvation of the Lord is the price for your breakthrough. The Lordship of Christ is the ability of God to deliver you and make you successful. Jesus took our illness, sickness, infirmity, diseases… He took our place. He overcame them all. And because he won, we win."[382]

This anthropocentric emphasis, though popular, is leading the church astray and exposing it to another Gospel which is not another but a perversion that damns. Can this tide be stemmed? Can the Kenyan church today find a solution? This writer believes that in these last days, with Christ's return drawing nigh, the church has her part to be a light, to warn, to teach and to take heed unto the flock that none be lost. This duty is encompassed in a great part in the teaching ministry of the church.

The Influence of Popular International Televangelists and their Writings

The influence of the media is unmistakable in this age, and this is not limited to the secular media. The church in Kenya has been greatly affected by popular print and audio-visual media. The presence of Christian book-stores and Christian television and radio stations should be seen as strengthening the church, but this is subject to the content availed through them. In the case of Kenya (and Africa in general), the media has done more harm than good due to the content it spreads. Esther Nyaboke in the abstract of her research project notes concerning the findings on the research of the effect of televangelism on the Worshippers of Nairobi,

> From the findings, it was established that televangelism influenced worship habits as evidenced by 93% of the Christian respondents who consumed televangelism services in the period under review. In terms of the impact of televangelism on church attendance amongst worshippers in Nairobi, the study found that only 7% watched T.V. programmes as an alternative to church service. In addition, only 11.9% of Christians preferred watching televangelism messages to church attendance.[383]

The finding that the majority of interviewees preferred watching television to attending church is cause for alarm and concern. It is a cause for alarm because the church is the institution established by Christ, and is the pillar and ground of truth, and if it is shunned by the body of believers, and is supplanted by modern popular media, then something must be wrong. It is a cause for concern because the church must have done something wrong that led to the situation, and it needs to take measures and steps to correct this trend. Nyaboke goes on to point out that it is the message that has drawn the masses. She writes,

> Majority of interviewees pointed that the "feel-good" messages or shallow theology being aired on T.V., made televangelism to be more attractive than church messages thus posing a real danger to the societal values that have been anchored in deep theological principles and doctrine. In terms of the worshipper's credibility perception of evangelistic messages aired on television, over 40% of the respondents said that televangelists were perceived to present programmes that promoted their popu-

---

[382] Ibid.

[383] Esther Nyaboke Mokaya, *Televangelism and the Changing Habits of Worshippers in Nairobi County*, (Masters of Arts Thesis: School of Journalism and Mass Communication of the University of Nairobi, 2015), p. ix. Electronic version obtained from URL: https://journalism.uonbi.ac.ke/sites/default/files/chss/journalism/journalism/ESTHER%20NYABOKE%20M OKAYA%20PROJECT%202015.pdf accessed on 18/01/2018

larity and personal gain. While majority of respondents and interviewees agreed the televangelistic messages are valid.[384]

This is a great indictment on the discipleship and teaching ministries of the church for allowing a message that is unbiblical in its foundation and emphasis like that presented by many televangelists to come into the church, turning many away from the church. One cause is that the church for a period now has not been taking heed unto doctrine. The presence of false teachers and brethren is not new, but the grasp that the televangelists have on both preachers and churchgoers alike is a cause for alarm especially considering that many of them preach a feel-good message devoid of any biblical basis, foundation or support. In examining the reasons for watching the programs and listening to the preachers Mokaya reports,

> From the above findings it emerged that a majority of the respondents, 67.2%, said that their primary motivation for watching the programmes was to grow as a Christian while a further 18% said they wanted to feel close to God. 7% said that they lacked time to go to church and therefore watched these programmes as an alternative to church service and 6.3% and 1.6% said they sought gratification in entertainment and relaxation from these programmes respectively.[385]

That Christians have to turn to the television to grow as a Christian is another big indictment on the condition of the teaching ministry of the church. The other reasons stated in Mokaya's findings do not give any comfort either, but rather show that there is a need to revisit how pastoral theology is being carried out in the church. One needs to also note that the popular televangelists screened on Kenyan Christian televisions include the likes of Joel Osteen,[386] Joyce Meyers, T.D. Jakes, Kenneth Copeland, John Haggee, the now deceased Myles Munroe, Jesse Duplantis, each of whom has his own version of self-entitlement messages that are man-centred and humanistic, making use of the Bible and the Word of God unlawfully presenting God's great purpose in grace is in some way or another to be just to take care of us while we are on earth and to save us from hell when we die. They go on to present "keys" and "insights" which are supposed to enable the readers and listeners to make the most of that great purpose they have presented. Television channels also air a host of continental televangelists like Prophet T.B. Joshua and Chris Oyakhilome, among a host of Kenyan charismatic preachers with their unconventional messages and strange claims.

FACTORS CONTRIBUTING TO THE DECLINE OF BIBLE TEACHING

The Bible is the Word of God, and many metaphors are used in it to illustrate its necessity and importance to every child of God. The Bible is also applicable to all gener-

---

[384]Ibid.

[385]Nyaboke, *Televangelism and the Changing Habits of Worshippers in Nairobi County* 37.

[386]Clint Archer, "Why Seminary? Exhibit A: Joel Osteen", *The Cripplegate*, last modified 2019, accessed January 18, 2018, http://thecripplegate.com/why-seminary-exhibit-a-joel-osteen/

Archer, revisiting Osteen's interview with Larry King, writes, "The question of whether seminary is necessary is one that perennially resurfaces among those who sense the urgency of the need to preach and feel compelled to dive right in, but also understand the benefit of thorough training, and want guidance about the balance." He then goes on to transcript at length the conversation between Larry King and Joel Osteen in which Larry King explores different aspects of Osteen's view of Christianity and ministry including training, ordination and faith in Christ. Osteen confesses his lack of training and avoids being dogmatic on the issue salvation by faith in Christ alone during the interview.

ations of man. In every culture, age, and context of life, the Bible is God's manual for faith and life to everyone who believes. Faith comes by hearing and hearing by the Word of God. This shows how important the Scriptures are to the life of the believer. Paul's injunction to Timothy to study to show himself approved unto God a workman that needeth not to be ashamed rightly dividing the Word of truth also establishes the necessity for the right use of the Scriptures. The right use of the Scriptures also ensures that all other practices are biblical and God-honouring. When one deviates in his view and use of scriptures, he will deviate from what he believes and what he does too. Thus, the right understanding, view and use of the Holy Scriptures is vital and central to the church's beliefs and practices.

Furthermore, the importance of the Holy Scriptures to the church and believers is clearly presented in the Bible. For example, Matthew 4:4 presents Scriptures as necessary for life as man does not live by bread alone but by every word that proceeds from the mouth of God. 2 Timothy 3:16-17 presents the nature of Scripture as God-breathed and is profitable for equipping man for life and service in every good work. Joshua 1:8 presents Scripture as the key or foundation of true success in all godly endeavours when Scripture is constantly and continually meditated upon. Romans 15:4 presents the reason why Scriptures was written, i.e. for instructing and encouraging God's people as they live in dangerous times. In Psalm 19:9-11, memorizing of Scripture is presented as man's safeguard against sinning. Romans 10:17 presents the Christian faith as tied to the Word of God as faith comes by hearing the Word. John 15:3 presents the Word of God as sanctifying and cleansing and so Scriptures are necessary for the Christian.

When considering factors that have contributed to the decline of Bible teaching in the church, the factors can be summarized under the phrase "the neglect of the Holy Scriptures." This neglect has taken many forms over the years. In some cases it has been the substitution of Scriptures where scriptures are set aside and in its place, visions, dreams and extra-biblical revelation are used. In other cases, it has been the dilution of scriptures which has taken form through the current Bible Translation and Modern Versions drive that employ a thought-for-thought method of translation instead of a word-for-word method. In other cases it has been the subordination of Scriptures which is by far the most subtle and popular method where time given to the scriptures through Bible reading and teaching is minimized. Emphasis is placed on other activities whether through the ever popular praise and worship sessions, the deceptive miracles and vision and dreams interpretation sessions, and also in the promotion of motivational speeches over biblical messages and the use of psychological counselling over biblical counselling.

The Neglect of Scriptures through Substitution

The modern worship service centres around man and his needs, not God and His Word. The accounts of worship in the Bible centre on the Word. For example, the Israelites having left Egypt and having come to the wilderness at the foot of Mount Sinai and spent about a year camped at its foot. It was during this period that God gave the people of Israel the Law and the instructions for building the tabernacle of worship for Israel. And God said that the people would be a kingdom of priests if they would obey His commandments. When the people heard the Word of the Lord, they said that they would do all that God had spoken to them. Then the first congregational worship service of Israel is recorded. As the Lord dictates how the gathering and meeting is to be, the following three elements can be drawn concerning worship:

Call to assemble and regulations for gathering (Exod. 19:10-15)

God designed the procedures He specified in verses 10-15 to help the people realize the difference between their holy God and their sinful selves. Notice that God separated Himself from the Israelites spatially and temporally. The temporary prohibition against normal sexual relations (v. 15) seems intended to impress the importance of this occasion on the Israelites and to help them concentrate on it. We should not infer from this command that normal sexual relations are sinful (cf. Gen. 1:28; 9:1, 7). Abstention was for ritual cleanness, not moral cleanness.[387]

From Exodus 19:10-15, it can be noted that man cannot approach God without proper consideration of the nature and attributes of God or as Constable puts it: "the difference between their holy God and their sinful selves."[388] Thus, the call to assemble is a call to the people to prepare themselves to approach God in a manner that will be acceptable to Him. When men assemble together to worship, they have to realize that they are coming into the very presence of God and thus need to prepare and present themselves in a manner worthy. This Moses does for the children of Israel by proclaiming the call to assemble before God in which he stipulates the manner in which everyone must approach God. In response, man must be to take his focus off himself and his desires and turn his focus unto God.

The Word of God proclaimed to the assembly (Exod. 20:1-17; 21:1-23:33)

The next element in this inaugural worship service, after the people have gathered together on God's terms and conditions, was the Word of God. It has been said that, at this point, the climax of the entire book of Exodus has been reached, and if this is so, then this too would most definitely form the climax of the worship service. As worship is response based on the revelation of God, it follows that before the people can be called on to respond, the Word of God has to be proclaimed. In this instance, the proclamation of God's Word takes the form of the proclamation of the Ten Commandments by the LORD Himself. Constable notes, "Notice that the Ten Commandments use verbs, not nouns. Nouns leave room for debate, but verbs do not. God gave His people ten commandments, not ten suggestions."[389] In this, Constable points out one very important aspect: the clarity of God's Word. In the presentation and proclamation of God's Word, there must not be any room for debate or ambiguity for these may lead to false and faulty responses. In this case, the clarity with which the Law is presented highlights its purpose and its God-honouring desired results. Davis observes,

> A careful study of both the Old and New Testament will reveal the fact that the Law had a five-fold purpose in the plan of God. (1) It was designed to reveal man's sinfulness (Rom. 3:19-20). (2) It uncovered or illustrated the hideous nature of sin (Rom. 7:8-13). (3) It revealed the holiness of God. (4) It restrained the sinner so as to help him come to Christ (Gal. 3:24). (5) It restrained wrong behavior so as to protect the integrity of the moral and social and religious institutions of Israel.[390]

---

[387] Thomas L. Constable, "Notes On Exodus", *Planobible Chapel*, last modified 2019, accessed February 12, 2019, https://planobiblechapel. org/tcon/notes/pdf/exodus.pdf.

[388] Ibid.

[389] Thomas L. Constable, *Notes on Exodus*.

[390] John J. Davis, *Moses and the Gods of Egypt* (Winona Lake: BMH Books, 1986), 207.

Congregational response and covenant (Exod. 20:18-21; 24:3-11)

The Word proclaimed reveals the presence of the LORD and His requirements of those who would approach Him in worship but this is not the only purpose. The Word also incites in man a response to God, His presence and His requirements. Thus, the third element of the worship service seen in this instance is the congregational response and covenant.

The people, in response to the manifestation of the presence of the LORD and on hearing the voice of the LORD, feared the LORD. Moses, in addressing the people, points out to them that the purpose of God revealing Himself in the manner that He did is that they may *"fear"* and *"sin not."*

These three elements can be also be found during the worship under Josiah as Temple worship was restored in 2 Kings 23, and also in the time of Nehemiah as the people gathered together in Nehemiah 8. This Old Testament pattern is maintained in the New Testament though it should be noted that there are differences in the administration of the third element, the congregational response. The focus and centrality of biblical worship remains the same, i.e. the Word of God. God's Word supplies the focus, guidelines and inspiration for worship. The departure from this in modern worship has brought with it the decline in both Bible reading and teaching. In its place, a man-centred focus has given prominence to visions, dreams, and extra-biblical prophecies. Though this in part is fulfilment of prophecy and a sign of the times with men not enduring sound doctrine but heaping unto themselves teachers having itching ears, yet in the same passage 2 Timothy 4:1-5, Paul exhorts Timothy to preach the Word, to make full proof of his ministry. The church has to be Word-centred even in perilous and apostate times.

The Neglect of Scriptures through Dilution

The neglect of Scriptures through dilution is probably the most rampant one that has led to the most abuse of the Bible than the others. This dilution has taken many forms ranging from the twisting and abuse of Scripture by politicians and other figures for monetary and other gains[391] and the abuse of Scripture by false prophets who attribute to themselves certain prophecies (e.g. David Owuor claims to be one of the two witnesses in Revelation 11[392]) to the production of new vernacular Bible translations that

---

[391] Article in the Religion News Service written in October of 2017, was titled, "Kenya's "Presidential Race Takes Pages from the Bible." The article in parts of it read, NAIROBI, Kenya (RNS) — Religion has long figured prominently into Kenyan politics. But the great lengths presidential candidates and their supporters have gone to connect themselves to the Bible and its heroes in the lead-up to this month's presidential election have disturbed many religious leaders and scholars. … <u>Politicians are trying to use this religious imagery to give force and legitimacy to their campaigns</u>, but no one should be fooled, said the Rev. Wilybard Lagho, the Mombasa Roman Catholic archdiocese vicar general. "<u>They want their supporters to believe this is a divine call, which is not. I think they are manipulating their supporters</u> [emphasis added]."
[Fredrick Nzwili, "Kenya's Presidential Race Takes Pages From The Bible - Religion News Service", *Religion News Service*, last modified 2019, accessed November 24, 2018, https://religionnews.com/2017/10/11/kenyas-presidential-race-takes-pages-from-the-bible/.]

[392] An article titled "Alert, Elijah Is Here! | Highway Of Holiness", *Highwayofholiness.Us*, last modified 2019, accessed February 12, 2019, https://www.highwayofholiness.us/alert-elijah-is-here/. says,

"On March 25th, 2018, at 2:00 pm eastern time, at the United States Capitol Building, on lawn nine (9) of the Capitol Grounds Demonstration Area, the Archbishop of the Ministry of Repentance and Holiness, USA, and National Overseer of the United States of America, Louis Lupo, along with the Senior Pastors and Ministers of the Gospel will announce the following: 'The Man of God, THE MIGHTIEST PROPHET OF THE LORD, He has Come! These are the Days of Elijah, prepare ye the Way!' (Mal 3:1, Mal 4:4-6, Revelation 11) … These are the stripes of Elijah and Moses, the Two Witnesses of Revela-

misrepresent the original texts of the Bible. These are just a glimpse of how Scripture is being abused in Kenya. Kenyans, being *"too superstitious ... ignorantly worship"* (as Paul said to the Athenians in Acts 17:22-23) something that is not God. They have fallen prey to manipulative people who used both Scriptures and scriptural themes "to give force and legitimacy to their campaigns."[393]

When it comes to the dilution through translations, the prevailing thought is that all Bibles and translations are the same; and the mindset prevalent in Kenya today is whatever translation one is comfortable with is "OK"; the important thing is that one has a Bible they can read. In the current drive on Bible translation in Kenya, spearheaded by Bible Translation and Literacy (BTL) to ensure that every tribe has access to a Bible in their mother tongue, BTL has chosen readability and relatability over faithfulness and accuracy in relaying God's Word. This is reflected in the video clip about its Bible translation journey. In the clip, by Live Studios Media, the journey of Bible translation is presented for the various people groups that still do not have access to a Bible in their language as well as the participation and partnership of the Deputy President of Kenya in the ongoing work. The video clip[394] begins with an elderly man draped in a shawl sitting down and pulling out a Bible with the narrator giving Nelson Mandela's observation: *"If you talk to a man in a language he understands, that goes to his head. If you talk to him in his language, that goes to his heart."*[395] Then a young man comes explaining that the elderly man is reading in his mother tongue. He explains that it is a reading taken from Isaiah 1:18 and goes on to state that "in the Marakwet language there is no scarlet and there is no snow, but right now with the Marakwet translation, the Scripture refers to as black as charcoal and as white as milk, so my father can really understand and relate with things he can see and relate well within the community."

What is distressing is that many people find that acceptable and commendable stating that the culture and context of the recipients counts for their understanding! They think that there are times that the translator should translate for the meaning and not just word for word. To many, relevance takes precedence over accuracy and faithfulness to the original biblical texts. What seems to be important is not what God said, but rather what makes sense to man in his culture and context. When attempting to discuss the issue, this writer was told that if translation was done accurately and faithfully with each word translated according to the original biblical texts, the Bible would be irrelevant in some contexts. And many feel that what is important is the meaning and not the form of the original text. In this case, red and snow were used as comparisons and therefore sub-

---

tion 11, and these are the fulfilled Prophecies of THE MIGHTIEST PROPHET OF THE LORD. This long-awaited announcement is most serious, most sobering, and most holy for this is not about money that we see at apostate altars of Baal known as "prosperity churches." The days of corruption are over in the Holy House of the LORD! The Message is clear: May those who have ears prepare for the glorious Coming of the Messiah. Be it Muslim, be it Hindu, be it Buddhist, be it Atheist, it does not matter now. You simply repent and receive Christ Jesus as LORD, and be born-again and walk in righteousness, because the Coming of the Messiah is at hand. "For I tell you, you will not see me again until you say, 'Blessed is he who comes in the name of the Lord." (Matt 23:39)."

[393] Nzwili, "Kenya's Presidential Race Takes Pages From The Bible - Religion News Service", https://religionnews.com/2017/10/11/kenyas-presidential-race-takes-pages-from-the-bible/.

[394] Available at URL: https://www.youtube.com/watch?v=e-RX0RYLFdU and viewed on 18/10/2018.

[395] The narration is transcripted in part in BTL's article titled "Mother Tongue Bible Changed My Father," BTL Admin, "Mother Tongue Bible Changed My Father", *Btlkenya.Org*, last modified 2019, accessed October 18, 2018, https://www.btlkenya.org/index.php/media/blog/item/35-mother-tongue-bible-changed-my-father.

stitution is allowed. The semantic domain for snow is its whiteness, but since snow is an unknown idea to most Africans, it therefore can be substituted with cotton, milk or anything else that is white. The same goes with the red in crimson as long as the substitution shares some similar traits with the original citation. Another example given during the discussion for this was that for communities that do not see the lion as the fiercest and who have never heard or seen the lion, 1 Peter 5:8 can have the devil presented by the animals that the people understand to be ferocious, e.g. the leopard. This is the sad state that this writer encountered and it is an issue that needs immediate addressing through teaching as it is one that contributes to the decline of Bible teaching in the church today.

The Africa Bible Commentary has an article on Bible Translation in Africa written by Aloo Osotsi Mojola. He gives mainly a historical overview on the work of the translation of Scriptures in the different parts of Africa mentioning both the early translations produced in North Africa and the Bible translation wave of the 19th century. Aloo recognizes the importance of Bible translation when he writes, "There can be no doubt that the phenomenal growth of Christianity in Africa owes an enormous debt to Bible translation."[396] However, he disregards the important issues in translation and favours the dynamic equivalence method of translation. This is seen in his description of the current revision of missionary translations as translations that are "created specifically with African audiences in mind."[397] The prevailing understanding and thought in the issue of translation today seems to be cultural sensitivity and contextualization instead of accuracy and faithfulness to the original text. This will no doubt lead to perversions just as it has happened in the English language and has begun to be evidenced for example by the Kalenjin Bible released recently in which the name of the LORD "Jehovah" as was in the previous Kalenjin Bible is replaced by a title for God "Kamuktaindet ne Toror" which in English would mean "High Lord." And the Holy Spirit is changed to the breath of the Lord "Kaabusetuap Kamuktaindet" in addition to omissions present due to the text used. The problem in Kenya is that those who are supposed to know and understand these things do not know and therefore cannot take a stand or teach on such vital issues.

Neglect through Subordination of Scriptures

The prominence given to praise and worship, to interpretation of visions and dreams and to miracles and signs has driven many away from the Bible. The Gospel music industry is evidence to that with many of the Gospel singers equating themselves to preachers and their music as on par with Bible messages. Most of them have no church affiliation and are under no particular pastoral care. The outcome has been music that is neither biblical nor Christian and yet is regarded as Gospel music. This is accompanied by a worldly lifestyle that is neither salt nor light to the world. Reginald Oduor, in his book *The Noise of our Songs* saw these dangers years back. In his preface, he gives his testimony concerning the disturbing trends that were emerging in his time, but are rampant today. He wrote,

> At Kenya Youth for Christ, I also began to appreciate the inherent dangers in gospel music. I noticed that as long as a person sang moving songs, he could have a false sense of spiritual well-being without adequately studying the Word! If that false feeling continued long enough, one's spiritual life would greatly deteriorate, and he would then wonder what really went wrong: had he not been ":singing for the Lord" with diligence? For that person to be helped, he would have to go back to <u>the only way that God had ordained for our spiritual nourishment — not song, but God's</u>

---

[396] *Africa Bible Commentary*, 1315.

[397] Ibid.

CHAPTER IV: THE CURRENT STATE OF BIBLE TEACHING IN THE CHURCH IN KENYA

Word [emphasis added]: "... man doth not live by bread only, but by every Word that proceedeth out of the mouth of the Lord doth man live" (Deut. 8:3).[398]

The substitution of God's Word by the present-day emphasis on praise and worship is leaving people with a false sense of assurance of spiritual well-being, when in truth they are spiritually malnourished. This substitution is fuelled by the notion that music is one of the avenues through which doctrinal teachings are passed. Roberta King rightly observes,

> Throughout the history of Christianity and God's interaction with the human race, music — mainly in the form of songs — has made a dynamic contribution in forwarding the work of the Kingdom of God. Martin Luther claimed that: Next after theology, I give to music the highest place and the greatest honor. I would not exchange what little I know of music for something great (Bainton 1951:346). Luther valued music immensely. The irony of his statement about possessing a limited knowledge of music is that Luther was very well-versed in music. He considered music a crucial element in theological education and ministry, emphasizing that "... before a youth is ordained into the ministry, he should practice music in school" (Plass 1959:980). For Luther, music went hand in hand with his theology. Not only did he honor music, but he employed music as the servant of his theology.[399]

Luther's understanding is best expressed in the phrase that is most commonly attributed to him: "Music is next to theology." The problem today is not the use of music to pass on doctrinal teachings, but the increasing perception that the use of music as a substitute to replace the ministry of the Word is acceptable. Luther's view of music did not undermine the ministry of the Word, rather it complemented it. Music is to be a tool to affirm the doctrines, the faith, and the hope of the church. It is primarily to express one's knowledge, faith, and gratitude to God, praising and extolling Him by declaring His attributes and works. And, secondarily, music is to remind, encourage and provoke one another to love and good works. For this to be accomplished, music has to be subordinated to the Scriptures. But the present praise and worship movement seeks to replace and supplant the Word from the worship service and is being used not to preserve, remind and affirm doctrines of the Bible, but rather create and form new and unbiblical doctrines.

In addition to this, the subordination of Scriptures has taken a more serious form in the recent decades when considering the number of Bible colleges and institutions that have become institutions of secular learning by adding secular courses to their curriculum or even totally phasing out theological training from their institutions. One of the recommendations Miller gave based on his research was the need to strengthen the Association of East African Theological Colleges (AEATC) to the intent that a strong AEATC would ensure proper theological training even prompting "Departments of Religious studies [to] develop further at the University colleges."[400] But the current trend is that of capitulation, with many of the Bible colleges turning into secular colleges due to the requirements for accreditation and in other cases financial constraints brought about by low enrolment.

---

[398] Reginald M. J. Oduor, *The Noise of our Songs: Disturbing trends in contemporary gospel music* (Nairobi, Kenya: Berean Publications Ltd., 1997), vii – viii.

[399] Roberta King, "The Role Of Music In Theological Education", *Biblicalstudies.Org*, last modified 2019, accessed February 12, 2019, https://biblicalstudies.org.uk/pdf/ajet/09-1-035.pdf.

[400] Paul M. Miller, *Equipping for Ministry* (Soni, Tanzania: Central Tanganyika Press, 1969), 214.

This has affected the Bible colleges of the Africa Inland Church (AIC) like Scott Theological College[401] which is now known as Scott Christian University offering graduate, undergraduate, diploma and certificate programs. Although it still has a school of theology as a department within the university, the introduction of secular colleges and particularly counselling psychology tells of the departure from its biblical emphasis. That Kapsabet Bible College seems to be going down the same path is indicated by the advertisement they placed in 2015 at the Kenyan Career website:

> Kapsabet Bible College was founded in1895 with an aim of training Pastors to serve in the Church. It has since trained over 1,000 pastors, leaders, chaplains, teachers and missionaries that are currently working in different parts of the world.
>
> Since its inception, the College has realized significant expansion of its facilities and infrastructure.
>
> Leveraging on these, the College intends to expand its training to include non-theological programs and research activities in the coming years.
>
> The Board of Directors of Kapsabet Bible College is thus seeking eminent scholars with an outstanding record of leadership for the position of The Principal and Head of Finance.[402]

When considering the qualifications and experience as well as the duties and responsibilities for the advertised positions, there is no indication of any spiritual require-

---

[401] Scott Theological College was established in 1962 as the national theological College of the Africa Inland Church, Kenya (AIC). Its purpose was to provide training for church ministries at a more advanced academic level than was available through the Bible Schools of the AIC. While functioning as the national theological College of the Africa Inland Church, the College has existed from the beginning to serve all churches.

The African Inland Mission, from whose ministry the Africa Inland Church developed, had begun its work in Kenya in 1895 under the leadership of Peter Cameron Scott. In the course of the years, several fine Bible training institutions were founded by the AIM. But as good as these schools were, as the educational level of the country advanced, there came a need for a higher level of biblical education. To meet this need, Scott Theological College, named in memory of Peter Scott, was opened in 1962. The College was located at Mumbuni, Machakos where land and buildings belonging to the Africa Inland Mission were made available for this purpose. ...

Together with this numerical growth the College has progressively upgraded the academic standards of its courses. In 1972 a decision was made to raise the entry requirement to a minimum of Secondary School Certificate, Level Three. The first students enrolled at this higher level graduated in 1978. Between 1978 and 1985 a total of 110 students, an average of 14 each year, graduated.

A further upgrading of standards occurred in 1982 with the introduction of a Bachelor of Theology (B.Th.) programme and the consequent raising of the entrance requirement to university entrance level. This development was made possible through an arrangement with Ontrario Bible College, an accredited degree granting college in Toronto, Canada. ...

In 1977 the College applied to the Accrediting Council for Theological Education in Africa (ACTEA) for accreditation of its training programme. This body had recently been established by the Association of Evangelicals of Africa and Madagascar to ensure high standards of theological education in Africa. Following an exhaustive evaluation process the College received its accreditation from ACTEA in December 1979. It was the first post-secondary theological college in Africa to receive such accreditation. In 1986 full accreditation of the College's Bachelor of Theology degree programme was granted by ACTEA. This accreditation has been maintained through periodical reviews to the present day. ["Scott Theological College |", *Kenya's How-To Website*, last modified 2019, accessed February 12, 2019, https://www.how.co.ke/scott-theological-college/]

[402] "Job Vacancies In Kapsabet Bible College", *Kenyancareer.Com*, last modified 2019, accessed February 12, 2019, http://www.kenyancareer.com/2015/05/job-vacancies-in-kapsabet-bible-college.html.

CHAPTER IV: THE CURRENT STATE OF BIBLE TEACHING IN THE CHURCH IN KENYA

ments or spiritual responsibilities that are tied to the positions. In another web post, dated 2018, the Kapsabet Bible College is identified as a "private technical and vocational college"[403] and the courses listed as offered at the college as per the advertisement placed are all non-biblical/theological courses.

This is the case not only with the Bible colleges of the AIC. Other theological training institutes of other denominations too, have been affected. For example, the theological training institution of the Africa Gospel Church (AGC) — Kenya Highlands Bible College[404] is now Kenya Highlands University. It has even dropped the term "Evangelical" which was in its initial name at accreditation (i.e. Kenya Highlands Evangelical University). Of the fourteen undergraduate programs it offers, only one is theological: the Bachelor of Theology program. The departure is quite marked noting the presence of the Bachelor of Arts in Counselling Psychology program. The same pattern is seen in its diploma and certificate programs.[405]

The subordination of Scriptures is seen also in the "unchristian" Religious Education taking place in Kenyan schools. Religious education has been part of the curriculum both in primary and secondary schools for a long time, and many schools both primary and secondary are still faith-based schools with some of the most popular national schools being mission schools. But the time when the curriculum was Bible-based, and counselling was biblical and pastoral with the children receiving Bibles from the Gideon's group and Pastoral Program in Schools done by pastors is long gone. Today, the Bibles recommended by the Kenyan Ministry of Education is either the RSV or the Good

---

[403] "Official Kapsabet Bible College Contacts, Courses ,Intakes ,Fee Structures And Location 2018", last modified 2019, accessed February 12, 2019, http://knecportal.co/ official-kapsabet-bible-college-contacts-courses-intakes-fee-structures-and-location-2018.

[404] The ideological heritage of educational instruction at the Kenya Highlands Bible College, which became the University, dates back to 1932 when missionaries of World Gospel Mission saw the need for training their converts. This instruction not only needed to cover biblical and ministry-related subjects, but also teacher training. Teachers were prepared for the sixteen primary schools the mission had started. These first teachers also served as preachers in their communities. A school first started in 1936 in the Sotik area as a Teacher's Bible School and met in various locations.

In 1944, the school was officially opened as Sotik Bible School and courses continued to combine training techniques in primary school teaching and Bible. The following year, the Bible School students were separated from the teacher training group as the need for trained leadership for the church grew. In 1950 the school was relocated from Sotik to Cheptenye in Belgut area.

Due to the need for more space to develop classrooms, dormitories, library and chapel facilities and staff housing, another plot was sought which would be separate from the established mission stations. The present site was acquired in 1953, and in 1955 Kenya Highlands Bible School was begun, offering a two-year Bible programme leading to the Christian Workers Certificate. In 1957 the course was upgraded to include a three-year programme leading to a diploma in Bible.

In 1962, the level of admission and training was again elevated to provide training on a secondary level in both biblical and secular subjects, and the name was changed to Kenya Highlands Bible College. In 1967 the college started offering secondary school education up to 1973 when it ceased offering "O" level. In 1970 the Bible College Council was constituted, drawing its membership equally from the church and the mission, and charged with the responsibility of managing the institution and improving the academic standards. In 1971 the college admitted its first class of post-secondary students into a four-year curriculum, modeled after degree-granting Bible colleges in North America, leading to the degree of Bachelor of Religion in Biblical Studies. ["Kenya Highlands University", *En.Wikipedia.Org*, accessed February 12, 2019, https://en.wikipedia.org/wiki/Kenya_Highlands_University#History.]

[405] This information can be found in their webpage: https://khu.ac.ke/academics/.

News Bible, with the latter being more promoted. Pastoral programs are being phased out and in their place a counselling department that is based on psychology is set up in all schools, and prayer days for schools have become times for motivational speeches and self-esteem building with the speakers appealing to the hearers' emotions through popular psychology whilst pretending to be biblical by seasoning their speeches with a few Bible verses here and there.

EVIDENCES OF THE DECLINE OF BIBLE TEACHING

In the preface to his book *Equipping for Ministry*, Miller gives an account of his experience during the two-year research he did, visiting the different communities and speaking to church leaders and pastors of different denominations. At one point he writes, "There were unforgettable days spent listening to African laymen discussing what Christ expected of their church in the future."[406] Those were days now long gone and totally forgotten as the church has taken a totally different direction. Miller worked on a research project that was aimed at addressing theological training in East Africa at the invitation of the Association of East African Theological Colleges. In his introduction, he points out,

> One solution would be to turn to the Bible alone for guidance. East African Christianity is united in a fervent belief in and love for the Scriptures. But the problem of the pattern of ministry for East Africa cannot be solved merely by a newly conducted study of the Scriptures. Biblical scholarship in every country and in most denominations has given up the notion that the Bible outlines one specific pattern of ministry for all time. The church leaders in East Africa largely agree with this view.[407]

The context of the paragraph given was the question facing theological colleges: the ideal pattern of ministry. The period of research also was a transitional one as the East African countries had gained independence and there was change in almost all areas of life. At that time, there were those who saw the need for the church to take up "an additional task in providing 'spiritual schools.' The government, as a secular institution in a multi-religious society, cannot teach the spiritual heritage of yesterday."[408] But sadly, half a century later, that fervent belief in and love for the Scriptures has waned and the vision of spiritual schools is dying if not dead already. Some problems that were foreseen are present today. The solutions that were offered are not being implemented today. Some challenges of that time are multiplied manifold today and "the deeper needs of man which still remain unmet, even after his ignorance is displaced by secular education, his disease by health, and his poverty becomes affluence"[409] even today still remain unmet. The church has chosen not to stress on the Gospel, but rather has turned to focus on the physical, material and temporal things of life.

Maurice Ogolla, in his article, "The Challenges Facing Religion in the Contemporary World: The Kenyan Situation", writes, "The challenges that continuously bedevil this major Kenyan religion include syncretism, secularism, materialism, modernity and education just to mention a few."[410] These challenges have affected greatly the church in Kenya and the practice of Christianity.

---

[406]Miller, *Equipping for Ministry*, 5.

[407]Miller, *Equipping for Ministry*, 11.

[408]Ibid., 13.

[409]Ibid., 15.

[410]Maurice Ogolla, The Challenges Facing Religion in the Contemporary World: The Kenyan Situation, *International Journal of Humanities and Social Science* (Vol. 4, No. 3: February 2014), 326.

CHAPTER IV: THE CURRENT STATE OF BIBLE TEACHING IN THE CHURCH IN KENYA

Secularism

The first challenge, and one that is currently distorting the Christian practice greatly and has changed the church scene in Kenya, is that of secularism. This is evidenced in the direction church services and worship has taken. The church is getting more and more worldly as a result of this. The common thought that indicates the inroads secularism has made in the thinking of many is expressed by Dickson Kagema in his article "The Use of Gospel Hip-hop as an Avenue of Evangelizing Youth in Kenya Today: A Practical Approach" where he writes,

> Rather than refuting Gospel hip-hop music as evil, the Church in Kenya should utilize it to evangelize the youth since they are more comfortable with it. There is a Kamba proverb which says that *Ileawa na kila yisaa* meaning "An animal is baited with what it eats" (Makewa 2008:5). Therefore, what is interesting and appealing to the youth should be used by the Church to reach them There is an urgent need for the Church to re-formulate a theology that positively enhances the life of the young people. At the end, it is the theological contents and not the tune or style of music that will inform the salvation and spirituality of the youth. ... It will be a mark of ignorance not to tap into the power of music since it is indeed a very relevant tool to use in youth ministries (Rukungu 2012:22). It is no doubt that the youth are proud to identify with Gospel hip hop music because it appeals to them (Kawira 2013). The vigorous and more vibrant music is what the youth in Kenya are looking for and will attend every forum including *Keshas* (Kiswahili word for Prayer night meetings) where the choice of music is open with a bias on hip-hop styles (Rukungu 2012: 23).[411]

This statement not only gives a picture of the prevailing popular thought in the church today, it is also of the paradigm shift in the church with the rise of pluralistic and humanistic emphasis. This rise in secularism gives the first evidence that Bible teaching has indeed declined. Indeed, there is an urgent need in the Church, but, that need is not a need "to re-formulate a theology," but, rather, it is a need to revisit and strengthen biblical theology through teaching avenues that will mature its members and make them wise unto salvation with the intent of presenting every man perfect in Christ Jesus. This shift in emphasis has replaced the glory of God with the fancies of man focusing on that which "positively enhances the life of the young people" rather than that which God requires of man. Furthermore, efforts are geared towards that which enhances life rather than that which glorifies God.

Syncretism

The second challenge pointed out by Maurice Ogolla is that of syncretism, a challenge that has been affecting the church in Kenya. The problem among Kenyan churches, he observed, is the lack of biblical separation and distinction that is required of Christians. In its place is a constant attempt at combining and reconciling the Christian faith with the African way. He writes,

> Syncretism means the attempt or tendency to combine or reconcile differing beliefs particularly in religion and/or philosophy (The American Heritage Dictionary of the English language, 1969).

---

[411] Dickson Nkonge Kagema, "The Use Of Gospel Hip-Hop As An Avenue Of Evangelizing Youth In Kenya Today: A Practical Approach", *Aijcrnet.Com*, accessed March 12, 2018, http://www.aijcrnet.com/journals/Vol_3_No_8_August_2013/19.pdf.

This has been a major challenge to Christianity in the sense that in Kenya and of course Africa, there is not even a single person who is a 100% Christian or 100% African. <u>Most Kenyan Christians practice only a percentage of African Religion and a percentage of Christianity</u>. As already noted above, <u>the African belief systems have not totally been cleared from an African's mind or way of life</u> and as such many a time, Kenyans who purport to have totally left such practices, which are intertwined with African religion, have simply not done or embarked on a serious retrospection or self examination. Many preachers have described most Kenyans as <u>"Christians by day and Africans by night"</u> [emphasis added].

This means, in most cases, that such people do certain rituals or consultations with diviners at night yet during the day they are actively involved in Christian activities. ... The Africans and Kenyans in particular, were forced to accept conversion into Christianity without understanding why their own religion was considered evil.[412]

In his last sentence, Ogolla points out not only the genesis of the problem, but also the key to its solution. There is a lack of understanding why Christianity cannot and should not be mixed with any other system, and there is a need to understand why all other religious practices and spiritual activities are to be considered evil. Syncretism as a challenge, is a great one, and is a difficult one due to the "prevailing wind of universalism,"[413] a term used by Kato as he explained the factors that made universalism a challenge to Christianity in Africa in his book *Theological Pitfalls in Africa*. As Kato explained the factors, he pointed out how universalism has contributed to the deeply rooted syncretism in Africa:

Biblical ignorance in the churches in Africa today and inadequate emphasis on theological education on the part of missionaries is another factor for the growth of universalism. Many pastors have swallowed the pill of incipient universalism without knowing the premise nor the end result. ... So a mammoth church has been established without the depth of theology that the church needs. Christian leaders are now vulnerable to the tactics of ecumenism with its basic universalistic premise.[414]

This biblical ignorance is what has contributed to the major and prevalent challenge that has created what Ogolla observes as "Christians by day and Africans by night" and has given rise to a syncretistic practice of Christianity in which "Most Kenyan Christians practice only a percentage of African Religion and a percentage of Christianity."[415] Ogolla goes on to cite examples which practically manifests syncretism when he writes,

All Christians to date marry in the African way first then go to Church for a Christian wedding or exchange of vows which again are not totally obeyed. This is evidently shown in the fact that death never ends African marriages as repeated in church vows "until death do us part." Children are sought by all Africans and can lead to the practice of polygamy in case of childlessness even if people are, so called, very strong Christians. Death is reacted to in almost the same way our fathers who were not Christians did and finally our names are still partly African and partly Western, for example, most of us are called Jacob Omollo, Peter Mbugua, Frederick Kasyoki, Paul Wanyonyi or Esther Nafula. Why must the African name

---

[412] Ogolla, *The Challenges Facing Religion in the Contemporary World: The Kenyan Situation*, 326.

[413] Byang H. Kato, *Theological Pitfalls in Africa* (Nairobi: Evangel Publishing House, 1987), 11.

[414] Ibid., 14-15.

[415] Ogolla, *The Challenges Facing Religion in the Contemporary World: The Kenyan Situation*, 326.

be added next to the Western one, yet we are Christians? Furthermore, we still follow the same order in building houses to our sons just as our fore fathers did. That is, the first son builds first then the others and the first daughter is married first then the others just to mention a few. The issue here is that as all these things happen, many who do these things call themselves strong Christians. These points may appear simple, but they reveal a lot about Kenyan Christians with regard to religion.[416]

Miller during his research raised this issue; yet it is still a problem half a century later. The question they pondered at that time was, "Can the church see her ministry in interpreting God's moral law while Africa seeks to blend many customary and tribal laws into new legal systems for the nation?"[417]

Materialism

The third area of challenge that Ogolla highlighted was that of materialism. This is by far the most subtle due to its appeal to most people who in general are under great financial constraints and difficulty. This has been taken advantage of mainly in the charismatic circles by the many prosperity televangelist preachers, prophets, and apostles. Ogolla explains,

> Another influence that is challenging the Kenyan Christian is materialism. This is very evident on our television programs. Pastors post their phone numbers for followers or well wishers to send money through M-Pesa to support programs that are never specified. It appears that many of the pastors particularly of the Neo-Pentecostal church start their churches in order to be rich. They are ready to go as far as bribing their followers to pretend that they have been healed miraculously yet, in reality, nothing like that is the case. The best example is pastor in Nairobi who bribed a prostitute to confess in church that she had been healed. She disguised herself as a sick visitor looking for assistance (mwakilishi-20/07/2012 on www.optiven.co.ke)

> We have heard it on TV again and again that the God of some churches is a rich one and members of such churches can never be so dedicated to church affairs, yet they remain poor. This dedication, however, calls for self giving both in wealth and health. One is poor, looking for wealth yet, he/she is asked to give in kind. It is in Kenya again where a pastor purporting to cure AIDS through prayer was interrogated by the police concerning her claims. It was found out that she organized with some laboratory technician of a particular hospital to declare the people sent there by her church free from the virus after prayers that coasted Kenya Shillings 50,000.[418]

The clamour for healing and prosperity is common and intrinsic to Kenyans in general due to the African traditional world-view in which prosperity (e.g. bumper harvests, healthy or increased herds, etc.) and health (e.g. a disease-free life, number of children one has, long life, etc.) are always seen as blessings from God and a sign of His pleasure, while the opposite will raise questions as to why God is displeased and will be considered as punishment meted out for some reason that needs to be found out and corrected. This view is often heard in miracle rallies and crusades with the ever-increasing

---

[416] Ogolla, *The Challenges Facing Religion in the Contemporary World: The Kenyan Situation*, 326.

[417] Miller, *Equipping for Ministry*, 15.

[418] Ogolla, *The Challenges Facing Religion in the Contemporary World: The Kenyan Situation*, 326-27.

popularity on "breaking down altars" and "generational curses" seen by the sheer numbers of preachers who refer to them as the causes of misfortune and poverty that bedevil their hearers. This has been pointed out by,

> Several charismatic groups (that) implied that wealth was a sign of God's favor and blessing to an individual. The pursuit of wealth for Christians in a way that would embarrass Christians in the 1970s has now become the quest of many Christians today. Individuals are moving to these churches because of the many promises given in this gospel. Pentecostalism which began as the work of the Holy Spirit has been hijacked by people who have turned the gospel of Christ to a licence of earning all kinds of evil instead of impacting the world with the Gospel. Despite the fact that the prosperity preachers are impacted by the word of God, others end up misusing and compromising Gods word with their interest at heart.[419]

CONCLUDING OBSERVATIONS

Kenneth O. Gangel in his article, "Marks of a Healthy Church," gives tangible and measurable marks which when used to measure the state of the church in Kenya, gives it an unhealthy verdict. In his article, Gangel was addressing the challenges that were facing the church in general as she pursues the concept which he terms as "Healthy Great Commission churches" which he goes on to define as "communities of Christ-centred people characterized by five balanced passions: winning the lost, building the believer, equipping the worker, multiplying the leader, and sending the called ones."[420] He then goes on to suggest marks of a healthy church asserting that "healthy churches are measured in spiritual terms, follow biblical patterns of ministry, are based on theological foundations, focus on a ministry model, and adopt scriptural models of leadership."[421]

When the health of the church is measured in spiritual terms, the focus turns to the Bible and emphasis is placed on Bible-teaching and doctrine. But when the health of the church is equated to numbers, then the focus changes and emphasis is placed on how to bring in the masses. This has led to the use of market and consumer-oriented methods at the expense of God's will as revealed in His Word. Gangel gives the view of the scripture on this by pointing out that in Acts, though there was numerical increase, the church stressed not on the numerical increase, but on the spiritual maturity particularly pointing out that after the increase of 3,000 souls at Pentecost, the focus of the life of the church is presented as based on the doctrines of the apostles, praying, fellowship, and breaking of bread. The church as a spiritual body continued in its spiritual activities with the numbers being attributed to the working of God with Luke stating in Acts 2:47 that *"the Lord added to the church daily such as should be saved."*

Contrary to this pattern, numbers is a very big issue in many churches in Kenya, with the numerical size of the church being equated to the spiritual status of the church. This has greatly abetted syncretism, materialism and worldliness in the church, since in pursuit of numbers, there is increasing focus on what is appealing to the target audience, rather than what pleases God. What is lost in this process is the spirituality of the church, which should be of more valued than the numbers, as Gangel rightly states, "Biblical

---

[419]Elina Kanaiza Milemba, *The Influence of Prosperity Gospel on the Well-being of the Youth: a case study of contemporary Christian churches, Nairobi County*, (Masters of Arts Thesis: Department of Sociology and Social Work of the University of Nairobi, 2015), 18.

[420]Kenneth O. Gangel, Marks of a Healthy Church, *Bibliotheca Sacra 158* (October – December, 2001), 467.

[421]Ibid., 467-68.

church health begins with a Christ-centred, Bible-centred congregation determined to be in their personal, family, and corporate life precisely what God wants of them, and it makes no difference whether their number is fifteen, fifteen hundred, or fifteen thousand."[422]

When the health of the church is measured by biblical patterns, both the focus and the methods of ministry will be drawn from the scripture and its injunctions. But when the health of the church is to be measured solely by vibrancy of its programs and their appeal and relevance to the audience, then the Christian distinctiveness is replaced by cultural preferences. This, as observed by Gangel, is one of the major abuses that has arisen from the modern and ever popular church-growth movement, a movement that is increasing in popularity and influence in Kenya.

The church in Kenya is not in a good state. Its condition is seen in the perspectives adopted by the men who minister to it and is seen in the focus they take as well as the path they pursue. The neglect of, and in some cases, hostility to theological principles and scriptural models is distressing. The increasing proliferation of falsehood and peddling of lies in the name of God just to draw followers in order to rake in millions shows the extent of the departure in Kenya and must be seen as a call to return to the Bible and Bible-based teaching.

---

[422] Gangel, <u>Marks of a Healthy Church</u>, 470.

CHAPTER V

PRESCRIPTIONS AND SUGGESTIONS FOR STRENGTHENING THE TEACHING MINISTRY OF THE CHURCH

The previous chapters and sections have sought to address the role and place of teaching in strengthening the church both from a scriptural perspective and from a historical one. In them, the state of the teaching ministry as well as the avenues available have been considered. The current state of the teaching ministry of the church is not good. There is little biblical teaching in the institutions that have been set up for theological training for they are turning into liberal arts institutions and into training centres for psychological counselling. The pulpit ministry is replacing biblical messages with those of self-esteem and with "feel good" motivational speeches. The church is in a downward spiral that it need not be in. Its state ought to be a different one, not the current discouraging one, since, as has been considered in the previous sections, teaching avenues and opportunities for strengthening the church are not lacking. But, alas, although avenues and opportunities abound, declension is on the increase due to the lack of emphasis in teaching, and the neglect to use the teaching avenues available for the church.

After considering all these things, there has to be a consideration of what needs to be done in order to remedy and correct the current state the church finds herself in and to stem the increasing spiritual declension in the church. The need to remedy the situation the church is in is an urgent one, and is one that is very possible. This section intends to give prescriptions and suggestions towards this effect. There is a need for a revival of biblical training and teaching in the church. There is an urgent need to return to the place where the pulpit and the pastoral ministry draws it authority, instruction, illustration, applications, and counsel from the Scriptures and models its practice to scriptural standards. This implies that, the suggestions and prescriptions that will be given in this section, and the response that will be expected from the church as it lives and serves in the Kenyan context will need to emphasize knowledge of Scripture and application of scriptural principles.

Kenyans generally consider themselves as religious, which, ought to be a good thing; but this is turning out to be their greatest danger in the light of the increasing spiritual declension. This declension has brought with it an influx of cults and cultic groups, an increase in charlatan religious peddlers and false teachers who make merchandise of the masses. This has been so rampant that the government has tried to intervene and made attempts to regulate the church and place restrictions for "preachers" and "church leaders". The Attorney General on behalf of the government issued a moratorium in 2014 stopping the registration of churches and societies. According to his office, the Attorney General's concern was to shield church goers from exploitation by men who prey on and make merchandise of those who attend their services. In a press release, the office of the Attorney General wrote,

> The moratorium stopping the registration of churches and societies was issued on 11th November 2014 by the Attorney General in line with his constitutional mandate to promote, protect and uphold the Rule of Law and defend public interest. This was necessitated by several reports indicting the officials of several religious institutions and societies of orchestrating certain unconscionable activities that left their congregants at a disadvantage. Such instances included the infamous 'panda mbegu' saga.[423]

---

[423] This article is drawn from a press release on a churches' law that was proposed by the Attorney General. ["Office Of The Attorney-General And Department Of Justice Press Statement On Proposed Churches Law", *Office Of The Attorney General And Department Of Justice*, accessed March 14, 2019, https://www.statelaw.go.ke/press-statement-on-proposed-churches-law/.]

CHAPTER V: PRESCRIPTIONS & SUGGESTIONS FOR STRENGTHENING TEACHING

The popularity of the "panda mbegu" which translates as "plant a seed" in English, probably illustrates the extent of the current declension in biblical teaching well. Instead of preaching the whole counsel of God, instead of maturing the believers in the most holy faith, grounding them in the most holy Word, teaching them to observe all whatsoever the Lord has commanded, church goers are lured and induced to give (selflessly, sacrificially, and in extreme cases, even senselessly pledging what they do not have) to the church. They are promised blessings of prosperity, health, and other material blessings from God as long as they give in faith to the "ministers" and their "ministries". It is this that caught the government's attention and prompted it to respond. The Attorney General went on formulate new rules which was titled the "Religious Societies Compliance Rules" which defined the standards for registration, operation and conduct for religious institutions and their leaders. In this proposal, the Attorney General's office listed documents required during the registration of religious societies and its branches and officers. The article on these states,

> 6.(1) In addition to the requirements for registration provided under rules 4 and 5, a religious society shall submit –
>
> (a) the following information relating to each of its local officers and local religious leaders –
>
> (i) a copy of the national identification card, personal identification number and one passport photograph;
>
> (ii) a certified copy of the theological certificate from a duly registered and accredited theological institution;
>
> (iii) a tax clearance or exemption certificate;
>
> (iv) a membership certificate and letter of recommendation from the relevant umbrella religious society;
>
> (v) a declaration of any familial relations of the religious leaders and officers;[424]

Among the propositions was the introduction of umbrella bodies that would exercise some form of control and regulate the practices of the religious societies under the same umbrella, and the introduction of a mandatory theological qualification for pastors and leaders together with the requirement to supply a clearance certificate and a certificate of good conduct. These rules were the government's response to the excesses and misuses of religion and radicalization in Kenya. They were shelved in 2016 after pressure from religious and political leaders and institutions. This push has taken a new form again in 2019 with the push coming from parliament this time round, with a member of parliament introducing a bill seeking to control the formation and registration of churches in Kenya. The Member of Parliament, Muturi Kigano, said that,

> People were opening churches to become rich through collection of tithes. "We have churches that are made up of three members with the husband being the bishop, wife acting as the pastor or archdeacon and their daughter as the treasurer. This cannot be allowed," … clerics no longer preached the virtues articulated by the scriptures. "They are preoccupied with what is called prosperity gospel that urges followers to get rich. It is about tithing generously and planting the seed,"[425]

---

[424] This is taken from the Legal Notice paper on The Societies (Religious Societies) Rules 2015 given by the then Attorney General of Kenya Githu Muigai.

[425] Brian Ojamaa, "Involve Clergy In Bill To Regulate Churches, Bishop Tells Legislator", *The Star*, accessed March 21, 2019, https://www.the-star.co.ke/counties/western/2019-02-19-involve-clergy-in-bill-to-regulate-churches-bishop-tells-legislator/.

The above article was one of the many written in response to this attempt at regulating churches. From the attempts and the reason given by the government for their intended involvement, the sad state of the church is highlighted, and what repeatedly comes out is the lack of teaching in the churches and the lack of training among the ministers and leaders. The church itself, though, has not been proactive in remedying its condition, but has been reactive, strongly responding to the interference by the government. Although sections of church leaders and religious bodies decry the condition of the church, no solution has been offered, and some have come out strongly against theological education of ministers. A column article by Kamotho Waiganjo on this issue, carried by the Standard newspaper on 23rd February 2019, states,

> If the church will not have thought through what a reasonable regulatory regime should look like, and proposed the same to government, a reactionary government may come up with a regime devastating for the church. ...
>
> Finally, outside of the normal requirements for identity cards and certificate of good conduct at registration, the regulatory regime should not concern itself with issues of doctrine and qualifications of pastors. These are issues of personal choice and come as a package within our constitutionally guaranteed freedom of worship. My advice to the church, make your proposals. The days of the "Pharaoh who knew not Joseph" could soon be with us.[426]

These are visible consequences of the lack of teaching in the church that also show the necessity for the church to review and remedy the current state, content, and condition of its teaching ministry. The consequences of the state of teaching as can be seen in the proliferation of cultic groups, in the wide following they have, and in the embrace of the errors they propagate show that many people do not discern truth from error, and would follow and embrace error with much zeal and dedication. Even among those who do not follow the error of the cultic groups, there is sympathy for the cults, and ignorance concerning their deception. To many, the choice of a church to attend is just a matter of personal preference. They think that all churches belong to God and lead to heaven. Some equate the choice of a church to choosing a house to live in. "It does not matter where you attend church, what is important is that you do attend a church" is the prevailing thought. This prevailing thought can be seen in the article by Waiganjo too. In his article, he says that the training, qualifications, and doctrines that a pastor has and which a church subscribes to "are issues of personal choice and come as a package within our constitutionally guaranteed freedom of worship."[427] This prevailing thought pattern is in the view of this writer, the root of the increasing rot in the church in Kenya.

The PERSPECTIVE hindering the teaching ministry of the church

The truth that teaching has not picked up in Kenya is evidenced by the number of untrained pastors and church leaders. Unlike in countries where one cannot be inducted or ordained to the pastoral ministry without proper preparation and formal training, in Kenya, the number of untrained pastors in active ministry and pastors entering ministry without proper preparation is alarming. The Pastoral Discipleship Network observes that "Over 85% of pastors in East Africa have not had access to theological training. Many pastors have expressed to us a desperate need for Bible education, while others do not feel

---

[426] Kamotho Waiganjo, "Rampant Abuse Of People's Faith Calls For Urgent Church Regulation : The Standard", *The Standard*, accessed March 21, 2019, https://www.standardmedia.co.ke/article/2001314067/rampant-abuse-of-people-s-faith-calls-for-urgent-church-regulation.

[427] Ibid.

CHAPTER V: PRESCRIPTIONS & SUGGESTIONS FOR STRENGTHENING TEACHING

they need training because they have made it thus far without it."[428] This fact is also illustrated by the testimony of Dennis Mock who when called to teach at a conference in Mombasa, Kenya, in 1988, discovered that the men he was speaking to "never had any opportunity for theological or ministry training."[429] This experience prompted him to found the Bible Training Centre for Pastors (BTCP) program and to develop and work on a basic curriculum that provides ten courses to equip pastors and leaders who have no theological or ministry training with the basic minimum training level necessary for pastoral ministry. The article on the history of BTCP goes on to explain that,

> Following his experience in Mombasa, Dennis wrote a comprehensive 10-course curriculum designed to equip pastors with essential Bible knowledge and basic pastoral skills. This curriculum was first taught in Nairobi, Kenya in 1990. Since that time, the Lord has expanded the ministry of BTCP around the world through ministry partners using the program in over 85 countries with 33 translations and 140,000 graduates as of 2017.[430]

The experience of Dennis Mock is not a unique one, as Flip Buys in his article on "Theological Training for Untrained Pastors" writes of the alarming figures that were presented in a meeting he attended in Philippines concerning the Training of Pastors in Churches (TOPIC). The report that was given was that,

> Studies have shown that there are at least two million preachers in these countries every Sunday who have never had any theological training whatsoever. In many African countries churches have an average of only one trained pastor for every 20 churches. A pastor from Uganda sitting next to me told us that his denomination has 1000 congregations but only 8 trained pastors. Another one from the Evangelical Christian Church in Zambia told us that his denomination has 675 churches with only 31 trained pastors.[431]

The fact of untrained pastors and leaders is presented as a crisis[432] and though different presentations are made on this, the lack of training among pastors and leaders is still unmistakable. The African Pastors Fellowship (APF) estimates that "over 3 million churches in the developing world are led by people with little or no qualifications for that responsibility."[433] APF places the percentage in Africa at 90%, EMIT places it at more

---

[428] "BIBLE TRAINING — Pastors Discipleship Network, Addressing A Desparate Need For Bible Education", *Pastors Discipleship Network*, accessed March 14, 2019, https://www.pdnafrica.org/bible-training.

[429] "The History Of BTCP", *Bible Training Centre For Pastors*, accessed March 14, 2019, https://bibletraining.com/get-to-know-us/who-we-are.

[430] ibid.

[431] Flip Buys, "Theological Training For Untrained Pastors", *Christianlibrary.org.au*, accessed March 14, 2019, https://www.christianlibrary.org.au/index.php/school-of-missions/226-theological-training-for-untrained-pastors.

[432] "More than 70% of the churches in Africa have a leader with no biblical or theological training! The strength and health of the church, its ability to fulfil its mission, is directly proportionate to developing skilled leadership. In Africa, religious leaders are a major force not only within their church, but also in broader society. Therefore, providing the church leaders with a strong biblical foundation, training in culturally relevant issues, and great leadership skills, are key to transforming communities." ["Pastoral Leaders: Training Church Leaders", *Emit.Global*, accessed March 14, 2019, https://emit.global/pastoral-leaders/.]

[433] "What We Do - African Pastors Fellowship", *African Pastors Fellowship*, accessed March 14, 2019, https://www.africanpastors.org/what-we-do/.

than 70% while the Pastors Discipleship Network (PDN) places it at over 85%.[434] Africa Rural Trainers (ART) says 800,000 pastors are untrained with the majority of the churches being in rural areas.[435] All these groups present these figures in their appeal for support and assistance in the training programs they have in Kenya and Africa. This need and crisis is graphically put by Keith Fernando who writes,

> Theological education has suffered from serious neglect across the African continent. There has undoubtedly been a massive response to the gospel, even after allowing for statistical exaggeration. However, one informed observer has estimated that if every person in leadership training — of every theological persuasion and at every level — were immediately put in pa position of pastoral responsibility, everyone of them would have to pastor ten churches of 600 members to cover the existing Christian population on the continent. There is a vast deficit of trained leadership in Africa.[436]

This deficit, in this writer's view, has to be attributed, not to "a serious neglect" as implied by Fernando, or to a lack of effort, but, chiefly, rather, to a predominant perspective that devalues Bible teaching and its necessity in strengthening the church. This is because the issue of training was the subject of the recommendations of Paul Miller's research which was published in 1969. Research that involved "more than 1600 persons"[437] among them church and denominational leaders.[438] In presenting the propositions[439] made during the discussions, Miller highlights the consensus on the need and place for theological teaching arrived at during that time as well as the recommendations that were given towards achieving them. The consensus was that,

> Because the apostolic authority seems now to reside in the Spirit-led body of Christ gathered around the Spirit-inspired Scriptures, aptness to teach becomes a central qualification. Even the divine grace which should be received by faith through the acted gospel, the sacraments, cannot be fully claimed by those untaught in the gospel. And so preaching with teaching becomes supremely important. ...
>
> The development of deep faith and Christ-like trust in God should be a primary goal of training. The aim is to produce a man of God, who can rightly interpret God's Word of truth.[440]

---

[434] "BIBLE TRAINING — Pastors Discipleship Network, Addressing A Desparate Need For Bible Education", *Pastors Discipleship Network*, accessed March 14, 2019, https://www.pdnafrica.org/bible-training.

[435] "Why ART Exists", *Africa Rural Trainers*, accessed March 14, 2019, https://africaruraltrainers.org.

[436] Philip E. Morrison, "Implications Of Paul's Model For Leadership Training In Light Of Church Growth In Africa", *Biblicalstudies.org.uk*, accessed March 14, 2019, https://biblicalstudies.org.uk/pdf/ajet/30-1_055.pdf.

[437] Paul Miller, *Equipping for Ministry*, 5.

[438] Miller further notes that "more than twenty African bishops, superintendent, or other top officials of their respective churches who gave their time without reserve. And their love and prayers in such a wholehearted way." [ibid., 5-6]

[439] Miller writes that "The series of forty-eight propositions drawn from the Biblical studies were fed into the nine study conferences throughout East Africa. Conference participants expressed strong appreciation for the Bible-centred approach. Each conference began with a discussion of the propositions from the Scriptures. Leaders could scarcely bring themselves to move on to other aspects of the study. No one challenged the selections of Scripture portions. The fort-eight propositions were enlarged and elaborated." [ibid., 194]

[440] Ibid., 199-200.

CHAPTER V: PRESCRIPTIONS & SUGGESTIONS FOR STRENGTHENING TEACHING

These propositions and the comments that follow seemed to thrust the teaching ministry of the church to the forefront with the pastor being both a preacher and a teacher. In order to realize this, the work went forth to make recommendations on how the theological college and training was to transform the life of the church and change the minds of the people. One of the recommendations was that "The fully trained person himself is one of those whose gift (or his aptness to teach) was discerned by the church and who was sent to a theological college for advanced training. When he returns, he calls together those who are gifted in teachings and equips them for their task."[441] The training that was recommended was broadened beyond the ordained ministry with the recommendations including "residential programmes" within the Bible colleges which would attend to the training of (a) "leading lay Christians who are to serve in strategic roles in society."[442], (b) "persons for specialized ministries such as chaplains in hospitals, chaplains in universities and larger schools, consultants in industry, chaplains in mental hospitals, and other such units in society."[443], among other groups that were targeted for specific training. The recommendation of "A Travelling College" and "Bible Correspondence Courses" was also put forth.

Considering, firstly, that these propositions and recommendations were put forth in the 1960s, one has to ask why is it that in this age, the majority of pastors and church leadership remains untrained? Secondly, that this research involved the churches of East Africa, and their leadership, one also has to ask what went wrong after the propositions and resolutions were made? Were they not implemented? What were the challenges, hurdles, and obstacles faced in the implementation? Many, when seeking to answer these questions, would point to the economic conditions and to the poverty as the main contributing factors. Some would claim that training is expensive, and so are books. Bible colleges are few, and since the living standards are low, people are preoccupied with meeting their basic needs and it becomes difficult to leave home and family to go to study at the Bible colleges. But the same people who cannot afford to pay for theological training or buy the books needed still can pay for secular trainings and purchase the required books. However, the same people who cannot afford to leave home and go to study or travel long distance or find time to attend Bible colleges and their training programmes have the time and resources to travel for other purposes. One Bible teacher complained about pastors in his class not being able to pay 500Kshs to purchase a book, but still could afford to travel from Nairobi to USA twice in a month for personal matters paying over 2,000Kshs for each trip. Another Bible teacher complained of church leaders attending his class but missing sessions saying that they are not able to find time to attend the two-hour sessions, but could find time to go for burial committee planning meetings and other social and welfare gatherings and stay for over 3 hours not minding the lateness of the time. The problem thus seems not to be a financial one, but rather a foundational one. The issue is not money or time but that of values. Effort, commitment, and zeal is placed on what is important and according to the value placed on the pursuit. Thus, there is little effort, commitment, and zeal towards teaching in the church due to its little value in the sight and mind of many.

There is a narrow and shallow view of the Christian ministry that disdains theology and theological training, looking at it as something that is at best an optional matter of preference and at worst an unnecessary hindrance to the leading and working of the Holy Spirit. When the issue of teaching and training comes up, more often than not, the first

---

[441]Ibid., 209.

[442]Ibid., 210.

[443]Ibid.

question is usually why is it needed and what is the value it adds to the ministry. It is in Kenya that one can be saved in a midweek evangelistic service on Wednesday and become a pastor by Sunday. Such a person when approached about training would claim that as long as he is saved, and has a burden for souls, and has the Holy Spirit and the Bible, he has all that is necessary and needful for ministry. He does not need any formal training to serve God!

This prevailing mindset has probably been one of the reasons why the effort towards training especially for pastors and church leaders, though a concerted one with many trying to address it, bears little fruit, and also why though there are many entering the pastoral ministry, Bible colleges are still dying at an alarming rate. At its worst, this mindset recommends those who have tried and failed at everything they have done to try the pastoral ministry and church work. It gives those who subscribe to it a false confidence in themselves, their ability and a false understanding of the role of the Holy Spirit in helping men to fulfil the work of the ministry without any sort of preparation or even calling.

This final chapter seeks to explore the strengthening of sound Biblical teaching in Kenya, and provide insights on what can be done to strengthen it, and how it should be done in order to ensure that the teaching ministry fulfils its role of strengthening and maturing the church in Kenya.

Strengthening, reviving and reforming theological training

Since in the previous chapters, Bible teaching was presented as teachings based on the biblical text, drawn out and presented with regard to biblical context and aimed at building, protecting, and warning the body of Christ as well as exposing the errors and dangers that face the church of Christ, the first prescription given in the strengthening of the teaching ministry of the church has to be the strengthening, revival and reformation of theological training. Paul Bowers rightly observes the importance of theological training and education to the church in Africa when he writes,

> Turning now to the question that focuses our reflection today, namely: Theological education in Africa: why does it matter?, may I suggest for your consideration a fundamental proposition, namely that theological schools form the backbone of organized evangelicalism in Africa. I propose that this is the case far more than most evangelical church leadership on the continent is aware, more than the Association of Evangelicals in Africa (AEA) may have always recognised, more than para-church leaders and mission strategists both here and overseas take into account, perhaps more true than even we ourselves are aware. And I believe it is not a recent development; I believe that theological schools have formed the backbone of organized evangelicalism in Africa for much of the past half century.[444]

Bowers' proposition with regard to the role of theological education presents the basis for this first prescription. Little emphasis and value has been placed on theological education, partly, as Bowers rightly attributes, to a lack of awareness. When he states that the evangelical church leadership is not fully aware role of the Bible college in strengthening and establishing "organised Evangelicalism in Africa.", this awareness must be understood as awareness of (i) the role and place of theological education in the church, (ii) the content and intent of theological education in equipping of ministers of the church and (iii) the need for disseminating theology from the pulpit to the pew and the equipping of every church member with right doctrine for right practice. When he further asserts that the Bible colleges have been the backbone of "organised Evangelicalism in Africa," the death of the

---

[444] Paul Bowers, "Theological Education In Africa: Why Does It Matter?", *Biblicalstudies.org.uk*, accessed March 28, 2019, https://biblicalstudies.org.uk/pdf/ajet/26-2_135.pdf.

CHAPTER V: PRESCRIPTIONS & SUGGESTIONS FOR STRENGTHENING TEACHING

Bible colleges in Kenya must be seen as leading to the death of evangelicalism, and the strengthening and revival of the theological institutions and education will likewise be the strengthening and revival of evangelicalism. How then is the church to go about the strengthening, reviving and reforming of theological training and institutions?

Address The Prevailing Mindset

The first step has to be addressing the prevailing mindset that devalues theological education and training. The Bible is the Word of God and it is living, and powerful, sharper than any two-edged sword. The Gospel is the power of God unto salvation to everyone who believes, and the Scriptures are able to make one wise unto salvation. Thus the one who is to handle the Word of God rightly is exhorted to study to show himself approved unto God. These are scriptural principles and understanding that are often disregarded and neglected in the discussions related to biblical teaching and education. They are thoughts that are not given much weight when consideration is made on the pulpit ministry and the persons to be inducted into it.

When care in the approach and handling of Scripture, diligence and accuracy in the searching of Scripture, faithfulness in the interpretation and exposition of Scripture are given emphasis, the teaching ministry of the church can be revived, but when neglected, as is common, those who are to teach, guide and instruct the church in the things of God turn to words that do not profit, words that subvert the hearers. Therefore, pastors are called to study not only to prepare for ministry, but also to do so in the course of ministry. The testimony of the Bible clearly points out that though the Bible can be understood and there is a blessing to those who read it and hear it read and taught.

The Bible is a book that requires more than a casual reading and haphazard teaching. Nehemiah 8:8 tells of how the reading of the Bible was accompanied by interpretation and exposition to enable those who had gathered to hear the Word to understand it. Ezra 7:10 gives a description of Ezra as one who was a ready Scribe, well grounded in the Law of Moses, and prepared both to do and to teach it. The Bible also warns those who take upon themselves the duty of teaching, that this responsibility is grave and those who teach bear a greater condemnation (Jas. 3:1). Since bad doctrine and teaching will always lead those being taught astray and will derail and stumble people, the Bible teacher has to be accurate and dogmatic in his teaching.[445]

In Malachi 2:7-8, there is an indictment against the priests who were the teachers in the Old Testament. Their office came with the responsibility of setting the standard for faith through their teaching and for life through their practice. But in the passage they are accused and charged because of their bad doctrines and teaching. The departure of the teacher and the leader inevitably leads to the departure of the students and followers. Bad doctrine will always lead astray and the people led astray will always stumble at the truth. The charge shows that there are standards to adhere to and expectations desired of teachers of the Law. This has to be reason enough to necessitate the training of teachers. They need to know the standards, and how they can attain them. Verse 8 would at many points be a

---

[445] In his book "Salt and Pepper", Vance Havner has a quote on the necessity of being dogmatic. He writes, "I believe in being dogmatic. When I go to the pharmacist to have a prescription filled, I want him to be dogmatic about the proportion of the ingredients. I do not want a doctor who says "your ailment could be this or might be that. we'll try these pills, and if they don't kill you we'll try something else." When I ride a train, I don't want the engineer to say, "I'm tired of this old timetable. It's too dogmatic. We are going to throw it away and follow no set schedule." I want to hear a dogmatic preacher who preaches from a dogmatic Bible." [Vance Havner, *Salt and Pepper*, (Westwood New Jersey: Fleming H. Revell Company, 1966), 11-12.]

fitting description of the state that the church in Kenya is at, and the blame would be rightly placed on the pulpits. In order to change this, biblical teaching has to return to the pulpit, and for this to happen, preachers have to receive theological training and instruction.

2 Peter 3:15-16 describes Scripture as having in it some things which are hard to be understood. These things have been subject of twisting and perversion by the unstable and unlearned. This points to the origin of bad teachings as well as stresses the need for learning and being knowledgeable in the Scriptures. Bad teachings not only lead people astray, they also destroy the one who propagates them. The unstable and unlearned men who twist and pervert Scripture do so at their own peril and to their own destruction. Clearly there is need for the preparation of all those who would serve God in the pastoral ministry. The Bible is understandable, but it also has some portions that are hard to be understood. The words of God need to be interpreted correctly, expounded and explained accurately, and applied relevantly. Keith Ferdinando puts this as one of the greatest challenges that the church in Africa faces. He writes stating that,

> So one of the greatest challenges facing African churches is that of communicating the gospel in its fullness, responding to the travesties and lies on offer, and building up believers who will have an impact on their societies as salt and light. It is a theological challenge, and the state of so much of the continent shows how critical it is. Corruption, Aids, ethnic violence, and political instability all demonstrate Africa's desperate need to have Christians who truly know God and deeply love him, and who can live out the gospel of Jesus Christ in every section of society. Theological education exists to equip the church to participate in God's mission in this world—it is about following Jesus, learning from him, growing to be like him, and so becoming fishers of men wherever he sends (Matthew 4:19).[446]

The picture painted and presented Ferdinando is an accurate one and one that any who lives in Kenya will acknowledge. But very few will relate it to the theology and teachings of the church. Ferdinando rightly observes that it is through theological education that the church is prepared and equipped to present the Gospel and to live up to biblical standards, so the one who would handle the Word of God needs to be prepared and equipped, and needs to be trained, and the one who would follow and imitate Christ also needs to be trained. The decline of theological education and teaching in Kenya is the cause of the decline in Bible teaching in the church, and the decline in Bible teaching in the church is the cause of the decline in biblical standards of Christian living.

Set Clear Standards For Bible Teaching And Theological Training

The second step that is to follow a change in perspective by the church and its members is that which gives clear vision and direction which the church and her members ought to take. A change in perspective must bring with it a clear vision and direction to the church. This vision and direction must be towards attaining biblical standards of faith and practice. Therefore, the church has to identify what it must do to ensure that its preachers and ministers are trained in the Holy Scriptures and their members are matured in the most holy faith. In order to set up its standards, the church has to consider its ministers and its members based on biblical standards requirements and call of both ministers and members. This will give the church a biblical perspective of what it means to be a minister in the church, and what is required of members in the church of God.

---

[446] Keith Ferdinando, "Theological Education – Why Bother? - Africa Inland Mission (Europe)", *Africa Inland Mission (Europe)*, accessed March 28, 2019, https://eu.aimint.org/why-bother-with-theological-education/.

CHAPTER V: PRESCRIPTIONS & SUGGESTIONS FOR STRENGTHENING TEACHING

After this, the church can then consider church history especially measures and changes that took place during periods of spiritual revival, and identify options and avenues available to raise the standards of its ministers and members.[447] The church has to (i) agree on the scope of the basic and irreducible minimum training that must be required for those who would minister, and (ii) formulate the basic minimum requirement it desires of its membership in terms of knowledge of the Bible, the creeds and the doctrines that the church adheres to. From this point it can go on to formulate a curriculum for Basic Bible Knowledge class for its membership and for those who would be confirmed into membership, or who would reaffirm their membership, or be baptized. For example, the Westminster divines formulated the requirements for all those who would be ordained. They put their proposals thus,

The Rules for Examination are these.

1. That the party examined be dealt withal in a Brotherly way, with mildness of spirit, and with special respect to the gravity, modesty, and quality of every one.

2. He shall be examined touching his skill in the Original tongues and his trial to be made by reading of the Hebrew and the Greek Testaments, and rendering some portion of some into Latin; And if he be defective in them, enquiry shall be made the more strictly after his other learnings And whether he hath skill in Logic and Philosophy.

3. What Authors in Divinity he hath read, and is best acquainted with; And trial shall be made in his knowledge of the grounds of Religion, and ability to defend the Orthodox Doctrine contained in them, against all unsound and erroneous opinions, especially these of the present age: of his skill in the sense and meaning of such places of Scripture as shall be proposed unto him, in cases of Con- science, and in the Chronology of the Scripture, and the Ecclesiastical History.

4. If he hath not before preached in public, with approbation of such as are able to judge, he shall, at a competent time assigned him, expound before the Presbytery such a place of Scripture as shall be given him.

5. He shall also within a competent time, frame a discourse in Latin upon such a Commonplace or Controversy in 'Divinity us shall be assigned him, and exhibit to the Presbytery such theses as expresses the sum thereof, and maintain a Dispute upon them.

6. He shall preach before the people, the Presbytery, or some of the ministers of the Word appointed by them, being present,

7. The proportion of his gifts in relation to the place unto which he is called, shall be considered.

8. Beside the trial of his gifts in Preaching, he shall undergo an examination in the premises two several days, and more, if the Presbytery shall judge it necessary.

---

[447]The Free Church of Scotland in its "Act of Declaration" writes, "When it pleased Almighty God, in His great and undeserved mercy, to reform this Church from Popery by presbyters, it was given to the Reformers, amid many troubles, to construct and model the constitution of the Church, in doctrine, worship, discipline, and government, according to the Word of God, and not according to the will of earthly rulers. … From the beginning these principles have been held as fundamental by the Reformed Church of Scotland; and as such, they were recognized in her earliest standards, …. For these principles, the ministers and members of this church, as well as the nobles, gentlemen, and burgesses of the land, from the first united in contending; … bound themselves one to another, as in the sight of God, to maintain and defend them against all adversaries." (**emphasis added**)[*Confession of Faith and Subordinate Standards*, v-vi.]

9. And as for him that hath been formerly ordained a Minister, and is to be removed to another charge, he shall bring a Testimonial of his Ordination, and of his Abilities and Conversation, whereupon his fitness for that place shall be tried by his Preaching there, (if it shall be judged necessary) by a further examination of him.[448]

The divines saw it as an absolute necessity (i) that the minister be skilled in the original languages and Latin in order to minister, (ii) that the minister be able to address contemporary issues of his time and show his understanding of the Scriptures and of the doctrines he believes, (iii) that the minister show his skill in logic and also his grasp of the church's history, and finally (iv) that the minister prove his ability to preach and present his views on assigned topics and discourses. These requirements were necessitated by the understanding of what the pastoral ministry would require of its candidates. The prevailing lack of willingness among pastors to receive theological training, and churches to have systematic and progressive training programs is due to a lack of understanding of what the pastoral ministry demands of the ministers, and how maturity is achieved among church members.

Train, Equip and Qualify Men for the Work of the Ministry

This is where the church in Kenya needs to re-evaluate and correct its mindset and approach to ministry. Paul says that "*we are labourers together with God*" (1 Cor 3:9), and there has to be the understanding that though it is God who calls and sends men into his vineyard, He has given the responsibility of preparing and equipping those men to the church. And as the church prays to "*the Lord of the harvest that he would send forth labourers into his harvest*", there also has to be a passing on and equipping of men as Paul instructed Timothy. The apostles' teachings were handed down "*to faithful men who shall be able to teach others also.*" Charles Williams talks at length about theological teachers in his book "The Function of Teaching in Christianity". In his discussions, he gives a paragraph that describes who the theological teacher should be. In his description, he writes,

> But the theological teacher is a specialist in the realm of the Bible and its practical application to human hearts and lives, human society and history. Hence, the theological teacher has always specialized for the mastery of his Bible, so far as possible. He feels that he is not qualified to teach it, or systems of theology supposed to be based on it, until he has a thorough knowledge of what the Book of books says to men. He is conscious that he should study it with the best helps and by the most helpful methods, old or new, and give the Bible writers a chance to say what they meant to say.[449]

This description ought to be the description of the pastor too, since it is the pastor who would be teacher. And if this description is to be transferred to the pastor, then the theological college has to be a place designed to enable him to achieve this description. In addition to the accurate preaching and teaching of the Word of God, there is also challenge of dealing with the falsehoods that are propagated and popularized in the Kenyan context. The truth has to be published, and errors and falsehood have to be exposed, and refuted. This necessitates the revival and strengthening of theological training in Kenya. In order to successfully and profitably train, equip and qualify men for the work of the ministry and for the maturity of its membership, the church has to:

---

[448] *Propositions Concerning Church Government and Ordination of Ministers, to the Right Honorable the Lords and Commons Assembled in Parliament, the humble advice of the Assembly of Divines now sitting by ordinance of Parliament at Westminster*, (Edinburgh: Evan Tyler, 1647), 16-17. (Spellings modernized by this writer)

[449] Charles B. Williams, *The Function of Teaching in Christianity*, (Nashville Tennessee: Sunday School Board, Southern Baptist Convention, 1912), 135.

CHAPTER V: PRESCRIPTIONS & SUGGESTIONS FOR STRENGTHENING TEACHING

Identify Persons or Groups that Need Discipling, Training and Mentoring for the Work of the Ministry

In order to successfully and profitably train, equip and qualify men for the work of the ministry and for the maturity of its membership, the church has to identify within its ranks all those who are involved in ministry and teaching. Some of them may see their need to be trained, while others may not see the need. Whether they see the need or not, they need to be trained. The church should not consider theological training and education as optional or as personal preference, and as such should not leave the decision to the individual or group of persons involved in ministry. It should be the church's burden, and the church has to execute it as such.

After formulating and setting clear biblical standards, the church should pursue the standards and aim at achieving them. In order to do this, the church has to actively pursue the teaching ministry first by training those who would be teachers. This is where the identifying, discipling and mentoring of men comes in.

Identify Available, Viable, and Credible Training Options

This second step follows and flows from the first. When the perspective towards theological education is changed, and men to be equipped identified, then there has to be an identification of where this education can be obtained. Identifying options available must consider their viability, their credibility and their theological soundness. Part of the reasons theological institutions are dying is because theological education is considered and largely pursued from a personal preference perspective. This in turn has opened the churches to a very great variety of false teachings since some who seek to pursue theological education have gone to train at liberal and apostate institutions. The main consideration for many pursuing theological education is purely monetary and prestige. They would choose to go anywhere irrespective of their doctrinal stand as long as they can study on scholarship, and can get an accredited or recognized certificate. While there, they imbibe whatsoever is taught, and return to teach the same.

This has to change. And it is the church that has to identify viable, credible options available to her and to give clear instructions and directions on where theological education is to be pursued. It is not to be left as optional. It has to be taken as institutional. The church has to have the final say in where its pastors and membership receives its theological education.

Promote a Working Ideal

The third step has to be the formulating and developing a working educational ideal that will be both effective in the Kenyan context and lasting. This step is necessary as it takes into consideration the context and ministry of the church and the needs that the church has when pursuing theological training. The options available for a working ideal should be considered in light and view of the aims and purpose the education seeks to fulfil. In discussing the purpose of theological education, Victor Cole presents two divergent perspectives that have been recognized worldwide. He writes,

> Historically two broad purposes have been recognized world-wide. These are the academic and the professional purposes. An ongoing dilemma has been how to reconcile the pure academic and the pure professional purposes of theological education. The education of the theologian has always been perceived as the education of the ministry, designed to prepare the clergy for ministry of the church. However, there

has been an ongoing tension between the perspective of pure education and that of pure vocation.[450]

Victor then goes on to discuss the two purposes, pointing out the findings of his research and the challenges in the African context. He points out that the "challenge, then of African theological education, as revealed in my research, is to both articulate and demonstrate these principles as convictions that guide what institutions or programmes of training actually do."[451] This implies that there has to be a clear plan of action that would translate the principles and "institutional ethos" of theological education into a practical work plan that is both adoptable and sustainable. Since there is still a distinction between laity and clergy in most churches in Kenya, theological training has been seen by most as strictly limited to those who would join the pastoral ministry. This has not solved the problems that face the church in Kenya due to the setup of the church. The denominational setup of most churches and the shortage of pastors have led to a system in which one pastor is assigned multiple churches and ministers to them with the assistance of lay leadership of the church.

For effective ministry, there has to be training of both the pastors and the lay leadership that assists him. There have been divergent approaches taken in the theological training of both pastors and lay leadership. Some approaches have tended to a formal academic equipment, while others to a more informal but practical ministerial training. But for effective training, there has to be both formal and informal training taking place in the church's setup. For example, Peter Mumo in his "Study of Theological Education in Africa Inland Church-Kenya" gives the AIC classification of formal theological training institutions. In his discussion, he points out that the formal theological education of the church has been classified mainly by the entry level of the target group. The AIC, according to Mumo's study, has two levels of theological education with "the first level, theological education ... provided to students who have low educational qualifications ... referred to as Biblical education."[452] He goes on to point out that this biblical education is offered to students who though have "acquired the skills of writing and reading"[453], have not completed their primary level of education i.e., "have not completed primary school education."[454] The second level of theological education is then offered to those with higher levels of education and is offered in what Mumo terms as "theological colleges." These colleges target students who would serve "as pastors, Church administrators and teachers in secondary schools, chaplains and teachers in Bible schools, institutes and colleges"[455] and thus have the same entry requirements as "the minimum entry requirement for public and private universities."[456]

Although this has been the approach the AIC has used over the years in the training of her pastors, and although it has served the church well, it has not always been effective. The church still had untrained lay leaders in churches where pastors have been

---

[450] Victor Babadije Cole, "Reformed Theology And Theological Education In Africa", *World Reformed Fellowship*, accessed March 29, 2019, http://wrfnet.org/resources/2009/04/reformed-theology-and-theological-education-africa.

[451] Ibid.

[452] Peter Mutuku Mumo, *A Study of Theological Education in Africa Inland Church-Kenya: Its Historical Development and Present State*, (Ph.D. Diss, University of Nairobi 1997), 85.

[453] Ibid.

[454] Ibid.

[455] Ibid., 86.

[456] Ibid.

CHAPTER V: PRESCRIPTIONS & SUGGESTIONS FOR STRENGTHENING TEACHING

few. This led to the development of an informal training programme to enable the church to provide trained men for her congregations. Mark Volkers, writing an article for the Evangelism and Missions Information Service (EMIS), points out the need for the founding of the Ahero Bible Training Centre, which is an AIC training institution. In the article titled "Lay Leaders: Trained and Dynamic or Untrained and Dangerous?" Volkers observed how the AIC changed its model due to the challenges that were unique to the Nyanza region of Kenya. He writes,

> The Africa Inland Church (AIC) in Kenya—the nationalized church begun by the Africa Inland Mission (AIM)—is desperately short of trained pastors in western Kenya. Despite a half-dozen excellent and well-staffed Bible colleges in the country, the shortage persists.
>
> Soaring school fees are one of the reasons, but so are challenges that crop up for students when they attend a Bible college in a different tribal area. Language is another hurdle. Some of the most qualified men who feel called to the ministry are eliminated because they're not fluent in either English or Kiswahili, the national language of Kenya.
>
> Some make it through the hurdles. Each year, Luo men and women from western Kenya graduate from AIC institutions. And each year, only a few of these graduates trickle back to their homeland to take up the work. The rest are offered higher paying pastorates in other parts of the country. It could be argued that they have every right to go to healthier climates than the Lake Region, and a worker is worth his wages.
>
> Yet the church in western Kenya wanes. Ben Koyo will wait in vain again on Sunday morning, because the pastor in charge of Kagimba has a whopping total of nine churches to look after. Rev. Kutte is committed and hard-working, but even the most talented pastor becomes more of an administrator than a pastor when he is expected to care for nine local churches. The pastor won't come today because he's busy making the rounds to all the other churches.[457]

This need led the church to try another approach in equipping its lay leadership. The usual approach that has been used by the AIC in areas that are far from their Bible colleges and that cannot afford to send students to study at the colleges has been their Theological Education by Extension (TEE[458]) programme. But although the TEE model has many advantages as is pointed out by Walter Gammage[459], this model too did not work in

---

[457] Mark Volkers, "Lay Leaders: Trained And Dynamic, Or Untrained And Dangerous?", *Missionexus.Org*, accessed March 29, 2019, https://missionexus.org/lay-leaders-trained-and-dynamic-or-untrained-and-dangerous/.

[458] "The historical origins of theological education by extension are familiar. Based on in-depth evaluation of the effectiveness of their past endeavors in a residential seminary, Ralph Winter, James Emery and Ross Kinsler of the Evangelical Presbyterian Seminary in Guatemala in 1963 inaugurated a new mode of theological education, widely known today as theological education by extension--or TEE. The concept of TEE soon spread to other countries and continents, including Africa, to such an extent that it has been termed "the largest non-governmental voluntary educational development in the world" and "the mast significant development in theological education in the twentieth century."" [George Foxall, "Continental Linkage And Support Services For TEE In Africa", *Biblicalstudies.org.uk*, accessed March 29, 2019, https://biblicalstudies.org.uk/pdf/ajet/08-1_041.pdf.]

[459] Henry Griffith in his article "Models of Theological Education Yesterday and Today" quotes Gammage concerning the benefits of TEE that, "Walter Gammage sees the TEE system to be good in that it can: (1) reach large numbers, (2) can reach mature family men who cannot attend a resident school, (3) be adaptable to different educational levels and cultural groups, (4) be suitable for part-time, tent making ministers, (5) provide for greater mobility in student enrolment, (6) cost less per student, (7) be well adapted to provide in-service theological education, and (8) use better educational methods such as programmed instruc-

the Western part of Kenya among the Luo people. The challenges faced by the TEE form of education as pointed out by Mark Volkers were unique and mainly traditional. Volkers explains,

> Theological Education by Extension (TEE) had been tried in the Lake Region over several years, but it never took off. In some parts of Kenya, TEE has had tremendous success and fruit, but not here. Though there are several reasons, two will suffice:
>
> 1. Lay leaders found it difficult to take their studies seriously when the instruction was presented "at home." The Luo people found it difficult to take the instruction seriously because they didn't go somewhere else to receive it. With thoughts of the farm, the cattle, and relatives right outside the hut, learning in the home area didn't work well.
>
> 2. Lay leaders found it difficult to discuss issues honestly while surrounded with family and clan members in the home area. Occasionally, Christianity and culture will clash. Polygamy, wife inheritance, funeral rites, and other thorny cultural issues were difficult for aspiring church leaders to discuss honestly while clan and family members listened.[460]

Thus, Ahero Bible Training Centre (ABTC) was created and a working educational ideal that took into account the challenges of the people and their context was formulated. To date, ABTC still trains its students in their mother tongue, and is open to all who can read and understand Luo. It currently has produced "more than 50 Bible studies and class notes for 24 courses, all in Luo. Now even those who don't study at ABTC can get Bible study material, or notes on everything from homiletics to New Testament survey in their mother tongue."[461]

This illustrates the necessity of this third step. Formulating and developing a working educational ideal that will be both effective has to address the following: (1) The goal of education — i.e. the end or aim to which all education is geared. This has to be done both objectively and subjectively. When done objectively, the goals and aims must be drawn from the Biblical injunctions, and must meet the Scriptural intention for training and teaching. When done subjectively, the goals and aims must be fitting and relevant to the context and situation of the church as well as appropriate to the audience targetted for teaching and training. Such that, what may seem elementary and rudimentary in some settings may be what is necessary and relevant in other settings. (2) The focus of education — i.e. the methods used in the process and approach to the education. This has to be done holistically, with the approaches to be used considered firstly in respect to the students to be taught and goal intended to be achieved by the training. Secondly in relation to education and opportunities for more advanced and in-depth studies that would be availed for the students being trained. Any form of training formulated must consider the whole body of divinity and clarify how the particular opportunity availed will fit in the grand scheme of theological teaching and education. (3) The mechanics of education — i.e. procedures and logistics that make it adoptable, relevant, and sustainable. As seen from the example of the AIC churches in Luo Nyanza region given above, there is necessity in clarifying and developing mechanics that will make theological training accessible, applicable and relevant if theological training is to be revived in Kenya. By taking into consideration these three

---

tion and group discussion rather than lecture." [Henry Griffith, "Models Of Theological Education Yesterday And Today", *Biblicalstudies.org.uk*, last modified 2019, accessed March 29, 2019, https://biblicalstudies.org.uk/pdf/ajet/07-1_045.pdf.]

[460] Mark Volkers, *Lay leaders: Trained and Dynamic or Untrained and Dangerous?*

[461] Ibid.

CHAPTER V: PRESCRIPTIONS & SUGGESTIONS FOR STRENGTHENING TEACHING

steps, the church provides both its leadership and membership with a systematic, progressive (i.e. continuous) theological training platform that will develop and mature the church and theological training both for church leadership and membership will be revived.

Affirming the textual basis for the teaching ministry of the church

The second prescription given in the strengthening of the teaching ministry of the church has to be concerned with the textual basis for the teaching ministry. This is so because the best training without the correct texts avails nothing. The Bible has a lot to say on the doctrine of Scripture. In 2 Timothy 3:15:17 both the attributes and purpose of Scripture are given. With regard to the purpose, the Scriptures are presented as *"are able to make you wise for salvation through faith in Christ Jesus."* As to the attributes it states that *"All Scripture is given by inspiration of God and is profitable."* In John 5:39, Jesus states that Scriptures testify of him and by this pointing to the topic of the Scriptures. Before the conquest of the Promised Land, Joshua was given instructions by the LORD. The directions given included his relation to the Scriptures with the LORD promising that diligent study and meditation on the Scriptures would bring him good success. Therefore, the place of the Scriptures itself in strengthening the church can never be underestimated.

Frank E. Gaebelein in his book *The Christian Use of the Bible* raises pertinent issues on the importance of the Scriptures as he presents his case for the reading and use of the Bible. He points out in his first chapter that "the use of any book depends upon its reading"[462] When this is applied to the reading of the Bible, the issue of the text of the Bible becomes one of great importance since the diligent reading and use of a wrong or corrupt text avails to no profit to the one exercised in it. Gaebelein in his discussions, further went on to quote Pascal who wrote "He who will give the meaning of Scripture, and does not take it from Scripture, is an enemy of Scripture."[463] Thus if there is to be any teaching in the church, it has to be drawn from and based on Scripture. There is currently a great deal of teaching, but, sadly, it is teaching that is not drawn from, nor based on Scripture. Teaching alone will not strengthen the church, the teaching that will strengthen the church has to be Bible teaching. In the concluding pages of his book, Gaebelein writes,

> Truly God has made perfect provision for the ministry and service to which He has called us. He has spoken both through His Son and through His Word. In His Son, the incarnate Word, He has accomplished our eternal redemption; in the written Word He has given us the one Book which, through teaching, conviction, restoration, and education in righteousness, is able to make us wise unto salvation through faith in Christ Jesus. But that is not all. In our hearts He has placed the Spirit of truth who quickened those men of God who wrote the Book. He, that same Spirit of truth, will also quicken us to understand it. And God has done all this that we might be adjusted in perfect conformity to His will for the accomplishment of good works to His glory. ... The man who devotes himself to the use of this Book in accord with its self revealed principles may count on the very blessings of heaven being showered upon his ministry. ... For God has never altered His promises to bless His Word. It will never return to Him void. It always accomplishes the purpose for which He has inspired it.[464]

Such is the understanding that should guide the subject of this second prescription. As much as effort is place on the training and equipping of men for the work of the minis-

---

[462] Frank E. Gaebelein, *The Christian Use of the Bible*, (Chicago: Moody Press, 1946), 13.

[463] Ibid., 15.

[464] Ibid., 110-112.

try, care should be taken to ensure that every effort taken in training and teaching is focused on training and teaching the Word of God, not words of men. When considering the textual basis for the teaching ministry of the church, there first has to be the understanding of the doctrine of the Scriptures and what ought to be believed concerning the Scriptures. Secondly, there must be a clear understanding and identifying of the text to be used especially in this age where there is a proliferation of versions and translations of Scripture. It is on these two considerations that the text which forms the basis and textbook of all church teaching is affirmed.

When discussing the issue of teaching, there is need to discuss the issue of the text used in teaching. There cannot be any proper teaching without the proper text. Sadly, the issue of the text of the Bible is one that is also considered as one of personal preference in Kenya, with many choosing based of readability or affordability. The differences between the texts, the theology presented by the different translations, and the methodologies employed during translations are issues that are either unknown or considered secondary, irrelevant and at times divisive. But, if as Gaebelein puts it, God has "given us the one Book which, through teaching, conviction, restoration, and education in righteousness, is able to make us wise unto salvation through faith in Christ Jesus", then the church has a duty to ensure that the text it is using to teach, convict, restore and educate is that one Book that God has given. Indeed then, if "the use of any book depends upon its reading", then attention has to be given to which book is being read. And if, as Pascal had put it that giving the meaning of Scripture without drawing it from the Scriptures itself makes on an enemy of Scripture, then, all teaching and exhortation that is given as from God but is not drawn from Scripture makes those who teach and exhort enemies of Scripture. Thus, the church must affirm the text that will be used as the basis of all teaching and instruction. Harold Lindsell in his book *The Bible in the Balance*, talks about "The Battle for the Bible." In his introduction, he writes,

> "*The Battle for the Bible*, asked two fundamental or foundational questions: (1) What is the source of our religious knowledge i.e., from where do we get answers to life's important questions …. (2) Is the source from which I get the answers to my basic questions reliable – i.e., does the source tell me the truth?
>
> The replies to these two questions were as follows. First, the foundation for the Christian faith lies in the two Words of God, the Word of God incarnate …, and the Word of God written, which is the Bible. The only Jesus the church can know is the Jesus of the Word of God written. Without the Bible there can be no knowledge of the Son of God and the Savior of the world. Therefore the written Word of God is foundational to the Christian faith." [465]

From the response to the first question, the assertion given in the two last sentences affirms that the Bible is the basis for both what ought to be believed and how believers ought to behave. Lindsell then goes on in response to the second question to assert the authority of the Bible as revelation and by it affirms the doctrine of inerrancy, that "this inspired Word of God is inerrant because the prophets and apostles laboured under the inspiration of the Holy Spirit who kept them from making errors even as he commanded their gifts and abilities." Lindsell presents the inerrancy of Scripture as the reason for its reliability and trustworthiness. Since the Bible is (i) the foundational to the Christian faith, and without the Bible there can be no saving knowledge of God, and (ii) trustworthy in all its parts it has to be the text for the teaching ministry of the church. No teaching can take

---

[465] Harold Lindsell, *The Bible in the Balance: A further look at the Battle for the Bible*, (Grand Rapids Michigan: Zondervan Publishing House, 1979),. 11

CHAPTER V: PRESCRIPTIONS & SUGGESTIONS FOR STRENGTHENING TEACHING

place in the church without the Bible and no teaching ought to take place in the church other than that which has the Bible for its foundation and as its textbook.

However, in the light of the proliferation of Bible versions in English, the following questions have to be discussed when considering the Bible as the teaching text of the church. Are all the texts the same? Is there a fixed text or is the choice of text a matter of personal preference? Can the church be strengthened without paying attention to what text is used? These are issues that should be of concern, yet these are questions that currently are considered divisive and unnecessary by many. Lindsell confesses that his first book which was *The Battle for the Bible* had "produced a fallout", showing that what ought to be believed and received concerning the Bible is a thorny and contentious issue. But he said he was "not unhappy" about the response that his book had produced as the conversation was continuing and hence the need for the debate. Kenya to a very great extent has been ignorant of the debates surrounding the doctrine of the Scriptures — i.e., the debate that concerns the inerrancy of Scripture, the inspiration of Scripture, and the most recent one, the preservation of Scripture. But if Scripture is to be presented as the teaching text of the church, then these doctrinal matters have to be affirmed biblically and a stand taken lest the error should creep in unawares and many be led astray through it. In order to address this and answer the questions posed above, two questions will be considered, questions which when answered biblically, would answer themselves. The questions are: (i) What ought to be believed concerning the text of the Bible? and (ii) which Text ought to be basis for teaching in the Church?

What Ought to Be Believed concerning the Text of the Bible?

The first question is one of doctrine. When considering the Bible, one must begin by considering his doctrine of the Bible. What does the Bible say about itself? When asked what the Bible is, many would answer that the Bible is the Word of God. But what does that mean? What does the Bible as the Word of God mean? It must mean its verbal and plenary inspiration. The written words of Scripture are God-breathed (2 Tim. 3:16), the very words of God themselves and that the human writers were simply instruments of God who wrote as they were borne (moved) by the Holy Spirit (2 Pet. 1:16-21). The men wrote not of their own will for they were borne (moved) by the Spirit of God. Thus, when the Bible is called the Word of God, the first thing that must be believed is the inspiration of the Bible which means that it is not the product of men but rather, the very Word of Him who sits on the throne (2 Pet. 1:19-21).

It must also mean the verbal and plenary preservation of the Bible. This means that the inspired words of Scripture have been providentially preserved through the ages such that when the Bible is called the Word of God, it is understood to be still the Word of God though time has passed. Thus, the Bible as the Word of God, is trustworthy in everything it says, including history, geography and science. As the Word of God, it is the final rule and authority in matters of faith and practice. This means that not only is any matter of dispute to be settled by appealing to the Bible but also every matter of practical Christian service and living is to be governed and measured by the Word.

The Verbal Plenary Inspiration of the Bible

The correct understanding of inspiration gives a right perspective of the Bible and its contents. Inspiration deals not only with the accuracy and reliability of the Bible, but also the words of the Bible. This is clearly seen in the Scripture's teaching on inspiration. Scripture (the written words) is inspired (2 Tim. 3:16); the men (human writers) were moved by the Holy Spirit (2 Pet. 1:20-21, cf. 2 Sam. 23:2; Mark 12:36; Acts 1:16; 28:25).

It is clear in the Bible that holy men were borne (moved) of the Holy Spirit, but it must be clarified that it is the words that are inspired, not the men. Thus, *inspiration* of the words and *moving* of the Holy Spirit are not to be confused especially in debates on whether cultural bias found its way into the inspired Word.

When Scripture talks about inspiration, it is not talking about the natural insight of men who wrote the Scriptures into truth, nor their religious perception or their experiences with God as they understood them. Neither does it teach that the men were mechanically controlled by God as they wrote the Scriptures and as such were passive instruments. When Scripture talks of its own inspiration, it talks about:

The Words of the Bible:

Inspiration focuses on the written Word. The words written are not words of men but those of God "which the Holy Ghost teaches" (1 Cor. 2:13) A. W. Pink states,

> What the Bible teaches about its own inspiration is a matter purely of Divine testimony, and our business is simply to receive the testimony and not to speculate about or seek to pry into its modus operandi. Inspiration is as much a matter of Divine revelation as is justification by faith. Both stand equally on the authority of the Scriptures themselves, which must be the final court of appeal on this subject as on every question of revealed truth.[466]

Constantly and consistently, Scriptures refer to its words as what the Holy Spirit said (Mark 12:36; Acts 1:16; 28:25; Heb. 3:7). And the writers were not ignorant of this but rather uniformly affirmed this (Exod. 4:11-12; 34:1, 27-28; 2 Sam. 23:2; Jer. 1:9).

The Writers of the Bible:

Inspiration also relates to the men who wrote the Scriptures. These men were not passive instruments, but were actively involved in the writing. When God moved the men, He did not override or ignore their circumstances in life, or their knowledge and skills (even their style of writing). There are times in which the human writers did not fully understand what they wrote (especially in eschatological and messianic prophecies), but, still the individual author's style, experience, and skills are evident in the books they wrote.

Inspiration as taught in the Scriptures is verbal plenary inspiration. This looks at the Bible in its entirety — the Bible as a whole is inspired, and in its parts — the individual words are inspired. Plenarily, the Word of God in its entirety and as a complete whole is tried (Ps. 18:30), and is pure (Ps. 119:140). Verbally too, the word of God in its component parts and individual words too is tried (Ps. 12:6-7), and is pure (Prov. 30:4-6). For example, Paul shows the deliberate use of the singular "seed" in the promise given to Abraham in Genesis instead of the plural to point to Christ (Gal. 3:16 cf. Gen. 22:18). It is necessary to emphasize that when talking about inspiration, the reference is the Scriptures in the original Hebrew, Aramaic and Greek Scriptures. The understanding of this doctrine is very well summed up by *A Higher Catechism of Theology*. In its final question under the topic of "Inspiration of Scripture", four points were put forth:

1. The Christian receives what are commonly called the canonical books of the Old and New Testaments as the mind and word of God given by His Holy Spirit through the instrumentality of holy men.

---

[466] A. W. Pink, *The Divine Inspiration of the Bible*, (Albany OR: USA, Ages Software, 1997), 74.

CHAPTER V: PRESCRIPTIONS & SUGGESTIONS FOR STRENGTHENING TEACHING

2. He must have a strong faith in the watchful providence of the Spirit over the work of His own hands: whether as to the unknown history of ages past, the present with its assaults and objections innumerable, or the unknown future of truth in the world.
3. He must expect that Spirit to breathe through the oracles within his soul His own effectual demonstration of the living and life giving power of the holy oracles.
4. And, in the proportion that his faith forms for him a high theory of the inspiration of the sacred writings will be his own delight in them and sanctification through their influence.[467]

The Verbal Plenary Preservation of the Bible

Inspiration deals with God's revelation of truth which man did not know and which man could not know apart from divine revelation. God used men whom He chose and prepared in order to write Scripture. The very words of God were written down exactly as God intended. This entire process was superintended by God the Holy Spirit. (2Tim. 3:16-17) In this passage all scripture is described using two adjectives: (i) God-breathed — i.e. inspired by God and (ii) profitable — i.e. beneficial and advantageous. Both these adjectives describe what Scripture is. The profitability of Scripture is here described to be in relation to four areas: (1) doctrine — i.e. learning and teaching the will of God, and to point out Jesus Christ till he should come; (2) reproof — i.e. proof, conviction, evidence to convince men of the truth; and to confound those who should deny it; (3) correction — i.e. straightening up again restoring things to their proper uses and places, correcting false notions and mistaken views; and (4) instruction in righteousness — i.e. upbringing, training, nurturing and communicating all initiatory religious knowledge; for schooling mankind in righteousness. Does not this demand the absolute necessity of the preservation of Scripture throughout all ages?

Scripture as the sole authority for the faith and practice of the saints not only clearly speaks of its divine origin and nature (2 Tim. 3:16-17, 2 Pet. 1:19-21), but also equally clear delineates the means and nature of its own preservation. While on the one hand, Inspiration deals with how man came to know God's Word and how he received it, Preservation deals with how successive generations came to possess God's Word and how God ensured the Word is not lost. A survey of the Scriptures helps present a picture that gives an understanding of the providential verbal and plenary preservation of Scriptures. This is seen in:

Passages Which Present the Attributes of God

Numbers 23:19 and Joshua 23:14 present the immutability and trustworthiness of God. What God has said, He will do, is the testimony of Moses to the children of Israel. Thus, if God accomplishes all that he says he will do, then that means that if he promises to preserve His Word then He will do it. The testimony Joshua gives to the children of Israel at the end of the book of Joshua is that none of God's words and promises to his people had failed. All that God had promised He had fulfilled, and they were witnesses to it. God can be trusted to fulfil his promises. Hence, when one reads the promises of God, he is to trust that what God says will not fail.

---

[467] Pope William Burt, *A Higher Catechism of Theology*, (London: T. Woolmer and Petermoster Taw, EC. 1883), 58.

Passages Which Present the Attributes of God's Word

Isaiah 40:8 and 1 Peter 1:23-25 describes the enduring nature of the Word of God. In those passages, God's Word is contrasted with the grass and the flowers of the field. The Bible clearly presents that unlike the grass and flowers of the field which are transient and temporary, God's Word is eternal and permanent. This is seen in the phrase *"the Word of the Lord endureth forever."*

Matthew 5:18, Matthew 24:35, Mark 13:31 and Luke 21:33 also presents the enduring nature of the Word of God. In these passages, the possibility of the Word of God perishing is emphatically negated. This is seen in the phrase that appears in all the verses *"shall not pass away."* This phrase is put in contrast with the passing away of more permanent ordinances of God namely, the heaven and earth. Implying that the Word of God will outlast the heaven and earth.

The Psalms is replete with verses which describe the Word of God as enduring, settled, founded forever. These verses include Psalm 100:5; 111:7-8; 119:89, 152, and 160. In addition to these psalms, Ecclesiastes 3:14 describes the eternal nature of God's work stating that *"Whatsoever God doeth, it shall be forever."* As the Scriptures are rightly attributed to God being called the Word of God, they too can be considered to be forever since Ecclesiastes affirms that whatsoever God does not only stands forever, but also *"nothing can be put to it, nor any thing taken from it."* which brings to mind what Paul says in 2 Corinthians 13:8 *"we can do nothing against the truth but for the truth."* implying the immutable attribute of God's Word.

Passages Which Warn against the Adulteration of God's Word

The Scriptures were written over a period of 1500 years. In the course of that period, the Scriptures itself warned against the adulteration of the Word. In Deuteronomy Moses has two verses warning against adding or subtracting. Moses warns the children of Israel in Deuteronomy 4:2 and 12:32, to take heed to themselves especially in relation to the statutes and commandments of the LORD. Theirs was to "observe to do" and in order to obey and please God, they had to be careful not to *"add thereto, nor diminish from it."*

Proverbs 30:5-6 also presents another warning on how God's Word is to be handled. Every Word of God is pure, and as such should not be adulterated in any way by addition. The Complete Word Study Old Testament has a comment on these verses which states,

> Verse five declares that every word of God is completely free of imperfections. This fact demands that the words of Scripture be no slighted or considered to be in error in any way. Furthermore, no part of it should ever be neglected or regarded as less important (2 Tim. 3:16). History is full of those who concentrated so heavily upon certain biblical concepts in favorite passages that they became blind to other important truths. Sound preaching and balanced devotions will not be restricted to the same portions of Scripture over and over again. It is curcial to remember that the Bible should be interpreted with the whole of its doctrines and principles in mind.[468]

The New Testament also has verses that warn against adulteration. And just as in the Old Testament, these warnings were given immediately after the Scriptures were penned. Paul in contrasting himself and the servants of God from the false apostles and "gospel merchants" asserts that the character of true servants of the Gospel is that they do not "corrupt the word of God" (2 Cor. 2:17) and they do not handle "the word of God de-

---

[468] Spiros Zodhiates, *The Complete Word Study Old Testament*, (Chattanooga, TN: AMG Publishers, 1994), 1634.

CHAPTER V: PRESCRIPTIONS & SUGGESTIONS FOR STRENGTHENING TEACHING

ceitfully" 2 Cor. 4:2). The last days are clearly presented as days of apostasy with a departure from the Word of God, and so, the passages which warn of that departure also warn against following those who twist and distort God's Word, urging faithfulness to the Word implying that even though there will be those who would twist Scripture for personal gains, God's people will not be destitute of God's Word. (2 Tim. 4:3-4; 2 Pet. 2:1-2; Jude 3-4). Finally, the book of Revelation ends with a solemn warning and injunction against addition or subtraction, with threatenings and curses attached to such attempts (Rev. 22:18-19).

Passages Which Present the Availability and Necessity of God's Word

Another set of passages that affirm the verbal and plenary preservation of Scripture is the set of passages that teach the availability and necessity of God's inspired Word to every generation. These verses include, Deuteronomy 30:11-14, which is quoted by Paul when he presented salvation to the Jews in Romans 10. The necessity of the Word of God for salvation demands its availability to every generation. 1 Peter 1:23-25 presents the means of man's salvation which is the Word of God described as an incorruptible seed. This precious and incorruptible and eternally preserved Word is tied to Him who *"liveth and abideth forever"* and *"endureth forever."*

Again, in 2 Peter 3:2, and in Jude 17, there is a call for believers to remember and to be mindful of *"the words which were spoken before"* Peter refers to the words spoken by the holy prophets, while Jude to the words spoken by the holy apostles. These injunctions to remember and bear in mind the words of those who wrote Scripture have to imply the availability of those words to the believers who are called to remember them. And since they are words that were written, this implies that those writings will be available to the generations required to remember them. Since the Scriptures were given with purpose, they are to be available in order to accomplish the purpose for which they were given, thus, their preservation.

Passages Which Confirm and Illustrate the Preservation of God's Word

Finally, there are passages that directly confirm the preservation of Scriptures and illustrate the same at different points of the Bible's history. Among these passages, is Psalm 12:6-7 which talks about the attributes of God's Word presenting the words of the LORD as *"pure words"* and the preservation of the same words affirming that the LORD will *"keep them"* and *"preserve them"* and this He will do *"forever."* In its context, these verses stand in contrast to the nature of man which is characterized by vanity and flattery. God on the other hand is faithful and trustworthy. His attributes are reflected in His words, hence, the character of God's *"pure words"* reflect the nature and attributes of God. The description that the words of the LORD are pure words, like silver refined in the furnace of fire, not only presents the attributes and nature of God's Word, that it is true and sincere, not veiled or deceptive, but also the value and preciousness of God's Word, which is likened to silver pure and refined to the highest degree. If this is the description of the Word of God given to man by inspiration of God, then it follows that man can unreservedly and unquestioningly put his faith and trust on God's Word. He can base his life and actions on God's Word; hence, the Word is the final authority for faith and practice. This is not to be limited to one generation only, but as history shows, is the testimony of all generations, for many have tried and proven the Word to be powerful and alive, to be true and trustworthy. God, indeed, as the psalmist asserts in verse 7 *"shalt preserve them from this generation for ever."* Evil has not abated, apostasy is on the rise, but in the midst of it all, God's standards, God's truths as written and inspired in God's Word, stands and remains written.

Jeremiah 36:1-32, on the other hand, presents a clear illustration on the preservation of Scripture. In verses 1-4, the picture given is that of the inspiration of Scripture with the Word of God coming to Jeremiah who in turn has it written down by the scribe Baruch by dictating it to him. Verses 5-20 record what occurred after the writing. The Word of God received different responses and reactions. The king upon hearing about the scroll, calls for it to be brought and read to him. What then follows is the destruction of the scroll in verses 21-23. The providence of God in the re-writing of the scroll that was burned is what is presented from verse 27 onwards. God reminded Jeremiah of all that had been written and Jeremiah dictates the same things to Baruch for recording. The second scroll added many other prophetic utterances to the former including the record of the responses to the reading of the first scroll as well as the burning of the first scroll and the judgments on the king. That addition was not human, but divine and apart from picturing the divine inspiration of Scriptures, also shows the particular care God took of His Word in preserving it. A similar incident had happened earlier in Israel's history after Moses broke the tablets upon which were written the Ten Commandments. The LORD commanded Moses to return up the mountain with new tablets and rewrote the Ten Commandments and gave them to Moses (cf. Exod. 31:28; 32:15-16; 34:1) again illustrating that God's written words will not be lost.

Apart from these illustrations, the revivals during the Old Testament monarchy during the reigns of Asa, Josiah and during the period of Ezra and Nehemiah, all revolve around the finding of Scriptures, which due to apostasy had been neglected. When the people strayed and sinned, they neglected the Word and worship of God. Each of the accounts of the revival is hinged on the return of the people to the Word of God. Though the Word was neglected for differing periods of time, it was never lost, and when discovered, it was acknowledged and accepted as the Word that God gave through Moses. Thomas Watson in his *A Body of Divinity*, first published in 1672, which were his sermons based upon the Westminster Assembly's Catechism, said this about Biblical Preservation:

> We may know the Scripture to be the Word of God by its miraculous <u>preservation in all ages</u>. The holy Scriptures are the richest jewel that Christ has left us; and the church of God has so kept these public records of heaven, that they have not been lost. The Word of God has never wanted enemies to oppose, and if possible, to extirpate it. They have given out a law concerning Scripture, as Pharaoh did the midwives, concern in the Hebrew women's children, to strangle it in the birth: but God preserved this blessed Book inviolable to this day. The devil and his agents have been blowing at Scripture light, but could never blow it our; a clear sign that it was lighted from heaven, Nor has the church of God, in all revolutions and changes, <u>kept the Scripture that it should not be lost only, but that it should not be depraved</u>. The letter of Scripture has been <u>preserved, without any corruption</u> in the original tongue. The Scriptures were not corrupted before Christ's time, for then Christ would not have sent the Jews to them. He said 'Search the Scriptures.' He knew these sacred springs were not muddied with human fancies.[469]

In the above paragraph, Watson affirms the preservation is evident in the Bible. He points out that the Scriptures have been preserve amidst opposition. This is the case that continued for many centuries while Scriptures were copied by hand. The invention of printing press, at the advent of the Protestant Reformation providentially changed the way copies were made and with it how copies would be preserved and passed from generation to generation. It was at this time too, that the need for Scriptures in vernacular languages

---

[469] Thomas Watson, *A Body of Divinity*, (Edinburgh: The Banner of Truth and Trust, Reprint 1965), 27. (emphasis added)

was thrust into the forefront and efforts to translate them increased. The Westminster Assembly when drafting the Confession of Faith affirmed the verbal and plenary inspiration of Scriptures and God's particular care and providence to keep the Word pure (verbal and plenary preservation of Scriptures) in chapter I paragraph 8 which also advocated for the translation of Scriptures from the original languages "into the vulgar language" so that everyone would be able to search the Scriptures and through them to fear the LORD. By this they inferred that when translated faithfully and accurately, Scriptures in the vulgar languages would convey the truth of the Word of God found in the original. This then leads to the second question to be considered which is: "Which text ought to be basis for teaching in the Church?"

Which Text Ought to Be the Basis for Teaching in the Church?

This second question is one that is to govern and direct the teachings presented in the church as well as the practice of the church. What text should and does the church use in its teaching and preaching ministries and programmes? How many books does the Bible have? Which are they? And how faithfully and accurately does the translation used reflect the original texts? The answers to these questions would give directions and guidance in the choice of Bible version both for reading and teaching in the church. What, then, are the issues involved and that need to be addressed in the seeking of answers to the above questions? In order to settle on the text which ought to be used for teaching in the church, the issues that have to be addressed include the Canon of the Bible and the translation of the Bible.

(i) The Canon of the Bible. In his article titled "The Limits and Growth of the Bible" found in *The Cambridge Companion to the Bible*, Professor Ryle gives the definition of the term "Canon" as,

> The word Canon is used to denote the authoritative collection of the Sacred Books of the Christian Faith. These books belong to two different groups, entitled the Old and New Testaments. The word "Canon," which is used of the whole collection of the Christian Scriptures, is also applied to its two divisions separately.
>
> The word is of Greek origin; its first meaning seems to have been a "measuring line" or "a carpenter s rule." Its root-idea is "straightness," and this is preserved in its secondary and metaphorical meaning, "standard" or "rule" (cf. Gal. vi. 16). Its use in a passive sense to denote "that which is measured," though not common, is well attested in secular literature.
>
> By Christian writers the word was at first especially applied to "Christian doctrine," which they termed "the Canon of the Church," "the Canon of the Truth," &c. Such a "standard" might be embodied in a creed, or defined by the discipline, worship, &c. of the Church.[470]

This definition of canonicity calls for a fixed and set standard. And when applied to the Bible, it points to the fixed and set books which form the Scriptures. Thus, the Canon[471] of

---

[470] B. D. Ryle, <u>Limits and Growth of the Bible</u>, *The Cambridge Companion to the Bible*, (London: C. J. Clay and Sons, 1893), 9-10.

[471] John F. McArthur in writing on "How We Got The Bible" gives the following three broad principles that the church used when recognizing the canon of the Bible. "Over the centuries, 3 widely recognized principles were used to validate those writings which came as a result of divine revelation and inspiration. First, the writing had to have a recognized prophet or apostle as its author (or one associated with them, as in the case of Mark, Luke, Hebrews, James, and Jude). Second, the writing could not disagree with or contradict previous Scripture. Third, the writing had to have general consensus by the church as an inspired book. Thus, when various councils met in church history to consider the canon, they did not vote for the canonicity

the Bible deals with the books that make up the Bible and the excluding of every other book.

(ii) The Translation of the Bible. The Bible in its original languages was written in Hebrew, Aramaic and Greek. Translation deals with the writing and conveying of the words of the original language to the chosen vernacular language. The issue of translation was a necessity since not everyone is able to read the original languages. The Word of God is to be accessible and to be read, known and understood by every man.

Since every matter to be believed, practised, and obeyed is to be drawn from and governed by the Scriptures and every matter of dispute to be settled by appealing to the Bible, the issues of the Canon and Translation of the Bible become fundamental issues for the church. Obedience to corruption and perversions is the same as disobedience since it all results in not doing the revealed will of God. Therefore, in determining the text which ought to be used in the teaching ministry of the church, there has to be an understanding of:

The Canonicity of the Bible

The Greek word "canon", appears five times in the New Testament (2 Cor. 10:13, 15, 16; Gal. 6:16; Phil. 3:16) and the phrase "canonical books" is used to refer to the books which are God-breathed or inspired books and are thus recognized as authoritative for Christian doctrine. Many when talking about the canon of the Bible present it as if it was established by the church, and as if it is the church which chose which books are to be put into the Bible. Although there are external evidences used in the recognition of the books of the Bible, it is the Bible that authenticates itself and the internal evidence (evidence found within the Bible) that set the Canon of the Bible. J. I. Packer rightly observes that, "The church no more gave us the New Testament canon than Sir Isaac Newton gave us gravity. God gave us gravity, by His work of creation, and similarly He gave us the New Testament canon, by inspiring the individual books that make it up."[472] Therefore, since canonicity is about the set or settled books which were inspired and thus are the Word of God, the Scripture itself is the first place to look in order to ascertain and determine the canonical books of the Bible (both the Old and New Testaments).

Canonicity of the Old Testament Books

When considering the internal evidence for the canon of the Old Testament, evidence is drawn both from the Old and New Testaments. In the Old Testament, the evidence is drawn from the text of Scripture itself, and the evidence drawn is usually what is used to ascertain the inspiration of the books of the Old Testament as well as the authority and authenticity of the Old Testament books. From the New Testament, the canon of the Old Testament is ascertained and fixed by none other than the Lord Jesus Christ and from the Old Testament quotations and allusions. In his introduction, Ryle writes:

> We are left face to face with the books themselves. When the external evidence fails us, it is to the internal evidence that we must turn. Scripture must tell its own tale. No record of the circumstances which led to the formation of the Sacred deposit having elsewhere been preserved to us, we must pierce down and investigate

---

of a book but rather recognized, after the fact, what God had already written." [John F. McArthur Jr., "How We Got Our Bible", *Onthewing.org*, accessed July 3, 2019, http://onthewing.org/user/Bible%20-%20How%20we%20got%20it%20-%20MacArthur.pdf.]

[472] J. I Packer, *God Speaks to Man*, (Philadelphia: Westminster Press, 1965), 81.

the signs of the strata themselves. We must see, whether their history has not there been told, and, if so, whether we cannot decipher it.[473]

Thus, in considering the Scriptures themselves in order to see what books are part of the canon, Christ's use of the Old Testament forms the primary source of authority. Christ asserts that the whole Bible centres around His person and work. He challenged the Jews to search the Scriptures (Old Testament books) affirming to them that the testimony of the Scriptures is the testimony of Jesus Christ (John 5:39). This points out that the books of the Old Testament canon must be books that would point to Christ. Christ also presented himself as fulfilling the messianic prophecies of the Old Testament Scriptures and as such quotations from messianic prophecies found in the New Testament also serve to guide in the identifying of the books of the Old Testament Canon. Thus, Christ, by His life's ministry (teaching and miracles) put His seal upon the genuineness and authenticity of the Old Testament and identified the books which form the canon of the Old Testament.

In Christ's teachings, He pointed to various parts of the Old Testament asserting that they are Scripture, as well as talking about "all Scripture" and "The Scriptures" pointing to the canon in its entirety. These references include Matthew 21:42, 22:29, 26:54, 56; Mark 12:10, 24, 14;49; Luke 4:21; John 5:39, 7:38, 10:35, 13:18, 17:12 (all of which are said by Jesus himself) and Mark 15:28, Luke 24:27, 32, 45, John 2:22, 7:42, 19:24, 28, 36, 37, and 20:9 (which are mainly references to Old Testament Messianic prophecies that were fulfilled by Christ). These references in the Gospels form 24 occurrences out of the 51 occurrences of the word Scripture in the New Testament. In talking about the Scriptures in its entirety, Christ gives the categories in which the Old Testament Scriptures are classified. Luke 24:27 states *"Beginning at Moses and all the prophets, he expounded to them in all the scriptures the things concerning himself"* and then further on in verses 44b-45 says *"which were written in the law of Moses, and in the prophets, and in the psalms concerning me. Then he opened their understanding that them might understand the scriptures."* From these verses, the three-fold division of the Old Testament Scriptures is established. Herbert writes concerning the divisions identifying which books are in which division stating that:

> For the sake of readers who may not before have given close attention to this subject, we here subjoin the contents of the Hebrew Canon of Scripture in the order and arrangement in which they appear in Hebrew Bibles: —
>
> i. 'The Law,' or Torah, which is equivalent to our Pentateuch.
>
> ii. 'The Prophets,' or Nebiim, which are divided into two groups —
>
> (a) The Former Prophets, or Nebiim rishonim; four narrative books, Joshua, Judges, Samuel, Kings.
>
> (b) The Latter Prophets, or Nebiim akharonim; four prophetical books, three 'great prophets,' Isaiah, Jeremiah, Ezekiel, and 'the Minor Prophets,' the twelve being united in a single book.
>
> iii. 'The Writings,' or Kethubim, which are divided into three groups —
>
> (a) The Poetical Books; Psalms, Proverbs, Job.
>
> (b) The Five Rolls (Megilloth); Song of Songs, Ruth, Lamentations, Ecclesiastes, Esther.
>
> (c) The remaining books; Daniel, Ezra and Nehemiah, Chronicles.[474]

---

[473] Herbert Edward Ryle, *The Canon of the Old Testament*, (London: Macmillan and Co., 1892), 9.

[474] Ibid., 11.

From these divisions of the Old Testament as recognized by Christ himself, one can clearly see that the Old Testament canon is composed of 39 books. Those who have documented the Old Testament quotations and allusions made in the New Testament have noted that not all the 39 books of the Old Testament are quoted or alluded to in the New Testament. For example, Ryle writes "Quotations are found in the writings of the New Testament from all the books of the Old Testament, Obadiah, Nahum, Ezra and Nehemiah, Esther, Song of Songs, and Ecclesiastes."[475] Yet, it can be seen that this need not affect the canonicity of the books. For example, the Minor Prophets are in the Hebrew Canon considered as on book titled "The Twelve," thus by virtue of they being part of that one book, Obadiah and Nahum would still be canonical though not quoted from or alluded to by the New Testament.

The other books also fall in groups that have references in the New Testament. Ezra and Nehemiah are in the third group under the "Kethubim" or "Writings". The other two books in that class have references made of them with Daniel's prophecy in chapter 9 mentioned by Christ in Matthew 24:15 and with an allusion made to the books of Chronicles in Matthew 23:35, and considering the similarities between the concluding verses of 2 Chronicles with the opening verses of Ezra together with the fulfilment of the prophecies of Jeremiah and Isaiah concerning the rebuilding of Jerusalem, and the authorship of Ezra and Nehemiah, the canonicity of the books of Ezra and Nehemiah can be established. Esther, Song of Songs, and Ecclesiastes are also classified under the "Kethubim" falling in the second group, that of "Megilloth" or "The Five Rolls" which contains also the book of Ruth and Lamentations.

Apart from the testimony of Christ, (which in itself should be sufficient) there is the testimony of the Old Testament books and writers. This testimony is presented in the text of the Old Testament Scripture in the form of authorship and authority of the books. For example, Moses after completing to write *"the words of this law in a book"* commanded that the book be put in the Ark of the Covenant under the charge and care of the priests and Levites for a witness to generations to come. (Deut. 31:24-30). The writers of the Old Testament themselves acknowledged the inspiration of God and attributed their writing to God (Exod. 6:2, 20:1; Isa. 8:1; Jer. 1:7-9, 11-14; 3:6; Ezek. 3:22; 9:4; 44:5; Amos 7:8, 15; Zech. 1:14; 11:13, 15). The general picture presented is that it is the Word of the LORD that is recorded. These and other texts that are used in presenting both the inspiration[476] of the Old Testament books and in giving evidence for the authority and unity of Scriptures also serve to affirm the canonicity if the books of the Old Testament.

Canonicity of the New Testament Books

When considering the internal evidence for the canon of the New Testament, evidence is drawn both from the Words of Jesus Christ and from the New Testament books themselves. When considering the words of Christ in determining the canon of the New Testament, the promise of the Holy Spirit and his specific ministry to the apostles as promised by Christ in the Gospel of John forms the basis for apostolic authority in determining the canon of the New Testament. In John 14:26 and 16:13 Christ promises the twelve that the Holy Ghost will *"teach you all things and bring all things to your remembrance what-*

---

[475] Ibid., 151.

[476] In his Historical Survey of the Old Testament, Eugene Merrill points out the centrality of Inspiration in the canonicity of the Old Testament when he says, "Perhaps the most important canonical criterion, however, was that of inspiration. Any literature not written under the supernatural influence of the Spirit of God was automatically excluded from consideration in the canon, even if it met all the other qualifications." [Eugene H. Merrill, *An Historical Survey of the Old Testament*, (New Jersey: The Craig Press, 1975), 6.]

soever I have said unto you." This points to the special inspiration of the apostles in the writing of Scripture. The twelve will remember all things that Jesus spake (which thing is naturally difficult for man), and will be taught all things by the Spirit. Christ then adds in John 16:13 that the twelve will be shown *"things to come"* by the Holy Spirit. In addition to the words of Christ, the apostle Paul in writing to the Ephesians, uses the imagery of a building to describe the church pointing out that as a building, the church is *"built upon the foundation of the apostles and prophets"* (Eph 2:20). Therefore, in determining the canonicity of the New Testament books, priority is given to the writings of the twelve apostles.

The Pauline epistles are affirmed as Scripture by the apostle Peter in 2 Peter 3:16, and this forms the primary reason for Pauline canonicity. Lukan writings are also considered canonical on the authority of Paul who, when writing to Timothy in his first epistle, quotes from both Luke 10:7 and Deuteronomy 25:4 in one verse terming them as Scripture in 1 Timothy 5:18. The first part *"thou shalt not muzzle the ox that treadeth out the corn"* is taken from Deuteronomy 25:4 while the second part *"the labourer is worthy of his reward"* is taken from Luke 10:7. These cover 16 books of the New Testament with Pauline being 14 (Romans to Hebrews) and two being Lukan (Gospel according to Luke and Acts of the Apostles). Of the remaining 11 books, ten bear the names of apostles (namely Matthew — *the Gospel according to Matthew*, John — *the Gospel according to John, 1st 2nd and 3rd John, and Revelation*, James — *the Epistle of James*, Peter — *1st and 2nd Peter*, and Jude — *the Epistle of Jude*), and the remaining book is the Gospel of Mark (Mark though not an apostle, had close connections with the apostles especially Peter).

Just as in the case of the Old Testament, the New Testament Canon is also affirmed and confirmed by the same evidence that is used to appeal to the inspiration and the authority of the books of the New Testament. In this regard, Archibald Alexander aptly sums it up thus,

> "Were there no other evidence of the truth of divine revelation than the existence of the holy Scriptures, that alone would be conclusive. The Bible is not a book compiled by a single author, nor by many authors acting in confederacy in the same age, in which case it would not be so wonderful to find a just and close connection in its several parts. It is the work of between thirty and forty writers, in very different conditions of life, from the throne and sceptre down to the lowest degree, and in very distant ages, during which the world must have put on an entirely new appearance, and men must have had different interests to pursue. This would have led a spirit of imposture to vary its schemes, and to adapt them to different stations in the world, and to different fashions and changes in every age. David wrote about four hundred years after Moses, and Isaiah about two hundred and fifty years after David, and John about eight hundred years after Isaiah. Yet these authors, with all the other prophets and apostles, wrote in perfect harmony—confirming the authority of their predecessors, labouring to enforce their instructions, and denouncing the severest judgments on all who continued disobedient. Such entire agreement in propounding religious truths and principles, different from any before or since Promulgated, except by those who have learned from them, establishes the divine mission of the writers of the Bible beyond dispute, proving that they all derived their wisdom from God, and spake as they were moved by the Holy Ghost. In all the works of God there is an analogy characteristic of his divine hand; and the variety and harmony that shine so conspicuously in the heavens and the earth, are not farther removed from the suspicion of imposture than the unity that, in the midst of boundless variety, reigns in that book which re-

veals the plan of redemption. *To forge the Bible is as impossible as to forge a world.*"[477]

The Transmission and Translation of the Bible[478]

The issues of transmission and translation of the Scriptures have to do with the Scriptures that are in use in the present generation, but, also, still relate to the doctrines of inspiration and preservation. Transmission of Scripture is a biblical doctrine that can be traced in Scripture right from the time of Moses. Deuteronomy 17:18 gives instruction that when God gives Israel a king, the king who ascends to the throne must ensure that "*he shall write him a copy of this law in a book out of that which is before the priests and the Levites.*" Hence, the Scriptures that were in the custody of the priests and Levites were to be transmitted and copied. This seems to have taken place and at the time of Christ, Jesus himself attested of the books he read in the synagogues of his time that they were indeed Scripture and that he fulfilled them. This presents the basis for the understanding of the transmission of Scripture.

Translation on the other hand, though related to transmission, in that it involves the existence of the Scriptures in every generation, differs from transmission. Transmission is the copying and passing of Scriptures in the original languages in which they were written, while translation is the rendering of the Scriptures in another language.[479] The need for translation may also be drawn from the doctrines of the inspiration and preservation of the Bible. If the Bible teaches that all Scripture is "God-breathed" meaning that, God through the person of the Holy Spirit supervised the writing process, ensuring that His words were recorded, and after that, providentially preserved those words through the ages, then, it follows that, the Word of God is to be available to all ages; hence transmission of Scriptures. And since, over the different periods of time, the languages that have been common to the people would also have changed, and since the transmission of Scriptures deals with the availability of the Scriptures to the different generations, it also follows that the translation of Scripture is necessary to ensure that each generation that possesses the Bible possesses it in a language that they can read and understand.

---

[477] Archibald Alexander, *The Canon of the Old and New Testaments Ascertained, or The Bible Complete without the Apocrypha and Unwritten Traditions*, (Grand Rapids MI.: Christian Classics Ethereal Library, 2006), 170-71.

[478] "There are three links in the chain "from God to us": inspiration, canoniztion and transmission. In the first, God gave the message to the prophets who received and recorded it. Canonization, the second link, dealt with the recognition and collection of the prophetic writings. In effect, the objective of the disclosure was complete when the sixty-six books of the Bible were written, and then recognized by their original readers. However, in order for the succeeding generations to share in this revelation the Scriptures had to be copied, translated, recopied and retranslated. This process not only provided the Scriptures for other nations, but for other generations as well. This third link is known as transmission of the Bible." [Norman L. Geisler & William E. Nix, *A General Introduction to the Bible*, (Chicago: Moody Press, 1977), 211.]

[479] "Translation is an operation performed on languages: a process of substituting a text in one language for a text in another." [J. C. Catford, *A Linguistic Theory of Translation, an essay in applied linguistics*, (Oxford: Oxford University Press, 1965), 1.]

This process of substituting one language for another forms the main understanding of translation whether it is done orally or in writing form. Postgate in his definition of translation writes, "'Translation' is 'transference,' that is merely transport from one medium to another. 'Version' on the other hand is 'turning' and change. By use Translation is limited to transference from one language into another; otherwise it might include all transference from any form of speech into any other form. But for this, and especially for the conversion of prose into verse, or of verse into prose, the name of 'Metaphrase' has been sometimes employed." [J. P. Postgate, *Translation and Translations; theory and practice*, (London: G. Bell and Sons LTD, 1922), 1. **(emphasis added)**]

CHAPTER V: PRESCRIPTIONS & SUGGESTIONS FOR STRENGTHENING TEACHING

When considering the translation of the Bible, the reality of different versions and translations of the Bible especially in the English language raises the need for understanding the process of translation and for giving guidance in the choosing of a Bible version to use in the teaching ministry of the church.

Since language, theology, and spiritual considerations have to be taken into account in the Bible translation process, four things must be taken into account in considering and evaluating translations, they are (i) the texts to be translated, (ii) the translators to do the work, (iii) the theological considerations of the translation, and (iv) translation techniques employed in the translation.

The Bible is a living book, and thus its translation into any language has to have an impact in the lives of those who read it. Since Scripture must impact the life of the church spiritually, it follows that the teaching ministry of the church must be hinged on the translation or version of Scripture used by the church. This was discovered early in the missionary endeavours to East Africa as Douglas Wanjohi notes in his thesis on "Scripture Translations in Kenya." He writes, "It was the Bible that gave the Christian faith its distinctive character and prompted people like H.M. Stanley to approach Mutesa, the King of the Baganda who, after hearing the word of the Book, asked for Dallington Maftaa of the U.M.C.A. in Zanzibar to remain in Uganda."[480]

The distinctive character of the Christian faith as drawn from the Bible is a spiritual, theological and practical one. The Bible when properly translated and accurately presented, changes lives. And as the King of the Baganda asked the missionaries to stay on after hearing the Bible read to him, even today, the teaching ministry of the church ought to draw its potency not just from the methods and avenues available, but from the Scriptures itself, hence, the importance of the Bible translation being used. The British and Foreign Bible Society came up with rules which were meant to "express the main principles according to which translations of the Holy Scriptures should be undertaken."[481] These rules, which were adopted by the American Bible Society, address the issue of Bible translation and revision gives guidelines which cover many issues from the need for revision, to the spirit with which it is to be undertaken, and addresses the issues of the texts to be used to the methods to be employed in translation. This shows that there are many considerations in the work of translation. All the consideration can generally be summarized under the following four fundamental issues below.

The Texts to be Translated

A translation, as the rendering of the text of Scriptures in another language, has to be an accurate reflection of the text in the original. Therefore, in considering which translation to use in the teaching ministry of the church, consideration has to be given to the original text from which the translation is drawn. In the case of Bible translations, as the guidelines adopted by the American Bible Society point out the primacy of the original languages in the choice of the source language (language from which the translation is to be drawn). They write that,

---

[480] Douglas Wanjohi Waruta, "Scripture Translations in Kenya", (Department of Religious Studies: University of Nairobi, 1975), 8. *Erepository.uonbi.ac.ke.* Accessed September 11, 2018. http://erepository.uonbi.ac.ke/bitstream/handle/11295/95524/Waruta%20 Scripture%20Translations%20In%20Kenya.pdf;sequence=1.

[481] *A Guide for Translators, Revisers & Editors, Working in Connection with the American Bible Society,* (New York: American Bible Society, 1932), 4.

The Board desires that, wherever practicable, versions should be made and revised from the original Hebrew, Aramaic, and Greek, advantage being taken of any previous translations in the particular language, and of versions in cognate languages.[482]

When it comes to the original texts of the Bible in the Hebrew, Aramaic and Greek, it has to be noted that there are different families of texts in existence. Hort presented four families of texts namely, the "Western" text family,[483] "Alexandrian or Egyptian" text family,[484] "Syrian" text family[485] and the "Neutral or Pre-Syrian" text family.[486] These families are drawn from the study of the manuscript texts with classification governed by the date of the text, place of origin of the text, and type of writing in the manuscript. Hort in his descriptions of the families clearly presents his preference of the so-called "Neutral" text which went on to form the basis for the Greek Text of the Revised Version. He presupposes that the other texts are edited and thus corrupted, hence textual criticism is necessary in finding out the original text. Marvin Vincent writes of this presupposition that,

> Briefly, then, while the majority of our extant manuscripts contain a revised, and therefore less original text, a comparatively small group contains texts which were not subject to this revision or were prior to it. Consequently, the evidence of this small group is usually to be preferred to that of the great mass of manuscripts and versions.[487]

The text that Westcott and Hort produced, which was used to revise the English Bible has since then become popularly known as the "Critical Text." Currently, the text families from which the English Versions are translated from are: (1) the Received Text[488], (2) the Critical Text[489] and (3) the Majority Text.

---

[482] Ibid., 6.

[483] "This appears to have originated in Syria or Asia Minor, and to have been carried thence to Rome and Africa, and also to have passed through Palestine and Egypt into Ethiopia. ... It appears to have been most widely diffused in Ante-Nicene times, and is the text of the Ante-Nicene Fathers who were not connected with Alexandria " [Marvin R. Vincent, *A History of the Textual Criticism of the New Testament*, (New York: The Maxmillan Company, 1899), 147-148.]

[484] "This seems to have proceeded from a learned and skilful hand in the beginning of the third century, or even earlier. It is found in the quotations of the Alexandrian Fathers – Clement, Origen, Dionysius, Didymus, Cyril – and in the Egyptian Versions, especially the Memphitic. It also appears, in part, in Eusebius of Caesarea. Its characteristic is that which might be expected from the influence of a Greek literary centre – a tendency to polish the language by correcting forms, syntax, etc." [ibid., 148.]

[485] "This was a mixed text, the result of a recension or revision of editors who desired to present the New Testament in a smooth and attractive form and accordingly borrowed from all sources." [ibid.]

[486] "This is represented by B and largely by a, and comes nearest to the apostolic originals. It cannot be assigned to any local centre, but belongs originally to all the Eastern world. It is characterised by careful copying, and is free from Western corruptions. It appears in places far removed from Alexandria. ... The readings of the neutral text when established, are to be accepted in the face of numerical preponderance of other texts." [ibid., 150-151.]

[487] Ibid., 151-152.

[488] "The Greek text from which the so-called Authorized Version of the English New Testament was made is commonly called the Textus Receptus, or Received Text. This text, in the main, is supported by the Greek manuscripts, as a whole, and by the versions and Fathers generally. With here and there a variation, it has been the generally accepted Greek text of the New Testament for the last eight or ten centuries at least." [S. W. Whitney, *The Revisers' Greek Text, a critical examination of certain readings, textual and marginal, in the original Greek of the New Testament adopted by the late Anglo-American Revisers*, (Boston: Silver, Burdett & Company, 1892), 15.]

[489] "That from which the Revised English Version of 1881 was made is called, by way of distinction, the Revisers' Text. This, as far as its peculiarities are concerned, is founded, in the main, upon certain

CHAPTER V: PRESCRIPTIONS & SUGGESTIONS FOR STRENGTHENING TEACHING

In the 1800s. Rationalism, and Higher Criticism were among other movements that led to the questioning of the text of the Bible. It was an attempt to subject the Bible to reason rather than faith; the question on how the Bible was handed down over the generations was raised. This questioning of the Bible focused mainly on the accuracy of the texts and the providential preservation of the text. Were the written texts available to the church reliable or compromised? Were they tampered with or preserved? These concerns led to the distinctions and families as commonly classified today. Gradually with time there was a movement to root out the Received or Accepted Texts, texts that had been used in the early translations of the English Bible. The introduction of Textual Criticism led to the process of trying to ascertain the original words. This eventually led to the publication of the Critical Text or the Westcott and Hort Text.[490] This text was mainly based on two corrupt manuscripts called Codex Vaticanus and Codex Sinaiticus, both manuscripts from the fourth century. From this initial start, changes and revisions have continued with the present text being 27th edition (revision) of the Nestle-Aland Greek Text, though the United Bible Societies have their own revision (based on the Nestle-Aland Text) which is in its fourth edition.

There are those who consider the older manuscript to be more authoritative being closer in date to the apostolic time, while, on the other hand, there are those who disagree. Burgon and Scrivener appealed for the consensus of manuscript evidence with Scrivener asserting that "all available authorities, and not the most ancient only, should be considered in the settlement of the text ... We accord to codex B at least as much weight as to any single document in existence"[491] Burgon on the other hand observed that "The antiquity of the most ancient manuscripts is due to their badness. They were known to be so bad that they were little used, and consequently remained untouched, and therefore have survived when better manuscripts have perished."[492] The distinction between these two main approaches to the Greek texts can be best summarized by the principles that the following table:

---

readings of less than half a dozen, and sometimes of only one or two, of the oldest extant Greek manuscripts in connection with such later ones and such versions and patristic writings as may correspond with them and support or seem to support their readings. A few moments' comparison of these two Greek texts with each other reveals many differences of greater or less importance between them. The plea in behalf of the alterations found in the Revisers' Text is, that between the first and the tenth or twelfth century changes were gradually introduced until the text became so largely corrupted as to need to be corrected by returning to the readings found in the oldest manuscripts, versions, and Fathers. These changes are of two kinds : (1) such as are supposed to be due to pure accident, and (2) such as seem to have been intentionally made by copyists and others." [ibid.]

[490]"The chief peculiarity of the Revised New Testament is that it represents a much older, and, in the judgment of all competent scholars, a more accurate G reek text. Naturally this makes it greatly superior to the Authorized Version. The latter was based upon the Greek Testament of Beza, from which it differs in only forty places. Now Beza, while a careful exegete, was not an expert textual critic. In his day the science of textual criticism had not yet been developed. ... To discover this original Greek text has been the task of textual critics, since the latter part of the eighteenth century. The labors of Bengel, Griesbach, Lachmann, Tischendorf and Tregelles convinced New; Testament scholars that the original text had been substantially recovered. While in minor details there was room for discus- sion, the position of both the English and American New Testament Companies was decidedly in favor of accepting the text resulting from the labors of these critics, in preference to the uncritical text on which the Authorized Version was based." [Matthew Brown Riddle, *The Story of the Revised New Testament, American Standard Edition*, (Philadelphia: The Sunday School Times Company, 1908), 27-29.]

[491]Ibid., p. 141.

[492]Vincent, *A History of the Textual Criticism*, 143.

Textual Principles Proposed by Tregelles[493]	Textual Principles by Proposed Scrivener[494]
1. To give the text on the authority of the oldest manuscripts and Versions, and with the aid of the earliest citations, so as to present, as far as possible, the text commonly received in the fourth century, always stating what authorities support, and what oppose, the text given.	1. That the true readings of the Greek New Testament cannot safely be derived from any one set of authorities, whether manuscripts, Versions, or Fathers, but ought to be the result of a patient comparison and careful estimate of the evidence supplied by them all.
2. In cases in which we have certain proofs which carry us still nearer to the apostolic age, to use the data so afforded.	2. That where there is real agreement between all documents containing the Gospels up to the sixth century, and in other parts of the New Testament up to the ninth century, the testimony of later manuscripts and Versions, though not to be rejected unheard, must be regarded with great suspicion, and unless upheld by strong internal evidence, can hardly be adopted.
3. In cases in which the oldest documents agree in certain undoubted transcriptional error, to state the reading so supported, but not to follow it, and to give grounds on which another reading is preferred.	
4. In matters altogether doubtful, to state distinctly the conflicting evidence, and thus to approximate toward a true text.	3. That where the more ancient documents are at variance with each other, the later uncial and cursive copies, especially those of approved merit, are of real importance as being the surviving representatives of other codices, very probably as early, perhaps even earlier than any now extant.
5. To give the various readings of all the uncial manuscripts and ancient Versions very correctly, so that it may be clearly seen what readings possess any ancient authority whatever. To these add the more important citations of the earlier writers to Eusebius inclusive. The places are also to be indicated in which the common text departs from the ancient readings.	4. That in weighing conflicting evidence we must assign the highest value, not to those readings which are attested by the greatest number of witnesses, but to those which come to us from several remote and independent sources, and which bear the least likeness to each other in respect to genius and general character.

Thus, in considering the text used, the modern English Versions of the Bible are based: on a text which gives pre-eminence to the older manuscripts — namely the Critical Text of Westcott and Hort. The assumption of the Critical Text is that, through the transmission process of the Scriptures, the original words were lost or corrupted whether intentionally or unintentionally, and as such, the closer the manuscript date is to the time of the apostles, the closer it is to the original words and so the more accurate. However, Burgon pointed out that "The antiquity of the most ancient manuscripts is due to their badness." This thus infers that the correct text for translation cannot be one that puts pre-eminence on

---

[493] Ibid., 134-135

[494] Ibid., 141

the older manuscripts, but rather on the text that appeals to the consensus of manuscripts. Edward F. Hills in explaining this writes:

> *First*, many trustworthy copies of the original New Testament manuscripts were produced by faithful scribes. *Second*, these trustworthy copies were read and recopied by true believers down through the centuries. *Third*, untrustworthy copies were not so generally read or so frequently recopied. Although they enjoyed some popularity for a time, yet in the long run they were laid aside and consigned to oblivion. Thus, as a result of this special providential guidance the True Text won out in the end, and today we may be sure that the text found in the vast majority of the Greek New Testament manuscripts is a trustworthy reproduction of the divinely inspired Original Text.[495]

The text which gives pre-eminence to the consensus of manuscripts (namely the Received Text) is the text to be used in translation. Burgon in his work *The Revision Revised* discusses the "facts which lie on the threshold of the science of Textual Criticism" in which he gives three points that form guidelines when considering the manuscript evidence. These three "instruments of Criticism — Copies, Versions and Fathers" affirm that the church as the custodian of the New Testament through continual copying and recopying and use of the Scripture, have transmitted through the generations the written Word of God. This is the same point brought forth by Hills. Burgon in explaining the three "instruments of Criticism" writes,

i. The provision, then, which the Divine Author of Scripture is found to have made for the preservation in its integrity of His written Word, is of a peculiarly varied and highly complex description. First, — By causing that a vast multiplication of Copies should be required all down the ages, — beginning at the earliest period, and continuing in an ever- increasing ratio until the actual invention of Printing, — He provided the most effectual security imaginable against fraud. ...

ii. Next, Versions. The necessity of translating the Scriptures into divers languages for the use of different branches of the early Church, procured that many an authentic record has been preserved of the New Testament as it existed in the first few centuries of the Christian era. ...

iii. Lastly, the requirements of assailants and apologists alike, the business of Commentators, the needs of controversialists and teachers in every age, have resulted in a vast accumulation of additional evidence, of which it is scarcely possible to overestimate the importance. For in this way it has come to pass that every famous Doctor of the Church in turn has quoted more or less largely from the sacred writings, and thus has borne testimony to the contents of the codices with which he was individually familiar. Patristic Citations accordingly are a third mighty safeguard of the integrity of the deposit.[496]

In considering the version to use for the teaching ministry of the church, the text used in translation of the version accepted is the primary standard and calibre by which the version is measured. This is because it is the Greek and Hebrew texts that form the foundation of the version. It is the Scripture that forms the foundation of the Christian's faith, and

---

[495] Edward F. Hills, *Believing Bible Study*, (Iowa: The Christian Research Press, 1967), 11.

[496] John William Burgon, *The Revision Revised. Three Articles Reprinted from The Quarterly Review. ' I. The New Greek Text. II. The New English Version. III. Westcott And Hort's New Textual Theory. To Which Is Added A Reply To Bishop Ellicott's Pamphlet In Defence Of The Revisers And Their Greek Text Of The New Testament Including A Vindication Of The Traditional Reading Of 1 Timothy III. 16*, (London: William Clowes and Sons Limited, 1883), 8-9.

the guide for the Christian's practice. A faithful and accurate translation of a corrupt text will still result in perpetuation of corruption. And as the Scriptures ask, *"If the foundations be destroyed, what can the righteous do?"* (Ps 11:3). The versions that the church must use are those translated from the Received or Accepted Texts. This conclusion is arrived at by considering what ought to be believed about the Bible, considering the doctrines of inspiration and preservation of Scriptures, canonicity and transmission of Scriptures. These doctrines point to the availability and presence of Scripture among God's people in all generations and as such, the text which has been received, accepted and used by the church through the generations become the texts to be used by the church in this generation. Dagg rightly observes that,

> Although the Scriptures were originally penned under the unerring guidance of the Holy Spirit, it does not follow, that a continued miracle has been wrought to preserve them from all error in transcribing. On the contrary, we know that manuscripts differ from each other; and where readings are various, but one of them can be correct. A miracle was needed in the original production of the Scriptures; and, accordingly, a miracle was wrought; but the preservation of the inspired word, in as much perfection as was necessary to answer the purpose for which it was given, did not require a miracle, and accordingly it was committed to the providence of God. Yet the providence which has preserved the divine oracles, has been special and remarkable. They were at first committed to the Jews, who exercised the utmost care in their preservation and correct transmission. After the Christian Scriptures were added, manuscript copies were greatly multiplied; many versions were prepared in other languages; innumerable quotations were made by the early fathers; and sects arose which, in their controversies with each other, appealed to the sacred writings, and guarded their purity with incessant vigilance. The consequence is, that, although the various readings found in the existing manuscripts, are numerous, we are able, in every case, to determine the correct reading, so far as is necessary for the establishment of our faith, or the direction of our practice in every important particular.[497]

This explanation gives the second consideration that attests to the authenticity of the Received texts. This consideration is that of its availability and continuity in use. Burgon discusses this at length and points out rightly that,

> The chief reasons of this are their continuous text, their designed embodiment of the written Word, their number, and their variety. But we make also such great account of MSS., because (i) they supply unbroken evidence to the text of Scripture from an early date throughout history until the invention of printing (2) they are observed to be dotted over every century of the Church after the first three (3) they are the united product of all the patriarchates in Christendom. There can have been no collusion therefore in the preparation of this class of authorities. The risk of erroneous transcription has been reduced to the lowest possible amount. The prevalence of fraud to a universal extent is simply a thing impossible.[498]

Burgon consistently stresses the continuity of the text through its use as evidence for its authenticity. In his *Revision Revised* he showed this by highlighting the importance of multiplication of copies, early translations and quotations and citations from the Christian fathers as they commented on the Bible. In his "The Traditional Text" cited above, he explains that the unbroken tradition of the text as evidenced in its use through

---

[497] J. L. Dagg, *Manual of Theology: A Treatise on Christian Doctrine* (Philadelphia: American Baptist Publication Society, 1871), 24.

[498] John William Burgon, *The Traditional Text of the Holy Gospels vindicated and established* ed. By Edward Miller, (London: George Bell and Sons, 1896), 25.

different ages, reduces the "risk of erroneous transcription." He then goes on to give seven notes of truth[499] which help in ascertaining which text is to form the basis for translation. The Received and Accepted Text thus, by virtue of having been used through different ages and across different places,[500] is the true text as opposed to the Critical Text which relies largely on the testimony of two codices.

The Translators to do the Work

The task of translation focuses on presenting the written Word of God in a language that is understood and known by the reader. This is not an easy task, neither is it one that can be done by anyone and everyone. In their quarterly magazine, The Trinitarian Bible Society carried an article on "Bible Translation Philosophy" which was written by A. C. Thomson. Thomson discusses the advancement in machine translations in this age pointing out that despite the advances, it remains "unthinkable to translate even human laws or literature by machine, let alone the Bible."[501] Thomson then goes on to explain why this is so, and who then should translate the Bible. He observes that the human element in translation greatly affects the translation in a way that any machine with comprehensive vocabulary database cannot. This shows that translation is not just a matter of vocabulary and syntax. The human aspect adds "the one thing that a computer can never envisage"[502] that is the ability to both assess and understand background, and reflect it in the translation. With regard to Bible translation, Thomson points out that the human element brings to the work of translation:

> Familiarity with the cultural priorities of the human author (and, for Bible translation, theological considerations, and above all, a saving knowledge of its Divine author), and the understanding which a given word or phrase will impart to the target audience.[503]

---

[499] Burgon writes, "Can any rules be offered whereby in any case of conflicting testimony it may be certainly ascertained which authorities ought to be followed? The court is full of witnesses who contradict one another. How are we to know which of them to believe? Strange to say, the witnesses are commonly, indeed almost invariably, observed to divide themselves into two camps. Are there no rules discoverable by which it may be probably determined with which camp of the two the truth resides ? I proceed to offer for the reader's consideration seven Tests of Truth, concerning each of which I shall have something to say in the way of explanation by-and-by. In the end I shall ask the reader to allow that where these seven tests are found to conspire, we may confidently assume that the evidence is worthy of all acceptance, and is to be implicitly followed. A reading should be attested then by the seven following NOTES OF TRUTH. 1. Antiquity, or Primitiveness; 2. Consent of Witnesses, or Number; 3. Variety of Evidence, or Catholicity; 4. Respectability of Witnesses, or Weight; 5. Continuity, or Unbroken Tradition; 6. Evidence of the Entire Passage, or Context; 7. Internal Considerations, or Reasonableness." [Burgon, *The Traditional Text of the Holy Gospels* 28-29.]

[500] Burgon writes, "Witnesses of different kinds ; from different countries ; speaking different tongues : witnesses who can never have met, and between whom it is incredible that there should exist collusion of any kind : such witnesses deserve to be listened to most respectfully. Indeed, when witnesses of so varied a sort agree in large numbers, they must needs be accounted worthy of even implicit confidence. ... Variety is the consent of independent witnesses, and is therefore eminently Catholic. Origen or the Vatican and the Sinaitic, often stand all but alone, because there are scarce any in the assembly who do not hail from other parts with testimony different from theirs, whilst their own evidence finds little or no verification. It is precisely this consideration which constrains us to pay supreme attention to the combined testimony of the Uncials and of the whole body of the Cursive Copies." [Burgon, *The Traditional Text of the Holy Gospels* 50-51.]

[501] A. C. Thomson, "Bible Translation Philosophy", *TBS Quarterly Record*, (Issue No. 619: April – June 2017), 29.

[502] Ibid., 30.

[503] Ibid.

Therefore, the human element in the Bible translation process can not be underestimated. It is a very necessary element as Thomson's observation above shows. This human element has to be understood not only in view of its importance in the translation process, but also in its connection to the God of the Bible. Thomson points out the necessity of the saving knowledge of God in translators, which means that Bible translation cannot be and is not to be undertaken by anyone.

> The translation of the Bible into any language is an event of the highest importance to those by whom that language is spoken. Rut when such a translation is to be read for successive centuries, by uncounted millions scattered over all the earth, and for whose use so many millions of copies have already been printed, it becomes a work of the highest moral and historical interest. Thus, the translation and printing of the Bible in English forms a most important event in modern history. Far beyond any other translation, it has been, and is, and will be, to multitudes which none can number, the living oracle of God, giving to them, in their mother tongue, their surest and safest teaching on all that can affect their eternal welfare.[504]

The work of translation is thus to be the concern of the church with the church fully consulted and involved in it.[505] The American Bible Society guidelines rightly put the caution against individual translation works noting that "the work of a single translator or reviser is inadmissible for publication."[506] This caution, though necessary, in itself is not a safeguard to ensure a good translation. It also does not undermine the labours of individual translators or revisers of the past like John Wycliffe, William Tyndale, John Rodgers and others as McClure rightly observes concerning their contribution to the English Authorized Version,

> The English Bible received its present form, after a fivefold revision of the translation as it was left in 1537 by Tyndale and Rogers. During this interval of seventy-four years, it had been slowly ripening, till this last, most elaborate, and thorough revision under King James matured the work for coming centuries.[507]

The caution rather serves to highlight the importance and value of the task of translation of the Bible, such that the church is to take particular care and concern to ensure the work is done by those who are fit to do it. This caution emphasizes "the benefit of this accumulated labour and pious care bestowed upon it by so many zealous and erudite scholars."[508] The nature and composition of the translators of the revision or translation committee will always reflect in the final product of their work. As to the competency of the translators of the Authorized Version, McClure goes on to write that,

> As to the capability of those men, we may say again, that, by the good providence of God, their work was undertaken in a fortunate time. Not only had the English language, that singular compound, then ripened to its full perfection, but the study of

---

[504] A. W. McClure, *The Translators Revived: a biographical memoir of the authors of the English version of the Holy Bible*, (New York: Charles Scribner, 1853), 11.

[505] Martin Luther said, "I think that if the Bible is to come up again, we, Christians, are the ones who must do the work, for we have the understanding of Christ, without which the knowledge of the language is nothing" [Martin Luther, *Works of Luther Vol VI, translated with introductions and notes*, (Philadelphia: A. J. Holman Company & The Castle Press, 1932), 380.]

[506] *A Guide for Translators, Revisers & Editors, Working in Connection with the American Bible Society*, 5.

[507] A. W. McClure, *The Translators Revived*, 59.

[508] Ibid., 60.

Greek, and of the oriental tongues, and of rabbinical lore, had then been carried to a greater extent in England than ever before or since.[509]

McClure voices such great confidence on the competency of the translators of the Authorized Version even pointing out to the reader that upon the completion of reading his accounts of their lives and work, all readers will agree with him as to the competency of the translators and with it, the high calibre of work they did. He asserts,

> When this pleasing task is done, it is confidently expected that the reader of these pages will yield to the conviction, that all the colleges of Great Britain and America, even in this proud day of boastings, could not bring together the same number of divines equally qualified by learning and piety for the great undertaking. Few indeed are the living names worthy to be enrolled with those mighty men. It would be impossible to convene out of any one Christian denomination, or out of all, a body of translators, on whom the whole Christian community would bestow such confidence as is reposed upon that illustrious company, or who would prove them- selves as deserving of such confidence.[510]

The translation is to be a reflection of the original; hence the translators are to be at home with the original languages. The translation when accurately and faithfully done reflects the inspired Word of God; hence the translators are to be men who both know and commune with God. This is why McClure rightly measures the translators of the Authorized Version by their learning and piety. The same learning and piety becomes reflected in the translation. The relationship between the translation and the original is as McClure puts it that the one is the best commentary to the other. He writes,

> For while a good translation is the best commentary on the original Scriptures, the originals themselves are the best commentary on the translation. Passages somewhat obscure in the translation often become very plain when we recur to the original, because we then distinctly see what it was that the translators meant to say.[511]

This sort of translation, that is accurate and faithful can be achieved only by a team of learned and pious men whose goal and aim is not the furtherance of their name or a showcase of their scholarship, but rather the glory of God and the edification of His church.

The Translation Techniques Employed

The aim of every translation has to be to accurately and faithfully make known the Word of God to those who read, speak and understand the language which the translation is being made. Edward Gilman rightly points out this as a fundamental Protestant principle. He writes,

> It is the right of the people to know exactly what is the Word of God, and to have the Scriptures in the form best fitted to their understanding. This, with Protestants, is a fundamental principle, in constant antagonism with the Romish theory, that the people are not to have access to the Scriptures in their own tongue.[512]

It is this principle that the technique employed either addresses or undermines. In their attempt to present the Word of God in language that is understandable, various

---

[509] Ibid., 64.

[510] Ibid.

[511] Ibid., 65.

[512] Edward W. Gilman, *Revision of the English Bible*, (Bangor, Maine: The New Englander, 1859), 146.

translation committees have over the years come up with different renderings of the Greek and Hebrew texts of the Bible chiefly because of the techniques they choose to adopt when translating. In defining translation, this section focused only on the one technique, namely, transference. And for a large part, this was the understanding early translators had of their work. Ryken observes this when he writes,

> Until the middle of the twentieth century, English Bible translation was governed by the assumption that the goal of Bible translation was to translate the words of the original Hebrew and Greek texts insofar as the process of translation allows. I know of no major, widely used English Bible before the middle of the twentieth century that did not primarily aim to reproduce in English the words of the original. William Tyndale, from whom English Bible translation largely flows, even coined words like intercession and atonement so as to be faithful to the actual words of the Greek text. Alister McGrath, in his book on the King James Version, claims that a careful study of the way in which the King James Bible translates the Greek and Hebrew originals shows that the translators tried (a) to ensure that every word in the original had an English equivalent, (b) to highlight all words added to the original for the sake of intelligibility, and (c) to follow the word order of the original where possible.[513]

But, there is another approach to translation that arose later and has come to prominence. This view presents translation not as transference, and its aim not as translating the words of the original source language into the receiving language as literally as the process allows for, but rather, translation is presented as a task in which the translator considers the meaning of what the original text says, and then relays that meaning in the language, culture and context of the receivers in their language. Ryken notes,

> Around the middle of the twentieth century, a theory of translation known as dynamic equivalence became the fashionable translation theory. Dynamic equivalence, more recently sailing under the name functional equivalence, has as its aim to reproduce not the words of the original text but the ideas or thoughts. The impetus for this theory came from translators who were translating the Bible into new languages on the mission field. The influential scholars behind the movement were Kenneth Pike and Eugene Nida. It was simply assumed that what was considered best for the mission field would also be best for English Bible translation. This is very significant, and it was in my view a serious mistake.[514]

Thus, in considering the technique employed by the translators in their work, there are two approaches. Formal Equivalence or word for word translation method and Dynamic Equivalence or thought for thought translation. With these two varying approaches to translation, how is one to choose a version to use? Kubo and Specht in their work *So Many Versions?* address this issue. They write,

> But how is such fidelity to be measured? By what standards is accuracy in translation to be judged? There is no simple answer to this question. There are varying standards of accuracy and differing philosophies of translation. On the one extreme are those who hold that faithfulness demands a literal word-by-word translation that retains, as far as possible, the original grammatical units. Words not actually in the original, but needed to complete the sentence in English, should be indicated by italics or other literary devices. On the other extreme are those who hold that the translator is not concerned with words so much as thoughts and ideas. He should strive for the principle of equivalent effect. The translation should have the same effect on those who read it

---

[513] Leland Ryken, *Bible Translation Differences: criteria for excellence in reading and choosing a Bible translation*, (Wheaton Illinois: Crossway Books, 2004), p. 6.

[514] Ibid.

CHAPTER V: PRESCRIPTIONS & SUGGESTIONS FOR STRENGTHENING TEACHING

as the original produced, or produces, on its readers. The translator should seek to grasp the message of the original and then attempt to put it into whatever English he feels will express it most accurately and satisfactorily.[515]

The formal approach of translation focuses on the words and the writers while the dynamic approach focuses on the understanding of the translators and of the readers. This writer holds on to the formal equivalence and thus the translator has to be concerned with and deal with the words. The dynamic approach to translation makes the work more interpretive while the formal approach is less interpretive.

A good translation is one that pays attention to the text, and as such, a good translation team will let the Bible speak for itself. In order for the Bible to speak for itself, the translation will have to be less interpretive and the translation will have to emphasize the transference of words rather than presentation of thoughts. What about the readers and their understanding, their culture and background? This has to find its answer not in the translators' ability to present the thoughts of the writers in the original, but rather, it is to be achieved through careful study of Scripture, with the Holy Spirit's guidance. Spurgeon rightly observes concerning the doctrine of man which would give balance in the approach to translation of Scripture when he writes,

> Once you believe man to be what the Scripture says he is — once you believe that his heart is depraved, his affection perverted, his understanding darkened, his will perverse — you must hold that if such a wretch as that is caved, it must be as a result of the work of the Spirit of God and of the Spirit of God alone.[516]

The doctrine of illumination through the work of the Holy Spirit has to be the chief consideration (instead of making the translators' ability to convey the writer's thoughts the chief consideration) for the readers to understand and interpret the Bible properly and accurately. Klooster in discussing illumination within the context of interpretation of Scripture observes that,

> Illumination is a work of the Holy Spirit in the reader, hearer, interpreter of the Scripture .... The Holy Spirit's illumination is indispensable for discerning the true meaning of the Spirit-breathed Scripture ... illumination is not the same term for regeneration, conversion, faith, internal testimony, and sanctification, but it cannot be separated from those activities of the Holy Spirit. It is not an additional activity, rather it is an aspect of each.[517]

When what both Klooster and Spurgeon point out about illumination is applied to the work of Bible translation, the translator's work becomes defined and focused. His task does not become one of understanding what was said on behalf of his readers, but relaying what is said to the readers in their language on behalf of the author. The questions he deals with become (i) "what does the original text say?" and not "What is the thought or meaning the author is trying to express?" (ii) "what are the lexical, syntactical, literary, cultural or stylistic elements evident in the text being translated?" and not "How did the earliest readers interpret or understand what the author was trying to relay?" The translator does not have to deal with the question "What has the text come to mean in these days?"

---

[515] Sakae Kubo & Walter F. Specht, *So Many Versions? 20th Century English Versions of the Bible,* (Grand Rapids Michigan: Zondervan Corporation, 1983), 342.

[516] Charles H. Spurgeon, *Spurgeon on the Holy Spirit,* (New Kingston: Whitaker house, 2000), 33.

[517] Fred H. Klooster, "The Role of the Holy Spirit in the Hermeneutic Process" *Hermeneutics, Inerrancy and the Bible,* Ed. Earl D. Radmacher and Robert D. Preus, (Grand Rapids Michigan: Zondervan Publishing House, 1994), 451-52.

because that would make the translation interpretive. When Bible talks about enlightening or darkening of the heart, it is presented spiritually rather than humanly. Paul in Ephesians 1:18-19, prays for the "eyes of understanding" of the believers to be "enlightened" with the onus of enlightenment placed upon the work of the Holy Spirit in the hearts and minds of the believers. In Ephesians 4:18, Paul again talks about the "understanding darkened" and this is by Paul in 2 Corinthians 4:3-4 attributed to the work of "the god of this world" and thus making the chief consideration in translation to be what the text means to the present day readers is a theologically unsound decision.

The issue of translations has for a long time been a non-issue in the vernacular languages in Kenya mainly because there was mainly only one mother-tongue translation in many of the Kenyan dialects. But the recent Bible Translation movement has been gathering momentum, not only with the drive to translate the Bible to the languages which still do not have a Bible, but also with the drive for new translations for tribes that already have a mother-tongue Bible is worrying, especially considering the words of Aloo Osotsi Mojola in his article in the *Africa Bible Commentary*, (bearing in mind that he is "currently regional Translation Coordinator for Africa for the United Bible Societies."[518]) He writes concerning Bible Translation in Africa that,

> The work of these pioneers provided a model for current translation work in Africa, which includes revision of missionary translations, the production of vernacular translations for people who still lack Bibles in their own language and for youth and children, culture sensitive study Bible in African vernaculars created specifically with African audiences in mind, African Bibles in new audiovisual and electronic media, and translations of liturgy for use in worship.[519]

These are worrying words because, a formal equivalence method of translation cannot produce a Bible "created specifically with African audiences in mind" but the use of the dynamic equivalence approach can. The dynamic equivalence approach has been the genesis of a great number of versions including the gender-sensitive and gender-inclusive version which pervert entire doctrines of the Bible, and is behind the drive for cultural-sensitive Bible which will no doubt distort Biblical doctrines.

The Theological Considerations of the Translators

The theological considerations of the translators deal with the guidelines and framework that govern the choices made by the translators in the course of their work. When making choices during the translation process, there has to be a doctrinal basis to guide. This basis brings balance to the whole work. What ought to be considered include what one believes about the Scriptures, what one believes about God, what one believes about man among other doctrines. The approach to adopt in Bible translation is not to be determined just by reviewing the two methods, measuring the pros and cons of each and making a decision. One's theology especially of the Bible has to guide all considerations. Which method of translation would the doctrines of the Bible require? If one believes in the Verbal Plenary Inspiration of Scripture, the Providential Preservation of Scripture, how would they handle the Bible during a translation process? If one believed in the role of the Holy Spirit in illumination of Scripture, and in the interpretation of Scripture, how would they approach the translation of the Bible? The theology of the translators brings out the spirituality of the translation, and this in turn feeds the spiritual health of the church. The Bible directly affects the spiritual health of the church, and as such, the choice of version

---

[518] Africa Bible Commentary, xvi.

[519] Ibid., 1315.

CHAPTER V: PRESCRIPTIONS & SUGGESTIONS FOR STRENGTHENING TEACHING

used ought to be one of great importance to the church. The problem today is how this choice is made, and the factors that are considered when making the choice of version to use. To many, choice of version has been left to personal preference, with no guidelines given. The outcome has been that versions have been chosen for use without taking into consideration matters of grave importance. Small observes,

> How are pastors and members to choose which translation to read and study? A Presbyterian Panel survey showed that most pastors use either the NRSV or the NIV, but why? For many, it is either default to denominational preference, presumed theological compatibility, or personal taste. All reasons for choice take little or no account of the fact that every translation from one language into another is, of necessity, an interpretation.[520]

Small rightly observes that "every translation from one language into another is, of necessity, an interpretation" and as such, every translation will reflect the theological considerations of its translators. It is sad that in the Bible versions consideration, little or no emphasis is laid on the theology of the translators and their translations. Choices of Bible version are made without clear and objective factors to govern them.[521] Although Small goes on to point out that this issue is not to be left to preference or taste, he, sadly, does not go on to discuss how the choice is to be made, or what ought to be considered. Thomas Strouse on the other hand does give clear directions on what version to use with reasons why. He writes,

> The student of the Bible must recognize that the Bible's underlying texts are extremely important. ... The student of the Word should use the Masoretic Text of the Hebrew OT because it is the standardized and traditional text of the OT, and the student should use the Received Text of the Greek NT because it is superior to the Critical Text and Majority Text textually, historically, and Christologically. Not only is the text of the Bible important, but so is the translation of the Bible. Since the Masoretic and Received Texts are superior, it follows that their resultant translation, the KJV, is superior. ... THE KJV IS THE WORD OF GOD IN THE ENGLISH LANGUAGE.[522]

Strouse clearly points out that the choice of version has to be based on textual and translational considerations. These two considerations cannot be discussed or addressed without any theological considerations, and as such, the theological considerations of the translators have to be a major factor in Bible versions. Small in his article goes on to note that "Most translations are the product of a committee of scholars"[523] and as such, the translation becomes a reflection of the theological positions taken by the translation com-

---

[520] Joe Small, "Choosing The Right Version Of The Bible | Presbyterian Foundation", *Presbyterianfoundation.Org*, accessed September 11, 2019, https://www.presbyterianfoundation.org/choosing-the-right-version-of-the-bible/.

[521] "Too often it is forgotten that the one only question which a Christian ought to ask about a text of the Bible, is not, What am I used to? And not, What would fall in with my taste or my liking or my view of the Gospel? But, What hath God said? What is the exact word written, so far as the pious toil and search of God-fearing men can verify it by the help of all the learning and all the experience which they can bring to bear upon it?" [C. J. Vaughan, *Authorized or Revised? Sermons on some of the texts in which the Revised Version differs from the Authorized*, (London: Macmillan and Co., 1882), 6.]

[522] David Cloud, "Testimonies Of KJV Defenders - Thomas Strouse", *Way Of Life Literature Inc.*, last modified 2004, accessed September 11, 2019, https://www.wayoflife.org/database/strouse.html.

[523] Small, "Choosing The Right Version Of The Bible | Presbyterian Foundation", accessed September 11, 2019, https://www.presbyterianfoundation.org/choosing-the-right-version-of-the-bible/.

mittee. In the process of translating, Small observes that "many of the most important decisions are negotiated accommodations, achieved by general agreement, and favouring only those solutions that prove the least offensive to everyone involved"[524] thus, theological considerations of the translators become a major factor in choice of version. And therefore when asking "who is involved, and how are we to decide which committee's word to take?",[525] the answer has to be drawn from a theological consideration of the translators.

The proliferation of Bible versions in the English language in part seems to be a fulfilment of an objection that went unheeded during the revision of 1881. Ellicott writing on the Revision of the English version in 1881 tried to address some concerns as well as present a case for the necessity of the revision that was to be undertaken, of which he was to be part of the revision committee. He addressed three that seemed to him to deserve consideration. He writes,

> These objections are only three in number; first, that revision would tend to unsettle; secondly, that it would probably loosen the bond between ourselves and Nonconformists, and indeed between the Church of England and the American and Colonial Churches, the present Authorized Version being common to all; thirdly, that it would encourage still further revisions, and that the great changes in our Version, which we all agree to deprecate, would be brought about by successive revisions, — in a word, that there would be no finality.[526]

In considering these three objections, Ellicott classified the third as the weightiest and most important objection to the revisers work. In his addressing the objections and in particular the third objection, he began by pointing out that the task of translation has to be one based on necessity and duty. He writes,

> One preliminary consideration, however, must be borne in mind, that even were these objections greater than they really will be found to be, there still remains on the other side the great argument of duty, which with some minds will outweigh every other consideration, whether of convenience or of religious policy. Now, if it be conceded that there are errors in our present Version, and if it also be conceded that they are fairly removable, and that any competent body of scholars could hopefully address itself to the work, then surely every principle of loyalty to God's word requires that this work should be done.[527]

His argument that translation of the Bible when considered as a duty to God demands from the translator loyalty to address himself to the work of God for his glory. The premise that comes out clearly is that which is presented by the "if" statements he gives. That premise presupposed the presence of errors in the version, and that the errors were removable, and so the committee set forth to remove them in loyalty to God's word. He then goes on to point out in address to the third objection that "The really *monumental* character of our Version is its best protection against progressive change."[528] This may be interpreted to mean that one test of good work is time, and that if a translation is properly done, there should be no need for further translations. This was the essence of the third objection, that the revision would open the floodgates of versions. This concern he agreed was the gravest and greatest, and with the passage of time, and in his statements, the ver-

---

[524] Ibid.

[525] Ibid.

[526] C. J. Ellicott, *Considerations on the Revision of the English Version of the New Testament*, (London: Longmans Green, Reader and Dyer, 1870), 188-89.

[527] Ibid., 189.

[528] Ibid., 200.

sion he hoped would be monumental was the revised version they were working on. But time has now shown and indeed confirmed that of the English versions, the version that has been indeed monumental has been the Authorized version. And the revision that they undertook especially of the Greek Text has turned out to do what he hoped would not happen. When discussing how the work would be conducted, Ellicott observed that,

> The third principle would be to preserve the mean between pretermission of what ought to have been corrected, and mere improvement in renderings when the necessity for the change was not distinctly appreciable. In other words, the revision would have to be alike conservative and sufficient carried out on the general principle of the least possible change on the one hand, and yet honourably imitative of that extreme vigilance, which (in the comparison in Chap. iii. of those passages as given in our own Version, with the same passages as given in Tyndale and the early Versions) we have already observed to be such a special and honourable characteristic of the Revision of 1611. To innovate, or, what is called ' improve,' is a grievous mistake on the one side; but it must not be forgotten that there is a directly contrary mistake, which, if made, might lead to very unwelcome consequences. If the revision were not fairly a sufficient one, it would certainly be followed at no great length of time by another attempt, and the very evil, of which we have been forced to admit the possibility in our last chapter, would become real and actual. To use a homely simile, if we create an appetite for revision we must be careful to satisfy it.[529]

The proliferation of versions after the Revised Version seems to point to an appetite for revision that was not satisfied, or else, a floodgate that was open, and that has given rise to all manner of translations including the gender-neutral ones. Either way, what remains clear is that from the Traditional and Received Texts, it is the Authorized Version that has stood the test of time, and is the English version that ought to be adopted for use by the church and its teaching and training institutes and programs.

Teaching and pastoral aids for strengthening the church

Theological Education

The decline of theological institutions is probably one of the biggest factors in the decline of teaching, and thus the revival of theological institutions may also be one of the biggest factor in reviving teaching and strengthening the church in Kenya. This decline was accurately and succinctly recorded by Reuben Kigame in an article he wrote for October-November 2018 edition of "The Shephard" a bimonthly Christian newspaper in Kenya. In the article Kigame wrote,

> In early April, I was invited to speak at this year's Kenya Students Christian Fellowship conference at Ng'iya Girls High School in Siaya County. Before I was called up to speak to the nearly 5,000 high school and college students, a student from the Kenya Highlands Evangelical University (formerly Kenya Highlands Bible College) stood up to say something about the study opportunities at the university.
>
> After listing several available courses, which did not include a single theological course or biblical study, he said the university was discussing with the Commission for University Education the possibility of dropping the word "evangelical" from the university's name. I sank into a temporary depression.

---

[529]Ellicott, *Considerations on the Revision of the English Version*, 211-12.

My mind went back to how many theological schools in Kenya have been melted into liberal universities offering and promoting the study of everything else but minoring in theology.

What was previously Nairobi Evangelical Graduate School of Theology (NEGST) is now the Africa International University (AIU). What was previously Nairobi International School of Theology (NIST) is now the International Leadership University (ILU).

I pray that the East Africa School of Theology (EAST), Nyang'ori Bible College and the Pan Africa Christian (PAC) University do not end up joining the pack in dropping their clear distinctiveness as Christian or theological schools.

While this trend is considered progressive and an economic solution to perennial financial challenges, it fails to consider several crucial aspects.

First, dropping clear, Christian/biblical distinctiveness is tantamount to being ashamed of the person and gospel of Jesus Christ. Jesus Himself did not have very polite words for such a decision. He said: "If you are ashamed of me, I will be ashamed of you before my Father and angels."

GOSPEL POWER

Paul said he was not ashamed of the gospel because it was the power of God unto salvation for the Jew and the Gentile. Thus, for Kenya's Christian institutions to go this direction is also to diminish the power of God unto salvation, including the physical reduction of trainees in the ministry as well as relegating theological education to a low status.

Second, this move teaches the younger generation as well as the public that Christian education is of a lower academic status compared to medicine, business studies, law, communication, engineering, etc.

I wonder what happened to the obvious status of theology as the "queen of the sciences" and the rigour of Christian philosophy as well as inventions in the name of God. I wonder how the leadership of these schools would take the fact that someone like Isaac Newton wrote 40 per cent more on theological subjects than he did science.

I wonder how they would view Albert Einstein's declaration that "religion without science is blind and science without religion is lame!" If the youth do not take up biblical education, the changers of these Christian schools into liberal arts colleges will have to answer for it.

Third, the more we kill Christian schools, the less the number of people going into ministry, hence a limited number of trained clergy, missionaries and professionals.

Our society being what it is today, the cry for a prophetic voice to guide the nation into righteousness is partly the product of undervaluing theological training and spiritual solutions to our problems as a nation.

If Christian schools do not value their own identities, then let us not expect the media, the government and society at large to value counsel from the Church and religious institutions. If we do not respect ourselves, why would we expect to be respected and given a voice to guide society?

Fourth, expanding into liberal arts training may look like the answer to the perennial economic challenges of Christian schools, but such a decision masks two other subtle problems.

The first is outright mismanagement of funds paid to the schools through graft or bad planning. The second may look small but is worse. It is the admission that Christian churches have no regard for such schools and cannot therefore support them through the huge tithes and offerings, or that the God who owns the silver and the gold has, all of a sudden, has become too bankrupt to fund the training of His servants.

The conclusion is hard, bitter and unpopular, but necessary: Those misleading these schools must either resign or allow Christians with a biblical vision to run these schools or else repent and restore the original status of these institutions.

The founders had a specific reason for setting them up. If we desire to set up Christian universities, let us leave the theological institutions alone and then invest from scratch in such new institutions.[530]

Kigame in this article raises issues that need thorough consideration. First he addresses the decline of theological institutions in Kenya, pointing out the major colleges that have been turned into liberal universities. He points out four crucial aspects that this decline presents firstly, about the institutions themselves, and secondly about the church in Kenya. This trend has substituted the gospel mission focus with a financial one. The abandoning of pastoral training because it is not financially self-sustaining and economically viable is a clear change of perspective. Theological education and training is not a financial or economic endeavour, rather it is a spiritual one, and a very crucial spiritual endeavour. The financial emphasis has diluted and replaced the spiritual focus with an academic one. Kigame points out that the shift has undermined the gospel witness, relegating theological education to an inferior or minor pursuit that should give way to the more important academic well paying pursuits like medicine, law, engineering, and teaching among others. This shift also strips the pulpit of its power as less and less men are properly prepared for the work of the ministry. Even if some institutions still have courses in theology or that are theology related, the courses are severely diluted by the content and by the learning environment. Joel Hawes preaching from 2 Timothy 4:2 recorded the importance of the learning environment of one preparing for ministry when he wrote,

> Formerly, a young man, looking to the sacred office, was fitted for college in the family of a pastor, and when he was graduated, he studied theology in the family of a pastor, and thus, in the whole process of his training, he was in a situation eminently favorable for growth in piety, and for cultivating an experimental acquaintance with the spirit and design of the sacred work for which he was preparing. How different from this is the modern mode of preparation for the ministry! ...

Let it not be thought that I undervalue theological seminaries, or a high standard of classical attainment. I speak simply of the present mode of preparing for the ministry as tending to cultivate the intellect rather than the heart, to raise the standard of scholarship at the expense of piety, of humble, earnest, self-devoted godliness; and just so far as this is the case, it operates to diminish the power of the pulpit ; to make preaching literary and scholar-like, rather than evangelical and searching ; to fit it for a display of talent and learning rather than for a direct and faithful commending of God's truth to the heart and conscience.[531]

What Hawes warned against in his time, seems to be the direction the church has taken. Can it yield differing results from what it did back when Hawes warned? Theological education cannot and must not be turned into an academic pursuit. It is not practical for the one seeking to join ministry to study theology in the home of a pastor due to certain

---

[530] Reuben Kigame, Sad Moment for Church as Theological Schools Die, *The Shepherd*, (October-November 2018), 2.

[531] Joel Hawes, *Decay of Power in the Pulpit: its causes and remedies: a sermon at the ordination of Prof. Timothy Dwight to the work of the Christian ministry, preached in the Center Church in New Haven, September 15, 1861*, (New Haven: E. Hayes, 1861), 5.

realistic constraints, with the calibre and testimony (both in terms of knowledge of the Word of God and the theological doctrines and disciplines) being a major constraint. Yet, the schools of theological education ought to be the place where the environment that the home of the pastor would have offered to the candidate for ministry is replicated. The situation that is eminently favourable to spiritual growth has to be a key consideration in training and preparation for the ministry. As such, Kigame's conclusion has to be heeded for the benefit of the teaching ministry of the church.

Although the house hold names and the theological institutions that were in the forefront of the teaching ministry of the church in Yester-years have capitulated, there are other institutions that are rising, — institutions that were little known, but have over the years proven true to the purposes of theological training. Although some of them may lack accreditation, yet the worth of a pastoral training institution or programme should not be measured by the papers it offers, but rather by (i) its faithfulness to the Bible and its teaching, (ii) its commitment to unwavering proclamation and adherence to the doctrines of the Bible. (iii) its warning against, shunning of, and exposing of falsehood, worldliness, and other manners of corruptions that would try to creep in to the pulpit. Hawes in presenting remedies that would restore the power of the pulpit writes,

> Another thing necessary to remedy the evil of which I have been speaking, and to increase the power of the pulpit, is to bring into greater prominency and force the peculiar doctrines of the gospel. There are many who seem to think that these doctrines have become old, are worn out, and can no longer be made to interest and move the minds of men. No mistake is greater. These doctrines old? So is the Bible old, and the plan of salvation, and God's perfections and ways of dealing with men. Are they therefore obsolete and useless, and to be laid aside as old wives' fables? No; the great distinctive truths of the gospel, the truths which relate to God and his government, to Christ and his salvation, to the soul and its destiny, to sin and redemption, to life and death, and heaven and hell — these truths are just as new, just as fresh, just as important to men now coming on the stage of life, as they were to the men to whom they were first announced, and so they will be to each successive generation to the end of time.[532]

Theological colleges are to be measured by their doctrinal emphasis, or lack of it. The watering down of doctrine must stop! Theological education must strengthen the pulpit for it to impact and strengthen the church. Men who are being prepared for the pulpit can never be measured by the standards of the world. Gardiner, speaking on the pulpit and its role in the influence of Christianity and the testimony of the church writes,

> Blessed are the people that "know the joyful sound." Favored is the man who bears even nothing more than the mark of the pulpit upon his conscience, exciting his fears, restraining his vices, and reaching forth its hand to keep him from the gulf of perdition before the time! If his heart is not the veriest sink of pollution, and his history the black record of the most loathsome vices and the foulest crimes, while he is thankful for other influences, let him lift his heart in gratitude to the "Father of lights," that his kind and gracious Providence has determined his residence under the droppings of the sanctuary![533]

The pulpit cannot bear such influence if those who occupy it are not acquainted with the doctrines they are to proclaim. The pulpit will be without power if those who ascend to it do not do so with full conviction and knowledge of the Word they are to declare.

---

[532] Joel Hawes, *Decay of Power in the Pulpit*, 17-18.

[533] Gardiner Spring, *The Power of the Pulpit: or, thoughts addressed to Christian ministers and those who hear them*, (New York: M. W. Dodd, 1845), 15.

CHAPTER V: PRESCRIPTIONS & SUGGESTIONS FOR STRENGTHENING TEACHING

Theological education has to be mandatory for the church, and as such, theological institutions have to maintain a standard that would empower the pulpits. Under a topic titled, "Fitting Education for Ministers," Gardiner Spring suggests three considerations that theological institutions should do in order to maintain standards that would empower the pulpit. Of these things, the first is supervision. He writes,

> Experience gives wisdom. No class of men have profited more by their experience, than those to whom the churches have intrusted the selection and education of poor and pious youth for the ministry. The enterprise is now probably as well conducted as it can be ; and if not, there is but one thing wanted to make the system as perfect as it is capable of being made. That one thing is the extension of the system of parochial schools throughout all our churches. These, under a wise supervision, would become not only the nurseries of the church, but the nurseries of the ministry. They furnish the very scenes, and associations, and employments which put the intellectual and moral character of this class of youth to the test ; and which, by that gradual development which is most to be relied on, would indicate the most worthy candidates for the Church's charity.[534]

Theological education and institutions would do a great disservice to the church if supervision of the students' study, social, spiritual and ministerial lives are left unmonitored. Churches must shun colleges that cannot give an account of the student apart from the academic transcripts and reports. Supervision was one of the aspects that accompanied the training of the youth who were taken in to the pastor's home.

The second thing that Gardiner points out is that of experience. This is not divorced from the first, but rather flows from and is tied to it. He writes,

> Many a young man has finished his course in our theological seminaries, who never ought to have thought of the ministry, and whom a faithful pastoral supervision would have so instructed ; while more have suffered in their usefulness as ministers, for the want of that personal inspection which, from the multitude of students, it has been impossible to exercise. ...
>
> *Let the teachers of those who are being educated for the ministry, the men of no inconsiderable experience in the pastoral office.* In the early organization of theological seminaries, the professors were of this character they came with the experience of settled pastors; not with clear heads only, but with warm hearts, and from the warm bosom of the churches which they loved.[535]

Instructors in theological institutions are not academicians, they are pastoral mentors and disciplers. As Gardiner rightly points out above, they ought to be men who possess knowledge of what they are teaching, and experience of active pastoral ministry. Theological education and institutions would do a great disservice to the church if its teachers are lacking either in knowledge of the Scriptures and the doctrines of the Bible or in experience of the pastoral office, the pulpit and ministries associated with it. Churches must shun colleges that are lacking in biblical pastoral experience and which do not offer practical ministerial learning opportunities.

The third thing pointed out by Gardiner is that of internship or apprenticeship. Just as the second was drawn from the first, so does this one flow naturally from the second. Gardiner writes,

---

[534] Ibid., 362.

[535] Gardiner Spring, *The Power of the Pulpit*, 379.

There is another thought also which is worthy of some consideration. It has been before intimated, that when a student at law, or at medicine, has finished his course at the law or medical school, so far as my knowledge extends, he is put under the tuition of a practising lawyer or practising physician. Let the same thing be done with our students in theology. On completing their theological course, let their respective presbyteries require them to spend three, or six months, with some settled pastor. They will find still, that they have something to learn they will receive important instruction, and at the same time will do good.[536]

Theological institution prepares men for the course of Christ and the work of the Gospel. The church is the institution Christ left to bear his Gospel to the world. The theological institutions cannot work independent of the church, and neither can the church disassociate itself from the Bible college. Each must do its part, but must also work in cooperation and collaboration with each other. Though the church currently has a shortage of men to fill their pulpits, she must not rush to ordain and fill them with men she has not tested and proven, even if they have graduated from reputable theological institutions. Apprenticeship also serves another important function, that of offering a smooth transition into the church context. The trained and equipped pastor is given an opportunity under a more experienced pastor to smoothly integrate his just concluded theological training with the ministry ahead of him within the church context.

Finally, this section would not be complete without recommendations identifying places that from the writer's experience, the educational model closely resembles that which has been presented in the discussion above. In Kenya, first and foremost, there is the Faith College of the Bible (FCB) and Bomet Bible Institute (BBI), in which this writer serves as a teacher. Bomet Bible Institute also offered this writer his first experience as a student of theology when he enrolled for study there in 2000. Apart from the academic rigours which emphasize the study of Biblical languages, Biblical Doctrines, Pastoral Theologies and Christian Education, these two institutions have for their faculty members teachers who are in active pastoral ministries and who attend both to the training of students and pastoral duties and as such often involve their students in pastoral practice and apply the context of the church in their teachings. The colleges also have ministerial opportunities to the churches as well as to institutions nearby. Both colleges to date have ministries to primary schools in which the students go to give Bible lessons to the children at appointed times. Both colleges have an afternoon set for outdoor evangelism every week, and a programme for end of term evangelism in which the students go to evangelize in churches where they are invited to immediately they the school term ends.

Faith College of the Bible (FCB) and Bomet Bible Institute (BBI) are both situated outside Nairobi. FCB is in Eldoret, while BBI in Bomet. Within Nairobi, there is another institution, Bible College of East Africa (BCEA). BCEA[537] was started by the Independent Board for Presbyterian Missions in 1965 and has been training men for the ministry since then. They have a campus in Arusha Tanzania which was started in 2006. BCEA is a conservative college, that places emphasis on spiritual duties and discipline of life and studies.

---

[536] Ibid., 388.

[537] "The Bible College of East Africa (Nairobi, Kenya) was founded in 1965 under the Independent Board for Presbyterian Foreign Missions (IBPFM; Philadelphia, PA, USA) upon the vision to train ministers not only for Kenya but also for the broader region of East Africa. As a result of this vision, the Bible College of East Africa, Tanzania (BCEA, TZ) was started in September 2006 at Arusha, Tanzania in order to provide sound biblical training against religious pluralism and apostasy in these days." ["Bible College Of East Africa Tanzania", *Findglocal.com*, accessed August 15, 2019, http://www.findglocal.com/TZ/Usa-River/168953509906031/Bible-College-of-East-Africa-Tanzania.]

CHAPTER V: PRESCRIPTIONS & SUGGESTIONS FOR STRENGTHENING TEACHING

When it comes to online courses, the Far Eastern Bible College (FEBC) has a good online programme. Far Eastern Bible College was started 1962 by Timothy Tow. The founding of the college was occasioned both by the need for trained men, and the need for defending the faith. In their website, they write,

> This idea arose partly from a pressing need to train a new generation of "evangelists, pastors, and teachers" (Eph 4:11) for the Church of Jesus Christ in the Far East, and partly from a theological confrontation with certain institutions in Singapore that had apostatised from the Faith. Setting up a biblically fundamental and positionally conservative School is one way of earnestly contending for the Faith once delivered unto the saints (Jude 3).[538]

The college thus, from onset was geared towards equipping men for the work of the ministry both in the pulpit of churches and in the missions field. Their goal and focus in this training is stated as providing "comprehensive theological biblical-education." They write,

> FEBC endeavours to provide a comprehensive biblical-theological education (Acts 20:27) that is based solely on the forever infallible and inerrant Scriptures (Ps 12:6–7, Matt 5:18, 2 Tim 3:16–17) so as to equip both Christian men and women for effective spiritual leadership and service (2 Tim 2:2, 2:15) in the proclamation of the Gospel of Jesus Christ (Matt 28:18–20), and in the defence of the Reformed Faith (Phil 2:16, Titus 1:9, Jude 3).[539]

The method used to accomplish this is both by on-campus full-time training and online or distance training. With regard to their distance learning programmes, "Video or audio lectures are delivered online and students are required to complete reading and writing assignments and take an exam at the end of each course. Courses are offered according to the academic calendar of the College."[540] The audio and video lectures are mostly recordings of the actual lectures that are taught in their normal full-time programs. This means that the same teachings given to the full time students are given to those who wish to study but are not able to go for full-time studies at the college campus in Singapore. The faculty lecturers of FEBC consist of ordained ministers within the Bible Presbyterian Churches in Singapore who are actively involved in the pastoral ministry and full time church workers.

The North American Reformed Seminary (TNARS) is also another provider of sound theological education online. TNARS is an unaccredited, online, non-profit distance learning seminary that is reformed in tradition following in the tradition of the Protestant Reformers. Though it is non-denominational, it adheres to the Westminster Confession of Faith. In their website, they state that their aim is "to educate the body of Christ completely free of charge."[541] Their focus is thus geared towards strengthening of the church and its method is each student learns under a mentor who is acknowledged by the college. They write,

---

[538] "Far Eastern Bible College | Introducing The College: A Short History Of The Far Eastern Bible College", *Febc.edu.sg*, accessed August 7, 2019, https://www.febc.edu.sg/v15/introducing_the_college.

[539] "Far Eastern Bible College | Word From The Principal", *Febc.edu.sg*, accessed August 7, 2019, https://www.febc.edu.sg/v15/word_from_the_principal.

[540] "Far Eastern Bible College | Distance Learning Online", *Febc.edu.sg*, accessed August 7, 2019, https://www.febc.edu.sg/v15/distance_learning_online.

[541] "Distinctives: A Different Approach To Seminary Education", *The North American Reformed Seminary*, accessed August 7, 2019, http://www.tnars.net/distinctives.html.

We teach through mentoring. The mentor guides and helps the student with his studies. We are interested in more than academics, so the mentor is also responsible to ascertain and help grow the student's application of biblical principles to their life. This is accomplished "one-on-one" and through interaction with the student's home church.[542]

As to their accreditation status, "They do not wish to seek accreditation but instead wish to accumulate their reputation by the biblical principal "by their fruits you shall know them", and also by the reputation of their graduates."[543]

Pastoral Tools and Library

Stewart Custer in the preface to his book "Tools for Preaching and Teaching the Bible" begins with a very potent statement which says, "The person who wishes to master the content of Scripture so that its content may master him will be greatly helped by the right study tools."[544] The potency of this statement is in its understanding of why one ought to master the Scriptures. The aim for the pursuit of tools is the mastery of the subject under pursuit. For the church to be strengthened through the teaching ministry, its teachers must be masters of the Scriptures and mastered by the Scriptures. As such, the use of tools is necessary. What tools are available for the teachers of the word in Kenya? Currently, the major distributor of evangelical books at affordable prices in Kenya is Africa Christian Textbooks (ACTS) which is an independent registered trust whose mission is to "strengthen local churches in Africa by providing evangelical, relevant and affordable literature for Christian leaders and Bible students in order to advance the cause of Christ."[545] They function both as a publisher and a bookseller and work in various countries within Africa. Their branch in Kenya is situated at Africa International University (AIU) which was formerly the Nairobi Evangelical Graduate School of Theology (NEGST). In their webpage, they give different strategies available for acquiring textbooks. They write,

There are several options for those who are serious about textbooks:

1. The school buys: your institution itself can buy a set of textbooks which will then be loaned out to the students and recovered at the end of the course — this is ideal since the teachers will always be able to rely on having something available.

2. The student buys: the teacher can recommend a textbook and make sure it is available for students to buy. The student will then own the book and be able to take it away with him after the course. Students may protest because of the cost but in the end they may appreciate this option the best. It also gives the teacher his or her own choice of a current book rather than relying on the choice made by the college some years earlier. Again advanced planning with ACTS is essential to in order have the book available on time.

3. The school buys using student funds: some institutions add a charge for textbooks as part of the school fees. This means they can supply the books to all the students without some

---

[542] "The North American Reformed Seminary", *Revolvy.com*, accessed August 7, 2019, https://www.revolvy.com/page/The-North-American-Reformed-Seminary?cr=1.

[543] Ibid.

[544] Stewart Custer, *Tools For Preaching & Teaching The Bible* (Greenville, S.C.: Bob Jones University Press, 1998)., preface.

[545] *About ACTS: Our Core Values – The Heart and Passion of ACTS* electronic article accessed on 7 August, 2019, available at URL: http://www.acts-ng.com/about-acts/

students complaining that they have no money. This way also the sponsors of the students are not tempted to view a book grant as an optional extra.[546]

ACTS as a publisher and distributor of books deals with a wide range of books and from varied theological positions. Another publisher of books in Kenya, but one which majors on the distribution of evangelical literature is Pilgrim Editorial. In their website, they say that,

> **Pilgrim Editorial** was founded in 1979, we have been editing and distributing quality evangelical literature for over thirty years. Our main commitment is with fidelity to the Scriptures, according to the line marked by biblical and historical Christianity. Our books are theologically sound and their approach is eminently practical, accessible to all kinds of readers.[547]

In Kenya, they are involved in the translation of theological and religious books into Swahili thus offering reformed books in Swahili through the efforts of Christian Literature in Kiswahili (CliK)[548] and Injili Bible Church. They are governed by four rules which they explain in their webpage. These rules are:

> **1. Proclamation and exaltation of Christ as the center of everything and the sovereignty of God in all spheres, in accordance with the doctrinal line of historical Christianity.** In the midst of the current religious confusion, it is vital that our message, as evangelical Christians, is not diluted in the multitude of modern innovations and sectarian approaches that hide behind labels such as "Christian", "Evangelical", "Biblical", etc. Our editorial advocates a determined return to the clear "ancient paths" of the Word and the history of the Church rather than the incursion of dark paths of doubtful origin and uncertain end.
>
> **2. Net biblical content of its publications and spiritual edification of the readers, with priority of the ministerial aspect over the commercial.** When so much literature called "Christian" consists only of mere subjective, philosophical or psychological reflections, when so many religious messages are based on the quicksand of human experiences rather than on the solid rock of divine revelation, it is imperative to make available of the people the "pure milk of the word" so that by it, it grows for salvation. Such an approach obviously does not produce great economic gains, but we believe, in the words of the great missionary Hudson Taylor, that "the work of God, done in the manner of God, will not lack God's provision."
>
> **3. Scrupulous respect for copyright, editorial rights and other regulations that control the publishing of books.** In these days when piracy invades all areas of human commercial activity, including Christian, it is essential to give a good testimony of honesty and legality, rather than succumbing to temptations and pressures to ignore elementary ethical principles under the false claim to "spread the Word of God." It is sad to see how some Christians take advantage and profit from the work and effort of others who maintain the biblical principle that "the worker is worthy of his salary."

---

[546] "ADVICE TO EDUCATORS ON THE USE OF TEXTBOOKS | ACTS", *Acts-ng.com*, accessed August 7, 2019, http://www.acts-ng.com/2012/01/05/a-call-for-educators/#more-170.

[547] "Who We Are-Pilgrim Editorial", *Editorial Peregrino*, accessed August 7, 2019, http://editorialperegrino.com/nosotros/quien-somos/.

[548] "Home - Clik Africa - Christian Literature In Kiswahili", *Clik-Africa.org*, accessed August 7, 2019, http://www.clik-africa.org/.

4. Rigorous fidelity to the original works in the translations. It was the Italians who coined the phrase "tradutore, traditore", and there is nothing easier than to betray the authors and their readers through translations that do not faithfully reflect the meaning of the original. There have been cases of editions in other languages that have suppressed entire paragraphs of the original work simply because the publishers disagreed with the author's theology. Sometimes, you have to look for the key in more prosaic causes, such as the lack of capacity of translators. In any case, Editorial Peregrino seeks not only to respect the original thinking of the authors, but also to employ trained translators who can transmit it with maximum fidelity and correctness in our language.[549]

Apart from these publishers and distributors who deal with textbooks, there are those which provide materials online. Among them, the website of the Mount Zion Bible Church provides sound resources. They deal mainly with reprinting sound biblical and doctrinal materials from the past. These materials can be found and accessed at their Chapel Library at www.ChapelLibrary.org. They also have the option in which they send their materials via post upon request.

Custer quotes from Spurgeon with reference to the purchase and possession of books as tools. He writes,

> If a man can purchase but very few books, my first advice to him would be, let him purchase the very best. If he cannot spend much, let him spend well. The best will always bee the cheapest. ... the next rule I shall lay down is, master those books you have. Read them thoroughly. Bathe in them until they saturate you.[550]

The words of Spurgeon give the attitude with which the tools available are to be accessed. Wisdom is to be exercised in the choice of books, attention is to be paid to what godly writers have handed down in print, and above all effort is to be put in developing one's spirituality and abilities for the service of God and the work of the ministry. The challenge of tools and materials in Kenya partly arise from the fact that most of the content is imported from abroad. Even ACTS which has tried to distribute books and materials affordably mainly deals with books and materials printed abroad. There is a very small amount of content that is developed in Kenya which is Biblically sound and developed by those in ministry here in Kenya. Thus, there is a need for the production of material that is able to strengthen the church locally especially that which will be relevant to address the specific challenges that are unique to the context of the church in Kenya.

Concluding Observations

The above prescriptions are vital for the teaching ministry of the church in Kenya because (i) they are prescriptions that ensure that the focus of the church is the Word of God. The church must never replace the Word of God with any other thing. All teachings in the church have to be teaching of the Word of God. As such, it is essential that those who would be teachers in the church be masters of the Word, and all those attending any teaching programmes of the church have with them the Word of God in a language that is clear to them, and have assurance and confidence that what they are reading and learning is indeed the Word of God; (ii) they are prescriptions that give guidance to the teachers of the Word of God and thus both enhance their abilities and giftedness in teaching and equip them to navigate the murky waters of theological perspectives in which diver-

---

[549] "The 4 Norms Of Editorial Peregrino", *Editorial Peregrino*, accessed August 7, 2019, http://editorialperegrino.com/nosotros/las-4-normas-de-editorial-peregrino/.

[550] Custer, *Tools for Preaching and Teaching the Bible*, preface.

gent views have been fronted and many institutions have capitulated; (iii) they are prescriptions that are relevant, taking into account the current need and the available options for the church in its local context.

Prescriptions that would enhance the teaching ministry of the church must be those that will guide the church back to the Scriptures. The teaching mandate of the church is centred on the Word of God. There is a need for solid biblical teaching in the church and thus the need for teachers who would study, know, and rightly divide and handle the Word of God. May God grant that the church would have such men!

CONCLUSION

Historical records document many achievements, but also note a great deal that was left undone and that needed to be accomplished. Progress over the years has been slow in some areas while in others great regression is seen. The neglect of a sustained Bible teaching ministry in the church from the time of the missionary endeavours to date has greatly affected the church today. The problems brought about by syncretistic and humanistic beliefs still persist today. Some of these problems would have been, and still can be, solved if a sustained and consistent sound Bible-based teaching program is adopted and used by the church.

The condition of the church though serious and at some points discouraging is not without remedy. History is replete with periods and generations when the church was in similar states characterized by spiritual declension and formalism, when worship and service were done out of mere routine. But the same history evidences that a return to a systematic, sustained and consistent teaching program in the church which involves a concerted effort remedied the situation and revived the church. There is therefore an urgent need for the church to return to the Bible and both re-introduce and emphasize systematic Bible-based teaching. This return should emphasize biblical and doctrinal teaching in the homes and in the church's programs. This teaching requires a concerted effort by pastors and church members. There is a need for the teaching, training, and equipping of all in the church so that through it, pastors can teach and preach God's Word faithfully, and heads of families can watch over the souls in their households, and every single member of the church can discern the times for they are evil.

The possibility of accomplishing this is attested to by history of the different generations, and in places which experienced a revival in religion was when the church returned to biblical teaching. The avenues available for teaching both in the homes and in the church further strengthen this possibility and thus the commitment to appropriate these avenues while trusting in God to revive His church, and the commitment to faithfully and systematically use the Word of God while depending on the Holy Spirit to apply it in the hearts, convincing, convicting and leading the church according to the truth of God's Word are the issues the church has to address and take responsibility for to consciously, continually and consistently pursue. There has to be a rethinking and a change of perspective in regard to how the church views the Sunday school and the Bible college and the role they have in the church's teaching ministry. The untrained ministry has to be replaced by a biblically trained ministry and the scope of teaching in the church has to be every man, and must aim at edifying, equipping, maturing and perfecting them in the grace and knowledge of the Lord Jesus Christ.

The situation may be bad, but it does not need to deteriorate further. Teaching has to be mandatory, not optional to the church. The Bible commands and illustrates it, history testifies of this, and the church is not left without avenues to practise it. It is this writer's hope that a biblical, practical, and pastoral teaching ministry will be encouraged and strengthened, and that the pulpit will be both a preaching and teaching platform especially in this age where many have erred in so many ways and have failed to adhere to God's commandment and stipulations concerning the faith and practice of the Christian life. Hopefully, with an understanding of what the pastor's duties are (duties which cannot be neglected or replaced), and of the need for instructing both the ministers of the Word and the need for teaching believers in all things which Christ has commanded, the church will return to the Bible and its doctrines, and teaching will once again have its God-appointed place in the church of God.

BIBLIOGRAPHY

BOOK SOURCES

A Dictionary of the Bible dealing with its language, literature, and contents including the Biblical theology. ed. By, James Hastings. Edinburgh: T&T Clark, 1898. sv. Doctrine.

A Guide for Translators, Revisers & Editors, Working in Connection with the American Bible Society. New York: American Bible Society, 1932.

Abercombie, James. *Lectures on the Catechism, on confirmation, and the liturgy of the Protestant Episcopal Church; delivered to the students of that denomination in the Philadelphia Academy.* Philadelphia: Bradford and Inskeep, 1811.

Adams, John. *Primer on Teaching: with special reference to Sunday School work.* Edinburgh: T & T Clark, n.d.

Africa Bible Commentary: a one volume commentary written by 70 African Scholars. Gen Ed., Tokunboh Adeyemo. Nairobi, Kenya: Word Alive Publishers, 2006.

Alexander, Archibald. *The Canon of the Old and New Testaments Ascertained, or The Bible Complete without the Apocrypha and Unwritten Traditions.* Grand Rapids MI.: Christian Classics Ethereal Library, 2006.

Alexander, James W. *Thoughts on Family Worship.* Morgan PA: Soli Deo Gloria Publications, 1998.

Ambrose, Isaac. *Works of Isaac Ambrose, sometime minister of Garstang in Lancashire.* London: Caxton Press, n.d.

Baker Theological Dictionary of the Bible. Ed. Walter A. Elwell. Grand Rapids Michigan: Baker Books, 1996. sv. Teach, Teacher.

Balikie, William Garden. *For the Work of the Ministry: a manual of homiletical and pastoral theology.* London: Strahan and Co., 1873.

_____. *The Preachers of Scotland from the sixth century to the nineteenth century.* Edinburgh: T & T Clark, 1888.

Barclay, Robert. *A Catechism and Confession of Faith: approved of and agreed unto by the General Assembly of the Patriarchs, Prophets, and Apostles, Christ Himself being the chief speaker in and among them.* Wilmington Delaware: James Wilson, 1821.

Barclay, Wade Crawford. *First Standard Manual of Teacher Training.* New York: The Methodist Book Concern, 1912.

Barnes, Albert. *Barnes' Notes on the New Testament: complete in one volume.* Michigan: Kregel Publications, 1962.

_____. *The Rule of Christianity in Regard to Conformity to the World: a sermon delivered in the First Presbyterian Church in Philadelphia, March 4, 1833.* Philadelphia: Harrison Hall, 1833.

Baxter, Richard. *Autobiography.* Christian Focus Publications: Ross-shire, 1998.

_____. "The Duties of Parents for their Children". *A Christian Directory: or a Body of Practical Divinity and Cases of Conscience in Five Volumes.* London: Printed for Richard Edwards, 1825.

Bean, James. *Family Worship: a course of morning and evening prayers for everyday in the month to which is prefixed a discourse on family religion.* London: Printed for C. and J. Rivington, 1826.

Beck, J. T. *Pastoral Theology of the New Testament.* Tr., James A. M'Clymont and Thomas Nicol. Edinburgh: T & T Clark, 1885.

Bedell, Gregory Thurston. *The Pastor: Pastoral Theology.* Philadelphia: J. P. Lippincott & Co., 1880.

Beza, Theodore. *The Life of John Calvin.* Translated by Francis Sibson with copious notes by an American editor. Philadelphia: J. Wm. S. Martien, 1836.

Bright, William. *Waymarks in Church History.* London: Longman, Green, & Co, 1894.

Brown, Charles Reynolds. "The Training of a Minister", in *Education for Christian Service,* by Members of the Faculty of the Divinity School of Yale University. New Haven: Yale University Press, 1922.

Brown, John. *A Compendious View of Natural and Revealed Religion in Seven Books.* Philadelphia: David Hogan, 1819.

_____. *Address to Students of Divinity by Rev. John Brown, Late minister of the Gospel in Haddington, Scotland.* np: nd.

Burgon, John W. *A Treatise on the Pastoral Office: addressed chiefly to candidates for holy orders, or those who have recently undertaken the cure of souls.* London: MacMillan and Co., 1864.

_____. *The Revision Revised. Three Articles Reprinted from The Quarterly Review.' I. The New Greek Text. II. The New English Version. III. Westcott And Hort's New Textual Theory. To Which Is Added A Reply To Bishop Ellicott's Pamphlet In Defence Of The Revisers And Their Greek Text Of The New Testament Including A Vindication Of The Traditional Reading Of 1 Timothy III. 16.* London: William Clowes and Sons Limited, 1883.

_____. *The Traditional Text of the Holy Gospels Vindicated and Established.* ed. By Edward Miller. London: George Bell and Sons, 1896.

Burt, Pope William. *A Higher Catechism of Theology.* London: T. Woolmer and Petermoster Taw, EC. 1883.

Calvin, John. *Calvin's Tracts containing Treatises on the Sacraments, Catechism of the church of Geneva, Forms of Prayer and Confession of Faith vol. II.* Trans. by Henry Beveridge . Edinburgh: Calvin Translation Society, 1849.

_____. *Commentaries on the Bible (22 volume set)*, MyBible v. 4.7.0.

_____. *Commentary on Philippians, Colossians and Thessalonians.* Trans. By John Pringle. Grand Rapids MI: Christian Classics Ethereal Library, n.d.

_____. *Commentary on the Psalms volume 1.* Grand Rapids, Michigan: Christian Classics Ethereal Library, 1999.

_____. *Institutes of the Christian Religion.* Trans. by, Henry Beveridge. Edinburgh: The Calvin Translation Society, 1845.

Carey, Eustace. *Memoir of William Carey D.D. late missionary to Bengal; professor of oriental language in the college of Fort William Calcutta.* London: Jackson and Walford, 1836.

Carey, S. Pearce. *William Carey.* London: The Carey Press, 1942.

Carey, William. *An Enquiry into the Obligations of Christians to use means for the Conversion of the Heathens; in which the religious state of the different nations of the world, the success of former undertakings, and the practicability of further undertakings, are considered.* London: Button and Son, Paternoster-Row, 1818.

Catechisms of the Scottish Reformation. Ed. by Horatius Bonar. .London: James Nisbet and Co., 1866.

Catford, J. C. *A Linguistic Theory of Translation, an essay in applied linguistics.* Oxford: Oxford University Press, 1965.

Centenary Memorial of the Rev. John Brown of Haddington: A Family Record. Compiled by John Croumbie Brown. Edinburgh: Andrew Elliot, 1887.

Chapell, F. L. *Biblical and Practical Theology.* Philadelphia: Harriet Chapell, 1901.

Custer, Stewart. *Tools For Preaching & Teaching The Bible.* Greenville, S.C.: Bob Jones University Press, 1998.

Dagg, J. L. *Manual of Theology: A Treatise on Christian Doctrine.* Philadelphia: American Baptist Publication Society, 1871.

Davies, John Hamilton. *The Life of Richard Baxter, of Kidderminster Preacher and Prisoner.* London: W. Kent and Co., 1887.

Davis, John J. *Moses and the Gods of Egypt.* Winona Lake: BMH Books, 1986.

Dictionary of the Apostolic Church. Ed. by James Hastings. New York: Charles Scribner's Sons, 1918. sv. Pastor.

Directions of the General Assembly concerning Secret and Private Worship, and mutual edification, for cherishing Piety, for maintaining Unity, and avoiding Schism and Division. with an Act for observing these Directions, and for censuring such as use to neglect Family Worship. AND An act against such as withdraw themselves from the Publick Worship in their own Congregations. Edinburgh: Evan Tyler, 1648.

"Doctrine". *A Dictionary Of The Bible Dealing With Its Language, Literature, And Contents Including The Biblical Theology.* Edinburgh: T&T Clark, 1898.

Doty, Thos K. *The Two-fold Gift of the Holy Ghost.* Cleveland O.: Christian Harvester Office, 1890.

Eddy, Franklin. *The Sabbath School Century: an authentic history of the rise and progress of Sabbath Schools for the past century. The work of Raikes, Fox, Pardee, Jacobs, Vincent, Eggleston, and many others.* Hamilton Ohio: J. H. Long, Steam Book and Job Printer, 1882.

Ellicott, C. J. Considerations on the Revision of the English Version of the New Testament. London: Longmans Green, Reader and Dyer, 1870.

Every Home A Godly Home. Singapore: Tabernacle Books.

Fisher, James. *The Westminster's Shorter Catechism Explained, by way of questions and answers part I, by several ministers of the Gospel.* Philadelphia: Presbyterian Board of Publication, 1850.

Fraser, Sir. Andrew. *William Carey: The Missionary Spirit.* London: The Baptist Missionary Society, n.d.

Gaebelein, Frank E. *The Christian Use of the Bible.* Chicago: Moody Press, 1946.

Gangel, Kenneth O. "Marks of a Healthy Church", *Bibliotheca Sacra 158*, (October – December 2001), p. 467.

Geisler Norman L. & William E. Nix. *A General Introduction to the Bible.* Chicago: Moody Press, 1977.

Gilman, Edward W. *Revision of the English Bible.* Bangor, Maine: The New Englander, 1859.

Good, James I. *Famous Reformers of the Reformed and Presbyterian Churches: a mission study manual on the Reformation.* Philadelphia: Heidelberg Press, 1916.

Hall, John. *The Chief End of Man: an Exposition of the first answer of the Shorter Catechism.* Philadelphia: Presbyterian Board of Publication, 1841.

Hamill, H. M. *The Sunday School Teacher.* New York: Fleming H. Revell Company, 1901.

BIBLIOGRAPHY

Harper, Francis Whaley. *Church Teaching for the Church's Children. An arrangement and exposition of the church catechism*. London: George Bell and Sons, 1877.

Havner, Vance. *Salt and Pepper*. Westwood New Jersey: Fleming H. Revell Company, 1966.

Hawes, J. J. "Christian Education". A report presented to the Brunswick Baptist Association at their 43rd Annual session as recorded in the *1941 Minutes of the Brunswick Baptist Association North Carolina*.

Hawes, Joel. *Decay of Power in the Pulpit: Its Causes And Remedies: A Sermon at The Ordination of Prof. Timothy Dwight to The Work of The Christian Ministry, Preached in the Center Church in New Haven, September 15, 1861*. New Haven: E. Hayes, 1861.

Heathcote, Charles William. *The Essentials of Religious Education*. Boston: Sherman, French & Company, 1916.

Hills, Edward F. *Believing Bible Study*. Iowa: The Christian Research Press, 1967.

Hodge, Charles. *A Commentary on Ephesians*. Edinburgh: Banner of Truth Trust, 1964.

Horne, Herman Harrell. *Jesus the Master Teacher*. New York: Association Press, 1920.

House, Erwin. *The Sunday School Handbook: a companion for Pastors, Superintendents, Teachers, Senior scholars and Parents*. Cincinnati: Hitchcock and Walden, 1868.

Hovey Alvah and J. M. Gregory. *Normal Class Manual for Bible Teachers*. Philadelphia: The Bible and Publication Society, n.d.

How, W. Walsham. *Lectures on Pastoral Work: delivered in the Divinity School, Cambridge, 1883*. London: WellsGardner, Darton & Co., 1884.

Hurlbut, Jesse Lyman. *Organising and Building up the Sunday School*, New York: Eaton & Mains, 1990.

James, George. *The Field and the Men for it, an address to the Divinity students of Queens College Kingston at the close of the session 1859-60*. Montreal: John Lovell, 1860.

Jerdan, Charles. *Scottish Clerical Stories and Reminiscences*. Edinburgh: Oliphants LTD, 1920.

Jones, E. D. *Aids to Sunday School Workers*. Philadelphia: American Baptist Publication Society, 1870.

Jones, Percy H. *William Carey: the pioneer of missions to India*. London: Pickering & Inglis, n.d.

Kato, Byang H. Theological Pitfalls in Africa. Nairobi: Evangel Publishing House, 1987.

Kigame, Reuben. "Sad Moment For Church As Theological Schools Die". The Shepherd, 2019.

Khoo, Jeffrey. "Role of the Bible College in Missions". *Frontlines in the Gospel Mission Fields.* Singapore: Maranatha BP Church, 2003.

Klooster, Fred H. "The Role of the Holy Spirit in the Hermeneutic Process" *Hermeneutics, Inerrancy and the Bible.* Ed. Earl D. Radmacher and Robert D. Preus. Grand Rapids Michigan: Zondervan Publishing House, 1994.

Kilbourne, E. A. *The Great Commission.* Tokyo Japan: Oriental Missionary Society, 1913.

Kubo Sakae & Walter F. Specht. *So Many Versions? 20th Century English Versions of the Bible.* Grand Rapids Michigan: Zondervan Corporation.

Life and Remains of the Rev. John Brown, The Late Minister of The Gospel at Haddington. Aberdeen: John and Robert King, 1845.

Lightfoot, J. B. *The Christian Ministry.* New York: Thomas Whittaker, n.d.

Lindsell, Harold. *The Bible in the Balance: A further look at the Battle for the Bible.* Grand Rapids Michigan: Zondervan Publishing House, 1979.

Luther, Martin. *Works of Luther Vol.* VI, Translated with Introductions and Notes. Philadelphia: A. J. Holman Company & The Castle Press, 1932.

Mackenzie, Robert. *John Brown of Haddington.* London: Hodder and Stoughton, 1918.

Masters, Peter. *Do We Have a Policy?: Paul's ten point policy for church health and growth.* London: The Wakeman Trust, 2002.

McClear, G. F. *A Class Book of the Catechism of the Church of England.* London & Cambridge: McMillan and Co., 1868.

McClure, A. W. *The Translators Revived: A Biographical Memoir of The Authors of The English Version of The Holy Bible.* New York: Charles Scribner, 1853.

Meade, Starr. *Training Hearts, Teaching Minds: Family Devotions Based on The Shorter Catechism.* Philipsburg New Jersey: P&R Publishing, 2000.

Menzies, Allan. *A Study of Calvin, and Other Papers.* London: Macmillan and Co., 1918.

Merrill, Eugene H. *An Historical Survey of the Old Testament.* New Jersey: The Craig Press, 1975.

Milemba, Elina Kanaiza. "The Influence of Prosperity Gospel on the Well-being of the Youth: a case study of contemporary Christian churches, Nairobi County." Masters of Arts Thesis: Department of Sociology and Social Work of the University of Nairobi, 2015.

BIBLIOGRAPHY

Miller, Paul M. *Equipping for Ministry*. Soni Tanzania: Central Tanganyika Press, 1969.

Miller, Randolf Crump. *Education for Christian Living*, 2nd ed. Englewood Cliffs N.J.: Prentice Hall, 1963.

Morgan, Irvonwy. *The Nonconformity of Richard Baxter*. London: The Epworth Press, 1946.

Morrison, J. H. *William Carey, cobbler and pioneer*. London: Hodder and Stoughton, n.d.

Mumo, Peter Mutuku. "A Study of Theological Education in Africa Inland Church-Kenya: Its Historical Development and Present State". Ph.D. Diss, University of Nairobi 1997.

_____. "Sunday Schools as the Foundation of Christian Nurture and their Relevance for Theological Education in Africa". *Handbook of Theological Education in Africa*, ed. By Isabel Apawo Phiri, and Dietrich Werner. Oxford: Regnium Books International, 2013.

Murphy, Thomas. *Pastoral Theology. The pastor in the various duties of his office*. Audubon, New Jersey: Old Paths Publications, 1996.

Oduor, Reginald M. J. *The Noise of our Songs: Disturbing trends in contemporary gospel music*. Nairobi Kenya: Berean Publications Ltd., 1997.

Ogolla, Maurice. "The Challenges Facing Religion in the Contemporary World: The Kenyan Situation". *International Journal of Humanities and Social Science*, (Vol. 4, No. 3: February 2014), p. 326.

Oosterzee, J. J. Van *Practical Theology, a manual for theological students*. Trans. by, Maurice J. Evans. London: Hodder & Stoughton, 1878.

Orr, James. "The Virgin Birth of Christ". *The Fundamentals, a Testimony to the Truth Vol. 1-4*. compliments of two Christian Laymen. Chicago, USA: Testimony Publishing Co., n.d.

Ouedraogo, Adama. "Prophets and Apostles", *Africa Bible Commentary: a one volume commentary written by 70 African Scholars*. Gen Ed., Tokunboh Adeyemo. Nairobi, Kenya: Word Alive Publishers, 2006.

Oxenden, Ashton. *The Pastoral Office: its Duties, Difficulties, Privileges, and Prospects*. Bible House, New York: Protestant Episcopal Society for the Promotion of Evangelical Knowledge, n.d.

Packer, J. I. *Fundamentalism and the Word of God*. Grand Rapids Michigan: Wm. B. Eerdmans Publishing Co., 1992.

_____. *God Speaks to Man*. Philadelphia: Westminster Press, 1965.

Paisley, Ian R. K. *An Exposition of the Epistle to the Romans*. Belfast: Ambassador Productions LTD., 1996.

Parry, Thomas. *The Indwelling Spirit*. New York: Alliance Press Company, 1906.

Pazmino, Robert W. *Foundational Issues in Christian Education: an Introduction in Evangelical Perspective*. Grand Rapids Michigan: Baker Books, 1997.

Pease, George William. *The Sunday School Teachers' Normal Course*. New York: Fleming H. Revell Co., 1895.

Plenning, L. *Life and Times of Calvin*. Translated by B. S. Berrington. London: Kegan, Paul, Trench, Trubner & Co., LTD, 1912.

Pond, Enoch. *Lectures on Pastoral Theology*. Andober: Warner F. Draper, 1866.

Postgate, J. P. *Translation and Translations; theory and practice*. London: G. Bell and Sons LTD, 1922.

Propositions Concerning Church Government and Ordination of Ministers, to the Right Honorable the Lords and Commons Assembled in Parliament, the Humble Advice of the Assembly of Divines Now Sitting by Ordinance of Parliament at Westminster. Edinburgh: Evan Tyler, 1647.

Riddle, Matthew Brown. *The Story of the Revised New Testament, American Standard Edition*. Philadelphia: The Sunday School Times Company, 1908.

Ridout, G. W. *Spiritual Gifts Including The Gift of Tongues: A consideration of the gifts of the Spirit and particularly the gift of tongues*. Kansas City Mo: Nazarene Publishing House, n.d.

Roberts, Seldon L. *Teaching in the Church School: a manual of principles and methods for church school teachers*. Philadelphia: The Judson Press, 1927.

Royer, Galen B. *Christian Heroism in Heathen Lands*. Elgin Illinois: Brethren Publishing House, 1914.

Ryken, Leland. *Bible Translation Differences: criteria for excellence in reading and choosing a Bible translation*. Wheaton Illinois: Crossway Books, 2004.

Ryle, B. D. "Limits and Growth of the Bible". *The Cambridge Companion to the Bible*. London: C. J. Clay and Sons, 1893.

Ryle, Herbert Edward. *The Canon of the Old Testament*. London: Macmillan and Co., 1892.

Ryle, J. C. *Training of Children*. Tampines Singapore: Christian Life Publishers, 1992.

Schenck, Ferdinand S. *Modern Practical Theology: a manual of homiletics, liturgics, poimenics, archagics, pedagogy, sociology and the English Bible*. New York: Funk & Wagnals Company, 1903.

Serampore Letters, being the unpublished correspondence of William Carey and others with John Williams. Ed. Leighton and Mornay Williams. London: G. P. Putnam's Sons, 1892.

Simpson, E. K. *The Pastoral Epistles: the Greek Texts with introduction and commentary.* London: The Tyndale Press, 1954.

Smyth, Thomas. *Calvin Defended: a memoir of the life, character and principles of John Calvin.* Philadelphia: Presbyterian Board of Publication, 1909.

Spurgeon, Charles H. *Spurgeon on the Holy Spirit.* New Kingston: Whitaker house, 2000.

Spring, Gardiner. *Power Of The Pulpit, Or, Thoughts Addressed To Christian Ministers And Those Who Hear Them.* New York: M. W. Dodd, 1845.

Stitzinger, James F. *Spiritual Gifts: Definitions and Kinds.* The Masters Seminary Journal, 14/2, Fall 2003. 161.

Tan, Paul Lee. *A Pictorial Guide to Bible Prophecy.* Hong Kong: Nordica International LTD., 1991.

Thayer, William M. *The Pioneer Boy, and How He Became President.* Boston: Walker Wise and Company, 1864.

The Complete Word Study Old Testament King James Version. Gen. Ed., Warren Baker. Chattanooga Tennessee: AMG Publishers, 1994.

The Heidelberg Catechism: the German text, with a revised translation and introduction. London: Andrew Melrose, 1900.

The International Standard Bible Encyclopaedia. Gen. Ed., James Orr, Grand Rapids Michigan: Wm. B. Eerdmans Publishing Co., 1955. sv. Teach, Teacher, Teaching.

The Life of the Rev. Richard Baxter, abridged from Orme's Life of Baxter. Philadelphia: Presbyterian Board of Publication, 1840.

The Popular and Critical Bible Encyclopaedia and Scriptural Dictionary fully defining and explaining all religious terms including biographical, geographical, Historical, archeological and doctrinal themes, Vol. III. Ed. by, Samuel Fallows. Chicago: The Howard Severance Company, 1902. sv. Pentateuchal Objections.

The School of Faith: The Catechisms of The Reformed Church. Translated and edited by Thomas F. Torrance. London: James Clarke & Co. LTD, 1959.

The Self-Interpreting Bible Library with commentaries, references, harmony of the Gospels, and the helps needed to understand and teach the text illustrated and explained in four volumes. New York: R. S. Pealeand J. A. Hill, 1896.

Theological Dictionary of the New Testament. ed. Gerhard Kittel and Gerhard Friedrich, trans. Geoffrey W. Bromiley. Grand Rapids Michigan: William B. Eerdmans Publishing Company, 1985. sv. didaskw

Thomson, Andrew. *Great Missionaries, a series of biographies.* London: T. Nelson and Sons, Paternoster Row, 1862.

Thomson, A. C. "Bible Translation Philosophy", *TBS Quarterly Record.* Issue No. 619: April – June 2017.

Tyng, Stephen II. *The Office and Duty of the Christian Pastor.* New York: Harper & Brothers Publishers, 1874.

Ursinus, Zacharias. *The Commentary of Zacharias Ursinus on the Heidelberg Catechism.* Translated from the original Latin by G. W. Williard. Cincinnati: T. P. Bucher Publisher, 1851.

Verkuyl, Gerrit. *Qualifying Men for Church Work.* New York: Fleming H. Revell Company, 1927.

Vincent, John H. *Sunday School Institutes and Normal Class.* New York: Carlton & Lanahan, 1872.

Vincent, Marvin R. *A History of the Textual Criticism of the New Testament.* New York: The Maxmillan Company, 1899.

Vinet, A. *Pastoral Theology: or the Theory of the Evangelical Ministry.* Translated and edited by Thomas H. Skinner. New York: Harper & Brothers Publishers, 1853.

Walker, F. Deaville. *William Carey, Missionary Pioneer and Statesman.* London: Student Christian Movement, 1926.

Wambui, Ngunju Alice and Wycliffe Amukowa. "Constraints Facing Teachers of Christian Religious Education in Using Life Approach in Secondary Schools in Nairobi East District in Kenya." article in *Academic Journal of Interdisciplinary Studies vol. 2 No. 2 July2013.* Published by MCSER-CEMAS-Sapienza University of Rome.

Wanjie, L. *God Meets US: Christian Religious Education From 2.* Nairobi: East African Educational Publishers, 1992.

Watson, Thomas. *A Body of Divinity.* Edinburgh: The Banner of Truth and Trust, Reprint 1965.

Wendel, Francois. *Calvin, the origins and development of his religious thought.* Translated by Philip Mairet. New York: Harper & Row Publishers, 1963.

Whitney, S. W. *The Revisers' Greek Text, a critical examination of certain readings, textual and marginal, in the original Greek of the New Testament adopted by the late Anglo-American Revisers.* Boston: Silver, Burdett & Company, 1892.

BIBLIOGRAPHY

Williams, Charles B. *The Function of Teaching in Christianity*. Nashville Tennessee: Sunday School Board Southern Baptist Convention, 1912.

Wilson, Annie E. *The Family Altar, helps and suggestions for family worship*. Richmond VA: Presbyterian Committee of Publication, 1898.

Winslow, Octavius. *Personal Declension and Revival of Religion in the Soul*. Edinburgh: The Banner of Truth Trust, 1978.

Zodhiates, Spiros. *The Complete Word Study Old Testament*. Chattanooga, TN: AMG Publishers, 1994.

ELECTRONIC AND INTERNET SOURCES

Admin, BTL. "Mother Tongue Bible Changed My Father". *Btlkenya.org*. Accessed October 18, 2018. https://www.btlkenya.org/index.php/media/blog/item/35-mother-tongue-bible-changed-my-father.

"Advice to Educators on The Use of Textbooks | ACTS". *Acts-ng.com*. Accessed August 7, 2019. http://www.acts-ng.com/2012/01/05/a-call-for-educators/#more-170.

"Alert, Elijah Is Here! | Highway Of Holiness". *Highwayofholiness.Us*. Last modified 2019. Accessed February 12, 2019. https://www.highwayofholiness.us/alert-elijah-is-here/.

Archer, Clint. "Why Seminary? Exhibit A: Joel Osteen". *The Cripplegate*. Accessed January 18, 2018. http://thecripplegate.com/why-seminary-exhibit-a-joel-osteen/.

Barker, P. C. "An Early Co-pastorate", *Pulpit Homiletics Commentary*, electronic version obtained from URL: http://biblehub.com/commentaries/homiletics/acts/11.htm accessed on 08/03/2018.

"Bible College Of East Africa Tanzania". *Findglocal.com*. Accessed August 15, 2019. http://www.findglocal.com/TZ/Usa-River/168953509906031/Bible-College-of-East-Africa-Tanzania.

"BIBLE TRAINING — Pastors Discipleship Network, Addressing A Desperate Need For Bible Education". *Pastors Discipleship Network*. Accessed March 14, 2019. https://www.pdnafrica.org/bible-training.

Bowers, Paul. "Theological Education In Africa: Why Does It Matter?". *Biblicalstudies.org.uk*. Accessed March 28, 2019. https://biblicalstudies.org.uk/pdf/ajet/26-2_135.pdf.

Buys, Flip. "Theological Training For Untrained Pastors". *Christianlibrary.Org.Au*. Accessed March 14, 2019. https://www.christianlibrary.org.au/index.php/school-of-missions/226-theological-training-for-untrained-pastors.

Cloud, David. "Testimonies Of KJV Defenders - Thomas Strouse". *Way Of Life Literature Inc*. Last modified 2004. Accessed September 11, 2019. https://www.wayoflife.org/database/strouse.html.

Chike, Chigor. "The Doctrine Of Salvation Among African Christians | Fulcrum Anglican". *Fulcrum Anglican*. Accessed February 18, 2017. https://www.fulcrum-anglican.org.uk/articles/the-doctrine-of-salvation-among-african-christians/.

Cole, Victor Babadije. "Reformed Theology And Theological Education In Africa". *World Reformed Fellowship*. Accessed March 29, 2019. http://wrfnet.org/resources/2009/04/reformed-theology-and-theological-education-africa.

Constable, Thomas L. "Notes On Exodus". *Planobible Chapel*. Accessed February 12, 2019. https://planobiblechapel.org/tcon/notes/pdf/exodus.pdf.

BIBLIOGRAPHY

"Controversy Is Wahome's Second Name". *Daily Nation*. Accessed December 20, 2016. http://www.nation.co.ke/news/Controversy-is-Wahomes-second-name/-/1056/2826286/-/iual5yz/-/index.html.

Dale, B. "1 Samuel 2 Pulpit Homiletics Commentary, Rejoicing in the Lord". *Bible Hub*. Last modified 2019. Accessed February 19, 2018. http://biblehub.com/ commentaries/homiletics/1_samuel/2.htm.

"Distinctives: A Different Approach To Seminary Education". *The North American Reformed Seminary*. Accessed August 7, 2019. http://www.tnars.net/distinctives.html.

"Deuteronomy 4 Commentary | Precept Austin". Precept Austin. Accessed February 6, 2018. http://www.preceptaustin.org/deuteronomy-4-commentary.

Donnelly, Edward. "Richard Baxter – A Corrective For Reformed Preachers". *Puritansermons.Com*. Last modified 2019. Accessed August 13, 2004. http://www.puritansermons.com/baxter/baxter15.htm.

"Ezra 7:10 Commentary | Precept Austin". *Precept Austin*. Last modified 2019. Accessed March 30, 2017. http://www. preceptaustin.org/index.php/ezra_710.

"Far Eastern Bible College | Distance Learning Online". *Febc.edu.sg*. Accessed August 7, 2019. https://www.febc.edu.sg/v15/distance_learning_online.

"Far Eastern Bible College | Introducing The College: A Short History Of The Far Eastern Bible College". *febc.edu.sg*. Accessed August 7, 2019. https://www.febc.edu.sg/v15/introducing_the_college.

"Far Eastern Bible College | Word From The Principal". Feedstuffs. Accessed August 7, 2019. https://www.febc.edu.sg/v15/word_from_the_principal.

Ferdinando, Keith. "Theological Education – Why Bother? - Africa Inland Mission (Europe)". *Africa Inland Mission (Europe)*. Accessed March 28, 2019. https://eu.aimint.org/why-bother-with-theological-education/.

Foxall, George. "Continental Linkage And Support Services For TEE In Africa". *Biblicalstudies.Org.Uk*. Accessed March 29, 2019. https://biblicalstudies.org.uk/pdf/ajet/08-1_041.pdf.

Frame, Randy. "Is Seminary Education Always Necessary For Pastoral Ministry? How Formal Education Can Help Build The Church". *CT Pastors*. Accessed September 17, 2018. http://www.seminarygradschool.com/article/Is-Seminary-Education-Always-Necessary-for-Pastoral-Ministry%3F.

Fraser, D. "1 Samuel 12 Pulpit Commentary Homiletics, The Good Man's Weapons". *Biblehub.Com*. Accessed March 8, 2018. http://biblehub.com/commentaries/homiletics/1_samuel/12.htm.

Gill, John. "Ezra 7 Gill's Exposition". *Biblehub.Com*. Last modified 2019. Accessed March 8, 2018. http://biblehub.com/commentaries/gill/ezra/7.htm.

Griffith, Henry. "Models Of Theological Education Yesterday And Today". *Biblicalstudies.org.uk*. Accessed March 29, 2019. https://biblicalstudies.org.uk/pdf/ajet/07-1_045.pdf.

Hawkins, Joshua. "Doctrine And The Pastoral Ministry". *Joshua Hawkins*. Accessed February 21, 2018. http://www.joshuahawkins.com/resources/articles/2011/07/doctrine-and-pastoral-ministry.

"History of Catechisms". Accessed August 13, 2004. www.kfpc.org/January17/tsld012.htm

"Home - Clik Africa - Christian Literature In Kiswahili". *Clik-Africa.org*. Accessed August 7, 2019. http://www.clik-africa.org/.

"Job Vacancies In Kapsabet Bible College". *Kenyancareer.com*. Accessed February 12, 2019. http://www.kenyancareer.com/2015/05/job-vacancies-in-kapsabet-bible-college.html.

Kagema, Dickson Nkonge. "The Use Of Gospel Hip-Hop As An Avenue Of Evangelizing Youth In Kenya Today: A Practical Approach". *Aijcrnet.com*. Accessed March 12, 2018. http://www.aijcrnet.com/journals/Vol_3_No_8_August_2013/19.pdf.

Kaiser, Henry J. "African Theologians Launch Bible Commentary to Guide Africans on Modern Problems, Including HIV/AIDS". *Thebody.com*. Accessed on February 20, 2019. http://www.thebody.com/content/art7534.html.

"Kenya Highlands University". *En.Wikipedia.org*. Accessed February 12, 2019. https://en.wikipedia.org/wiki/Kenya_Highlands_University#History.

King, Roberta. "The Role Of Music In Theological Education". *Biblicalstudies.org*. Last modified 2019. Accessed February 12, 2019. https://biblicalstudies.org.uk/pdf/ajet/09-1-035.pdf.

Lange, John Peter. "Acts 11 Lange Commentary On The Holy Scriptures". *Biblehub.com*. Accessed March 8, 2018. http://biblehub.com/commentaries/lange/acts/11.htm.

Mackennal, A. "Ezra 7 Pulpit Commentary Homiletics, Ezra And His Mission". *Biblehub.com*. Last modified 2019. Accessed March 8, 2018. http://biblehub.com/commentaries/homiletics/ezra/7.htm.

McArthur Jr., John F. "How We Got Our Bible". *Onthewing.org*. Accessed July 3, 2019. http://onthewing.org/user/Bible%20-%20How%20we%20got%20it%20-%20MacArthur.pdf.

Morad, Stephen. "The Beginnings Of Christianity In Kenya". *William Carey International University*. Last modified 2019. Accessed February 3, 2017. http://www.wciu.edu/docs/resources/Course10_readerGC2_C10R_Morad_Beginnings_of_Christianity_in_Kenya.pdf.

BIBLIOGRAPHY

Morrison, John. *The Great Commission and Christian Education: a pointed challenge to Christian parents and church leaders.* Electronic version obtained from URL: http://www.gcswarriors.org/about-us/christianeducationresources/The%20Great%20Commission%20and%20Christia n%20Education%20by%20John%20Morrison.pdf

Morrison, Philip E. "Implications Of Paul's Model For Leadership Training In Light Of Church Growth In Africa". *Biblicalstudies.org.uk.* Last modified 2019. Accessed March 14, 2019. https://biblicalstudies.org.uk/pdf/ajet/30-1_055.pdf.

Ndeda, Mildred A. J. "The Struggles Of New Religious Movements In The Kenyan Religious Space: The Case Of Repentance And Holiness Movement". *Les Cahiers D'Afrique De L'Est / The East African Review.* Accessed May 5, 2019. http://journals.openedition.org/eastafrica/404.

Nyaboke, Esther. "Televangelism And The Changing Habits Of Worshippers In Nairobi County". *Journalism.Uonbi.Ac.Ke.* Last modified 2019. Accessed January 18, 2018. https://journalism.uonbi.ac.ke/sites/default/files/chss/journalism/journalism/ESTHER%20NYABOKE%20MOKAYA%20PROJECT%202015.pdf.

Nzwili, Fredrick. "Kenya's Presidential Race Takes Pages From The Bible — Religion News Service". *Religion News Service.* Last modified 2019. Accessed November 24, 2018. https://religionnews.com/2017/10/11/kenyas-presidential-race-takes-pages-from-the-bible/.

Oduor, Peter. "The Kenyan Church And The Gospel Of Prosperity". *Daily Nation.* Wednesday, February 13, 2013. Accessed September 12, 2019. https://www.nation.co.ke/lifestyle/dn2/The-Kenyan-church-and-the-gospel-of-prosperity/957860-1691986-fk8kt4/index.html.

"Official Kapsabet Bible College Contacts, Courses, Intakes, Fee Structures And Location 2018". Last modified 2019. Accessed February 12, 2019. http://knecportal.co/ official-kapsabet-bible-college-contacts-courses-intakes-fee-structures-and-location-2018.

Ogolla, Maurice. "The Challenges Facing Religion In The Contemporary". *Studyres.com.* Last modified 2019. Accessed March 12, 2018. https://studyres.com/doc/14808240/the-challenges-facing-religion-in-the-contemporary.

Ojamaa, Brian. "Involve Clergy In Bill To Regulate Churches, Bishop Tells Legislator". *The Star.* Last modified 2019. Accessed March 21, 2019. https://www.the-star.co.ke/counties/western/2019-02-19-involve-clergy-in-bill-to-regulate-churches-bishop-tells-legislator/.

Orr, J. "2 Kings 12 *Pulpit Homiletics Commentary,* A Mixed Character". *Bible Hub.* Accessed 19 February 2018. http://biblehub.com/ commentaries/homiletics/2_kings/12.htm

"Pastoral Leaders: Training Church Leaders". *Emit.Global*. Last modified 2019. Accessed March 14, 2019. https://emit.global/pastoral-leaders/.

Perkins, Linda. "Pastoral Training Is Changing". *CT Pastors*. Last modified 2019. Accessed February 21, 2018. https://www.christianitytoday.com/pastors/2018/February-web-exclusives/pastoral-training-is-changing.html.

Pink, A. W. *The Divine Inspiration of the Bible*. Albany OR: USA, Ages Software, 1997.

Roberts, Elizabeth. "Faithfulness Among The Frauds In Kenya". *The Gospel Coalition*. Last modified 2019. Accessed August 22, 2019. https://www.thegospelcoalition.org/article/christianity-in-kenya-faithful-in-the-midst-of-frauds/.

"Scott Theological College". Kenya's How-To Website. Last modified 2019. Accessed February 12, 2019. https://www.how.co.ke/scott-theological-college/.

Small, Joe. "Choosing The Right Version Of The Bible | Presbyterian Foundation". *Presbyterianfoundation.org*. Accessed September 11, 2019. https://www.presbyterianfoundation.org/choosing-the-right-version-of-the-bible/.

Stoddard, Elizabeth. "The Ubiquity Of Religion In Kenya". *Berkleycenter.georgetown.edu*. Accessed August 8, 2019. https://berkleycenter.georgetown.edu/posts/the-ubiquity-of-religion-in-kenya.

"The 4 Norms Of Editorial Peregrino". *Editorial Peregrino*. Accessed August 7, 2019. http://editorialperegrino.com/nosotros/las-4-normas-de-editorial-peregrino/.

"The Men Who Claim To Be Africa's 'Miracle Workers'". *BBC News*. Accessed October 28, 2017. http://www.bbc.com/news/world-africa-38063882.

"The History Of BTCP". *Bible Training Centre For Pastors*. Last modified 2019. Accessed March 14, 2019. https://bibletraining.com/get-to-know-us/who-we-are.

"The North American Reformed Seminary". *Revolvy.com*. Accessed August 7, 2019. https://www.revolvy.com/page/The-North-American-Reformed-Seminary?cr=1

Tucker, R. "1 Corinthians 12 Pulpit Commentary Homiletics, The Order Of Offices In The Christian Church". *Biblehub.Com*. Last modified 2019. Accessed March 8, 2018. http://biblehub.com/commentaries/homiletics/1_corinthians/12.htm.

"UK Extradites 'Miracle Pastor' To Kenya". *BBC News*. Accessed October 28, 2017. http://www.bbc.com/news/world-africa-40824267.

Van Buren, Paul. "An Uneducated Pastor". *Pastorpaulvbsblog.Blogspot.Com*. Last modified 2019. Accessed September 17, 2018. http://pastorpaulvbsblog.blogspot.com/2012/11/an-uneducated-pastor.html.

Vine, W. E. "Vine's Complete Expository Dictionary Of Old And New Testament Words. Ed. Merrill F. Unger, William White Jr.". *Ultimatebiblereferenceli-*

BIBLIOGRAPHY

brary.Com. Last modified 2019. Accessed February 7, 2018. http://www.ultimatebiblereferencelibrary.com/Vines_Expositary_Dictionary.pdf. sv. Teach

Volkers, Mark. "Lay Leaders: Trained And Dynamic, Or Untrained And Dangerous?". *Missionexus.Org*. Accessed March 29, 2019. https://missionexus.org/lay-leaders-trained-and-dynamic-or-untrained-and-dangerous/.

Voss, Barry. "Six Lessons Christians Must Learn From Church History". *Faithlifeministries.Net*. Last modified 2019. Accessed February 8, 2019. http://faithlifeministries.net/six-lessons-christians-must-learn-from-church-history/.

Vukani, Madoda. "Flag Continues To Follow Cross". *The Sunday Mail*. Last modified 2019. Accessed October 28, 2017. http://www.sundaymail.co.zw/flag-continues-to-follow-cross/.

Waiganjo, Kamotho. "Rampant Abuse Of People's Faith Calls For Urgent Church Regulation : The Standard". *The Standard*. Last modified 2019. Accessed March 21, 2019. https://www.standardmedia.co.ke/article/2001314067/rampant-abuse-of-people-s-faith-calls-for-urgent-church-regulation.

Wambui, Ngunju Alice, and Wycliffe Amukowa. "Constraints Facing Teachers Of Christian Religious Education In Using Life Approach In Secondary Schools In Nairobi East District In Kenya". *Academic Journal of Interdisciplinary Studies* (2013). Accessed February 18, 2017. https://www.researchgate.net/publication/271040628_Constraints_Facing_Teachers_of_Christian_Religious_Education_in_Using_Life_Approach_in_Secondary_Schools_in_Nairobi_East_District_in_Kenya.

Waruinge, Maureen. "Five Strange Miracles Some Pastors Perform Archives – Radio Jambo". *Radio Jambo*. Last modified 2019. Accessed October 28, 2017. https://radiojambo.co.ke/tag/five-strange-miracles-some-pastors-perform/.

Waruta, Douglas Wanjohi. "Scripture Translations In Kenya". *Erepository.uonbi.ac.ke*. Accessed September 11, 2018. http://erepository.uonbi.ac.ke/bitstream/handle/11295/95524/Waruta%20_Scripture%20Translations%20In%20Kenya.pdf;sequence=1.

"What We Do — African Pastors Fellowship". *African Pastors Fellowship*. Last modified 2019. Accessed March 14, 2019. https://www.africanpastors.org/what-we-do/.

"Who We Are-Pilgrim Editorial". *Editorial Peregrino*. Accessed August 7, 2019. http://editorialperegrino.com/nosotros/quien-somos/.

"Why ART Exists". *Africa Rural Trainers*. Last modified 2019. Accessed March 14, 2019. https://africaruraltrainers.org.

Zuck, Roy B. "Hebrew Words For Teach". *Pdfs.semanticscholar.org*. Accessed February 6, 2018. https://pdfs.semanticscholar.org/fab9/d8817376b5059157812a4afd6a4314f28e88.pdf

ABOUT THE AUTHOR

CURRICULUM VITAE

PERSONAL DETAILS:

Name: Nelson Noel Ng'uono Were.
Address: Faith College of the Bible.
 P. O. Box 158 Eldoret, 30100,
 Kenya
 Email – noelwerre@hotmail.com
 Tel No. +254-734450827 or +254-718611466

EDUCATION AND TRAINING:

- 2017–2020 Doctor of Religious Education (in ministry program) at Far Eastern Bible College, Singapore.

- Dissertation: *Pastors as Teachers: The Teaching Ministry of the Church and Its Role in the Strengthening of the Church in Kenya Today.*

- 2005–2006 Master of Theology at Far Eastern Bible College, Singapore.

- Thesis: *Biblical Greek Exegesis.*

- 2003–2005 Master of Divinity at Far Eastern Bible College, Singapore.

- Thesis: *Biblical Greek Syntax.*

- 2001–2004 Bachelor of Theology at Far Eastern Bible College, Singapore.

- Thesis: *The Identity of the Unsaved.*

- 2000 a one year study at Bomet Bible Institute, Kenya.

- 1994–1997 Diploma in Electrical Power Engineering at the Mombasa Polytechnic, Kenya.

TEACHING EXPERIENCE:

- 2010– to date: Lecturer at Faith College of the Bible, Eldoret Kenya.

- 2010– to date: Visiting Instructor at Bomet Bible Institute, Bomet Kenya.

- 2012–2013 Visiting Instructor at Kisumu Bible School, Kisumu Kenya.

- 2007–2009 Instructor at Bomet Bible Institute, Bomet Kenya.

- 2007–2009 Visiting Instructor at Faith College of the Bible, Eldoret Kenya.

- 2005–2006 Teaching Assistant at Far Eastern Bible College, Singapore.

WORK EXPERIENCE:

- 2010– to date: Pastor at Holy Trinity Church in Africa – Eldoret Parish, Eldoret Kenya.

- 2019– to date: Independent Tribunal Committee Chairman of Holy Trinity Church in Africa

- 2015– to date: Deputy Principal and Academic Dean at Faith College of the Bible, Eldoret Kenya.
- 2016–2018 Deputy Secretary General of Holy Trinity Church in Africa.
- 2014–2015 Education Board Chairman of Holy Trinity Church in Africa.
- 2008–2009 Pastor at Singorwet Africa Gospel Unity Church, Bomet Kenya.
- 2007 Assistant to Pastor at Bomet Africa Gospel Unity Church, Bomet Kenya.
- 1993–1999 Sunday School and Youth worker (Lay Reader) at Tudor Holy Trinity Church in Africa, Mombasa Kenya.
- 1990–1993 Sunday School teacher at Tudor Holy Trinity Church in Africa, Mombasa Kenya.

PUBLICATIONS:

Were Nelson Ng'uono. "Africa Bible Commentary: A Review Article" *The Burning Bush* (Vol. 13, No. 2, July 2007): 97-116.

Were Nelson Nelson Noel Ng'uono. *"A Biblical Greek Syntax Guide."* Cleveland, Georgia: The Old Paths Publications Inc., 2015.

Were Nelson. "The Numbers in Ezra 2 and Nehemiah 7: A Solution in Favour of the Inerrancy of the Verbally and Plenarily Preserved Text" *The Burning Bush* (Vol. 13, No. 2, July 2007).: 101-105.

Were Nelson. "Comforting Nature of God's Word" *Bible Witness* (Vol. 10, Issue 4, July-August 2010): 9-11.

www.ingramcontent.com/pod-product-compliance
Lightning Source LLC
Chambersburg PA
CBHW080236250426
43670CB00043BA/2561